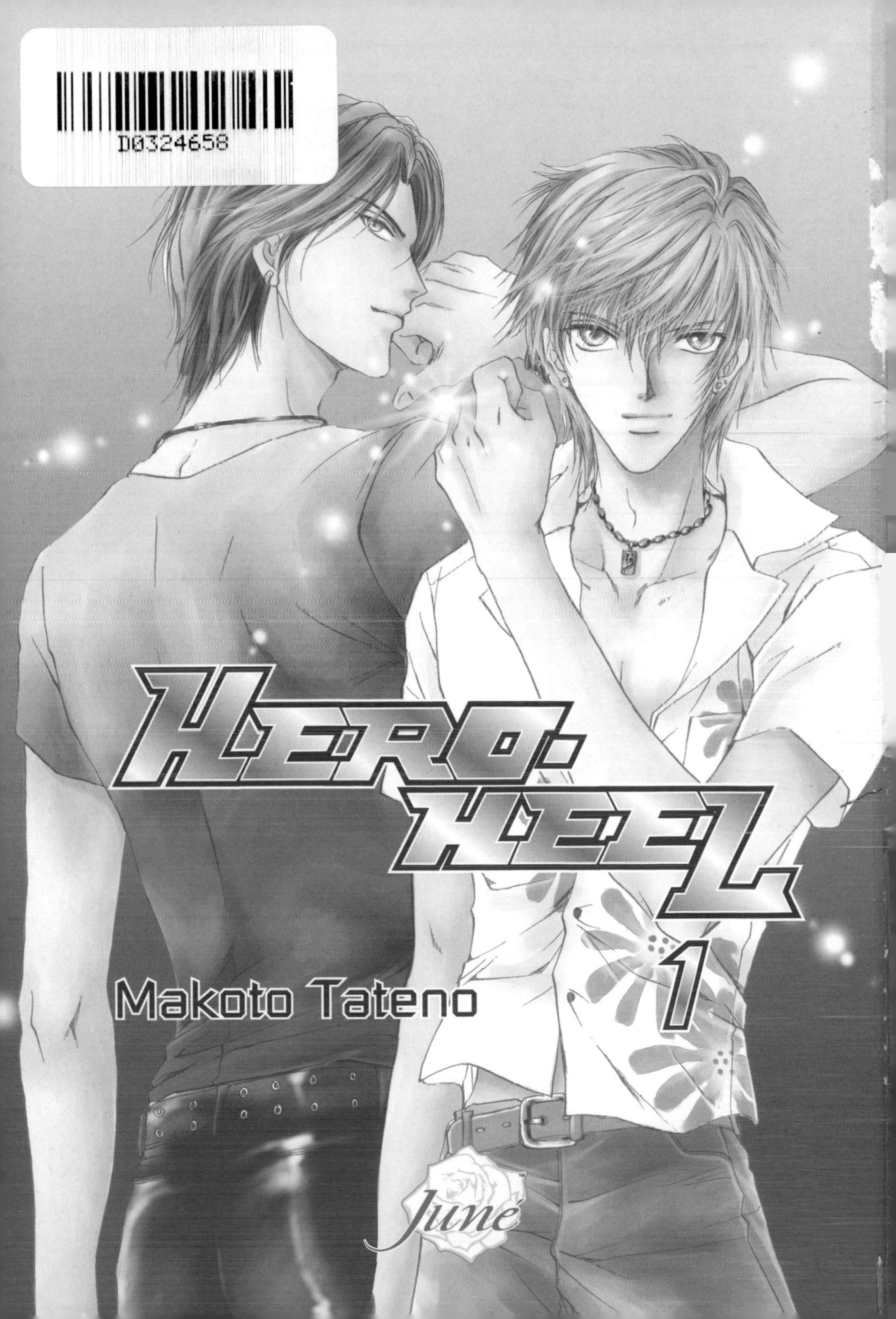
HERO HEEL
1
Makoto Tateno
Juné

HERO HEEL 1

Translation — Katherine Schilling

Editing — Wendy Lee

Lettering — Geoff Porter

Graphic Design/Layout — Wendy Lee/Daryl Kuxhouse

Editor in Chief — Fred Lui

Publisher — Hikaru Sasahara

English Edition Published by
DIGITAL MANGA PUBLISHING
A division of DIGITAL MANGA, Inc.
1487 W 178th Street, Suite 300
Gardena, CA 90248

www.dmpbooks.com

First Edition: November 2006
ISBN-10: 1-56970-870-3
ISBN-13: 978-1-56970-870-5

1 3 5 7 9 10 8 6 4 2

Printed in China

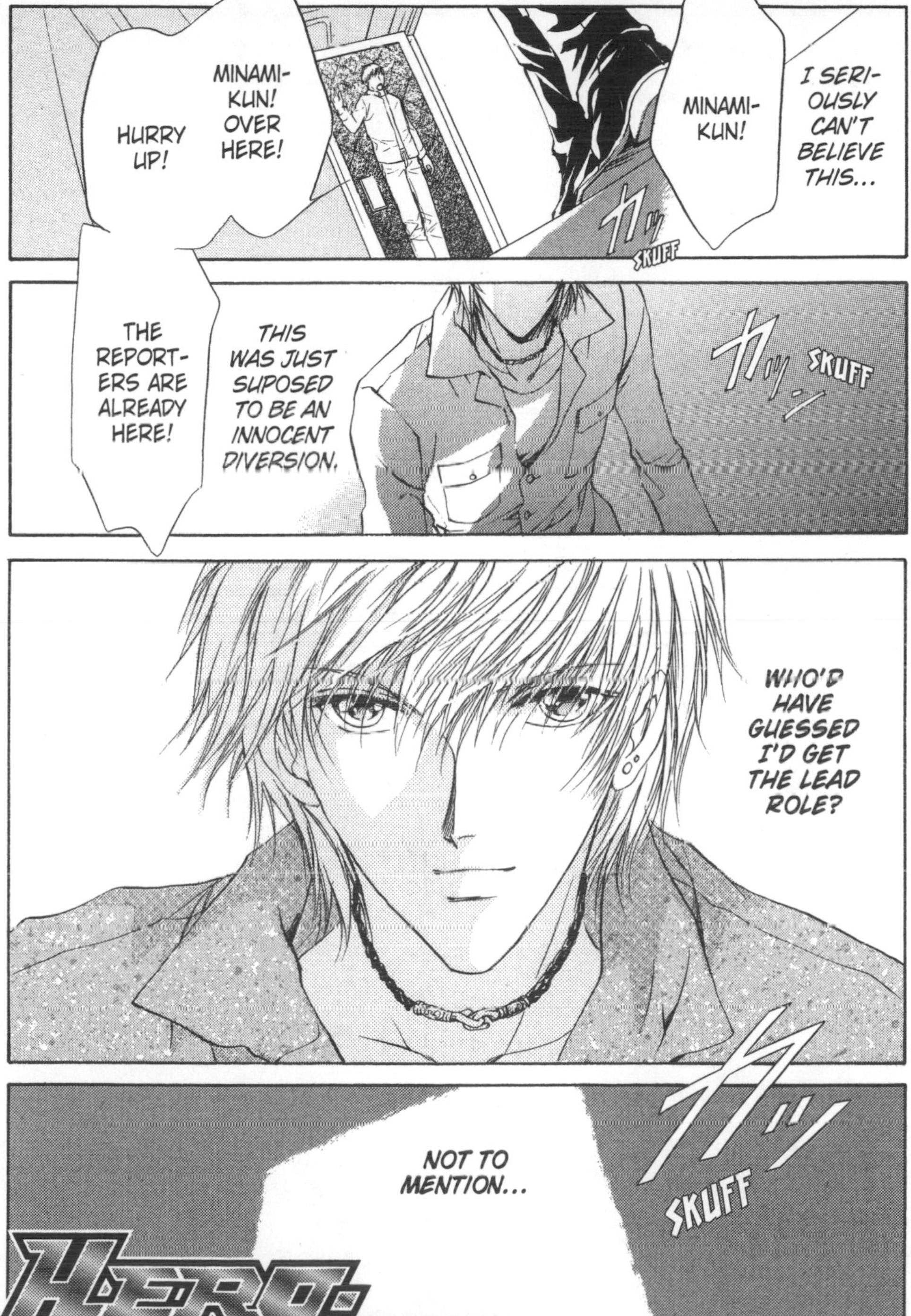
I SERI-OUSLY CAN'T BELIEVE THIS...
MINAMI-KUN!
SKUFF
MINAMI-KUN! OVER HERE!
HURRY UP!
THE REPORT-ERS ARE ALREADY HERE!
SKUFF
THIS WAS JUST SUPOSED TO BE AN INNOCENT DIVERSION.
WHO'D HAVE GUESSED I'D GET THE LEAD ROLE?
SKUFF
NOT TO MENTION...
HERO HEEL
—英雄と悪漢—
—HERO & VILLAIN—
Scene.1

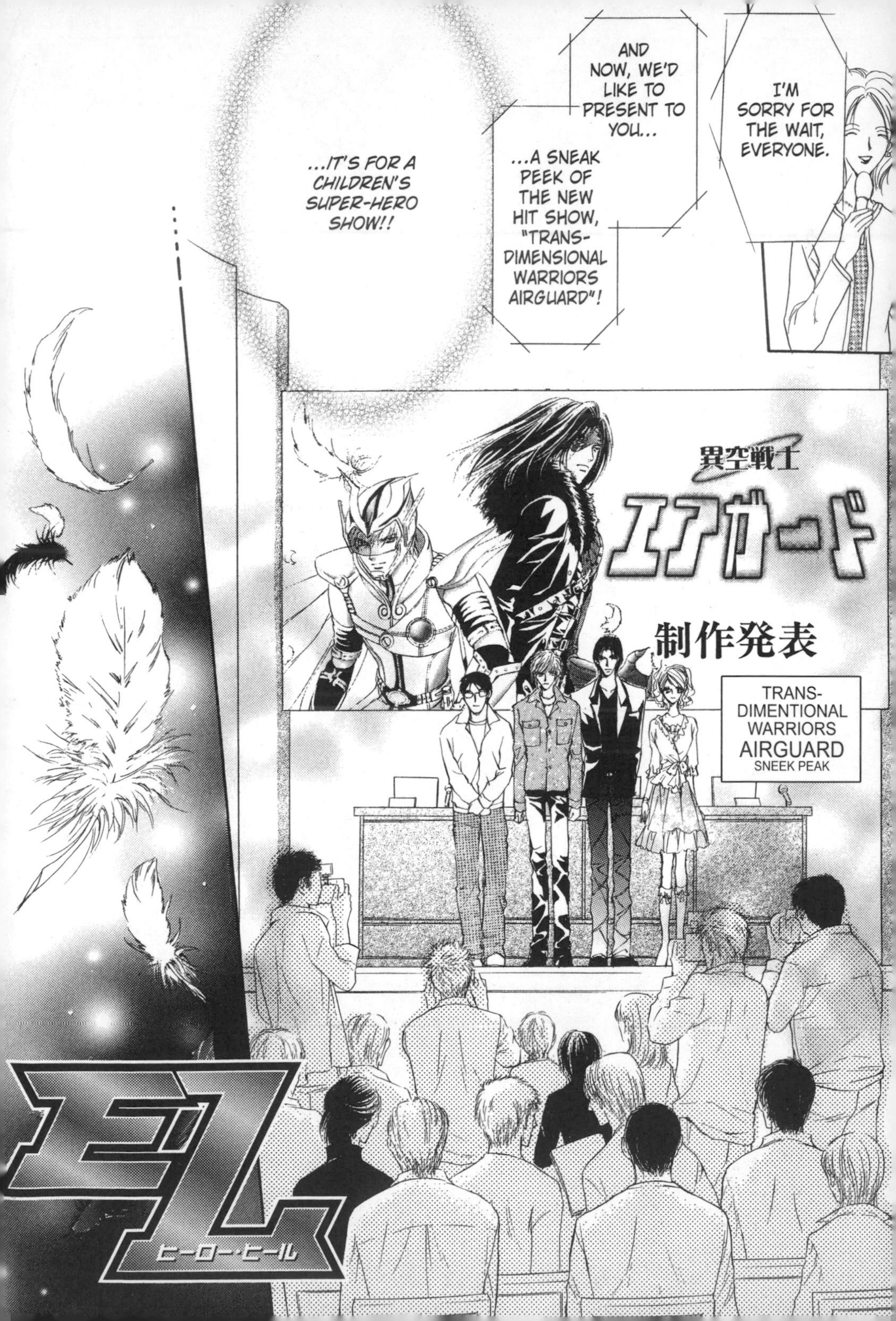
I'M SORRY FOR THE WAIT, EVERYONE.
AND NOW, WE'D LIKE TO PRESENT TO YOU...
...A SNEAK PEEK OF THE NEW HIT SHOW, "TRANS-DIMENSIONAL WARRIORS AIRGUARD"!
...IT'S FOR A CHILDREN'S SUPER-HERO SHOW!!
異空戦士
エアガード
制作発表
TRANS-DIMENTIONAL WARRIORS AIRGUARD SNEEK PEAK
ヒーロー・ヒール

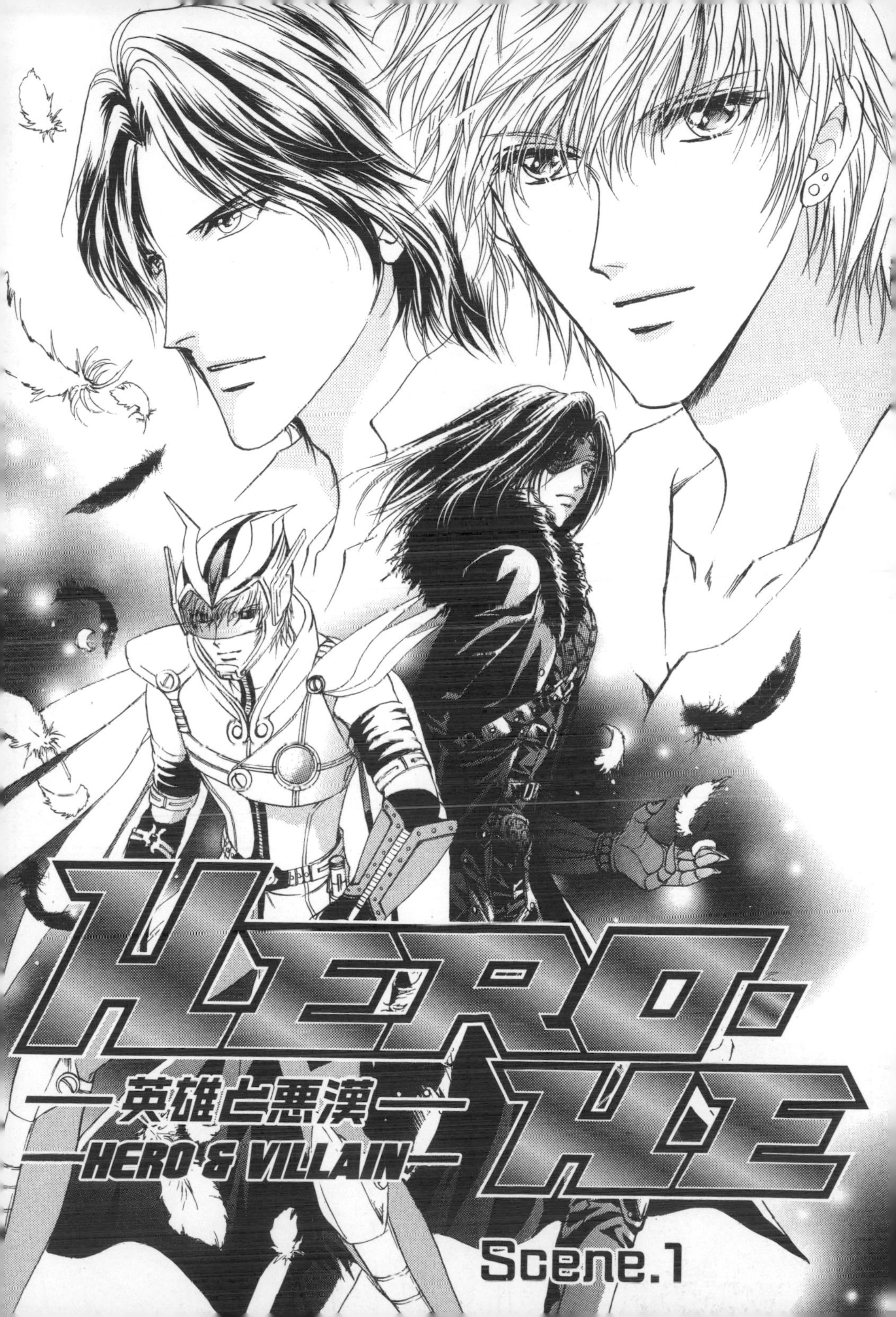
ヒーロー・ヒール
―英雄と悪漢―
―HERO & VILLAIN―
Scene.1

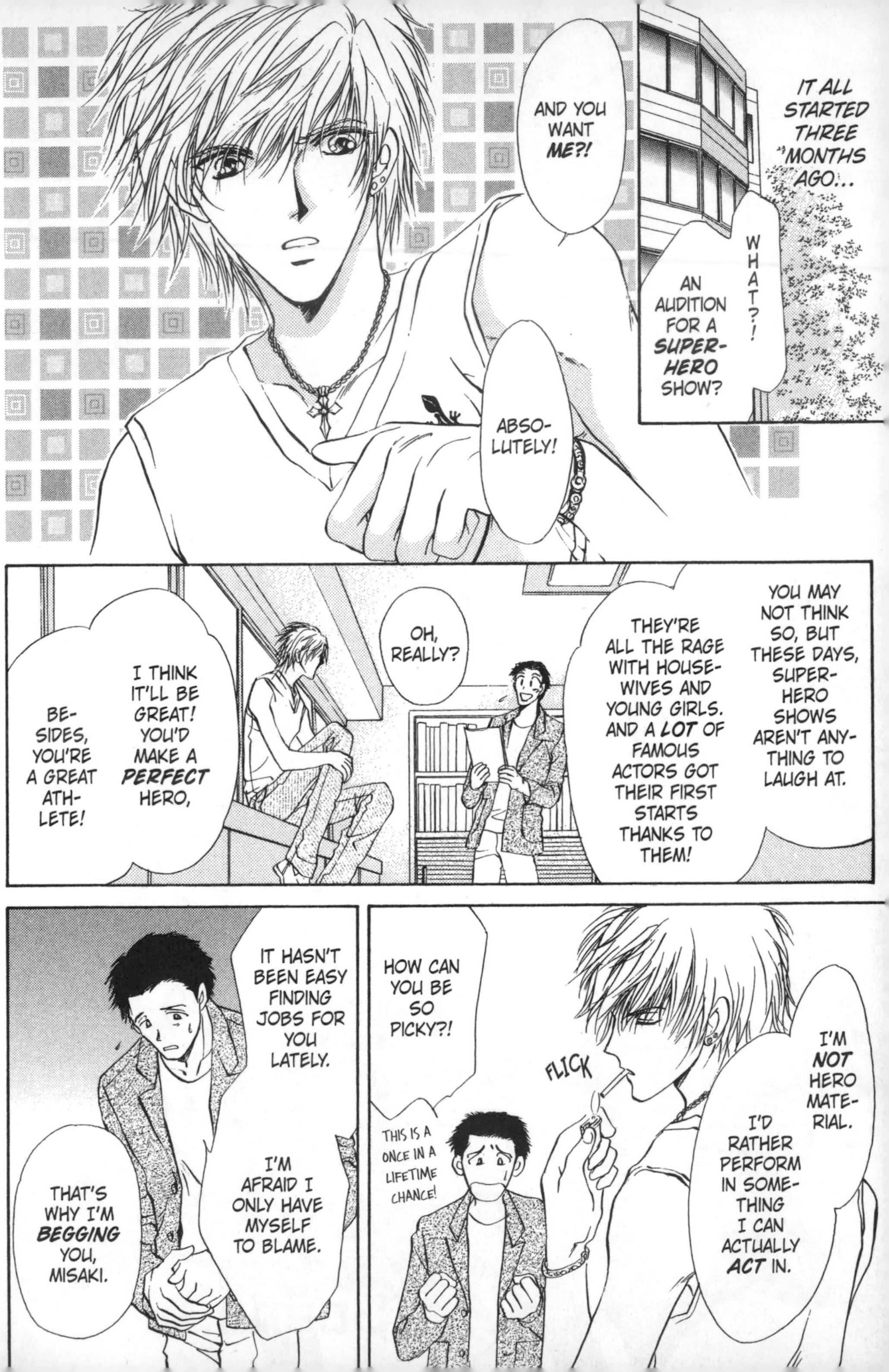
IT ALL STARTED THREE MONTHS AGO...
WHAT?!
AN AUDITION FOR A SUPER-HERO SHOW?
AND YOU WANT ME?!
ABSOLUTELY!
YOU MAY NOT THINK SO, BUT THESE DAYS, SUPER-HERO SHOWS AREN'T ANYTHING TO LAUGH AT.
THEY'RE ALL THE RAGE WITH HOUSE-WIVES AND YOUNG GIRLS. AND A LOT OF FAMOUS ACTORS GOT THEIR FIRST STARTS THANKS TO THEM!
OH, REALLY?
I THINK IT'LL BE GREAT! YOU'D MAKE A PERFECT HERO,
BE-SIDES, YOU'RE A GREAT ATH-LETE!
I'M NOT HERO MATE-RIAL.
I'D RATHER PERFORM IN SOME-THING I CAN ACTUALLY ACT IN.
FLICK
HOW CAN YOU BE SO PICKY?!
THIS IS A ONCE IN A LIFETIME CHANCE!
IT HASN'T BEEN EASY FINDING JOBS FOR YOU LATELY.
I'M AFRAID I ONLY HAVE MYSELF TO BLAME.
THAT'S WHY I'M BEGGING YOU, MISAKI.

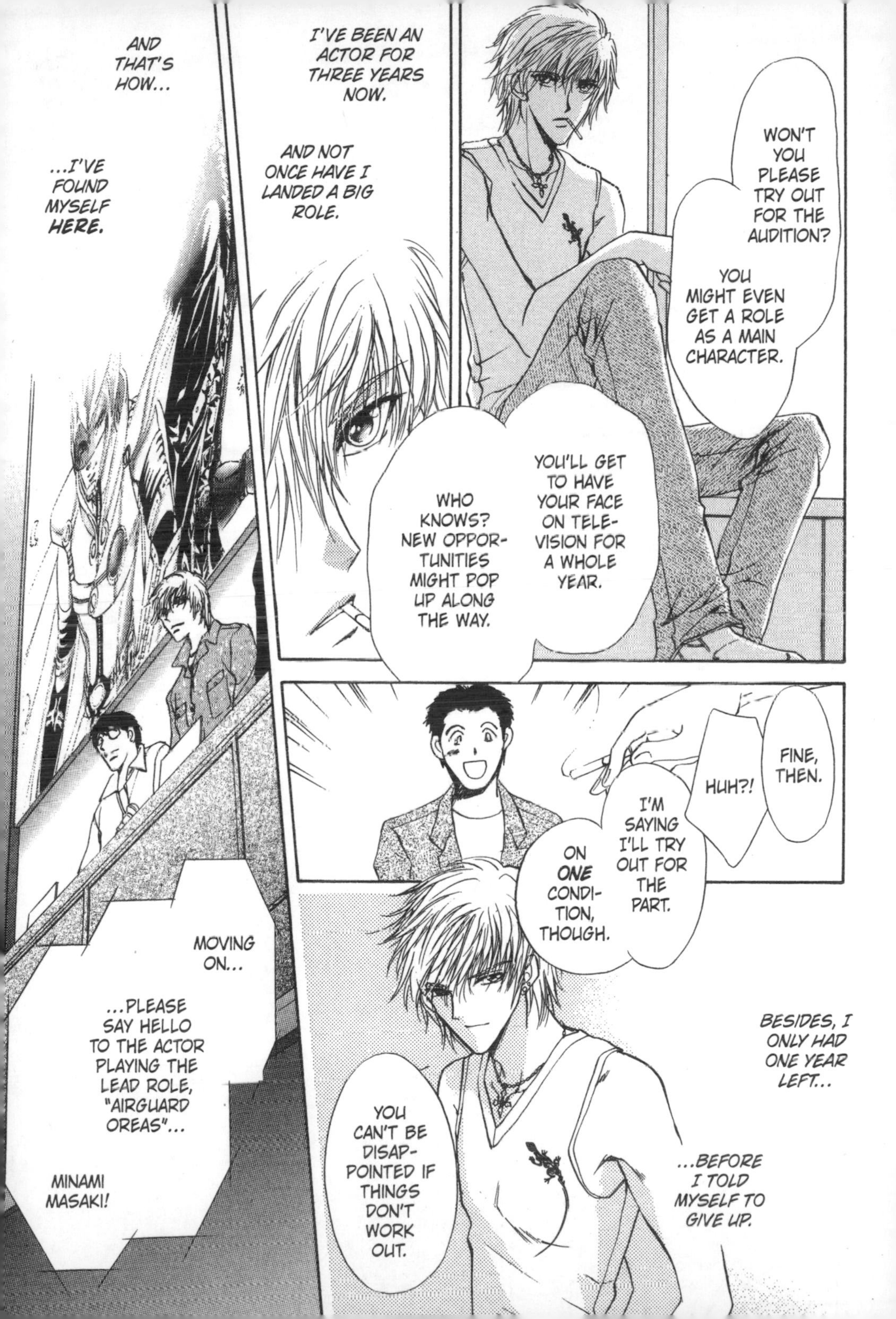
WON'T YOU PLEASE TRY OUT FOR THE AUDITION?
YOU MIGHT EVEN GET A ROLE AS A MAIN CHARACTER.
YOU'LL GET TO HAVE YOUR FACE ON TELE-VISION FOR A WHOLE YEAR.
WHO KNOWS? NEW OPPOR-TUNITIES MIGHT POP UP ALONG THE WAY.
I'VE BEEN AN ACTOR FOR THREE YEARS NOW.
AND NOT ONCE HAVE I LANDED A BIG ROLE.
FINE, THEN.
HUH?!
I'M SAYING I'LL TRY OUT FOR THE PART.
ON ONE CONDI-TION, THOUGH.
BESIDES, I ONLY HAD ONE YEAR LEFT...
...BEFORE I TOLD MYSELF TO GIVE UP.
YOU CAN'T BE DISAP-POINTED IF THINGS DON'T WORK OUT.
AND THAT'S HOW...
...I'VE FOUND MYSELF HERE.
MOVING ON...
...PLEASE SAY HELLO TO THE ACTOR PLAYING THE LEAD ROLE, "AIRGUARD OREAS"...
MINAMI MASAKI!

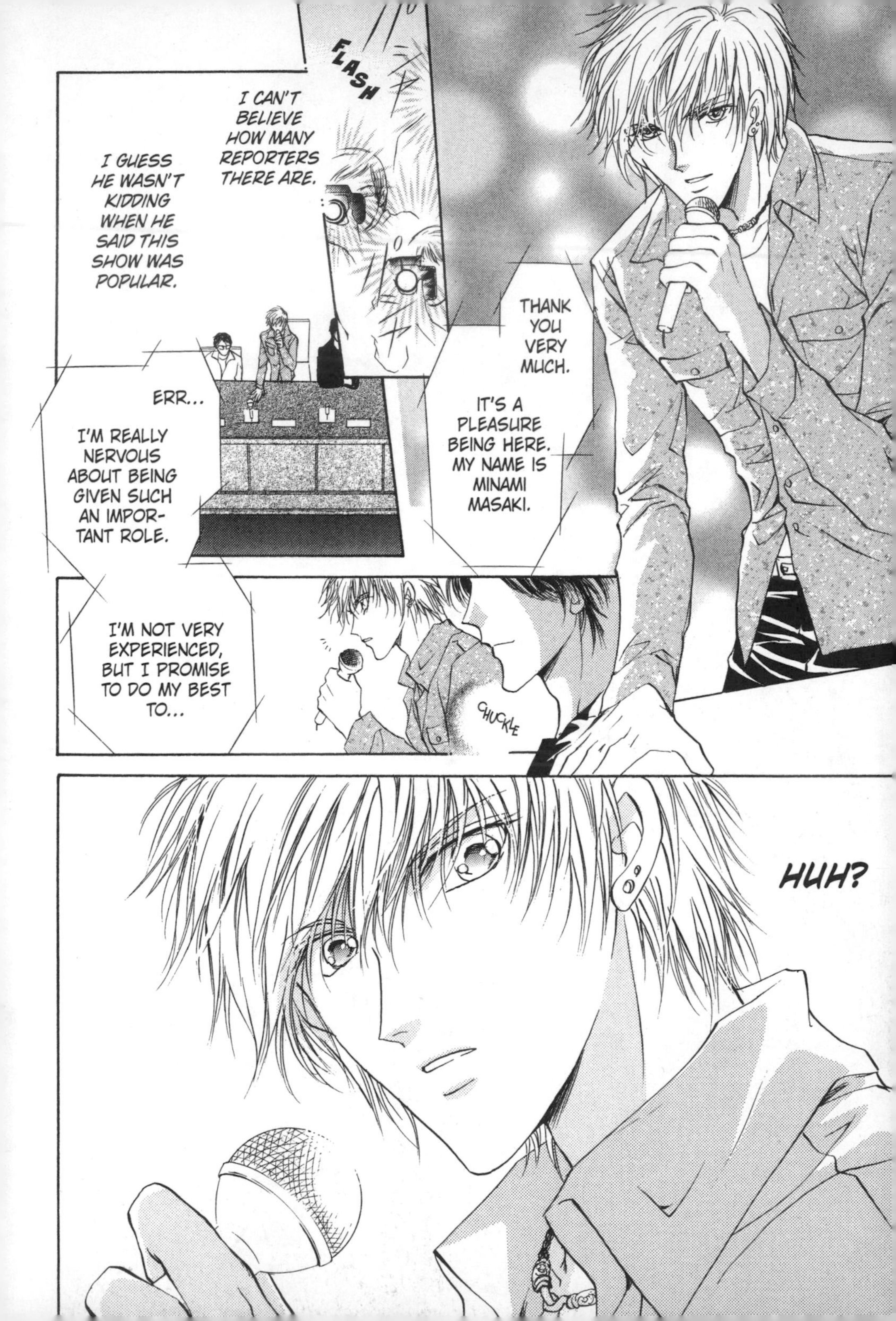
THANK YOU VERY MUCH.
IT'S A PLEASURE BEING HERE. MY NAME IS MINAMI MASAKI.
FLASH
I CAN'T BELIEVE HOW MANY REPORTERS THERE ARE.
I GUESS HE WASN'T KIDDING WHEN HE SAID THIS SHOW WAS POPULAR.
ERR...
I'M REALLY NERVOUS ABOUT BEING GIVEN SUCH AN IMPOR-TANT ROLE.
I'M NOT VERY EXPERIENCED, BUT I PROMISE TO DO MY BEST TO...
CHUCKLE
HUH?

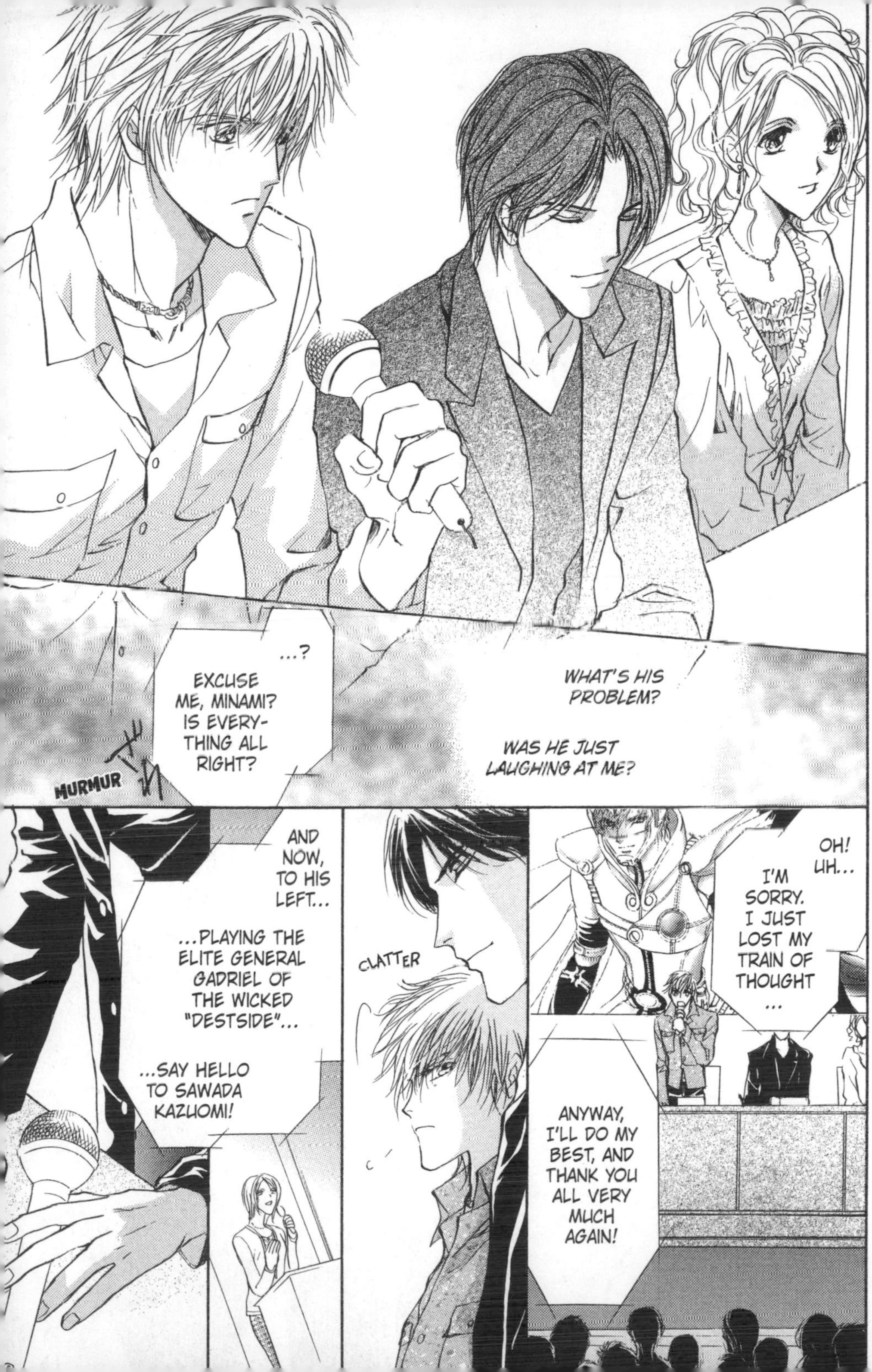
WHAT'S HIS PROBLEM?
WAS HE JUST LAUGHING AT ME?
...?
EXCUSE ME, MINAMI? IS EVERY-THING ALL RIGHT?
MURMUR
OH! UH...
I'M SORRY. I JUST LOST MY TRAIN OF THOUGHT...
ANYWAY, I'LL DO MY BEST, AND THANK YOU ALL VERY MUCH AGAIN!
CLATTER
AND NOW, TO HIS LEFT...
...PLAYING THE ELITE GENERAL GADRIEL OF THE WICKED "DESTSIDE"...
...SAY HELLO TO SAWADA KAZUOMI!

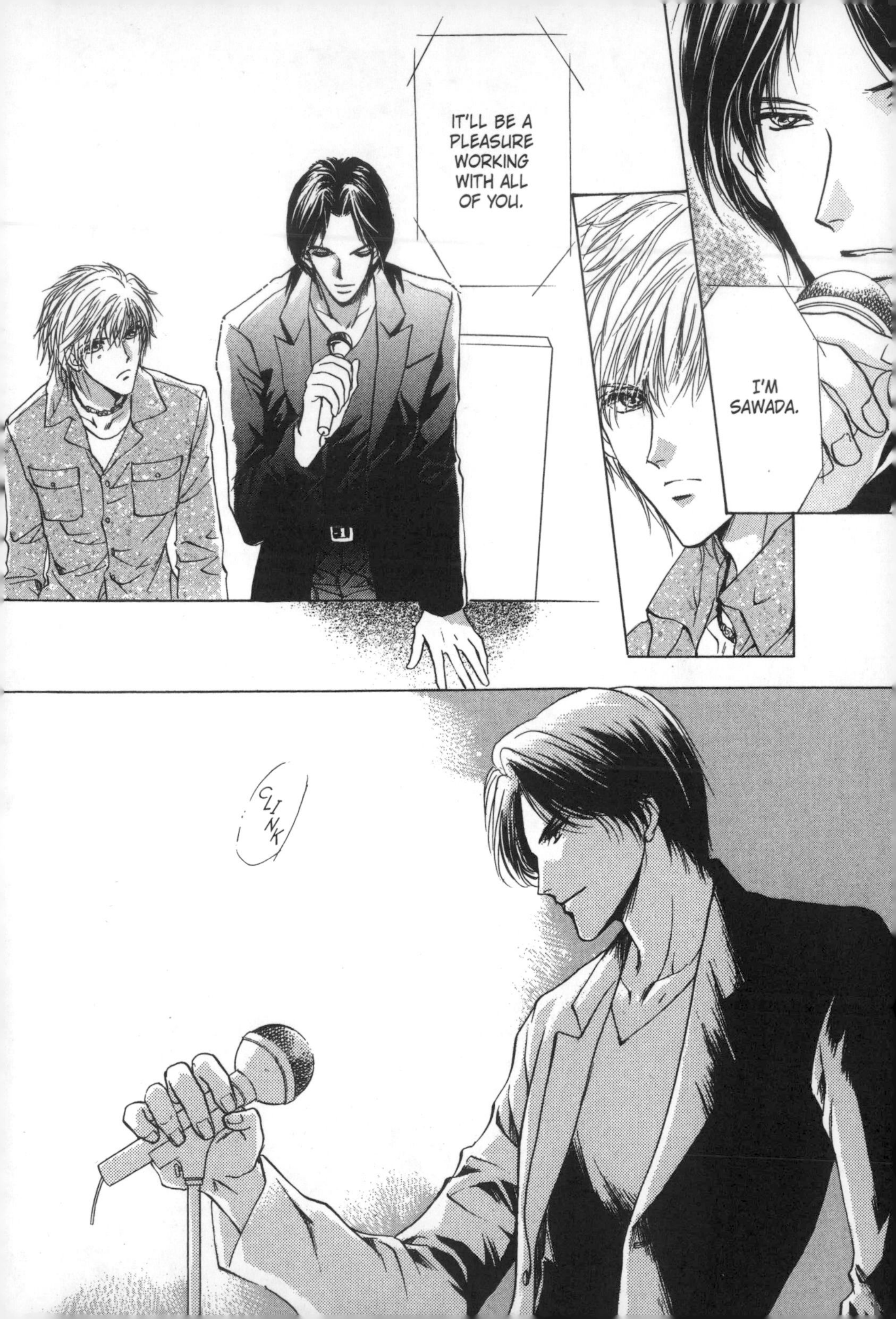
I'M SAWADA.
IT'LL BE A PLEASURE WORKING WITH ALL OF YOU.
CLINK

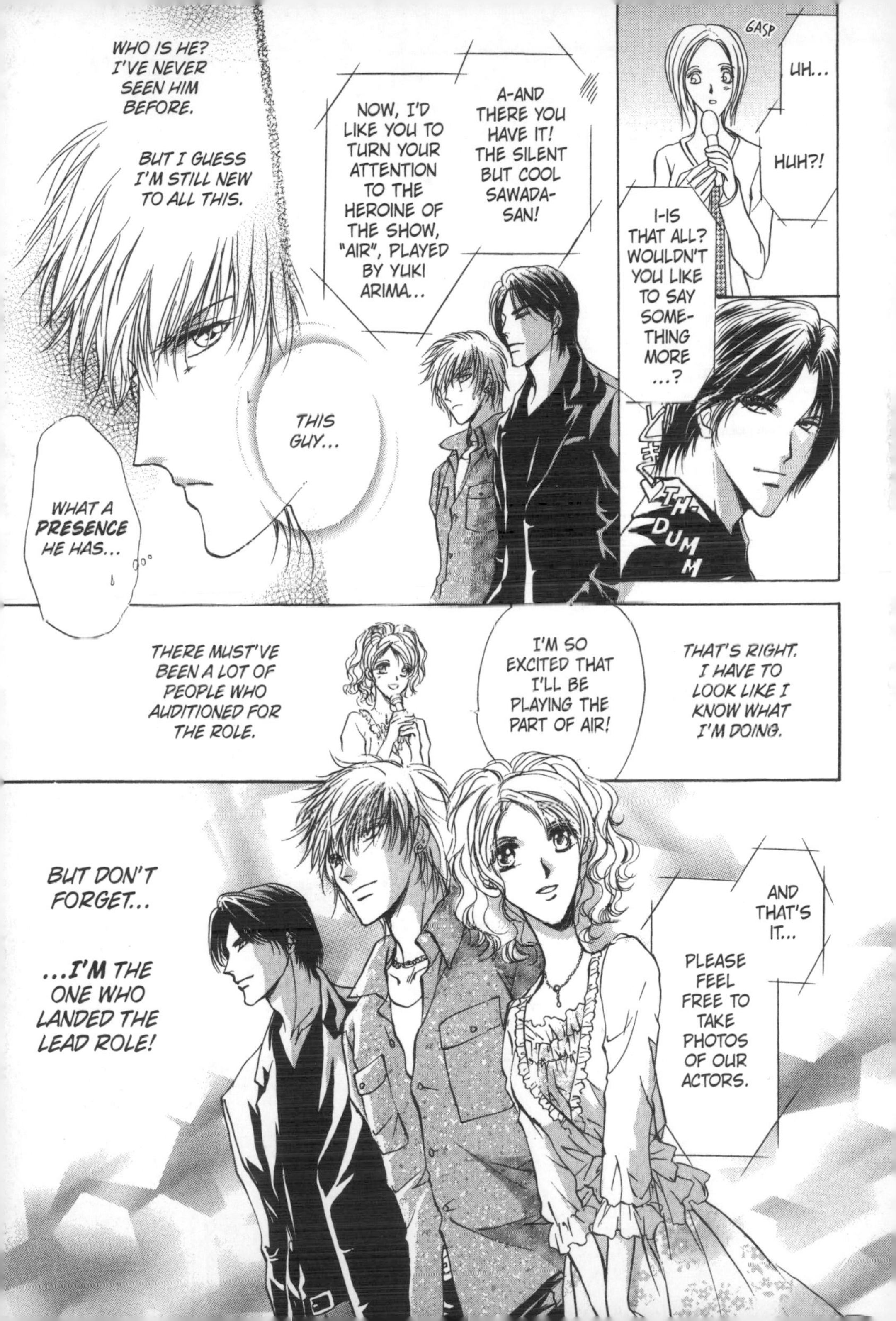
GASP
UH...
HUH?!
I-IS THAT ALL? WOULDN'T YOU LIKE TO SAY SOME-THING MORE ...?
TH-DUMM
A-AND THERE YOU HAVE IT! THE SILENT BUT COOL SAWADA-SAN!
NOW, I'D LIKE YOU TO TURN YOUR ATTENTION TO THE HEROINE OF THE SHOW, "AIR", PLAYED BY YUKI ARIMA...
WHO IS HE? I'VE NEVER SEEN HIM BEFORE.
BUT I GUESS I'M STILL NEW TO ALL THIS.
THIS GUY...
WHAT A PRESENCE HE HAS...
THAT'S RIGHT. I HAVE TO LOOK LIKE I KNOW WHAT I'M DOING.
I'M SO EXCITED THAT I'LL BE PLAYING THE PART OF AIR!
THERE MUST'VE BEEN A LOT OF PEOPLE WHO AUDITIONED FOR THE ROLE.
AND THAT'S IT...
PLEASE FEEL FREE TO TAKE PHOTOS OF OUR ACTORS.
BUT DON'T FORGET...
...I'M THE ONE WHO LANDED THE LEAD ROLE!

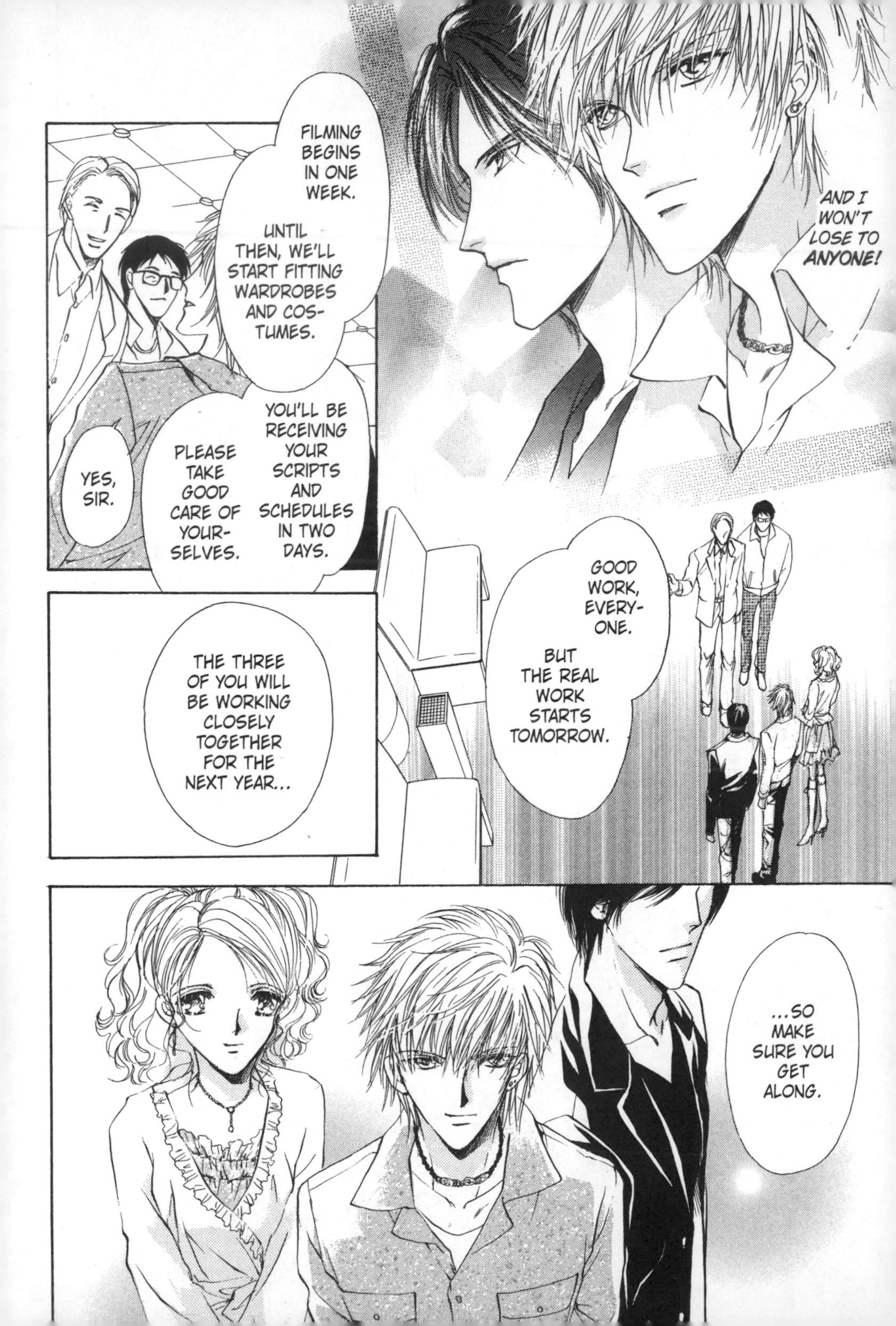
AND I WON'T LOSE TO ANYONE!
FILMING BEGINS IN ONE WEEK.
UNTIL THEN, WE'LL START FITTING WARDROBES AND COS-TUMES.
YOU'LL BE RECEIVING YOUR SCRIPTS AND SCHEDULES IN TWO DAYS.
PLEASE TAKE GOOD CARE OF YOUR-SELVES.
YES, SIR.
GOOD WORK, EVERY-ONE.
BUT THE REAL WORK STARTS TOMORROW.
THE THREE OF YOU WILL BE WORKING CLOSELY TOGETHER FOR THE NEXT YEAR...
...SO MAKE SURE YOU GET ALONG.

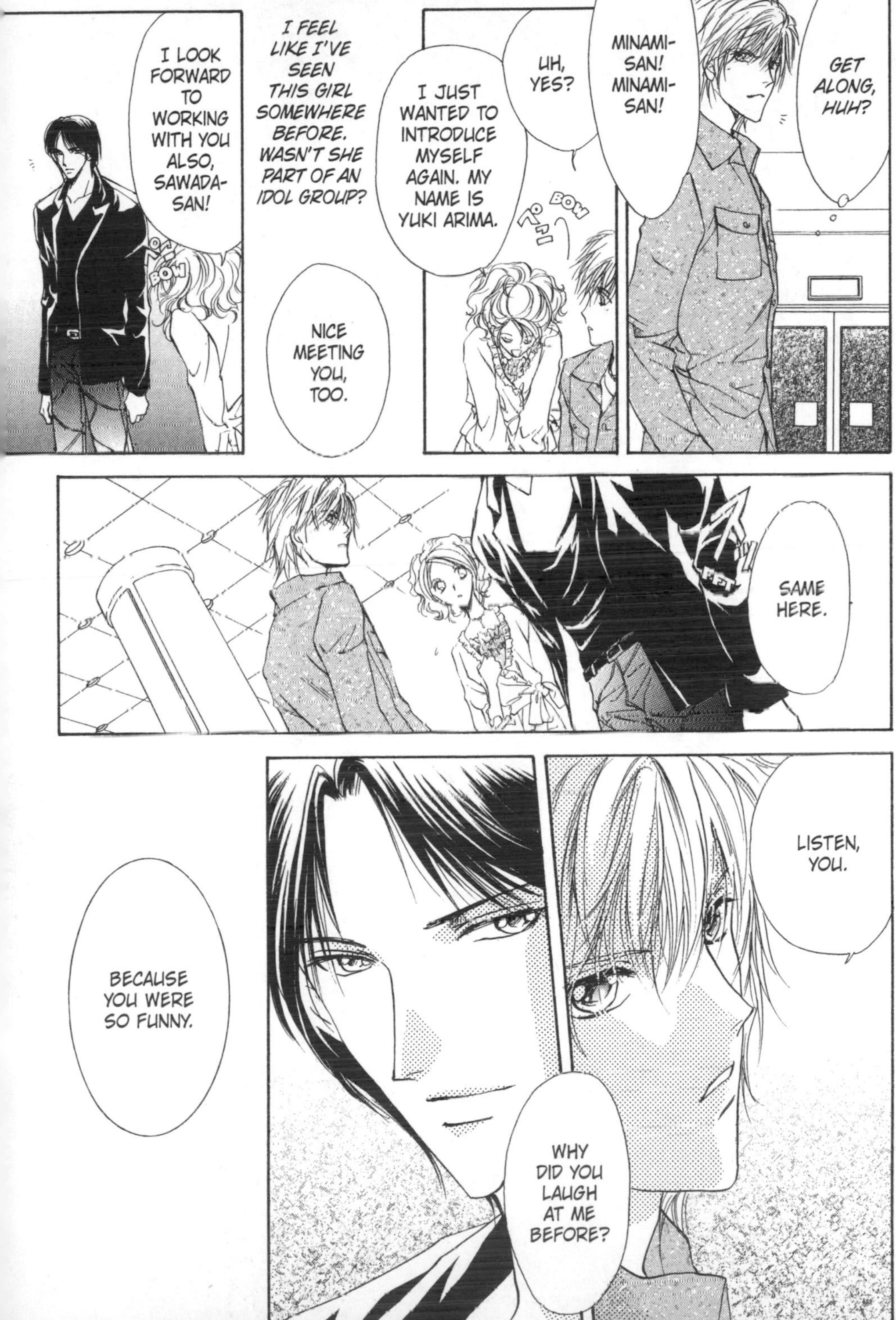
GET ALONG, HUH?
MINAMI-SAN! MINAMI-SAN!
UH, YES?
I JUST WANTED TO INTRODUCE MYSELF AGAIN. MY NAME IS YUKI ARIMA.
BOW
NICE MEETING YOU, TOO.
I FEEL LIKE I'VE SEEN THIS GIRL SOMEWHERE BEFORE. WASN'T SHE PART OF AN IDOL GROUP?
I LOOK FORWARD TO WORKING WITH YOU ALSO, SAWADA-SAN!
BOW
SAME HERE.
LISTEN, YOU.
WHY DID YOU LAUGH AT ME BEFORE?
BECAUSE YOU WERE SO FUNNY.

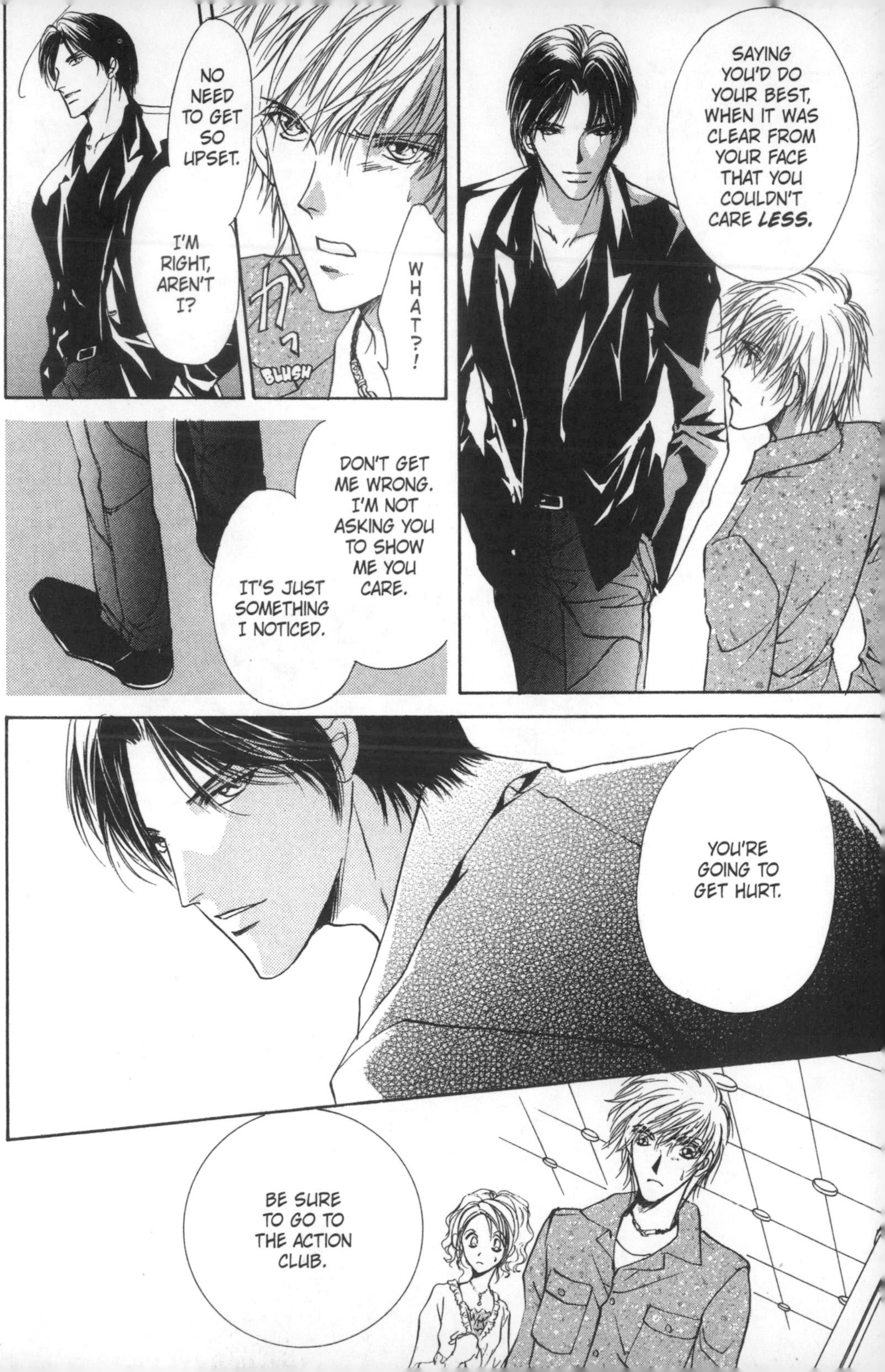
SAYING YOU'D DO YOUR BEST, WHEN IT WAS CLEAR FROM YOUR FACE THAT YOU COULDN'T CARE LESS.
WHAT?!
BLUSH
NO NEED TO GET SO UPSET.
I'M RIGHT, AREN'T I?
DON'T GET ME WRONG. I'M NOT ASKING YOU TO SHOW ME YOU CARE.
IT'S JUST SOMETHING I NOTICED.
YOU'RE GOING TO GET HURT.
BE SURE TO GO TO THE ACTION CLUB.

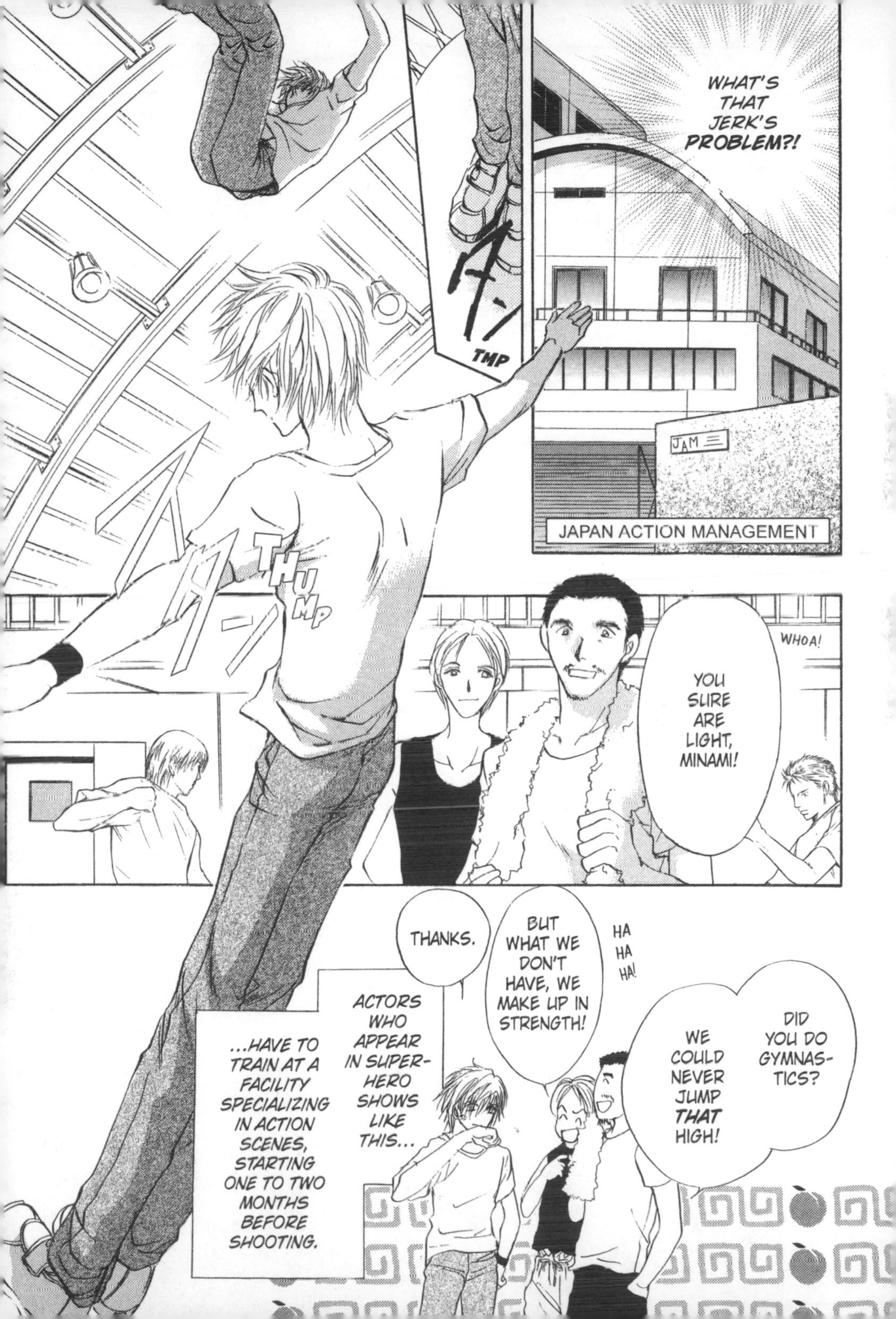
WHAT'S THAT JERK'S PROBLEM?!
JAM
JAPAN ACTION MANAGEMENT
TMP
THUMP
WHOA!
YOU SURE ARE LIGHT, MINAMI!
DID YOU DO GYMNASTICS?
WE COULD NEVER JUMP THAT HIGH!
HA HA HA!
BUT WHAT WE DON'T HAVE, WE MAKE UP IN STRENGTH!
THANKS.
ACTORS WHO APPEAR IN SUPER-HERO SHOWS LIKE THIS...
...HAVE TO TRAIN AT A FACILITY SPECIALIZING IN ACTION SCENES, STARTING ONE TO TWO MONTHS BEFORE SHOOTING.

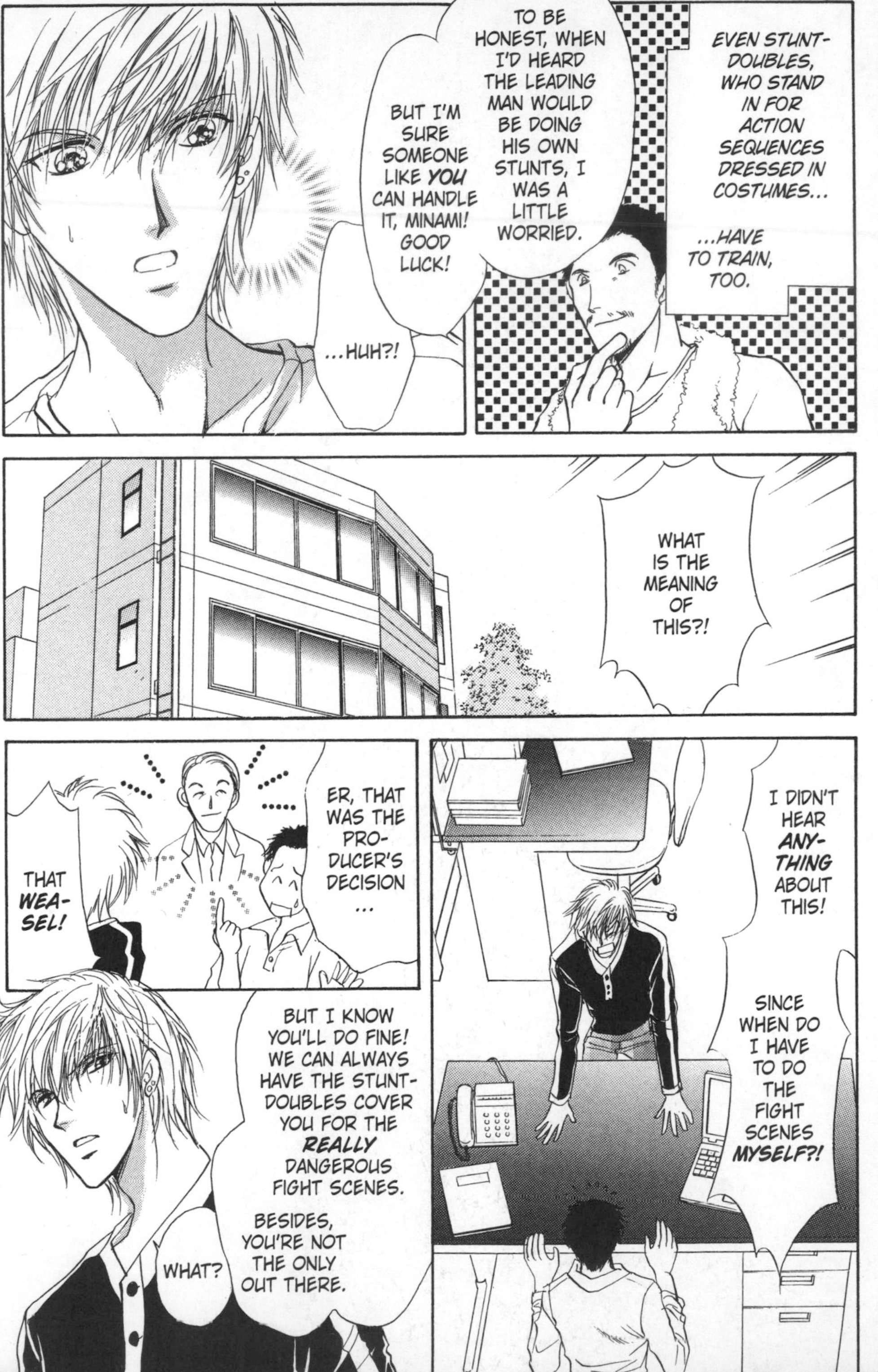
EVEN STUNT-DOUBLES, WHO STAND IN FOR ACTION SEQUENCES DRESSED IN COSTUMES...
...HAVE TO TRAIN, TOO.
TO BE HONEST, WHEN I'D HEARD THE LEADING MAN WOULD BE DOING HIS OWN STUNTS, I WAS A LITTLE WORRIED.
BUT I'M SURE SOMEONE LIKE **YOU** CAN HANDLE IT, MINAMI! GOOD LUCK!
...HUH?!
WHAT IS THE MEANING OF THIS?!
I DIDN'T HEAR **ANY-THING** ABOUT THIS!
SINCE WHEN DO I HAVE TO DO THE FIGHT SCENES **MYSELF?!**
ER, THAT WAS THE PRO-DUCER'S DECISION ...
THAT **WEA-SEL!**
BUT I KNOW YOU'LL DO FINE! WE CAN ALWAYS HAVE THE STUNT-DOUBLES COVER YOU FOR THE **REALLY** DANGEROUS FIGHT SCENES.
BESIDES, YOU'RE NOT THE ONLY OUT THERE.
WHAT?

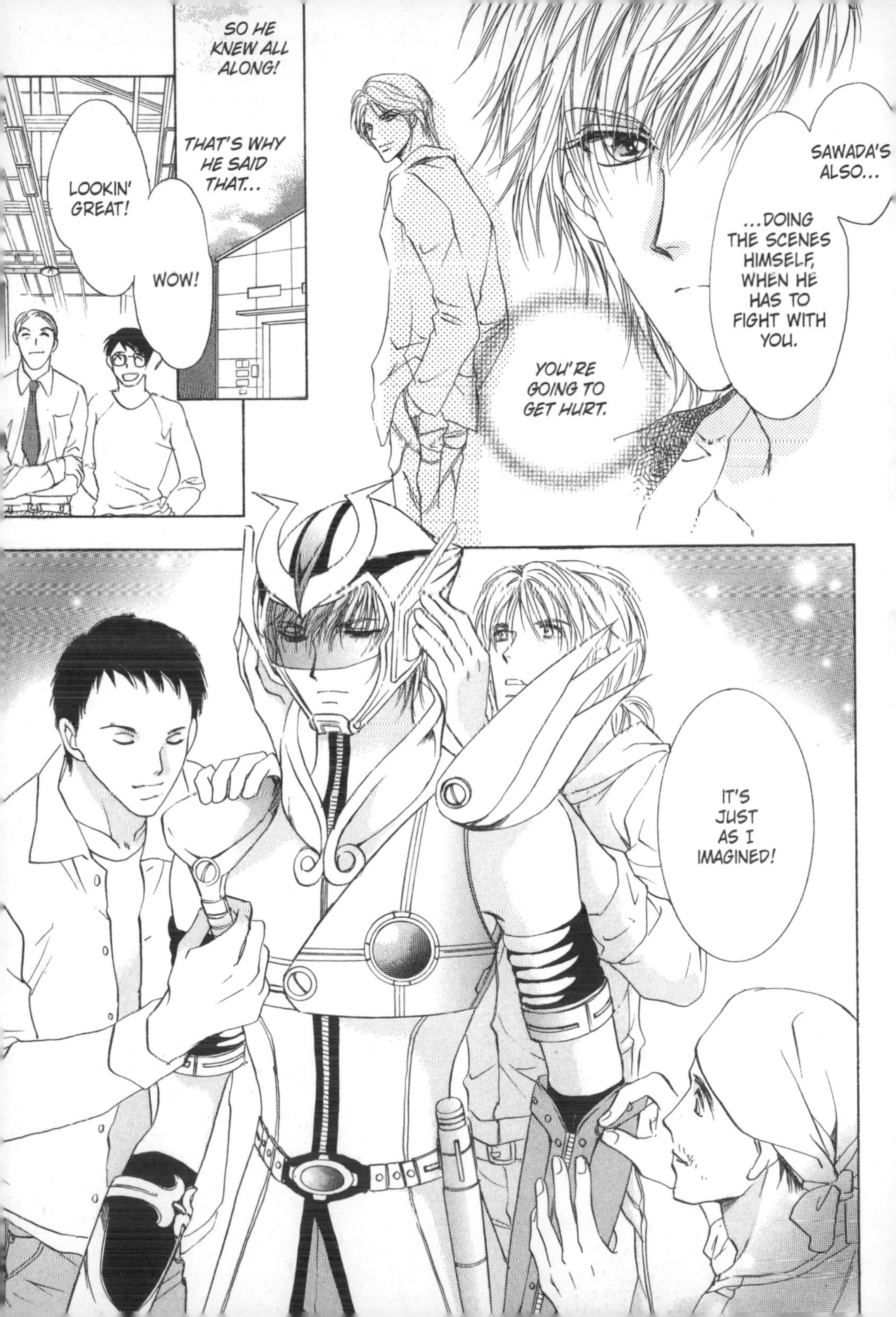
SAWADA'S ALSO...
...DOING THE SCENES HIMSELF, WHEN HE HAS TO FIGHT WITH YOU.
YOU'RE GOING TO GET HURT.
SO HE KNEW ALL ALONG!
THAT'S WHY HE SAID THAT...
WOW!
LOOKIN' GREAT!
IT'S JUST AS I IMAGINED!

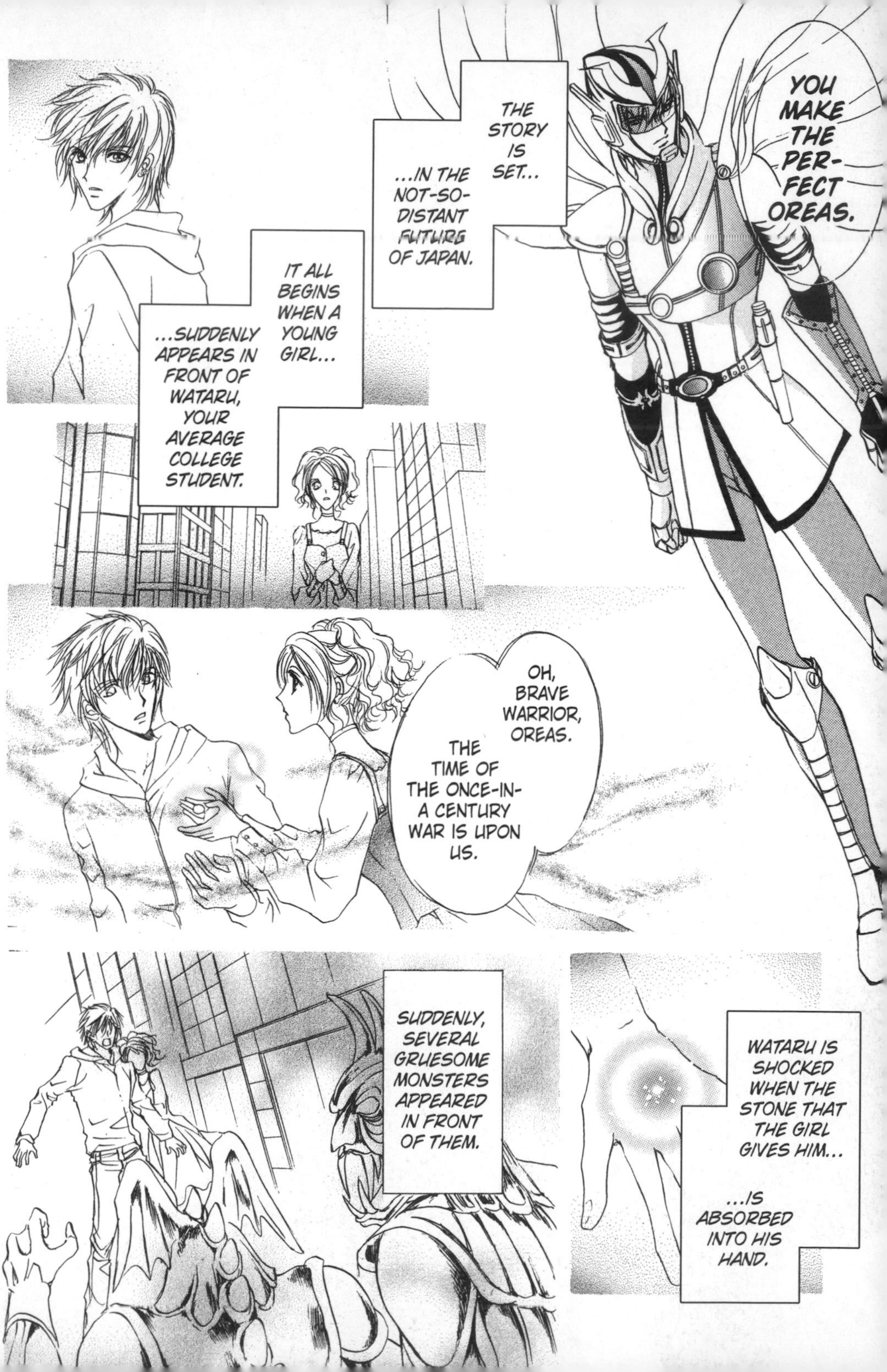
YOU MAKE THE PERFECT OREAS.
THE STORY IS SET...
...IN THE NOT-SO-DISTANT FUTURE OF JAPAN.
IT ALL BEGINS WHEN A YOUNG GIRL...
...SUDDENLY APPEARS IN FRONT OF WATARU, YOUR AVERAGE COLLEGE STUDENT.
OH, BRAVE WARRIOR, OREAS.
THE TIME OF THE ONCE-IN-A CENTURY WAR IS UPON US.
WATARU IS SHOCKED WHEN THE STONE THAT THE GIRL GIVES HIM...
...IS ABSORBED INTO HIS HAND.
SUDDENLY, SEVERAL GRUESOME MONSTERS APPEARED IN FRONT OF THEM.

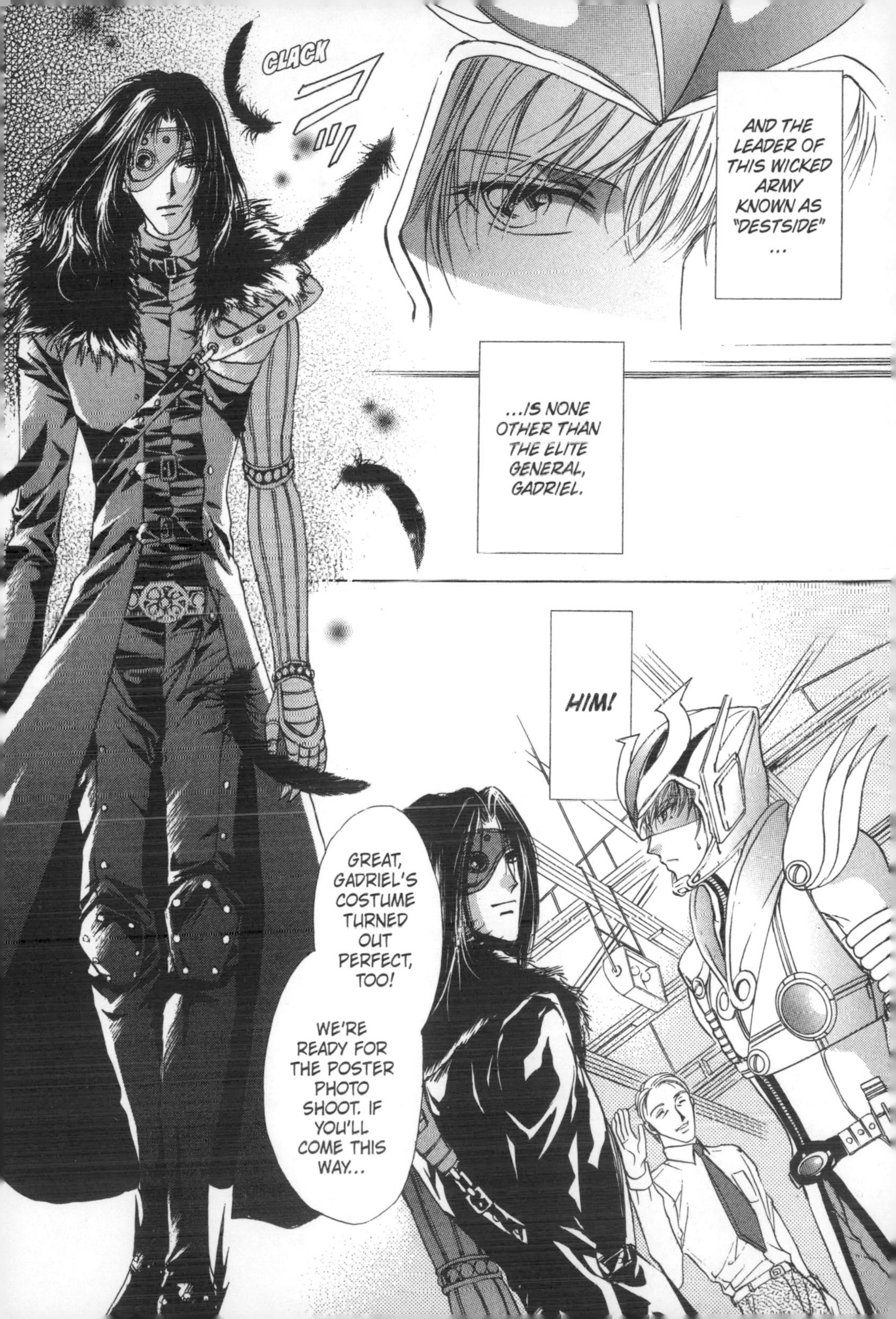
AND THE LEADER OF THIS WICKED ARMY KNOWN AS "DESTSIDE" ...
...IS NONE OTHER THAN THE ELITE GENERAL, GADRIEL.
HIM!
GREAT, GADRIEL'S COSTUME TURNED OUT PERFECT, TOO!
WE'RE READY FOR THE POSTER PHOTO SHOOT. IF YOU'LL COME THIS WAY...
CLACK

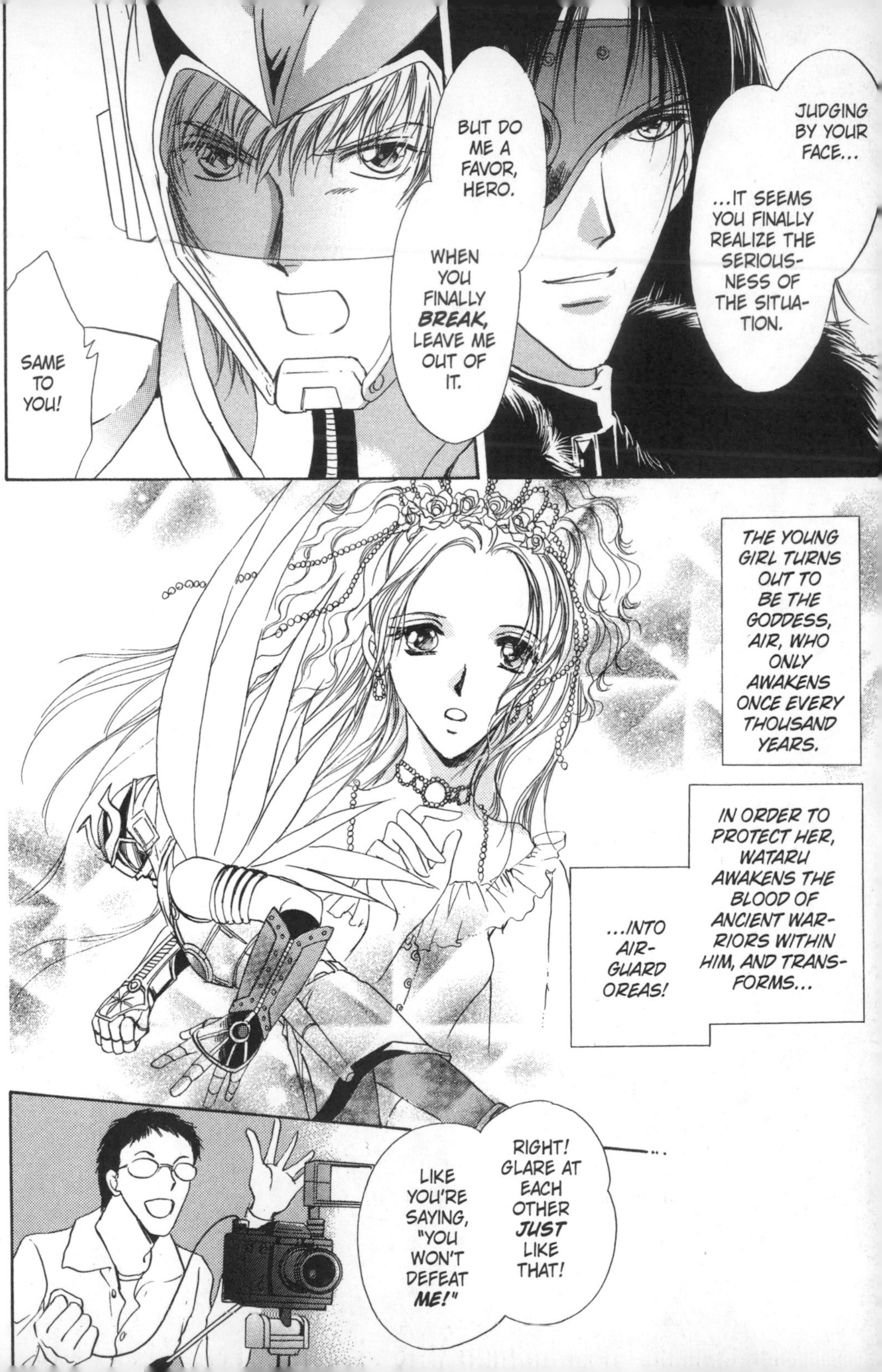
JUDGING BY YOUR FACE...
...IT SEEMS YOU FINALLY REALIZE THE SERIOUSNESS OF THE SITUATION.
BUT DO ME A FAVOR, HERO.
WHEN YOU FINALLY **BREAK**, LEAVE ME OUT OF IT.
SAME TO YOU!
THE YOUNG GIRL TURNS OUT TO BE THE GODDESS, AIR, WHO ONLY AWAKENS ONCE EVERY THOUSAND YEARS.
IN ORDER TO PROTECT HER, WATARU AWAKENS THE BLOOD OF ANCIENT WARRIORS WITHIN HIM, AND TRANSFORMS...
...INTO AIR-GUARD OREAS!
RIGHT! GLARE AT EACH OTHER **JUST** LIKE THAT!
LIKE YOU'RE SAYING, "YOU WON'T DEFEAT **ME!**"

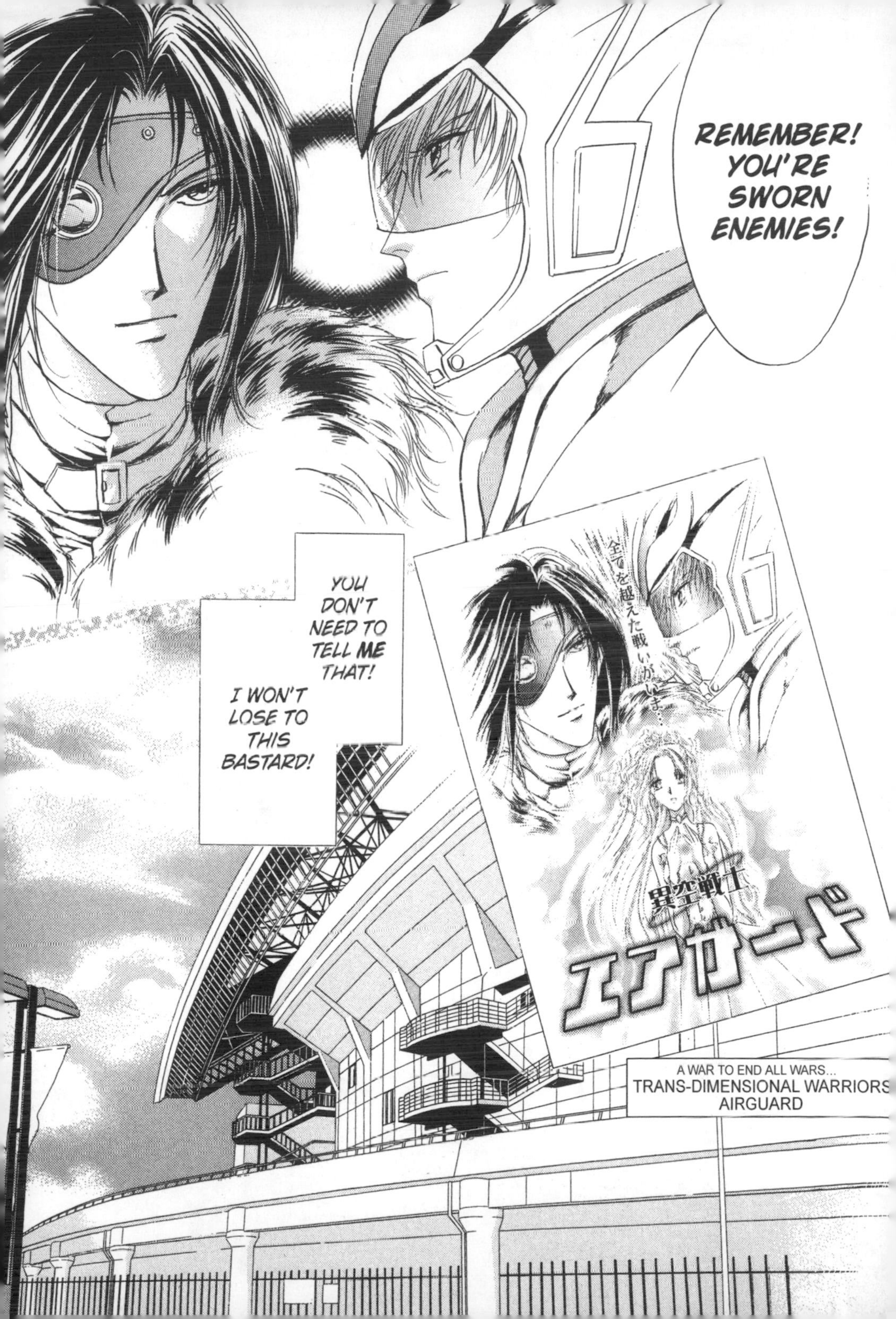
REMEMBER! YOU'RE SWORN ENEMIES!
YOU DON'T NEED TO TELL ME THAT!
I WON'T LOSE TO THIS BASTARD!
全てを越えた戦いがいま…
異空戦士
エアガード
A WAR TO END ALL WARS...
TRANS-DIMENSIONAL WARRIORS
AIRGUARD

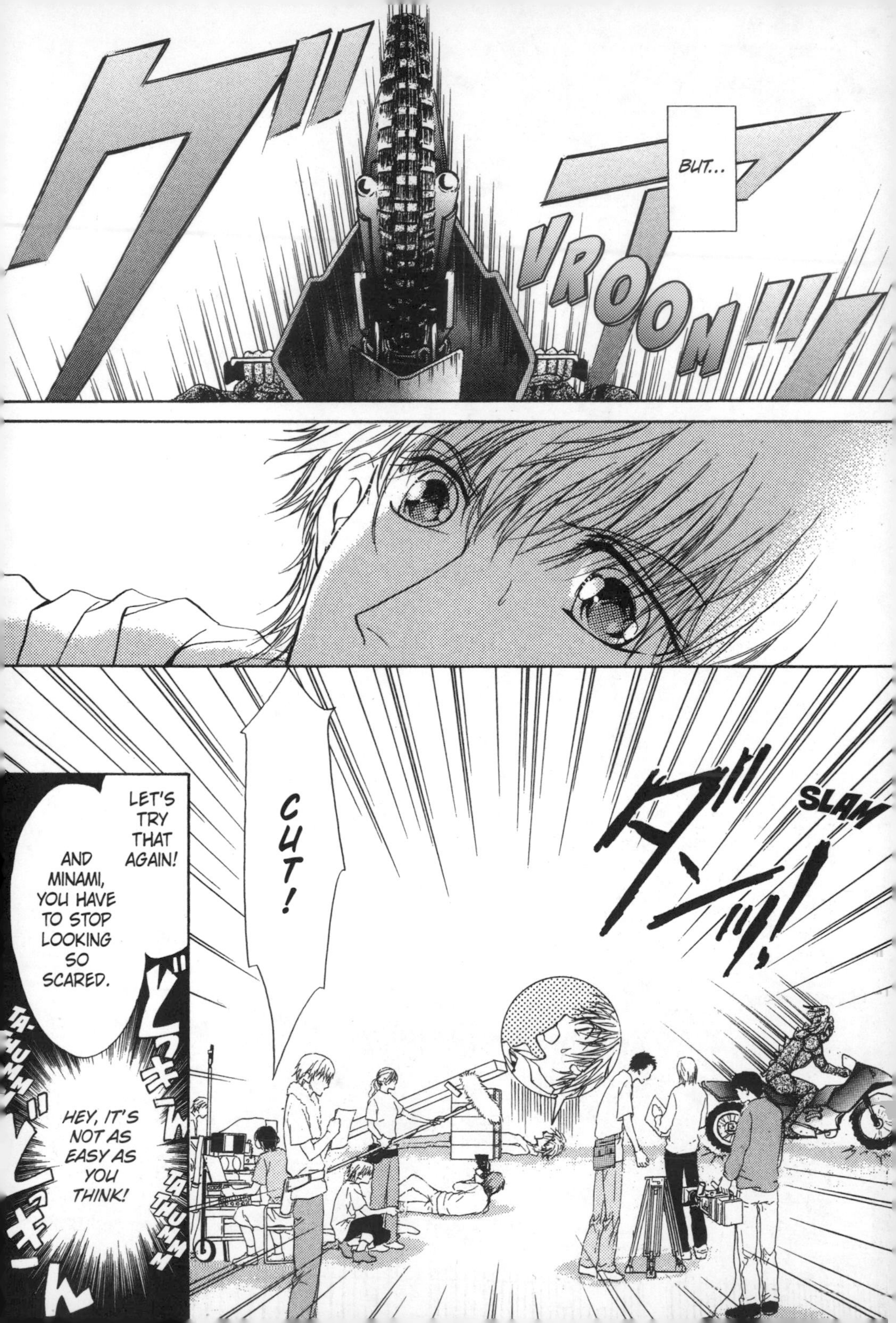
BUT...
VROOM!!
SLAM
CUT!
LET'S TRY THAT AGAIN!
AND MINAMI, YOU HAVE TO STOP LOOKING SO SCARED.
TA-THUMM
HEY, IT'S NOT AS EASY AS YOU THINK!
TA-THUMM

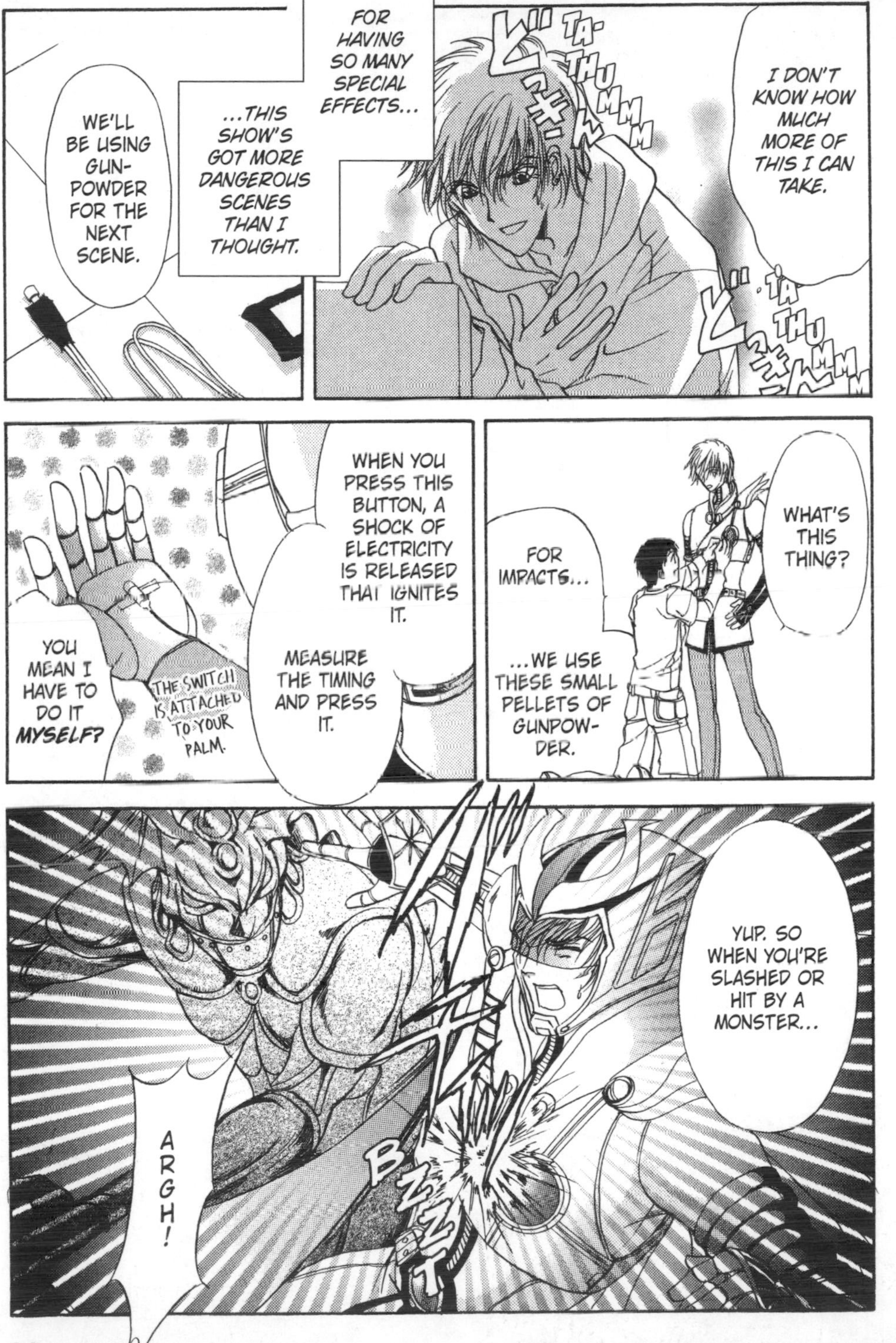
I DON'T KNOW HOW MUCH MORE OF THIS I CAN TAKE.
TA-THUMMMM
FOR HAVING SO MANY SPECIAL EFFECTS...
...THIS SHOW'S GOT MORE DANGEROUS SCENES THAN I THOUGHT.
TA-THUMMMM
WE'LL BE USING GUN-POWDER FOR THE NEXT SCENE.
WHAT'S THIS THING?
FOR IMPACTS...
...WE USE THESE SMALL PELLETS OF GUNPOW-DER.
WHEN YOU PRESS THIS BUTTON, A SHOCK OF ELECTRICITY IS RELEASED THAT IGNITES IT.
MEASURE THE TIMING AND PRESS IT.
THE SWITCH IS ATTACHED TO YOUR PALM.
YOU MEAN I HAVE TO DO IT *MYSELF?*
YUP. SO WHEN YOU'RE SLASHED OR HIT BY A MONSTER...
BZZZT
ARGH!

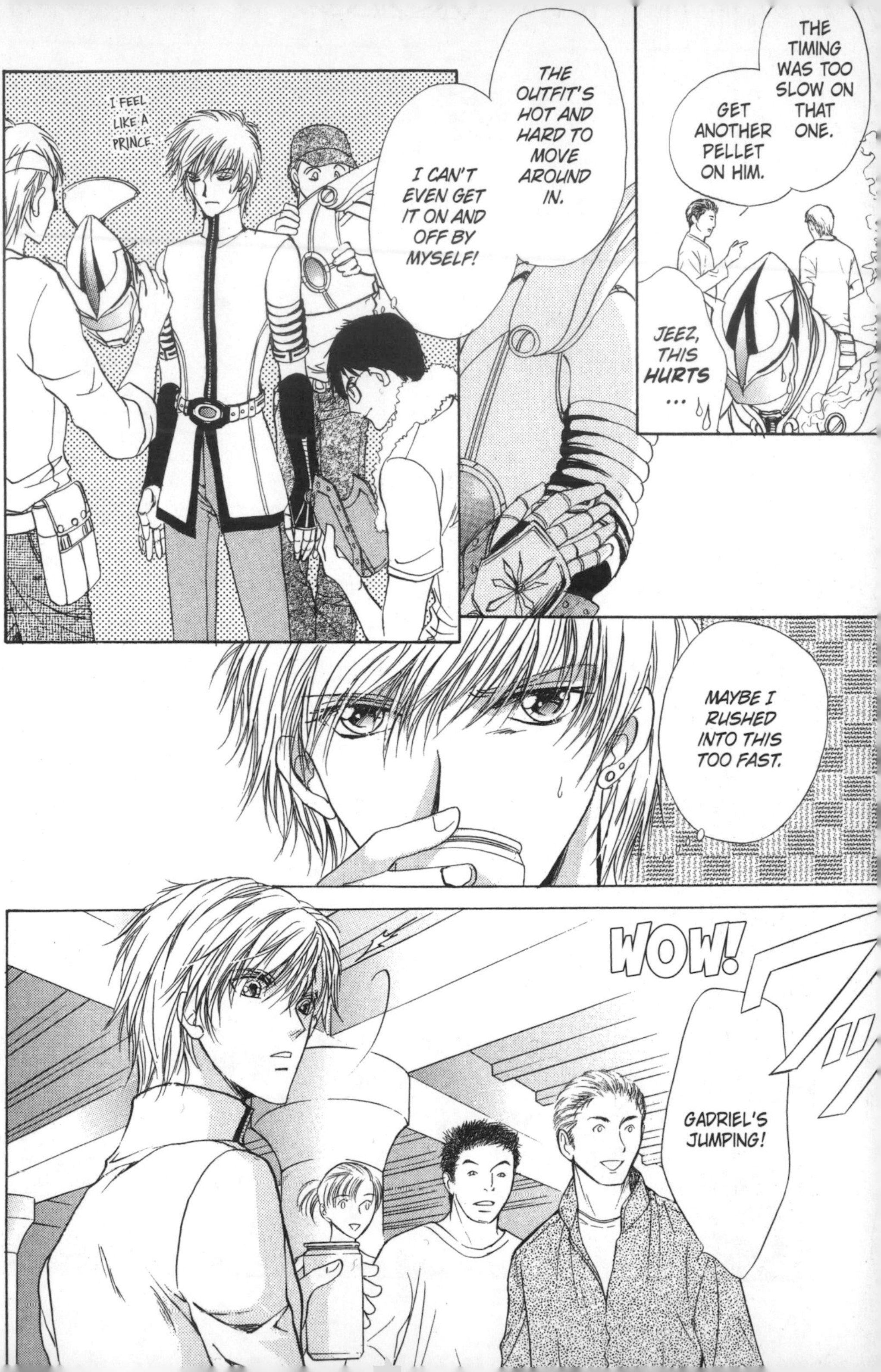
THE TIMING WAS TOO SLOW ON THAT ONE.
GET ANOTHER PELLET ON HIM.
JEEZ, THIS HURTS ...
THE OUTFIT'S HOT AND HARD TO MOVE AROUND IN.
I CAN'T EVEN GET IT ON AND OFF BY MYSELF!
I FEEL LIKE A PRINCE.
MAYBE I RUSHED INTO THIS TOO FAST.
WOW!
GADRIEL'S JUMPING!

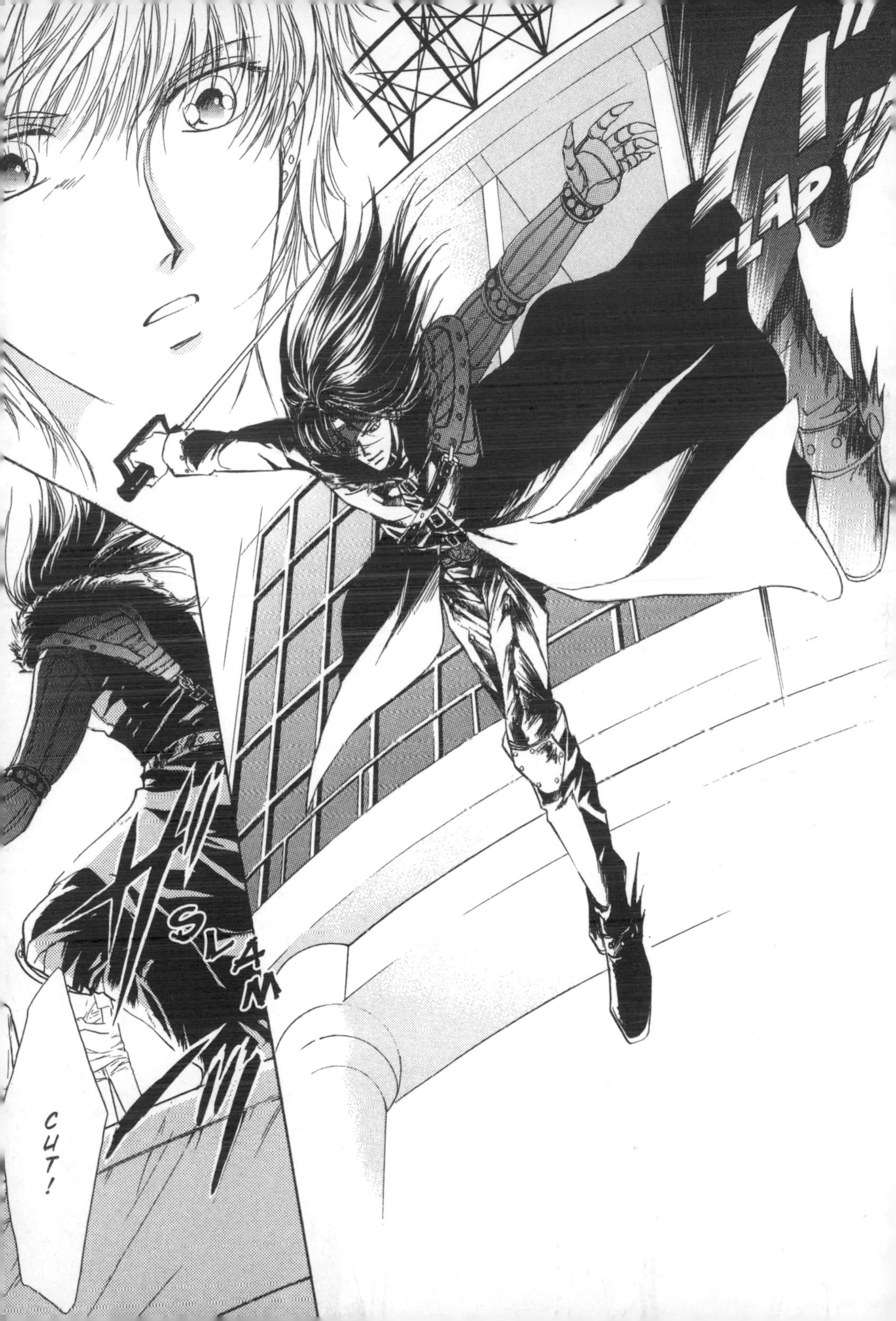
FLAP
SLAM
CUT!

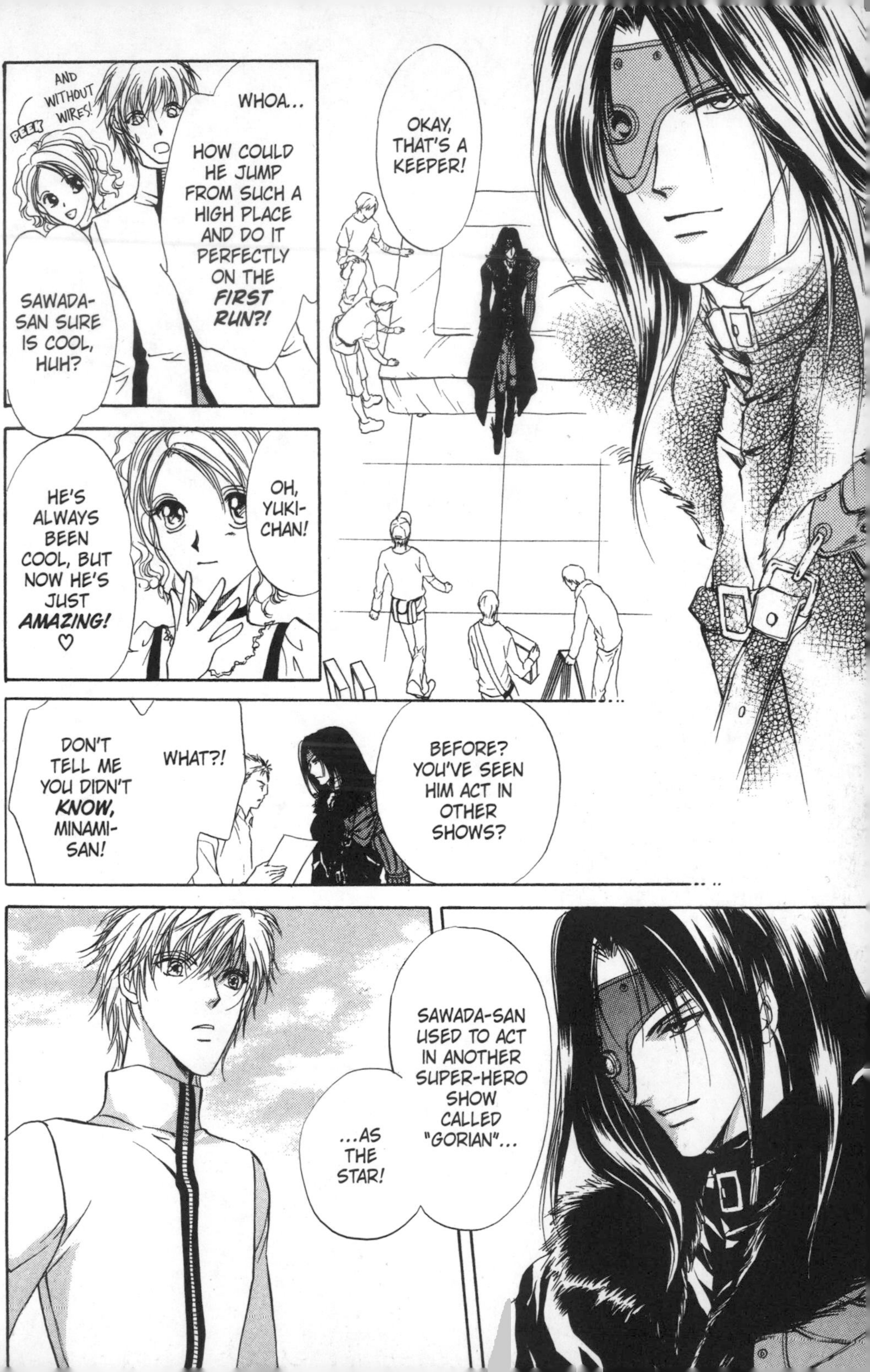
OKAY, THAT'S A KEEPER!
WHOA...
HOW COULD HE JUMP FROM SUCH A HIGH PLACE AND DO IT PERFECTLY ON THE *FIRST RUN?!*
AND WITHOUT WIRES!
PEEK
SAWADA-SAN SURE IS COOL, HUH?
OH, YUKI-CHAN!
HE'S ALWAYS BEEN COOL, BUT NOW HE'S JUST *AMAZING!* ♡
BEFORE? YOU'VE SEEN HIM ACT IN OTHER SHOWS?
WHAT?!
DON'T TELL ME YOU DIDN'T *KNOW,* MINAMI-SAN!
SAWADA-SAN USED TO ACT IN ANOTHER SUPER-HERO SHOW CALLED "GORIAN"...
...AS THE STAR!

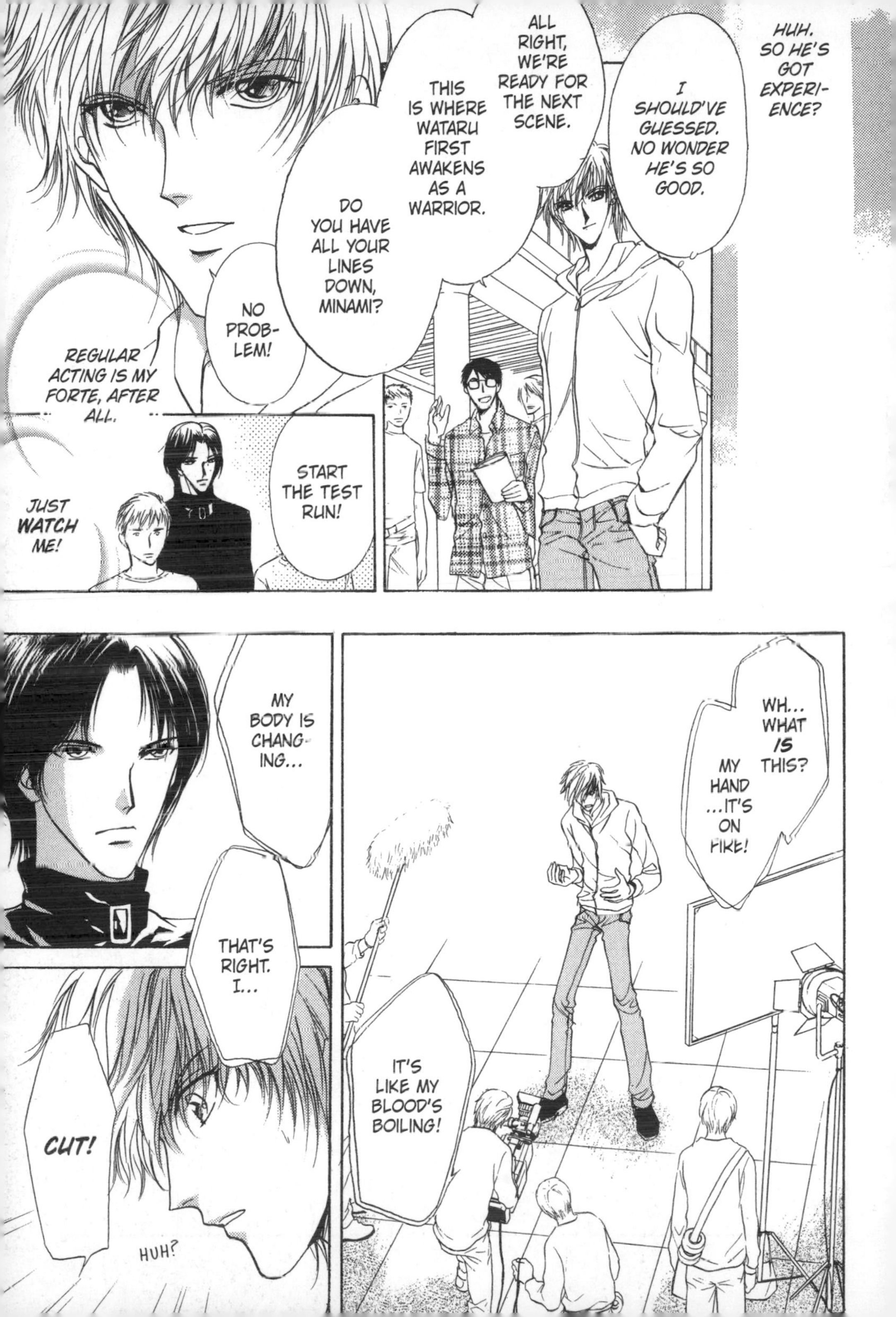
HUH. SO HE'S GOT EXPERIENCE?
I SHOULD'VE GUESSED. NO WONDER HE'S SO GOOD.
ALL RIGHT, WE'RE READY FOR THE NEXT SCENE.
THIS IS WHERE WATARU FIRST AWAKENS AS A WARRIOR.
DO YOU HAVE ALL YOUR LINES DOWN, MINAMI?
NO PROBLEM!
REGULAR ACTING IS MY FORTE, AFTER ALL.
START THE TEST RUN!
JUST WATCH ME!
WH... WHAT IS THIS?
MY HAND ...IT'S ON FIRE!
IT'S LIKE MY BLOOD'S BOILING!
MY BODY IS CHANGING...
THAT'S RIGHT. I...
CUT!
HUH?

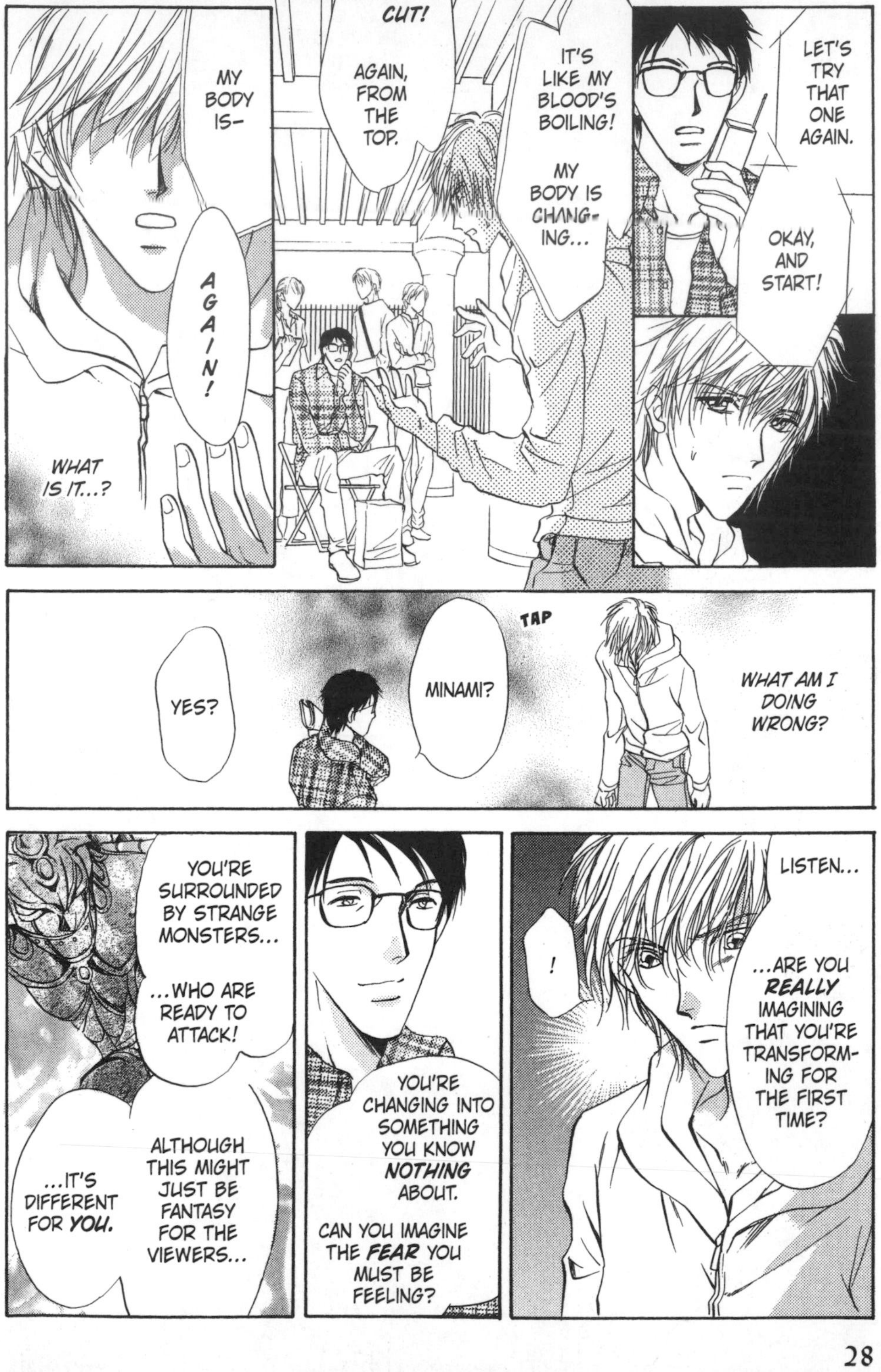
LET'S TRY THAT ONE AGAIN.
OKAY, AND START!
IT'S LIKE MY BLOOD'S BOILING!
MY BODY IS CHANG-ING...
CUT!
AGAIN, FROM THE TOP.
MY BODY IS—
AGAIN!
WHAT IS IT...?
WHAT AM I DOING WRONG?
TAP
MINAMI?
YES?
LISTEN...
...ARE YOU REALLY IMAGINING THAT YOU'RE TRANSFORMING FOR THE FIRST TIME?
!
YOU'RE CHANGING INTO SOMETHING YOU KNOW NOTHING ABOUT.
CAN YOU IMAGINE THE FEAR YOU MUST BE FEELING?
YOU'RE SURROUNDED BY STRANGE MONSTERS...
...WHO ARE READY TO ATTACK!
ALTHOUGH THIS MIGHT JUST BE FANTASY FOR THE VIEWERS...
...IT'S DIFFERENT FOR YOU.

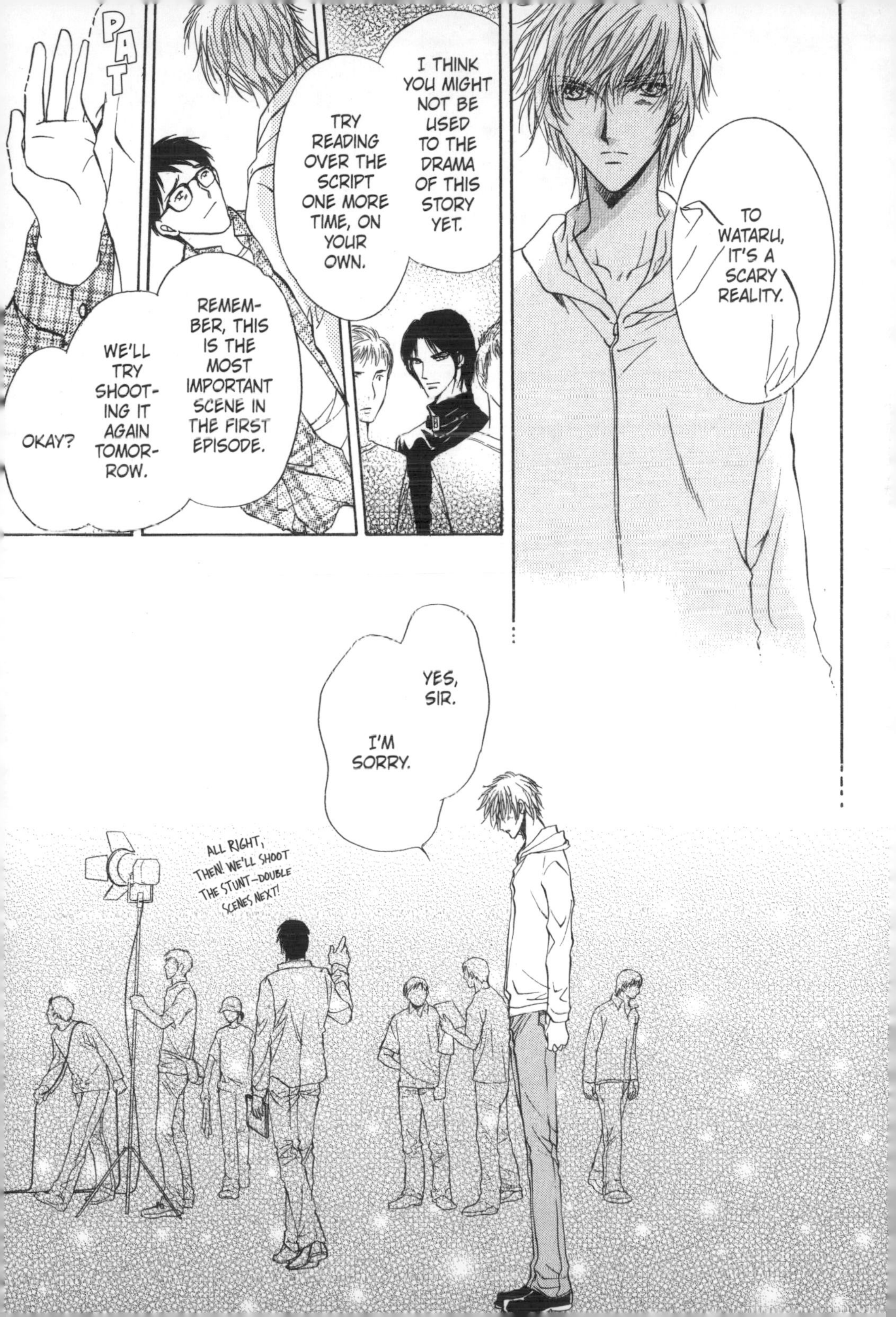
TO WATARU, IT'S A SCARY REALITY.
I THINK YOU MIGHT NOT BE USED TO THE DRAMA OF THIS STORY YET.
TRY READING OVER THE SCRIPT ONE MORE TIME, ON YOUR OWN.
REMEMBER, THIS IS THE MOST IMPORTANT SCENE IN THE FIRST EPISODE.
WE'LL TRY SHOOTING IT AGAIN TOMORROW.
PAT
OKAY?
YES, SIR.
I'M SORRY.
ALL RIGHT, THEN! WE'LL SHOOT THE STUNT-DOUBLE SCENES NEXT!

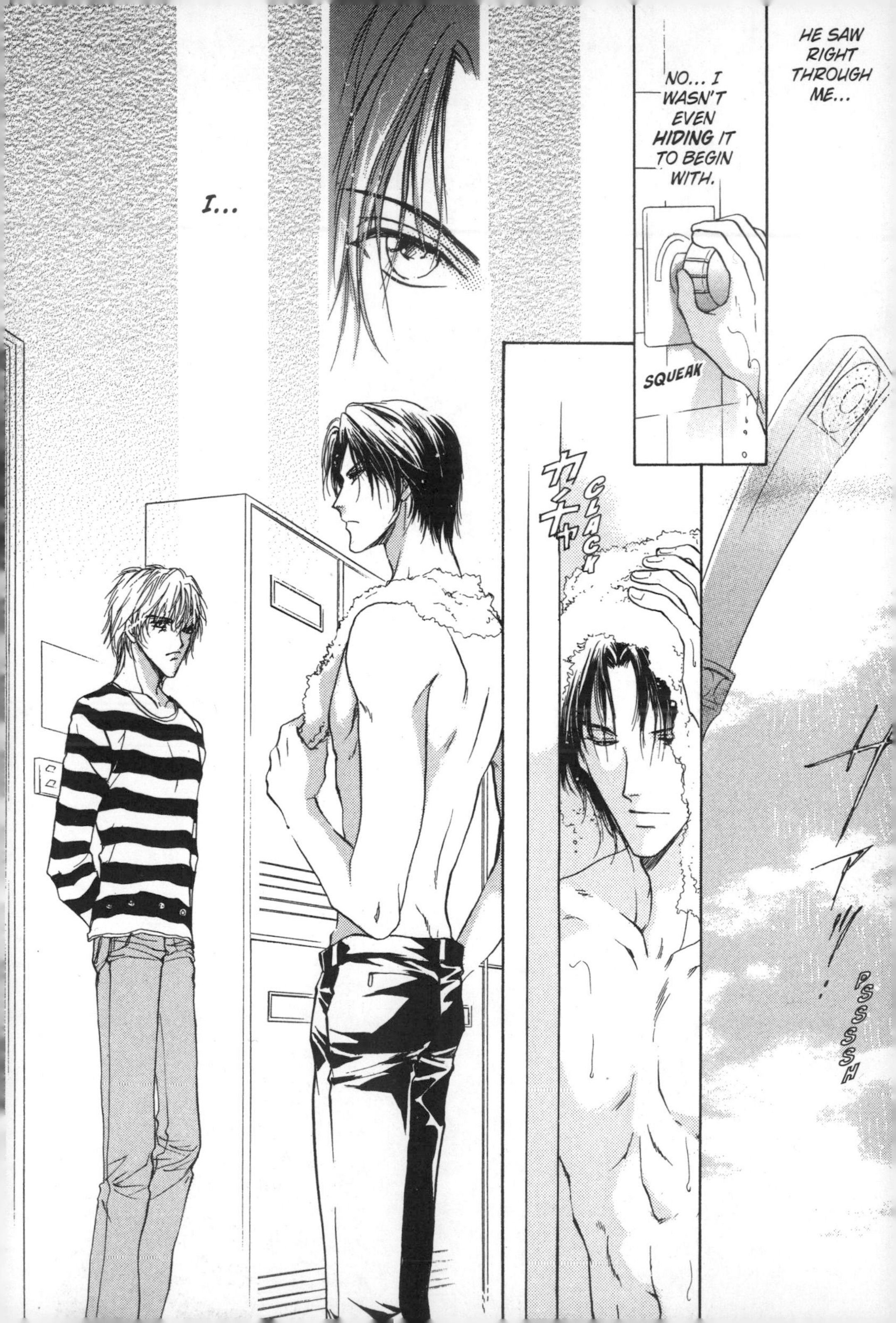
HE SAW RIGHT THROUGH ME...
NO... I WASN'T EVEN HIDING IT TO BEGIN WITH.
SQUEAK
I...
PSSSSH
カチャ CLACK

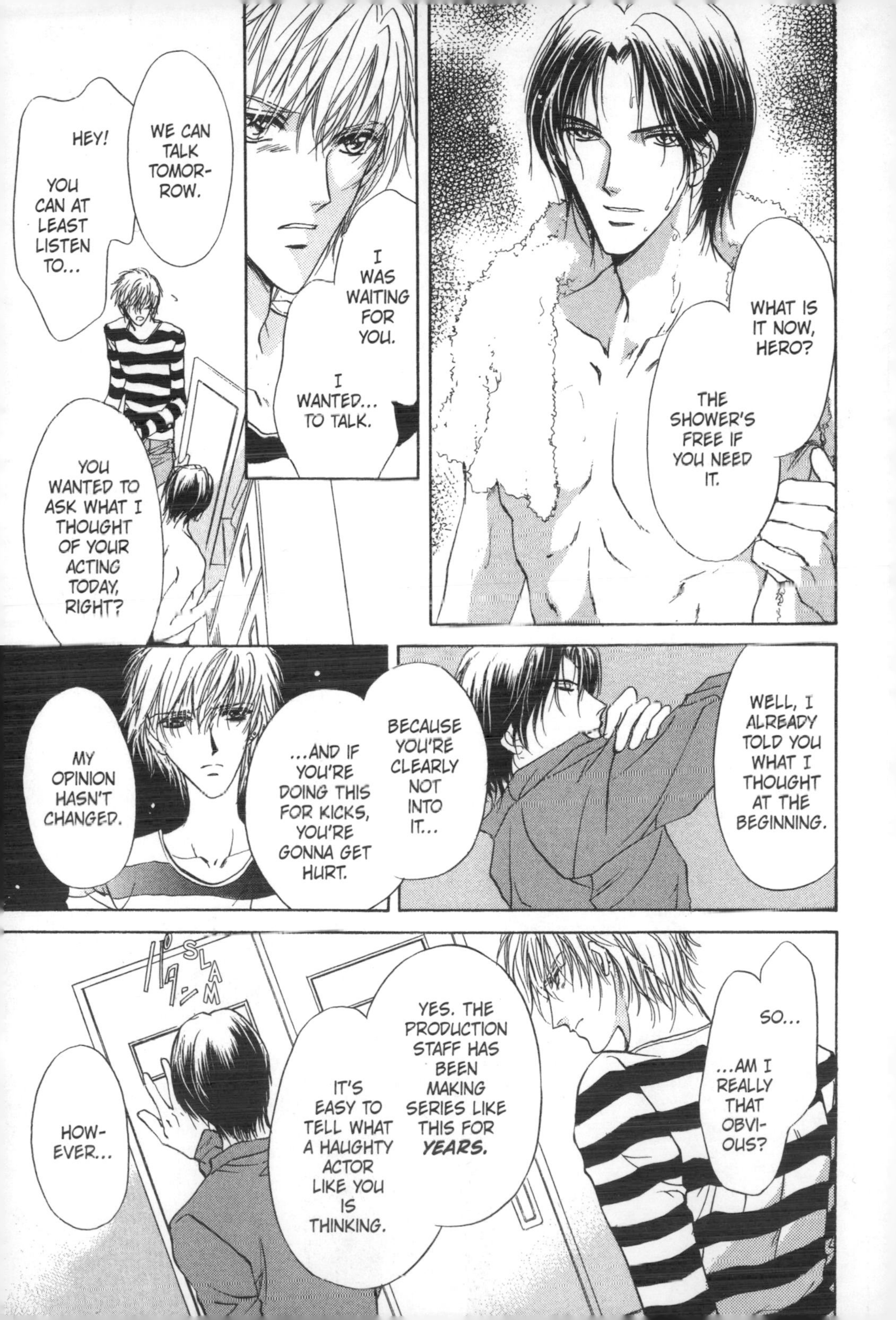
WHAT IS IT NOW, HERO?
THE SHOWER'S FREE IF YOU NEED IT.
I WAS WAITING FOR YOU.
I WANTED... TO TALK.
WE CAN TALK TOMOR-ROW.
HEY!
YOU CAN AT LEAST LISTEN TO...
YOU WANTED TO ASK WHAT I THOUGHT OF YOUR ACTING TODAY, RIGHT?
WELL, I ALREADY TOLD YOU WHAT I THOUGHT AT THE BEGINNING.
BECAUSE YOU'RE CLEARLY NOT INTO IT...
...AND IF YOU'RE DOING THIS FOR KICKS, YOU'RE GONNA GET HURT.
MY OPINION HASN'T CHANGED.
SO...
...AM I REALLY THAT OBVI-OUS?
YES. THE PRODUCTION STAFF HAS BEEN MAKING SERIES LIKE THIS FOR *YEARS.*
IT'S EASY TO TELL WHAT A HAUGHTY ACTOR LIKE YOU IS THINKING.
SLAM
HOW-EVER...

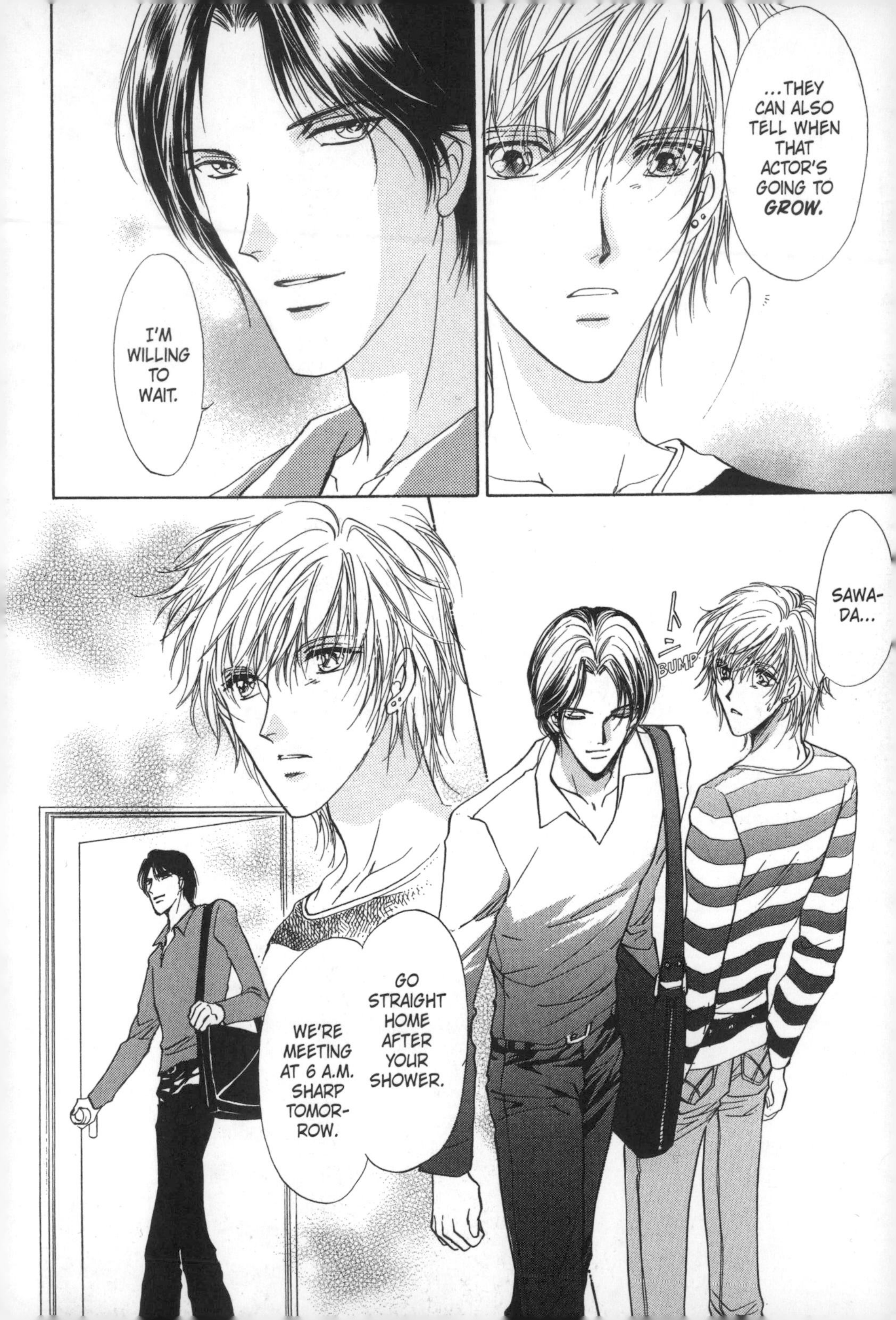
...THEY CAN ALSO TELL WHEN THAT ACTOR'S GOING TO GROW.
I'M WILLING TO WAIT.
SAWA-DA...
BUMP
GO STRAIGHT HOME AFTER YOUR SHOWER.
WE'RE MEETING AT 6 A.M. SHARP TOMORROW.

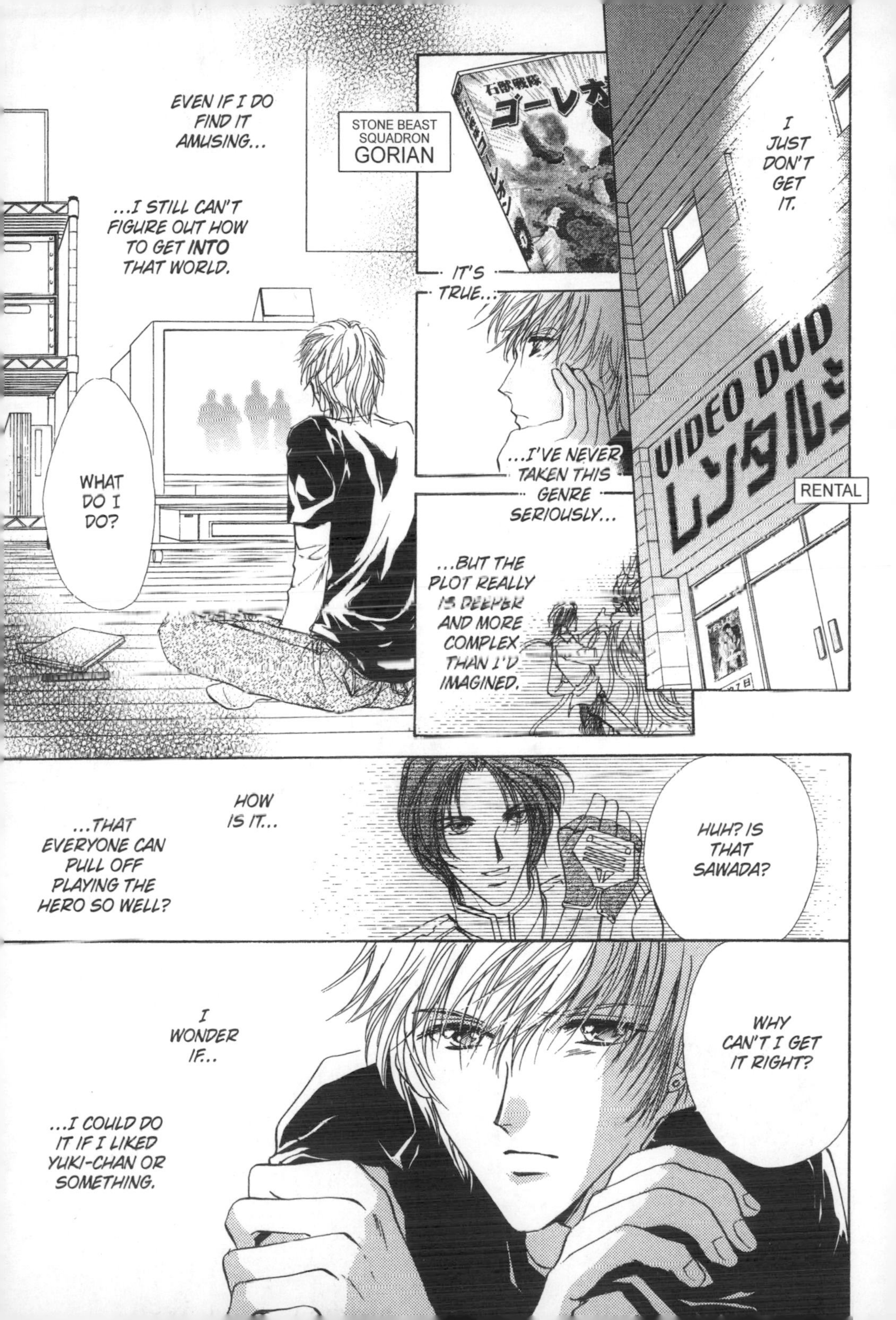
I JUST DON'T GET IT.
VIDEO DVD
レンタル
RENTAL
石獣戦隊
STONE BEAST SQUADRON GORIAN
IT'S TRUE...
...I'VE NEVER TAKEN THIS GENRE SERIOUSLY...
...BUT THE PLOT REALLY IS DEEPER AND MORE COMPLEX THAN I'D IMAGINED.
EVEN IF I DO FIND IT AMUSING...
...I STILL CAN'T FIGURE OUT HOW TO GET INTO THAT WORLD.
WHAT DO I DO?
HUH? IS THAT SAWADA?
HOW IS IT...
...THAT EVERYONE CAN PULL OFF PLAYING THE HERO SO WELL?
WHY CAN'T I GET IT RIGHT?
I WONDER IF...
...I COULD DO IT IF I LIKED YUKI-CHAN OR SOMETHING.

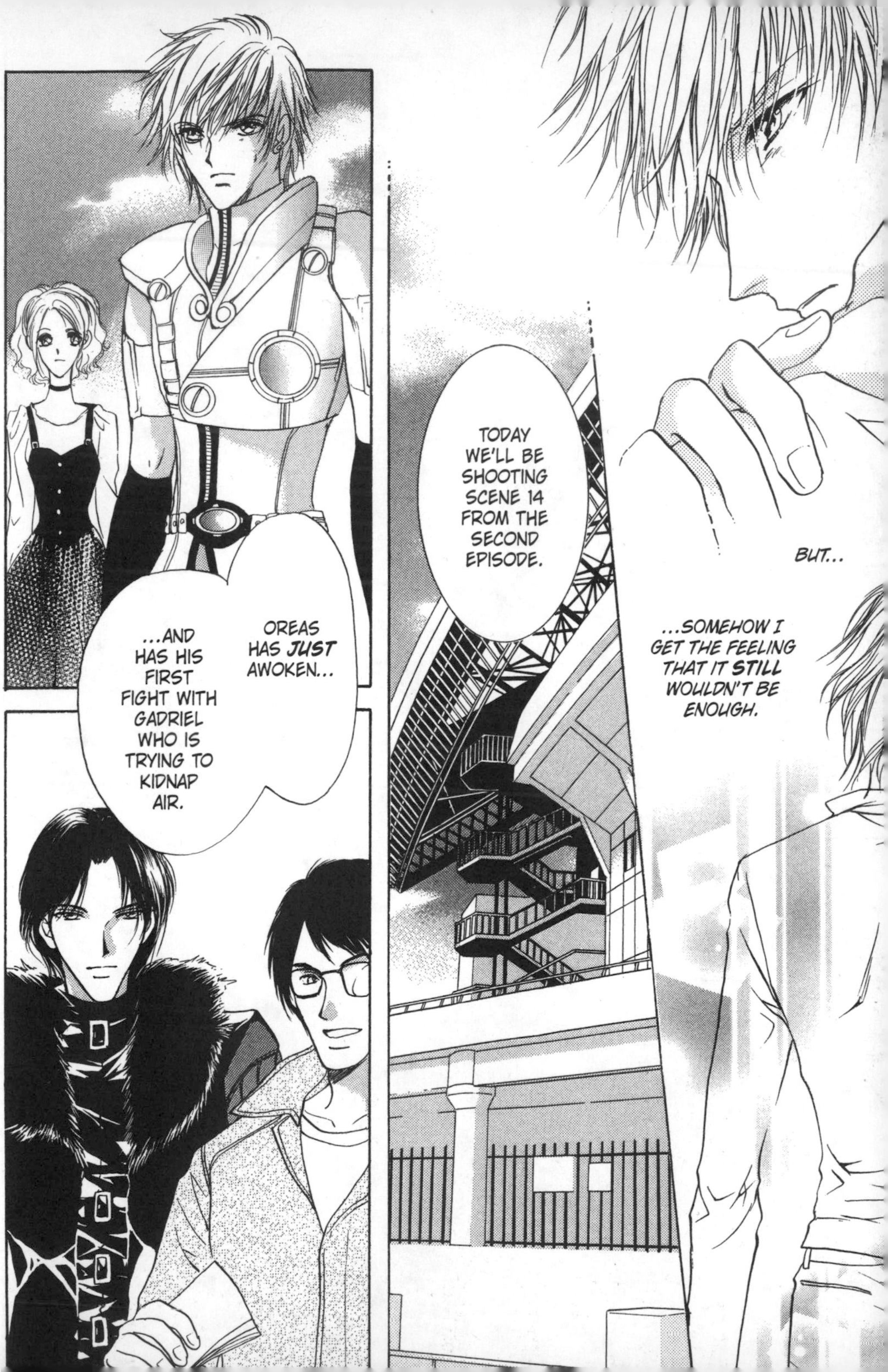
BUT...
...SOMEHOW I GET THE FEELING THAT IT STILL WOULDN'T BE ENOUGH.
TODAY WE'LL BE SHOOTING SCENE 14 FROM THE SECOND EPISODE.
OREAS HAS JUST AWOKEN...
...AND HAS HIS FIRST FIGHT WITH GADRIEL WHO IS TRYING TO KIDNAP AIR.

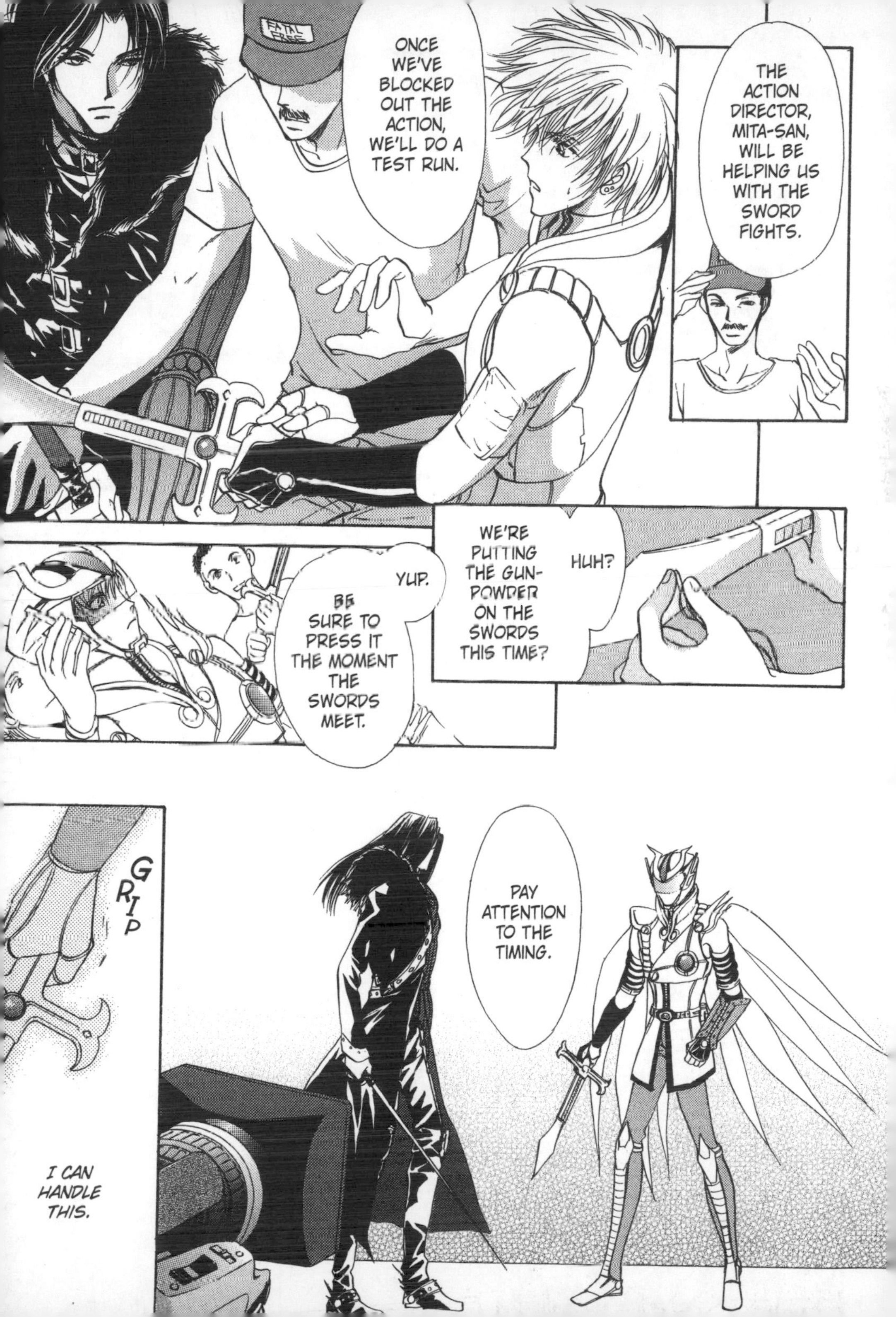
THE ACTION DIRECTOR, MITA-SAN, WILL BE HELPING US WITH THE SWORD FIGHTS.
ONCE WE'VE BLOCKED OUT THE ACTION, WE'LL DO A TEST RUN.
HUH?
WE'RE PUTTING THE GUN-POWDER ON THE SWORDS THIS TIME?
YUP.
BE SURE TO PRESS IT THE MOMENT THE SWORDS MEET.
PAY ATTENTION TO THE TIMING.
GRIP
I CAN HANDLE THIS.

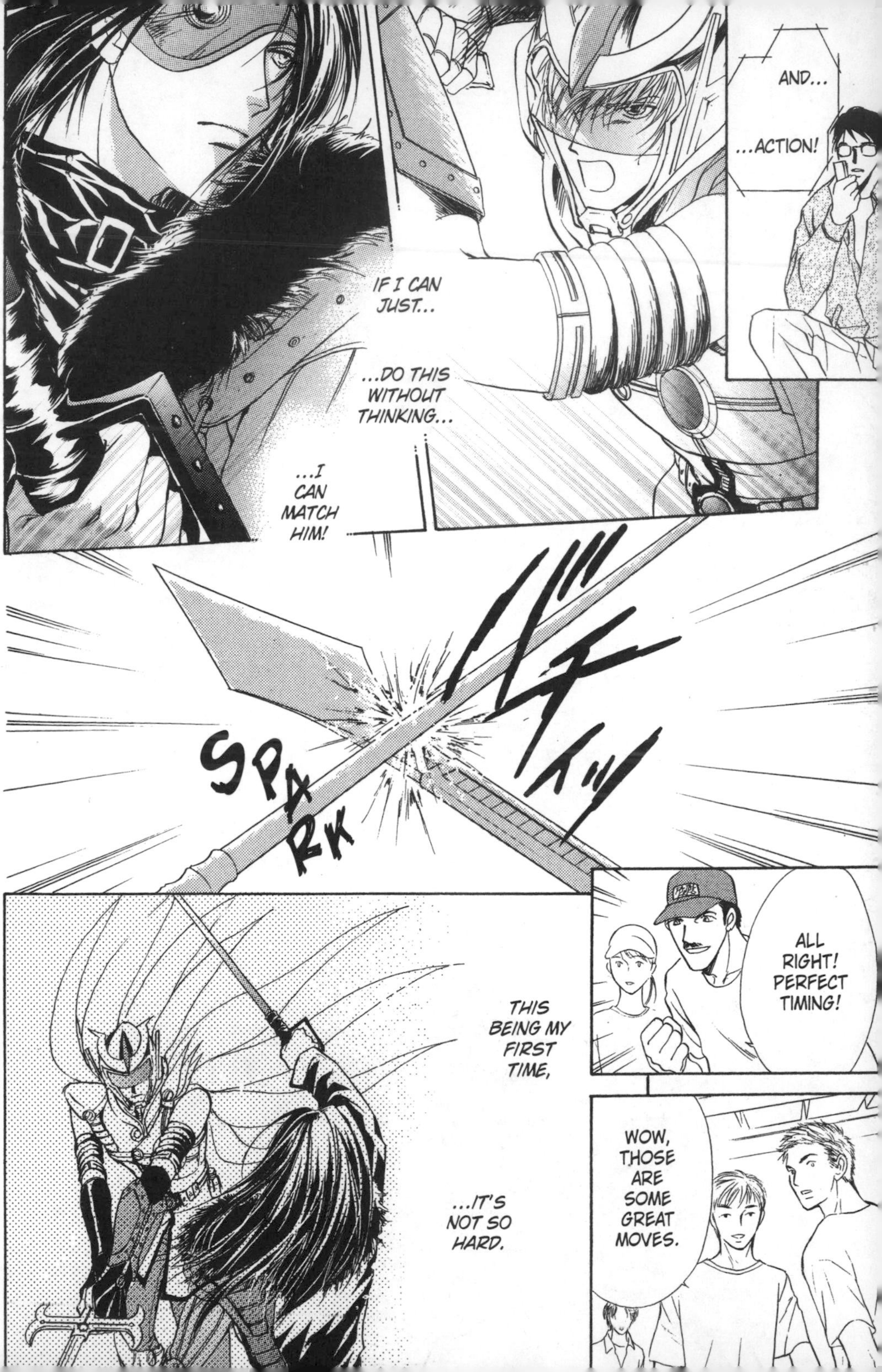
AND...
...ACTION!
IF I CAN JUST...
...DO THIS WITHOUT THINKING...
...I CAN MATCH HIM!
SPARK
ALL RIGHT! PERFECT TIMING!
WOW, THOSE ARE SOME GREAT MOVES.
THIS BEING MY FIRST TIME,
...IT'S NOT SO HARD.

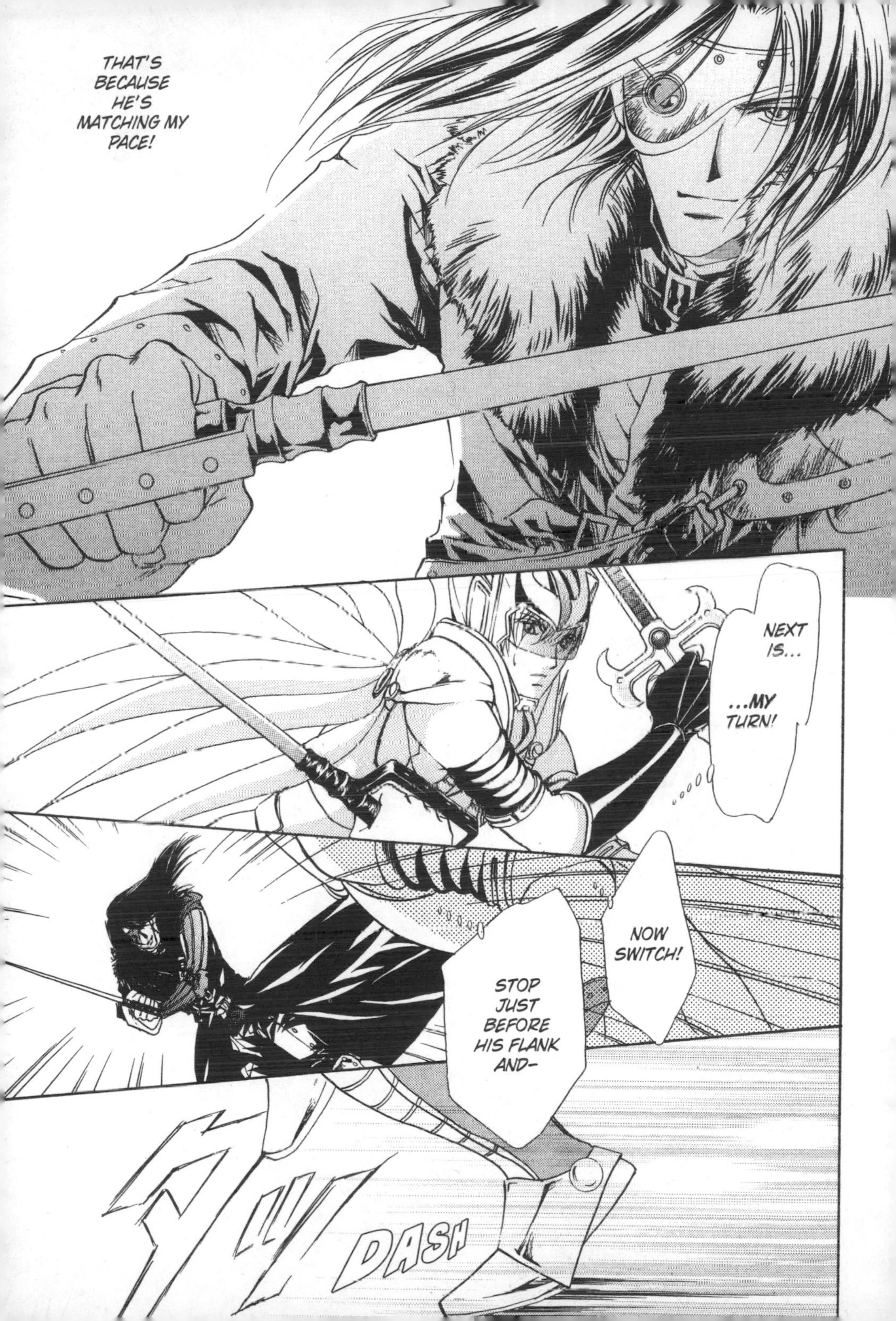
THAT'S BECAUSE HE'S MATCHING MY PACE!
NEXT IS...
...MY TURN!
NOW SWITCH!
STOP JUST BEFORE HIS FLANK AND-
DASH

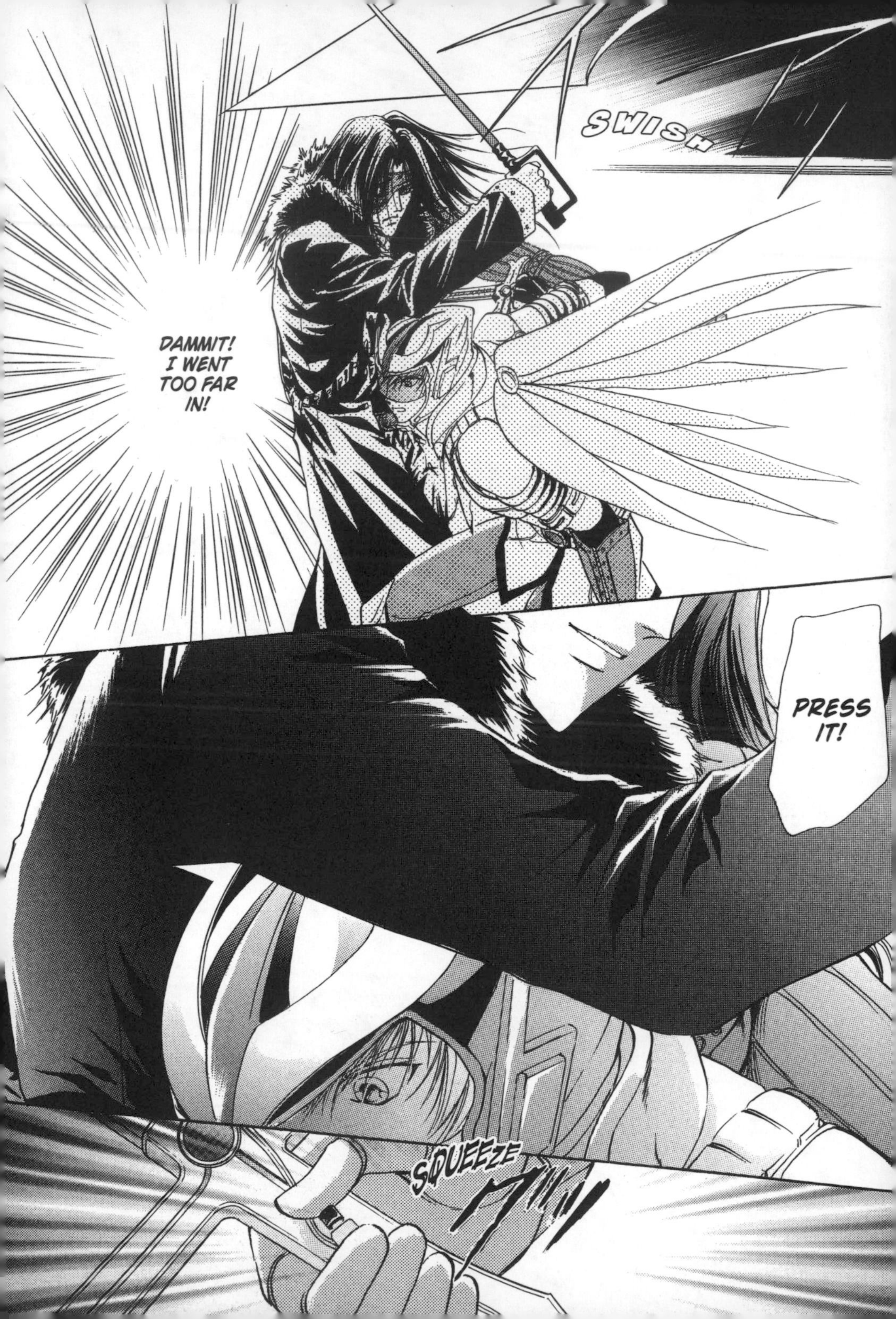
SWISH
DAMMIT! I WENT TOO FAR IN!
PRESS IT!
SQUEEZE

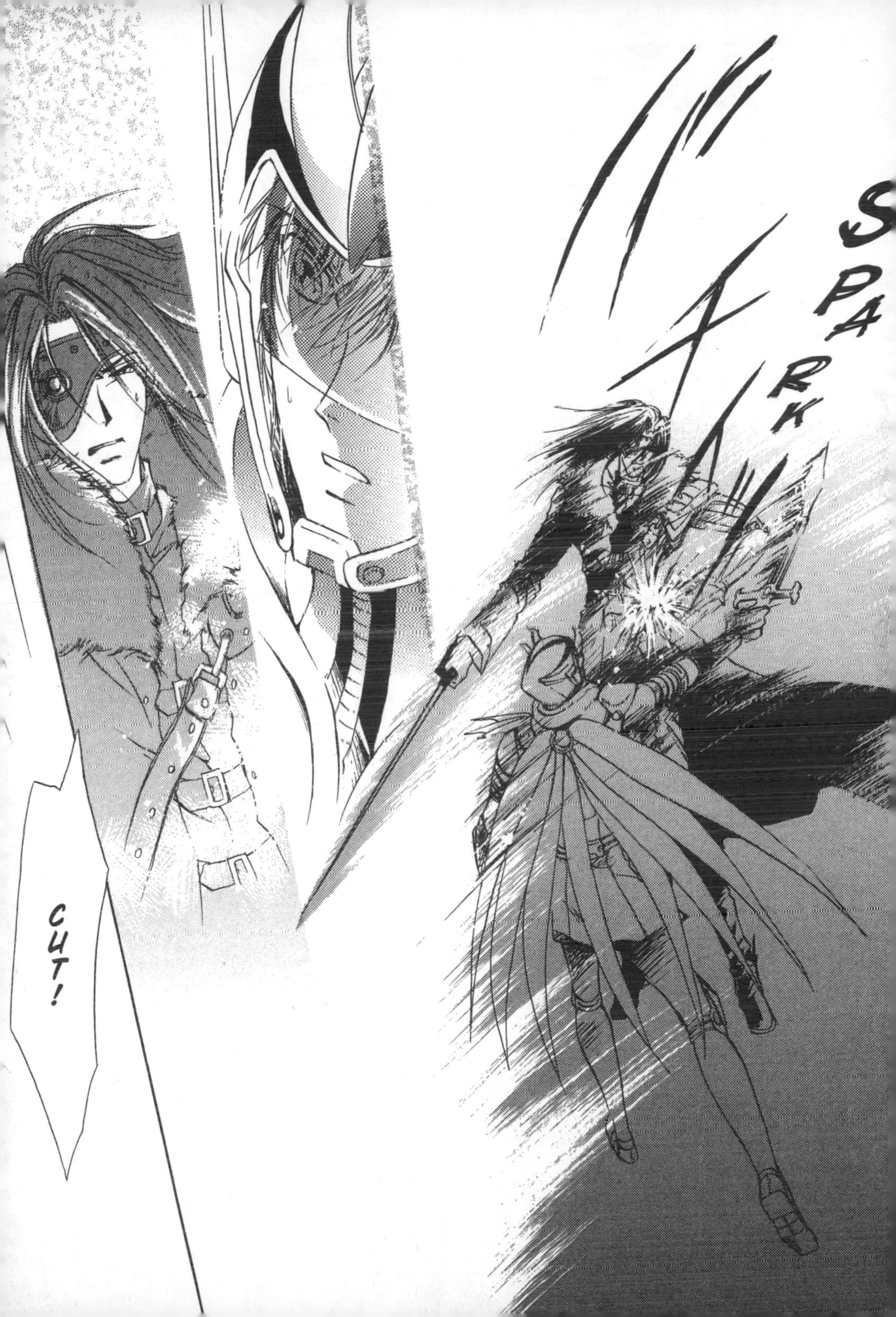
SPARK
CUT!

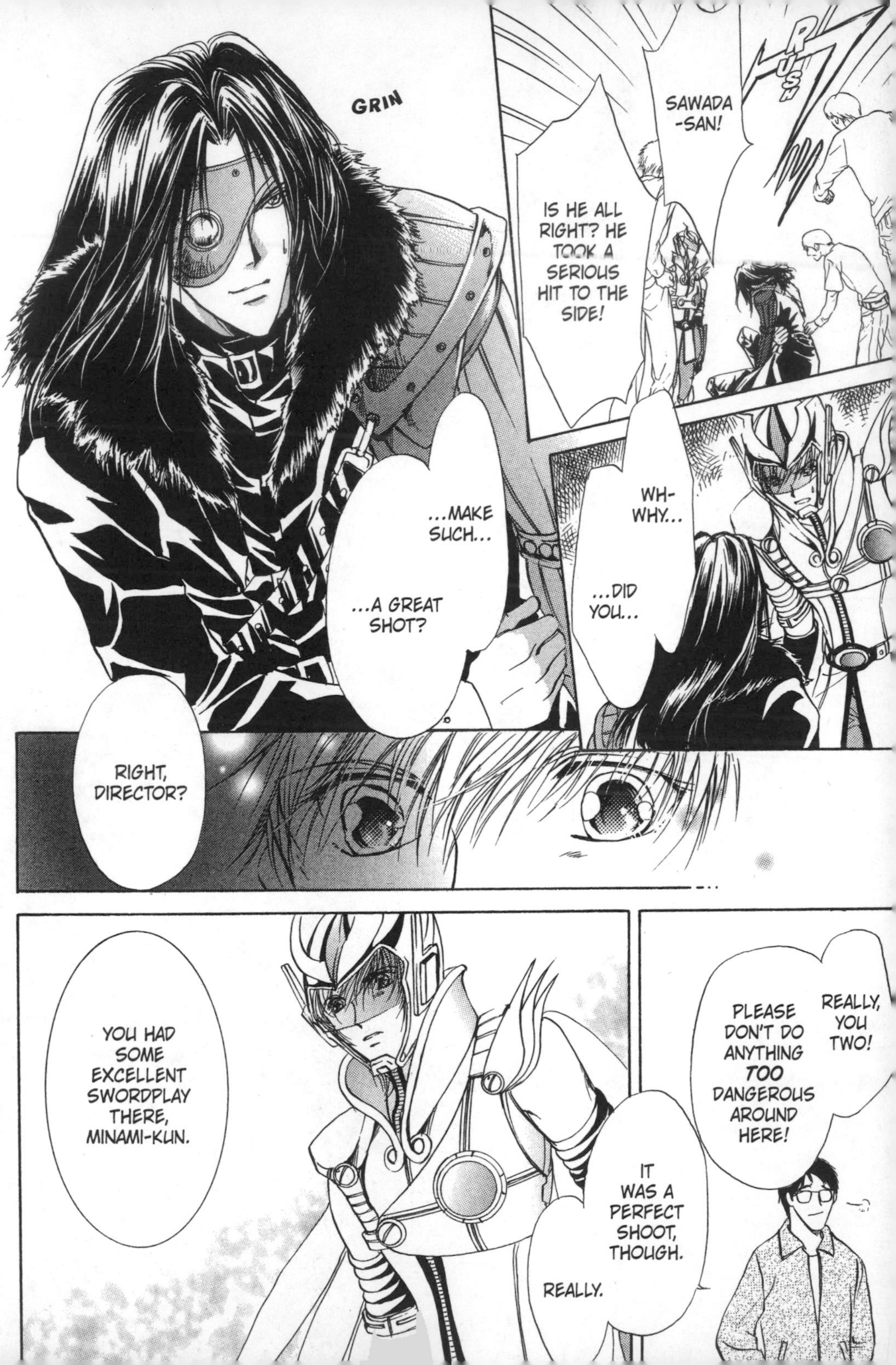
RUSH
SAWADA-SAN!
IS HE ALL RIGHT? HE TOOK A SERIOUS HIT TO THE SIDE!
WH-WHY...
...DID YOU...
GRIN
...MAKE SUCH...
...A GREAT SHOT?
RIGHT, DIRECTOR?
REALLY, YOU TWO!
PLEASE DON'T DO ANYTHING *TOO* DANGEROUS AROUND HERE!
IT WAS A PERFECT SHOOT, THOUGH.
REALLY.
YOU HAD SOME EXCELLENT SWORDPLAY THERE, MINAMI-KUN.

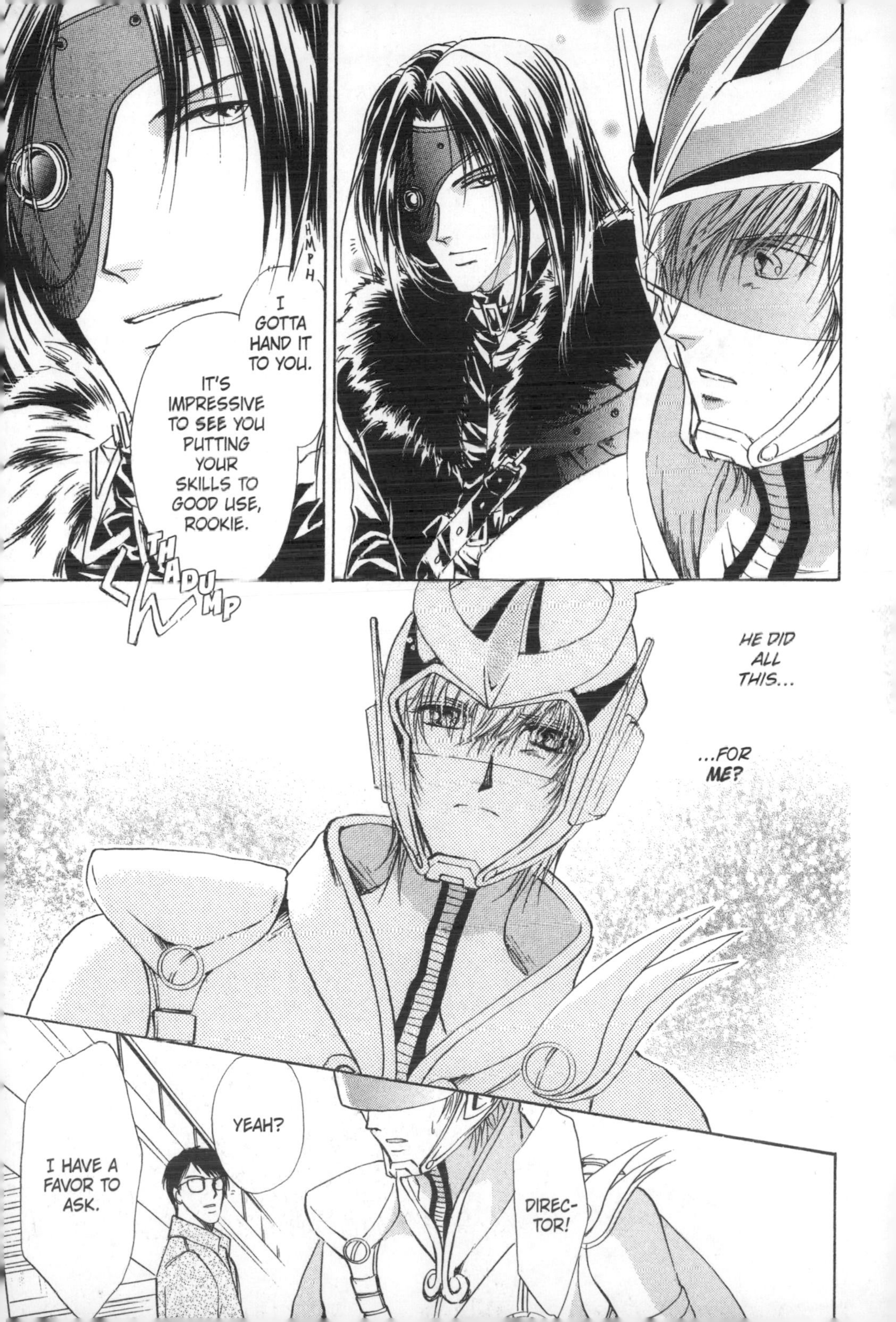
HMPH
I GOTTA HAND IT TO YOU.
IT'S IMPRESSIVE TO SEE YOU PUTTING YOUR SKILLS TO GOOD USE, ROOKIE.
THADUMP
HE DID ALL THIS...
...FOR ME?
DIRECTOR!
YEAH?
I HAVE A FAVOR TO ASK.

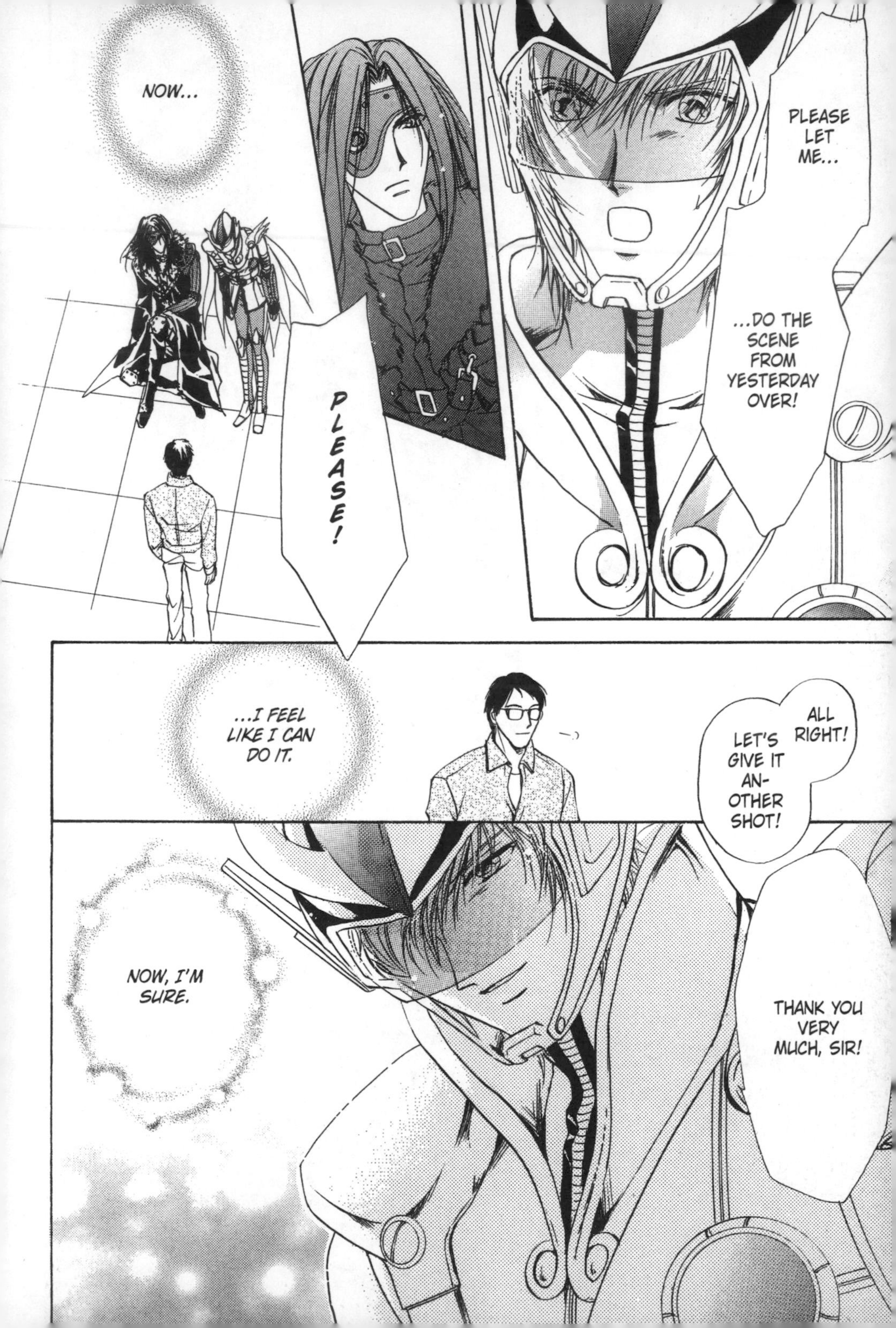
PLEASE LET ME...
...DO THE SCENE FROM YESTERDAY OVER!
PLEASE!
NOW...
ALL RIGHT! LET'S GIVE IT AN-OTHER SHOT!
...I FEEL LIKE I CAN DO IT.
THANK YOU VERY MUCH, SIR!
NOW, I'M SURE.

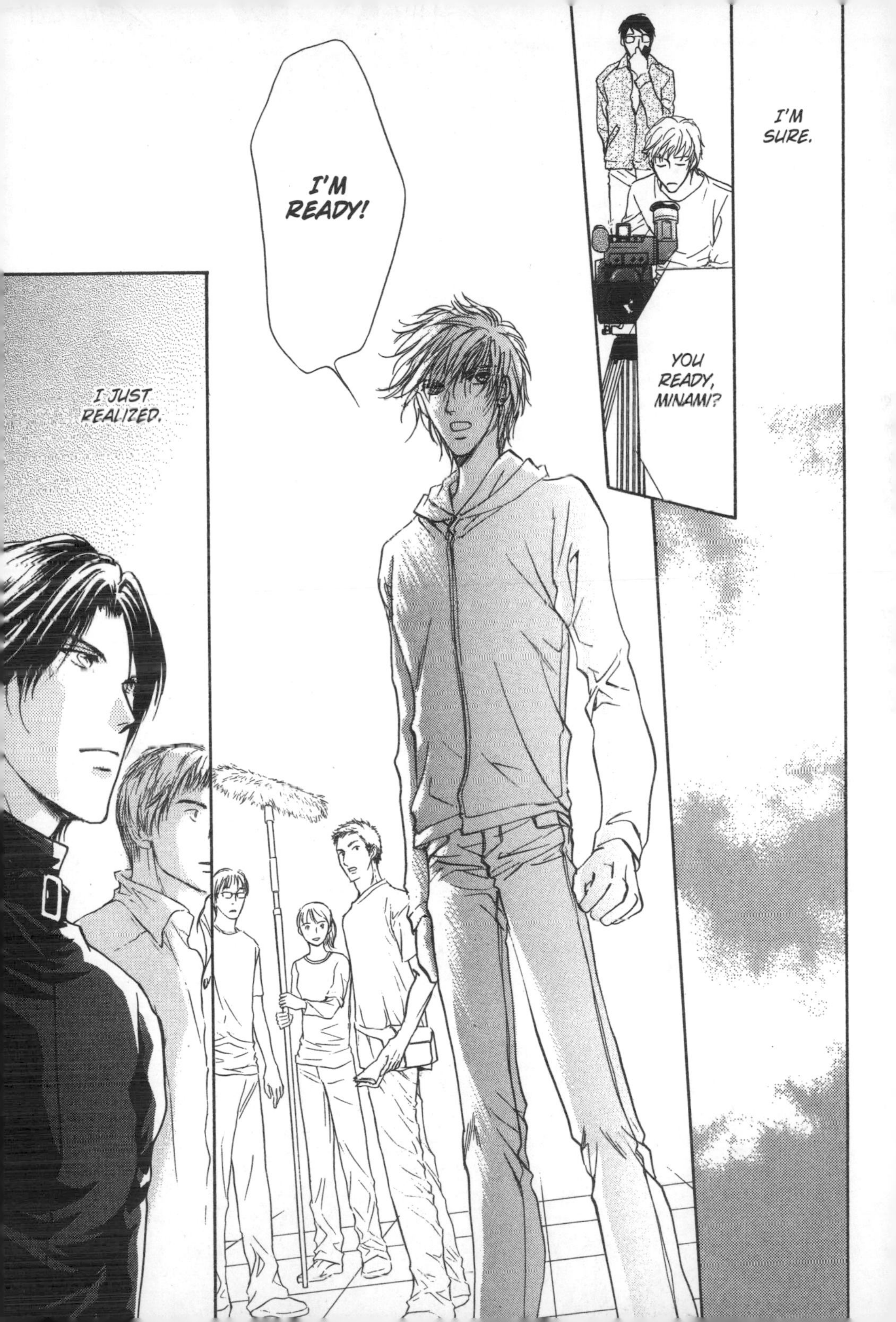
I'M SURE.
YOU READY, MINAMI?
I'M READY!
I JUST REALIZED.

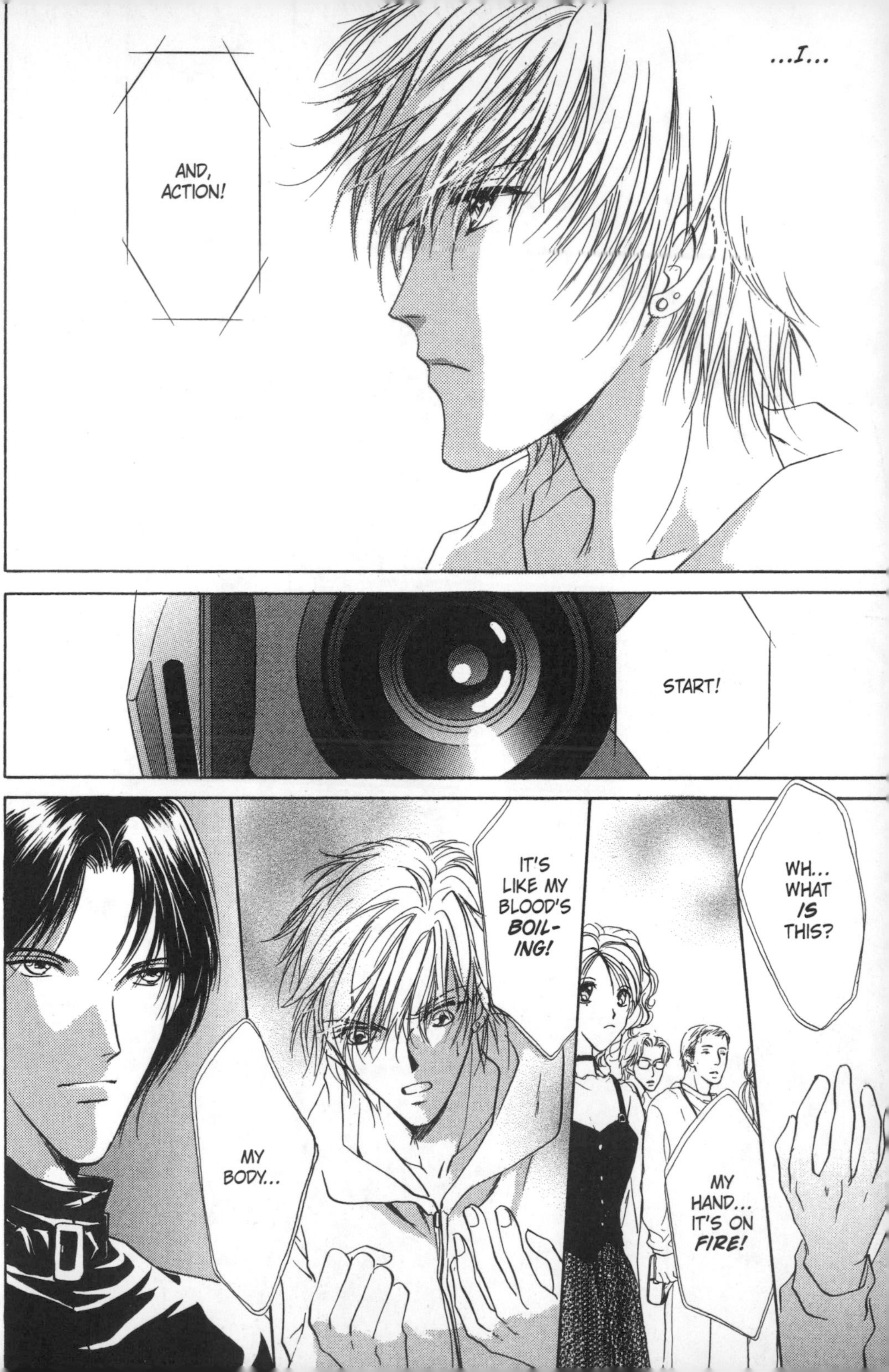
...I...
AND, ACTION!
START!
WH... WHAT IS THIS?
MY HAND... IT'S ON FIRE!
IT'S LIKE MY BLOOD'S BOILING!
MY BODY...

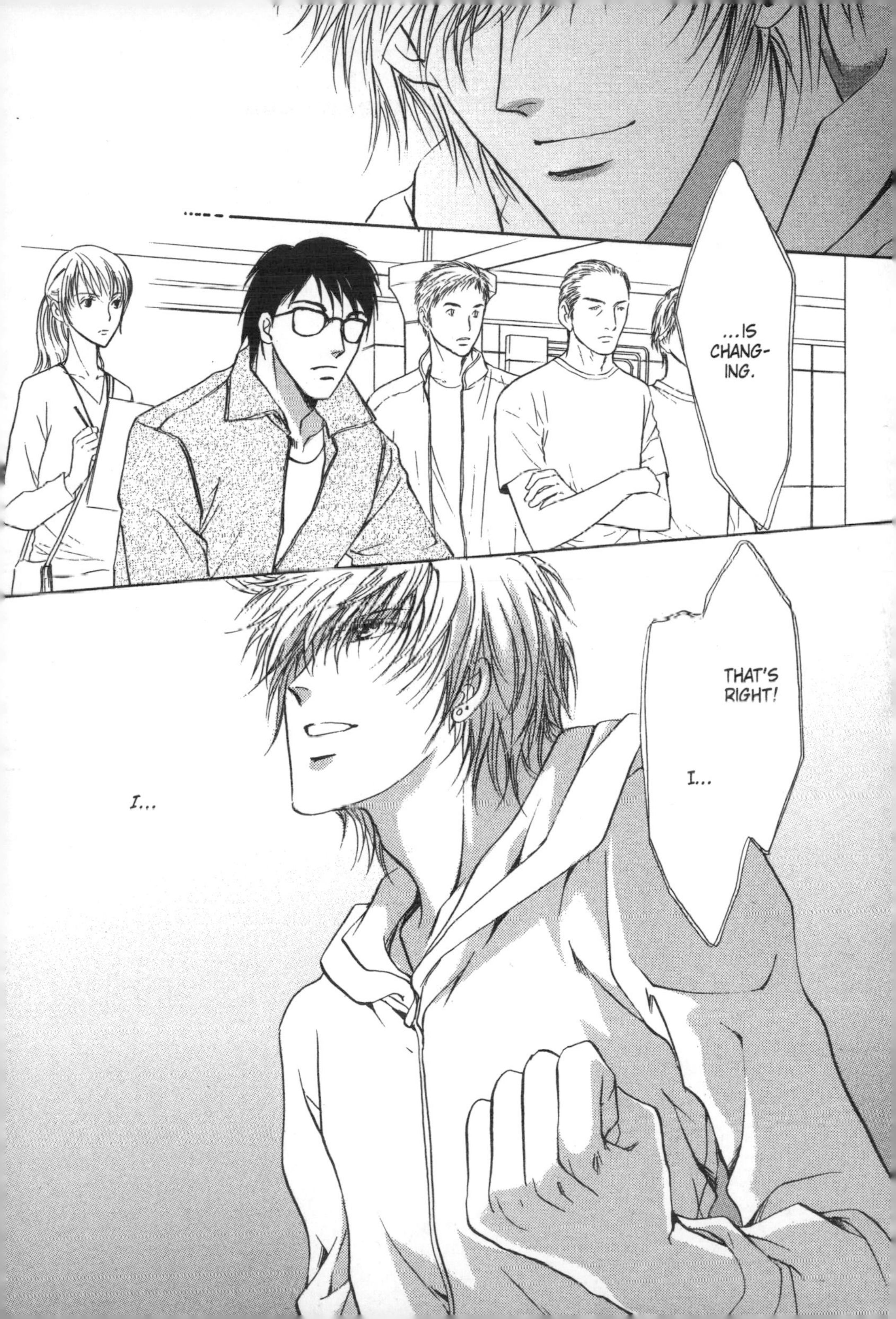
...IS CHANG-ING.
THAT'S RIGHT!
I...
I...

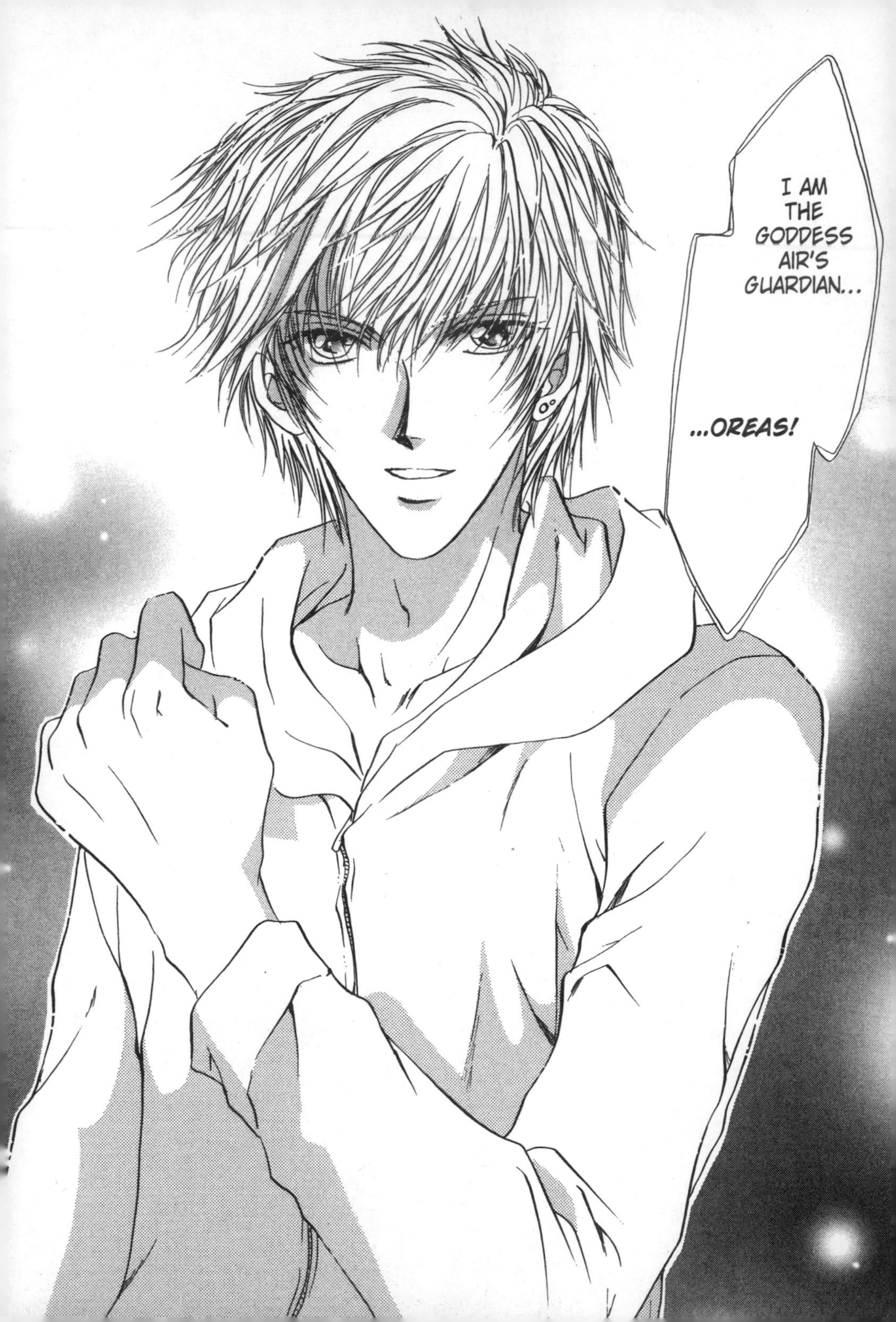
I AM THE GODDESS AIR'S GUARDIAN...
...OREAS!

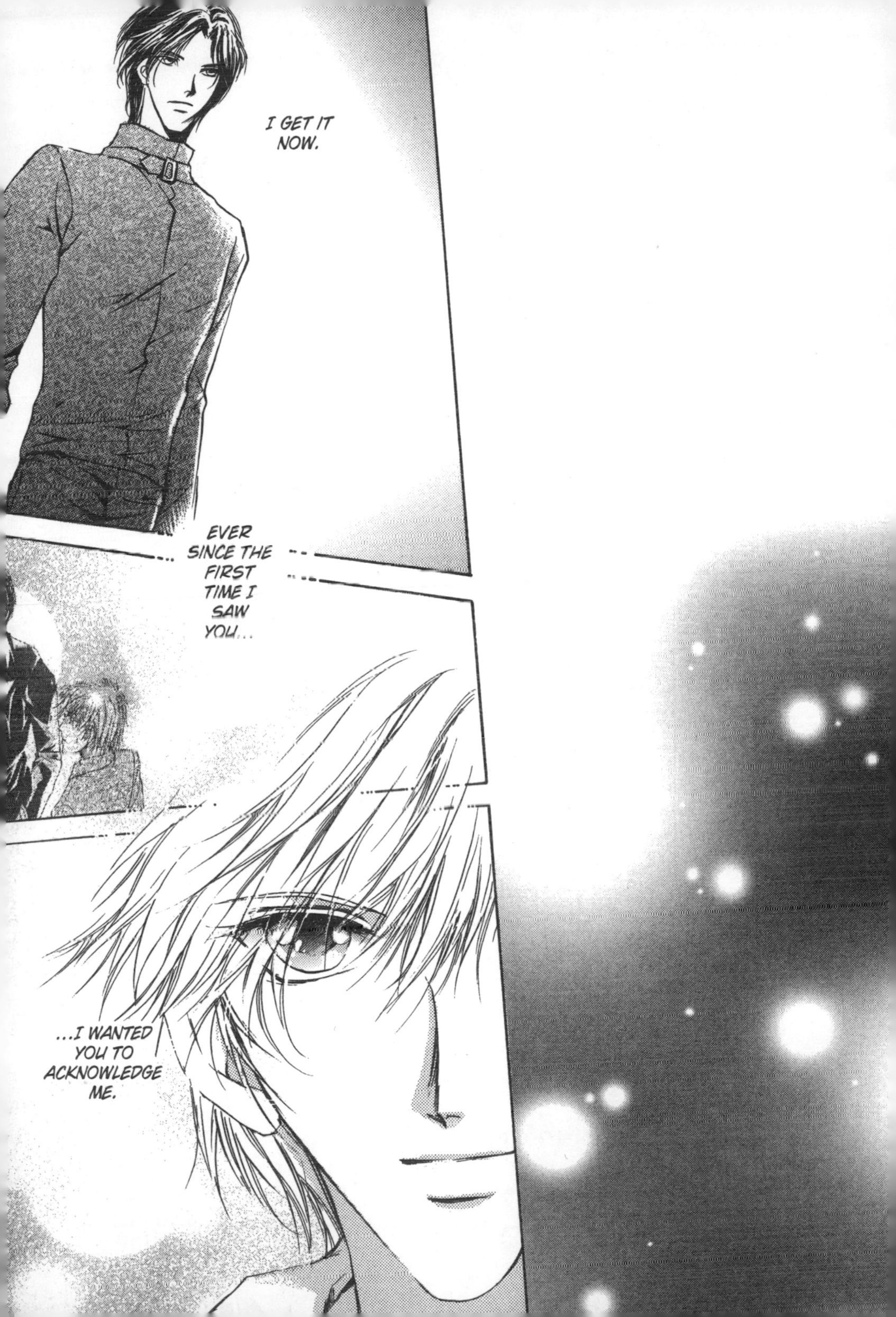
I GET IT NOW.
EVER SINCE THE FIRST TIME I SAW YOU...
...I WANTED YOU TO ACKNOWLEDGE ME.

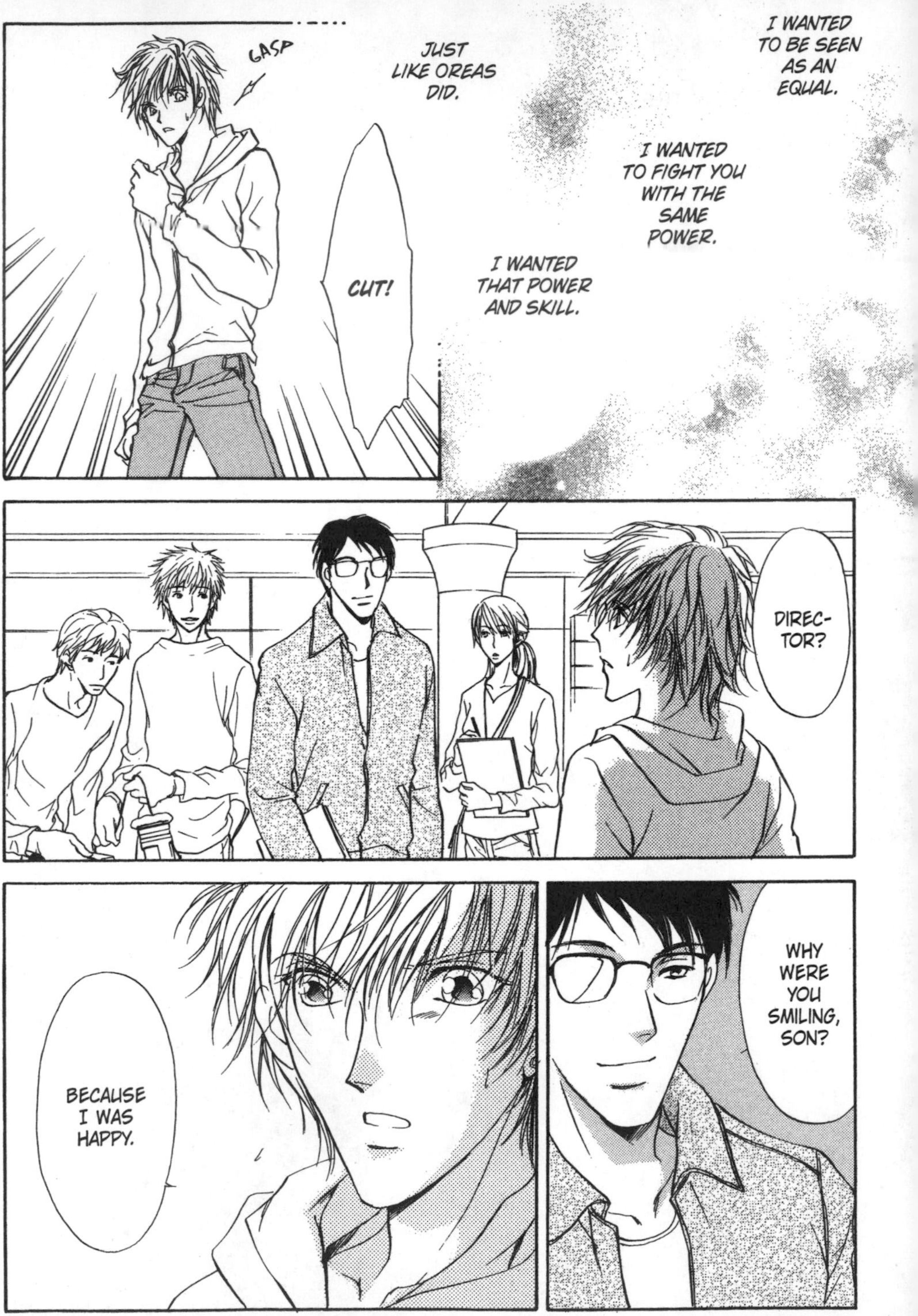
I WANTED TO BE SEEN AS AN EQUAL.
I WANTED TO FIGHT YOU WITH THE SAME POWER.
I WANTED THAT POWER AND SKILL.
JUST LIKE OREAS DID.
CUT!
GASP
DIREC-TOR?
WHY WERE YOU SMILING, SON?
BECAUSE I WAS HAPPY.

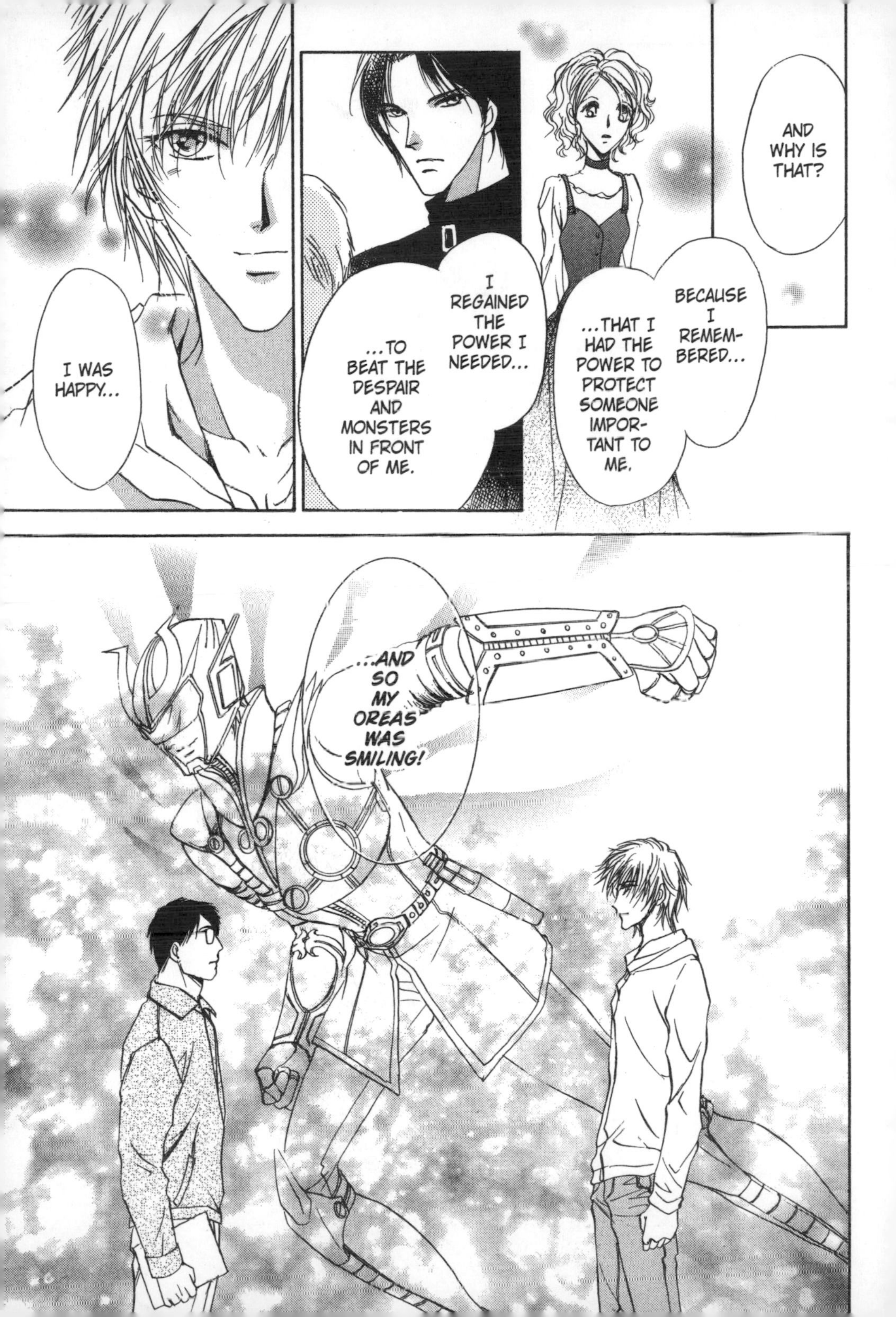
AND WHY IS THAT?
BECAUSE I REMEMBERED...
...THAT I HAD THE POWER TO PROTECT SOMEONE IMPORTANT TO ME.
I REGAINED THE POWER I NEEDED...
...TO BEAT THE DESPAIR AND MONSTERS IN FRONT OF ME.
I WAS HAPPY...
...AND SO MY OREAS WAS SMILING!

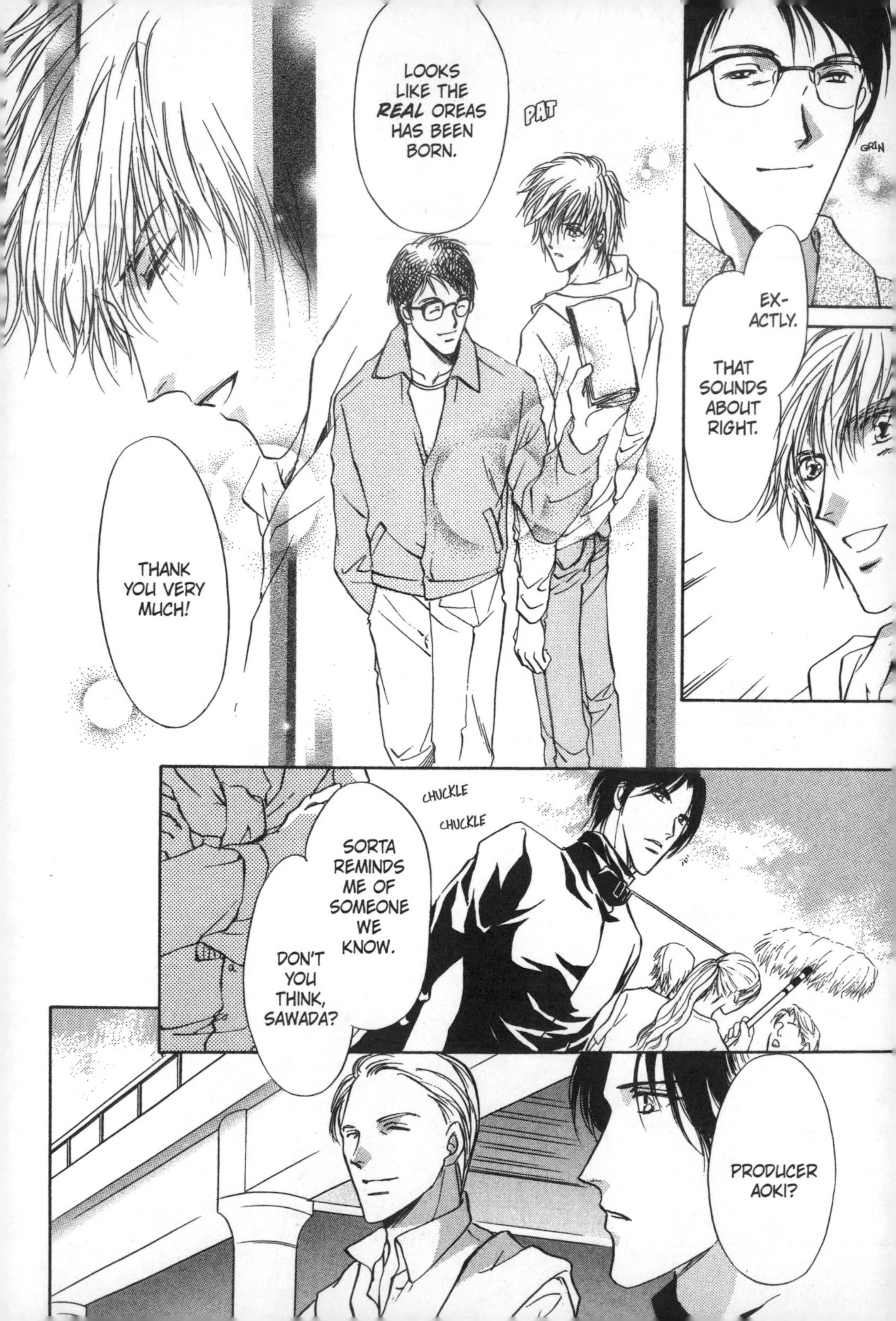
GRIN
EX-ACTLY.
THAT SOUNDS ABOUT RIGHT.
LOOKS LIKE THE REAL OREAS HAS BEEN BORN.
PAT
THANK YOU VERY MUCH!
CHUCKLE
CHUCKLE
SORTA REMINDS ME OF SOMEONE WE KNOW.
DON'T YOU THINK, SAWADA?
PRODUCER AOKI?

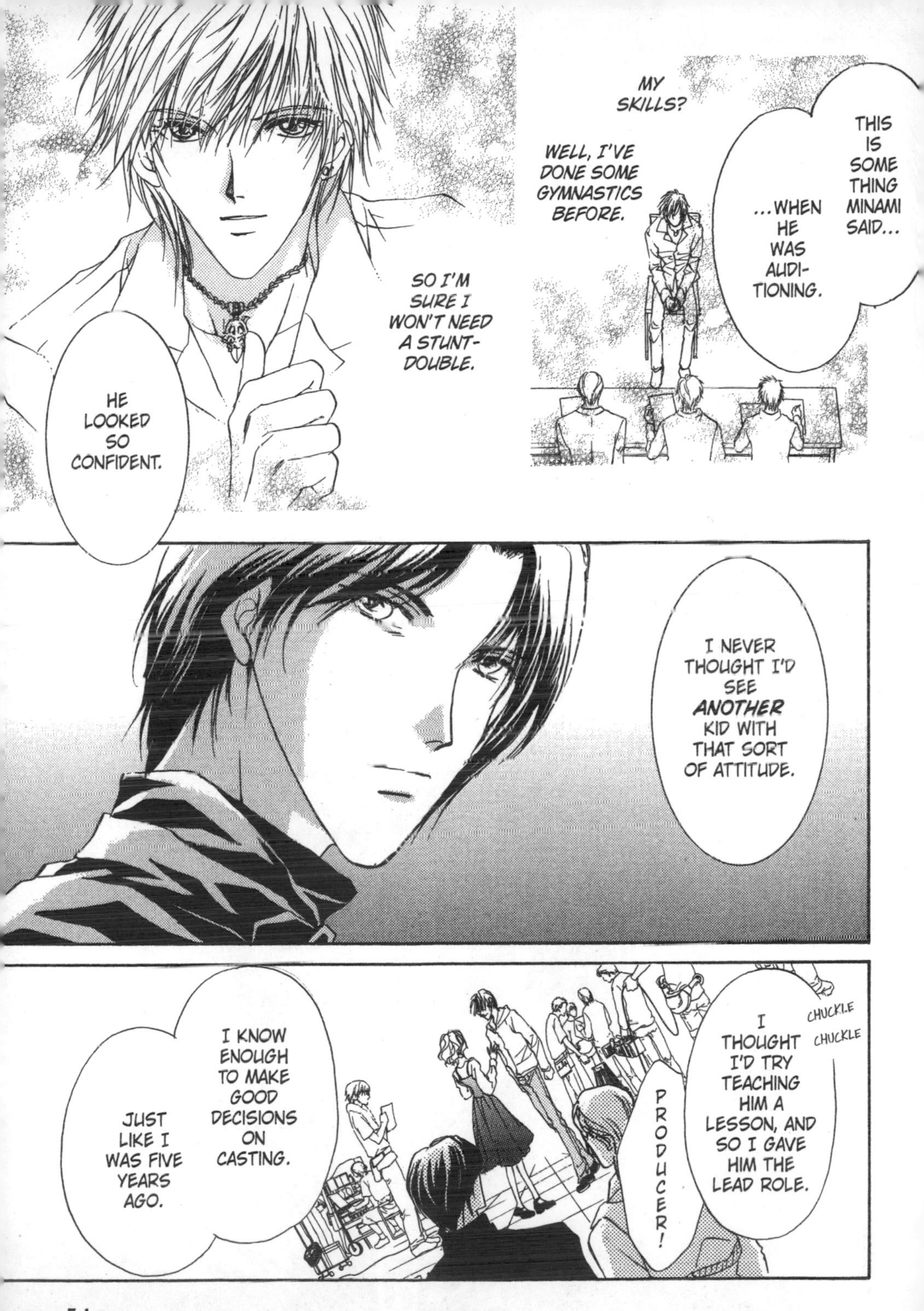
THIS IS SOME THING MINAMI SAID...
...WHEN HE WAS AUDITIONING.
MY SKILLS?
WELL, I'VE DONE SOME GYMNASTICS BEFORE.
SO I'M SURE I WON'T NEED A STUNT-DOUBLE.
HE LOOKED SO CONFIDENT.
I NEVER THOUGHT I'D SEE ANOTHER KID WITH THAT SORT OF ATTITUDE.
CHUCKLE CHUCKLE
I THOUGHT I'D TRY TEACHING HIM A LESSON, AND SO I GAVE HIM THE LEAD ROLE.
PRODUCER!
I KNOW ENOUGH TO MAKE GOOD DECISIONS ON CASTING.
JUST LIKE I WAS FIVE YEARS AGO.

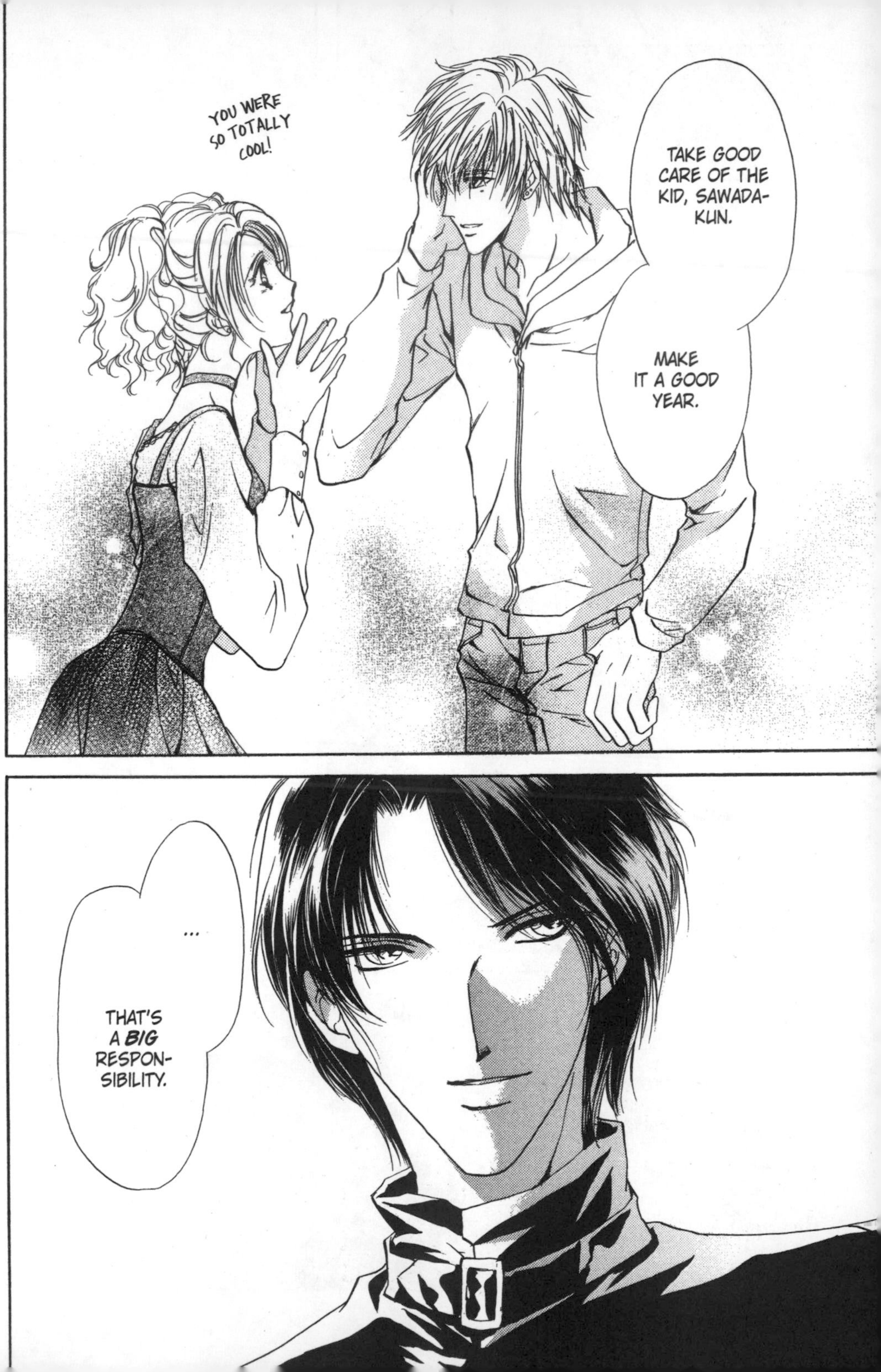

TAKE GOOD CARE OF THE KID, SAWADA-KUN.
MAKE IT A GOOD YEAR.
YOU WERE SO TOTALLY COOL!
...
THAT'S A *BIG* RESPONSIBILITY.

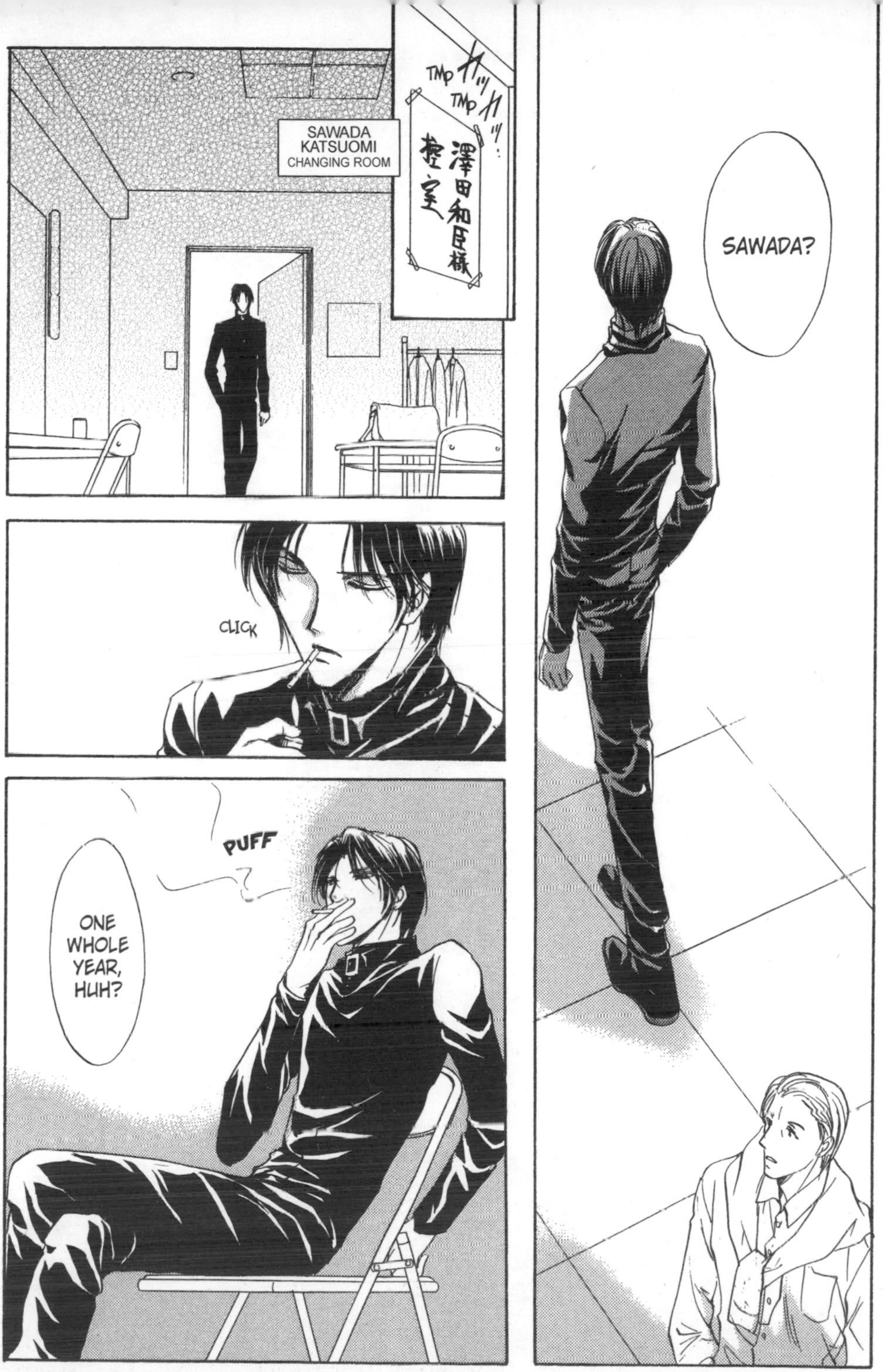
SAWADA?
TMP
TMP
SAWADA KATSUOMI CHANGING ROOM
澤田和臣様
控室
CLICK
PUFF
ONE WHOLE YEAR, HUH?

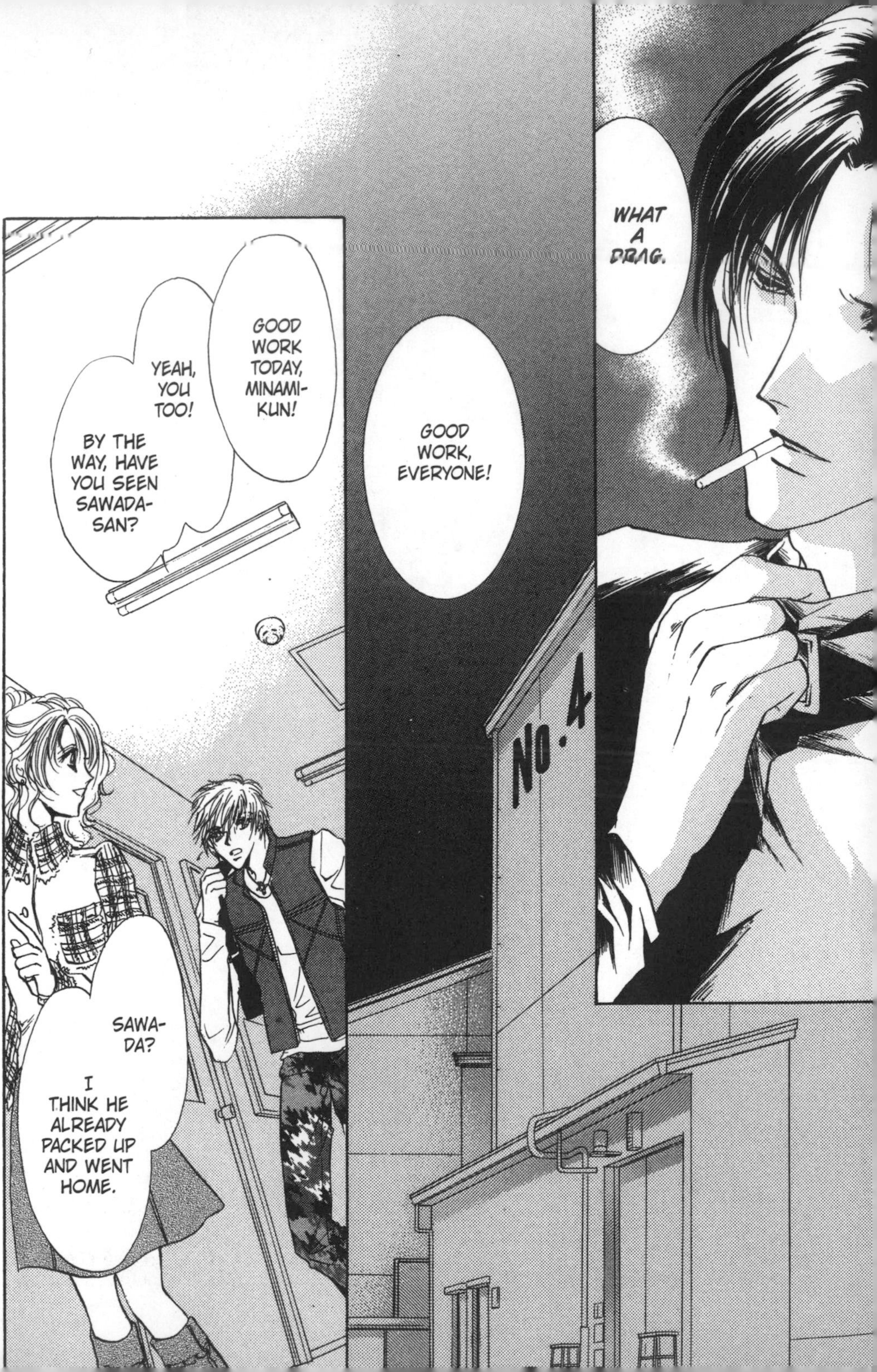
WHAT A DRAG.
GOOD WORK, EVERYONE!
GOOD WORK TODAY, MINAMI-KUN!
YEAH, YOU TOO!
BY THE WAY, HAVE YOU SEEN SAWADA-SAN?
SAWADA?
I THINK HE ALREADY PACKED UP AND WENT HOME.

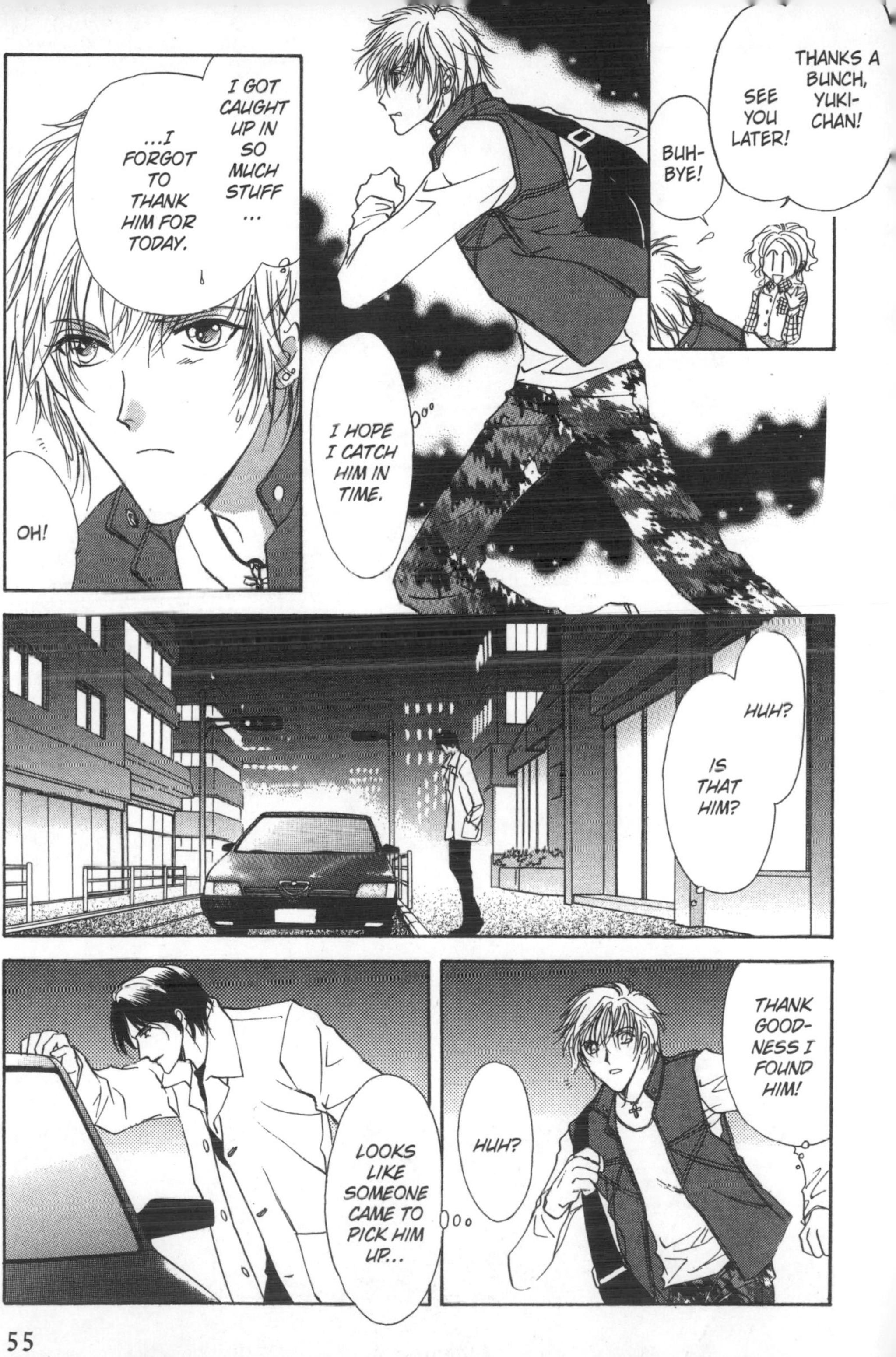
THANKS A BUNCH, YUKI-CHAN!
SEE YOU LATER!
BUH-BYE!
I HOPE I CATCH HIM IN TIME.
I GOT CAUGHT UP IN SO MUCH STUFF...
...I FORGOT TO THANK HIM FOR TODAY.
OH!
HUH?
IS THAT HIM?
THANK GOODNESS I FOUND HIM!
HUH?
LOOKS LIKE SOMEONE CAME TO PICK HIM UP...

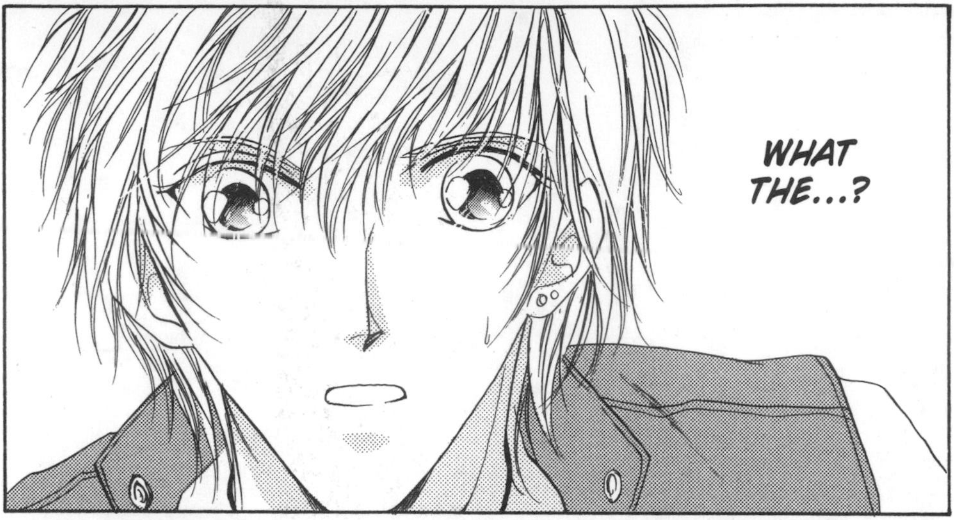
WHAT THE...?

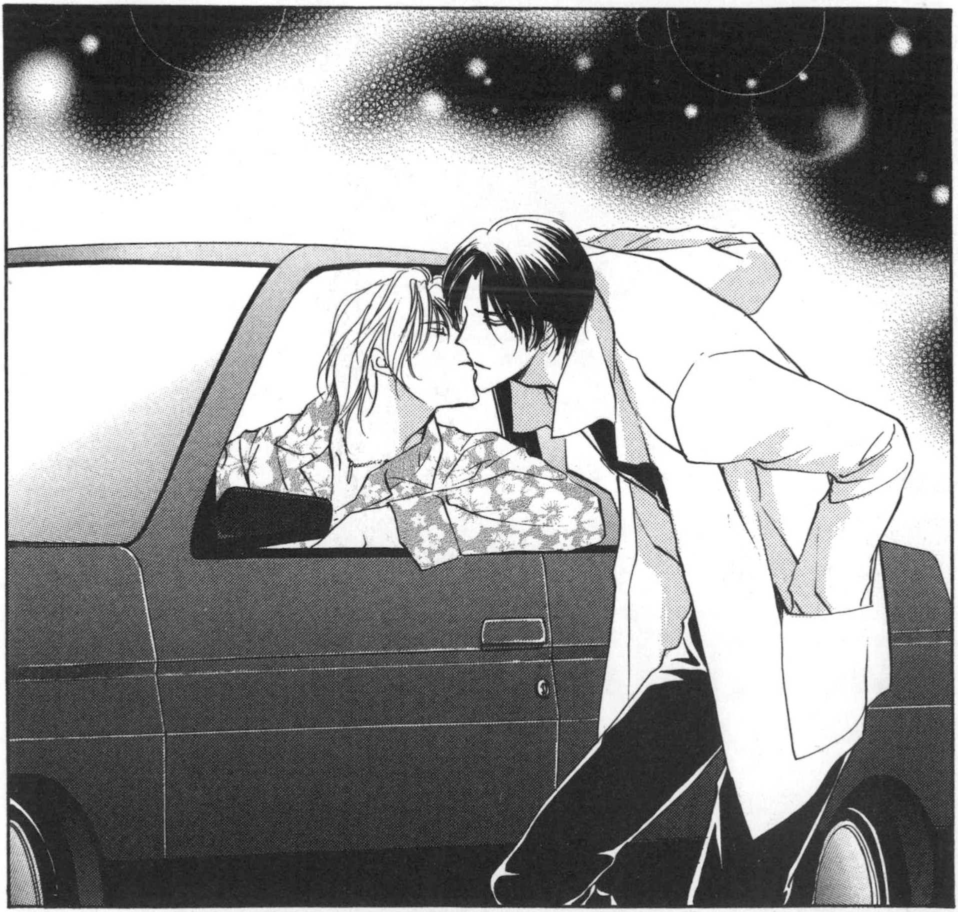

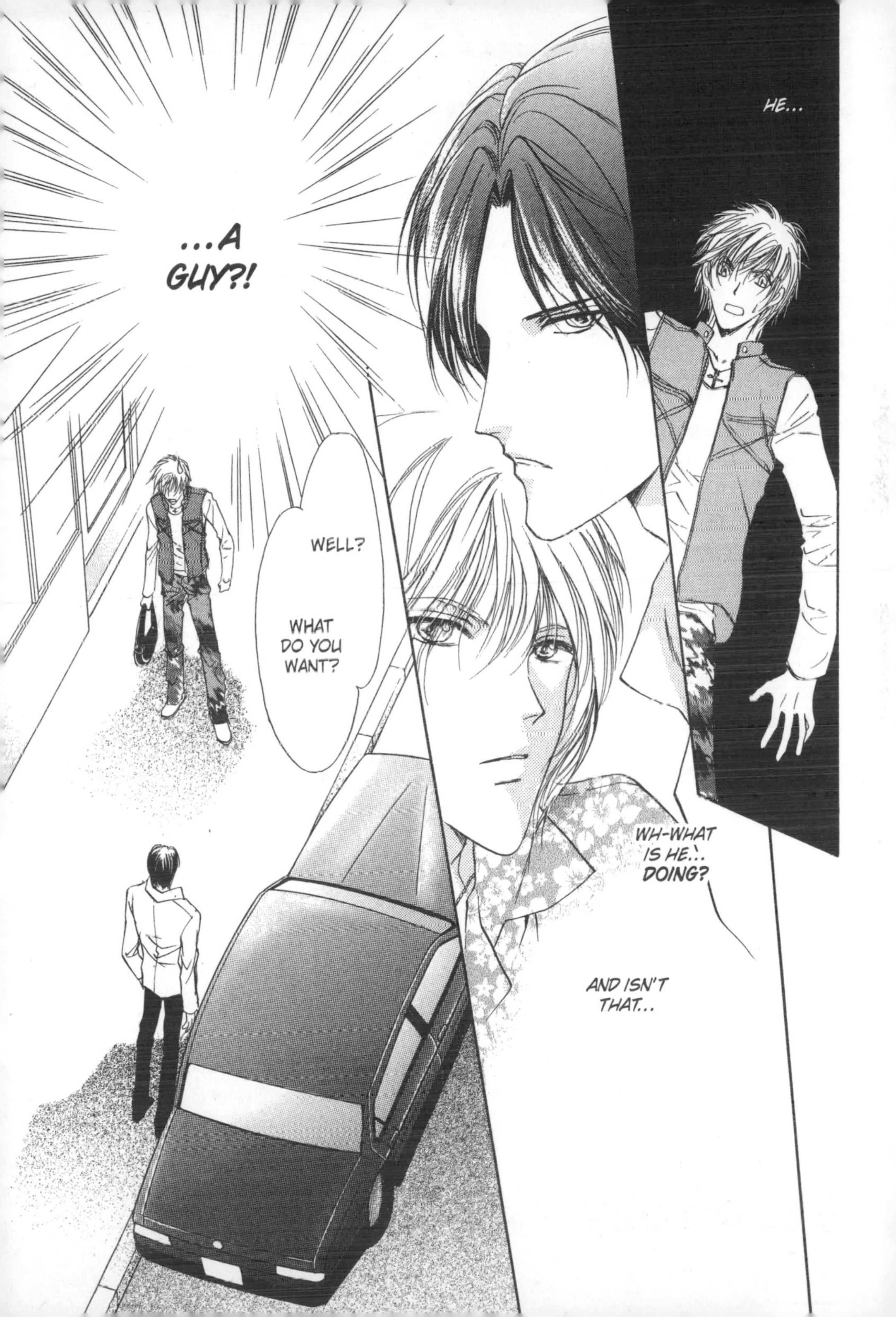
HE...
WH-WHAT IS HE... DOING?
AND ISN'T THAT...
...A GUY?!
WELL?
WHAT DO YOU WANT?

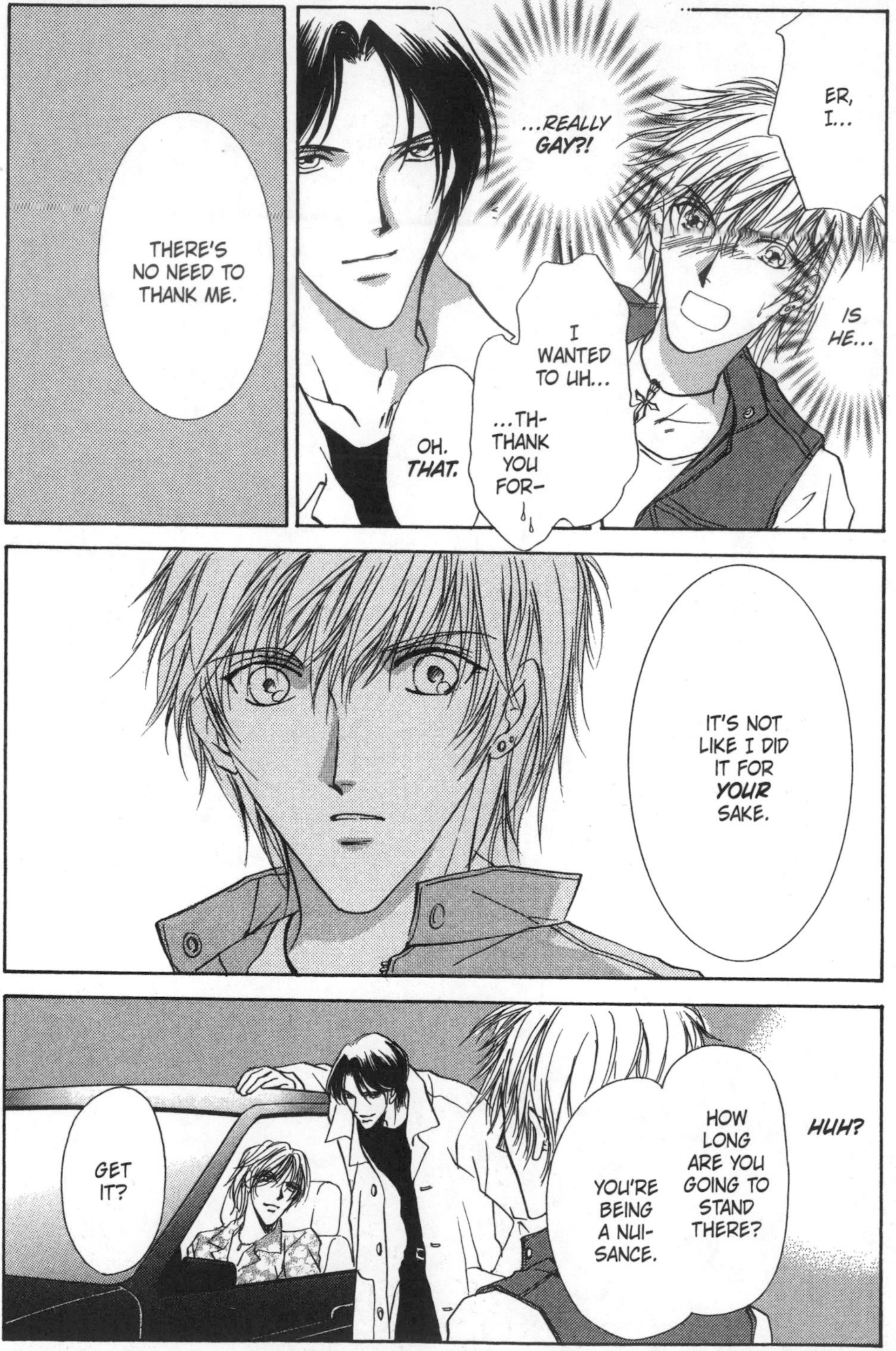
ER, I...
...REALLY GAY?!
IS HE...
I WANTED TO UH...
...TH-THANK YOU FOR-
OH. THAT.
THERE'S NO NEED TO THANK ME.
IT'S NOT LIKE I DID IT FOR YOUR SAKE.
HUH?
HOW LONG ARE YOU GOING TO STAND THERE?
YOU'RE BEING A NUI-SANCE.
GET IT?

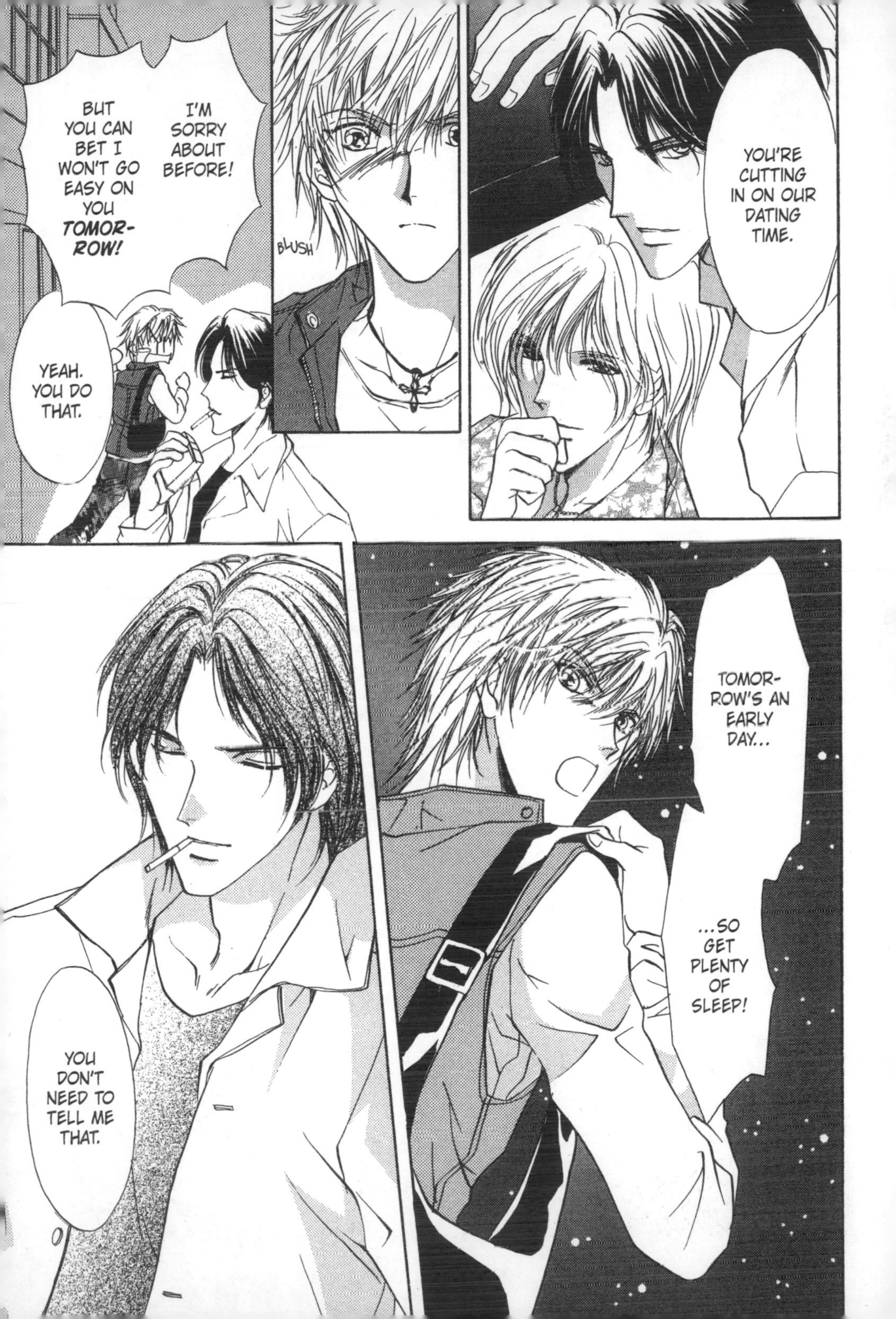
YOU'RE CUTTING IN ON OUR DATING TIME.
BLUSH
I'M SORRY ABOUT BEFORE!
BUT YOU CAN BET I WON'T GO EASY ON YOU *TOMORROW!*
YEAH. YOU DO THAT.
TOMORROW'S AN EARLY DAY...
...SO GET PLENTY OF SLEEP!
YOU DON'T NEED TO TELL ME THAT.

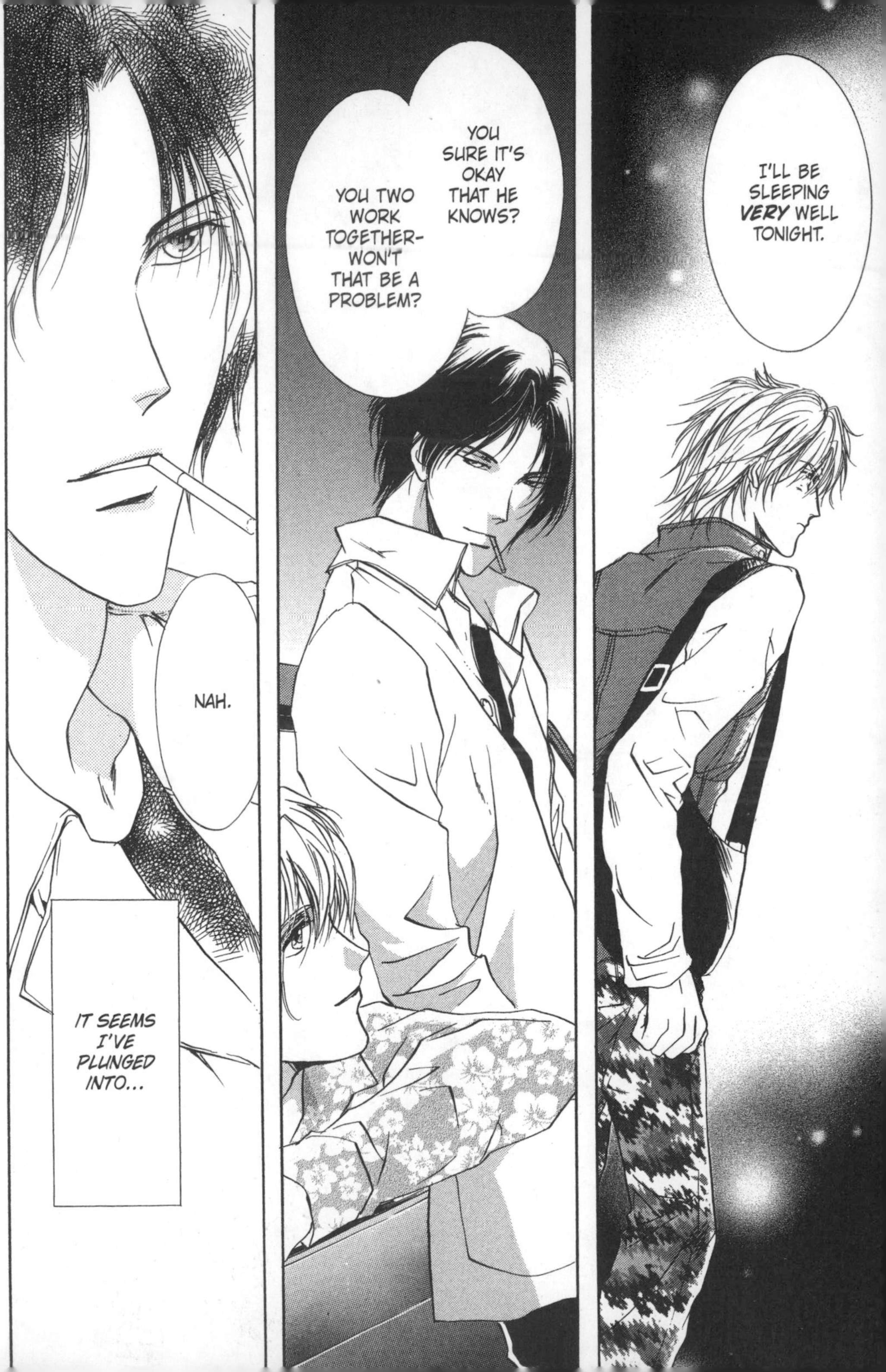
I'LL BE SLEEPING *VERY* WELL TONIGHT.
YOU SURE IT'S OKAY THAT HE KNOWS?
YOU TWO WORK TOGETHER-WON'T THAT BE A PROBLEM?
NAH.
IT SEEMS I'VE PLUNGED INTO...

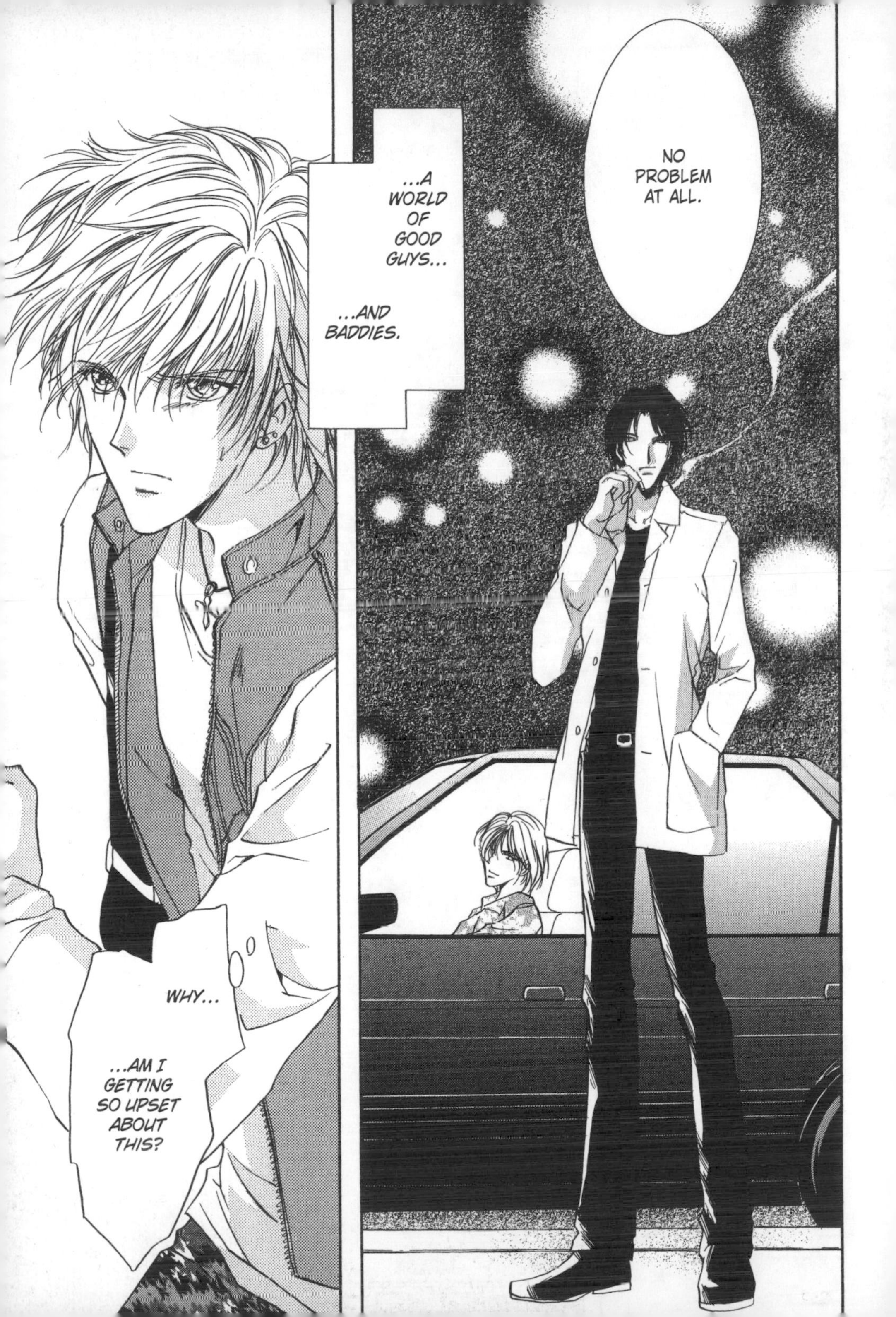
NO PROBLEM AT ALL.
...A WORLD OF GOOD GUYS...
...AND BADDIES.
WHY...
...AM I GETTING SO UPSET ABOUT THIS?

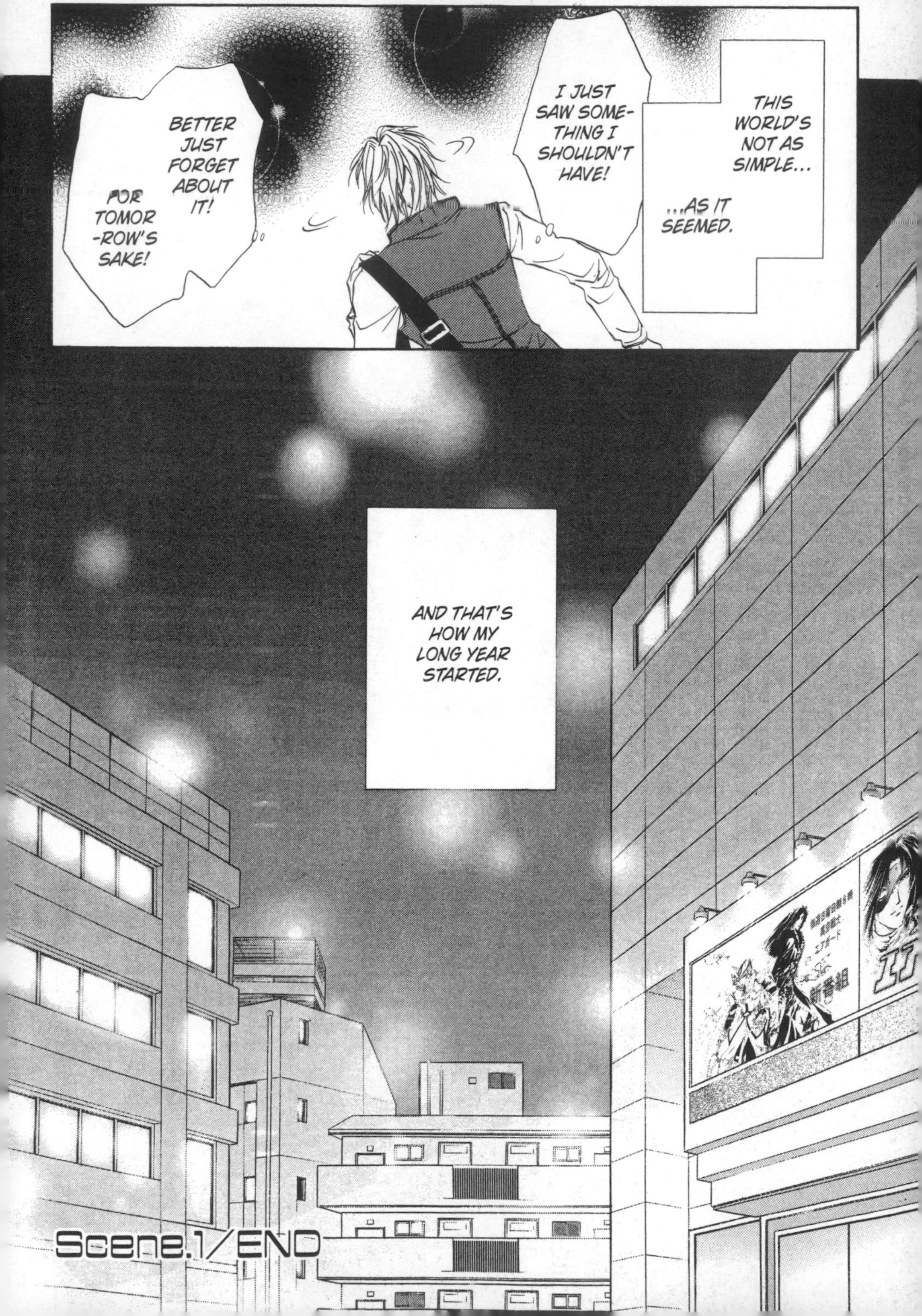
THIS WORLD'S NOT AS SIMPLE...
...AS IT SEEMED.
I JUST SAW SOME-THING I SHOULDN'T HAVE!
BETTER JUST FORGET ABOUT IT!
FOR TOMOR-ROW'S SAKE!
AND THAT'S HOW MY LONG YEAR STARTED.
新番組
Scene.1/END

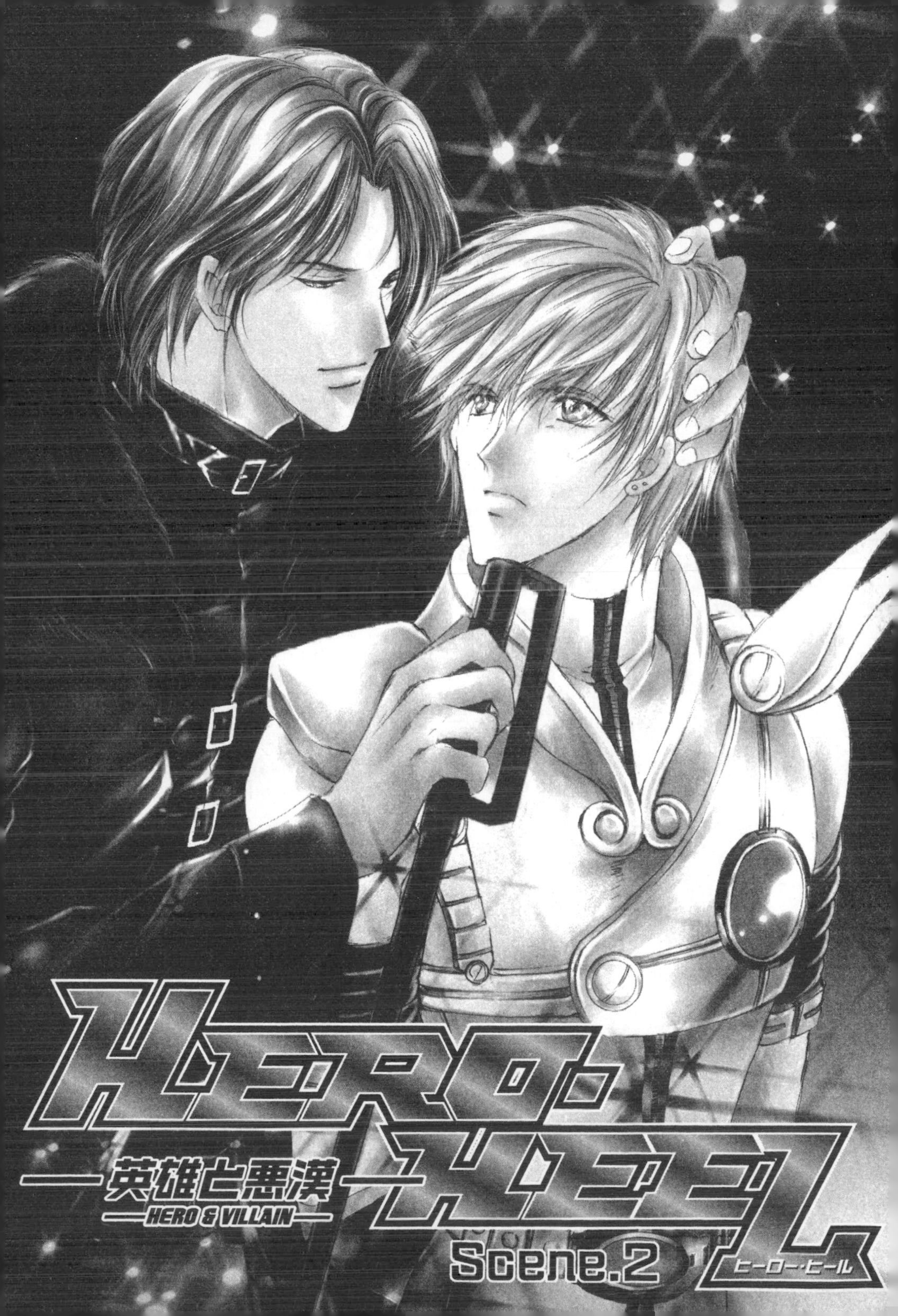
HERO HEEL
—英雄と悪漢—
—HERO & VILLAIN—
Scene.2
ヒーロー・ヒール

HERO HEEL

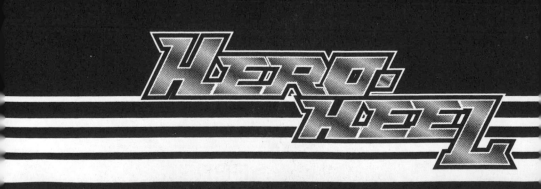

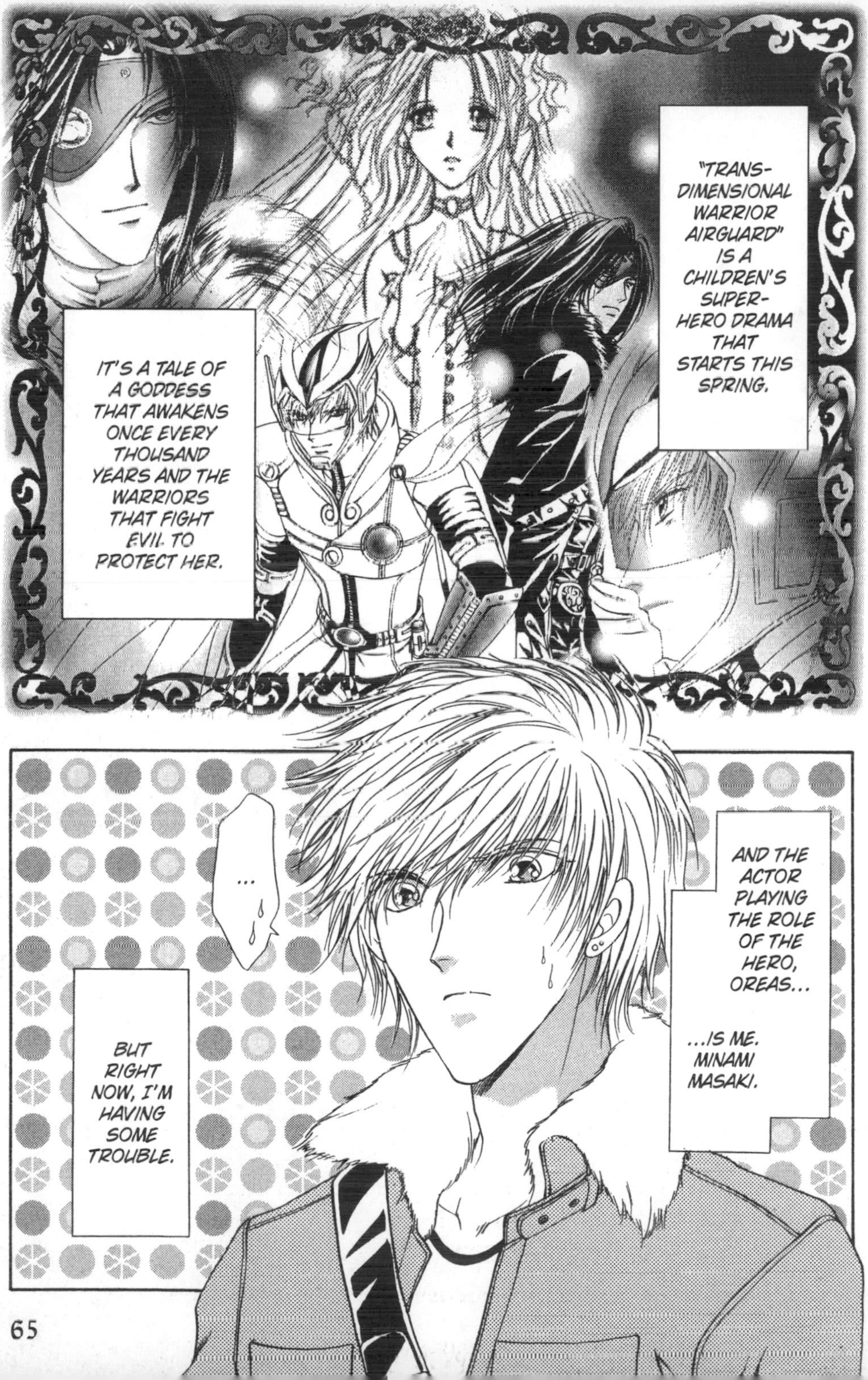
"TRANS-DIMENSIONAL WARRIOR AIRGUARD" IS A CHILDREN'S SUPER-HERO DRAMA THAT STARTS THIS SPRING.
IT'S A TALE OF A GODDESS THAT AWAKENS ONCE EVERY THOUSAND YEARS AND THE WARRIORS THAT FIGHT EVIL TO PROTECT HER.
AND THE ACTOR PLAYING THE ROLE OF THE HERO, OREAS...
...IS ME. MINAMI MASAKI.
...
BUT RIGHT NOW, I'M HAVING SOME TROUBLE.

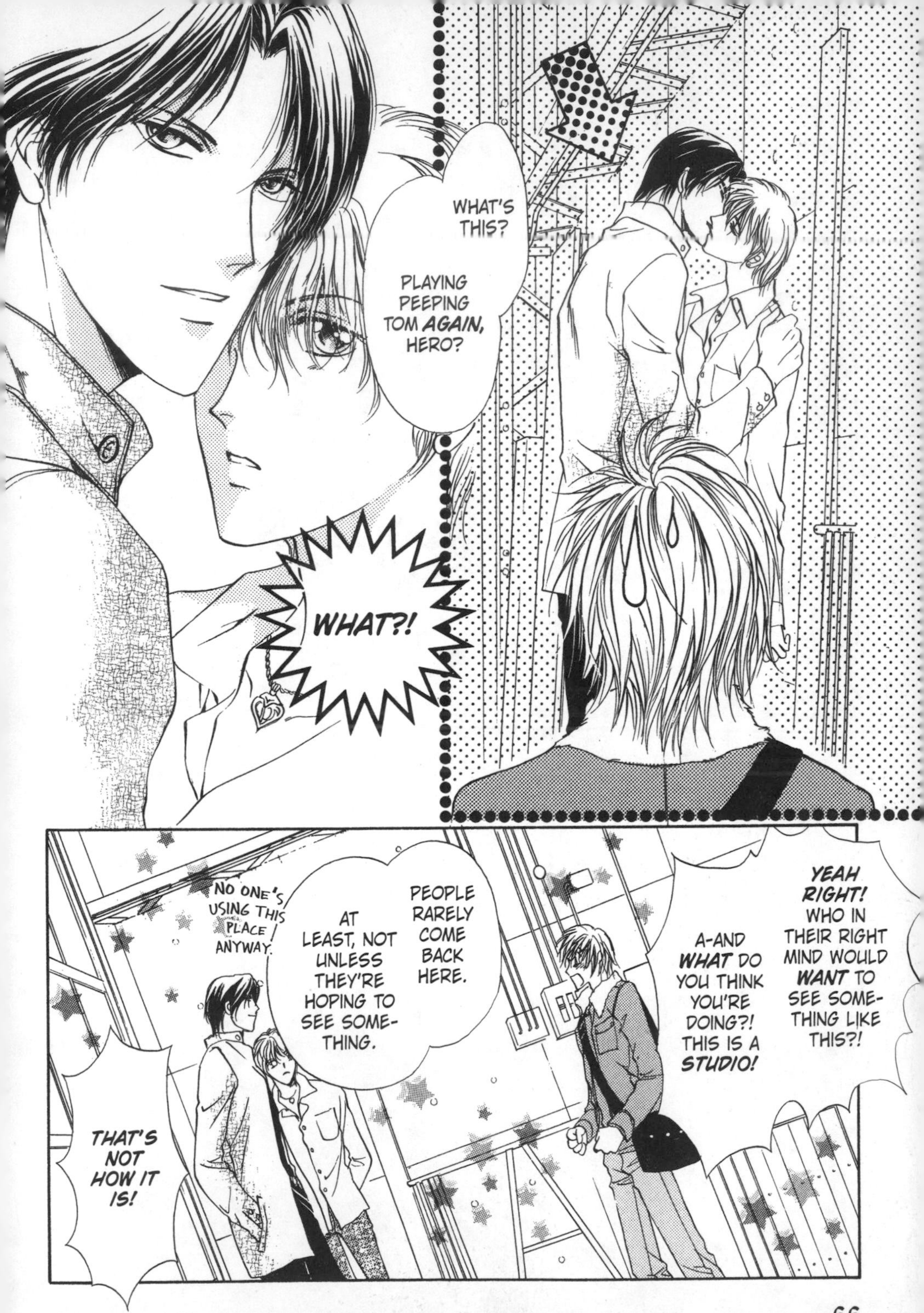
WHAT'S THIS?
PLAYING PEEPING TOM *AGAIN,* HERO?
WHAT?!
YEAH RIGHT! WHO IN THEIR RIGHT MIND WOULD *WANT* TO SEE SOME-THING LIKE THIS?!
A-AND *WHAT* DO YOU THINK YOU'RE DOING?! THIS IS A *STUDIO!*
PEOPLE RARELY COME BACK HERE.
AT LEAST, NOT UNLESS THEY'RE HOPING TO SEE SOME-THING.
NO ONE'S USING THIS PLACE ANYWAY.
THAT'S NOT HOW IT IS!

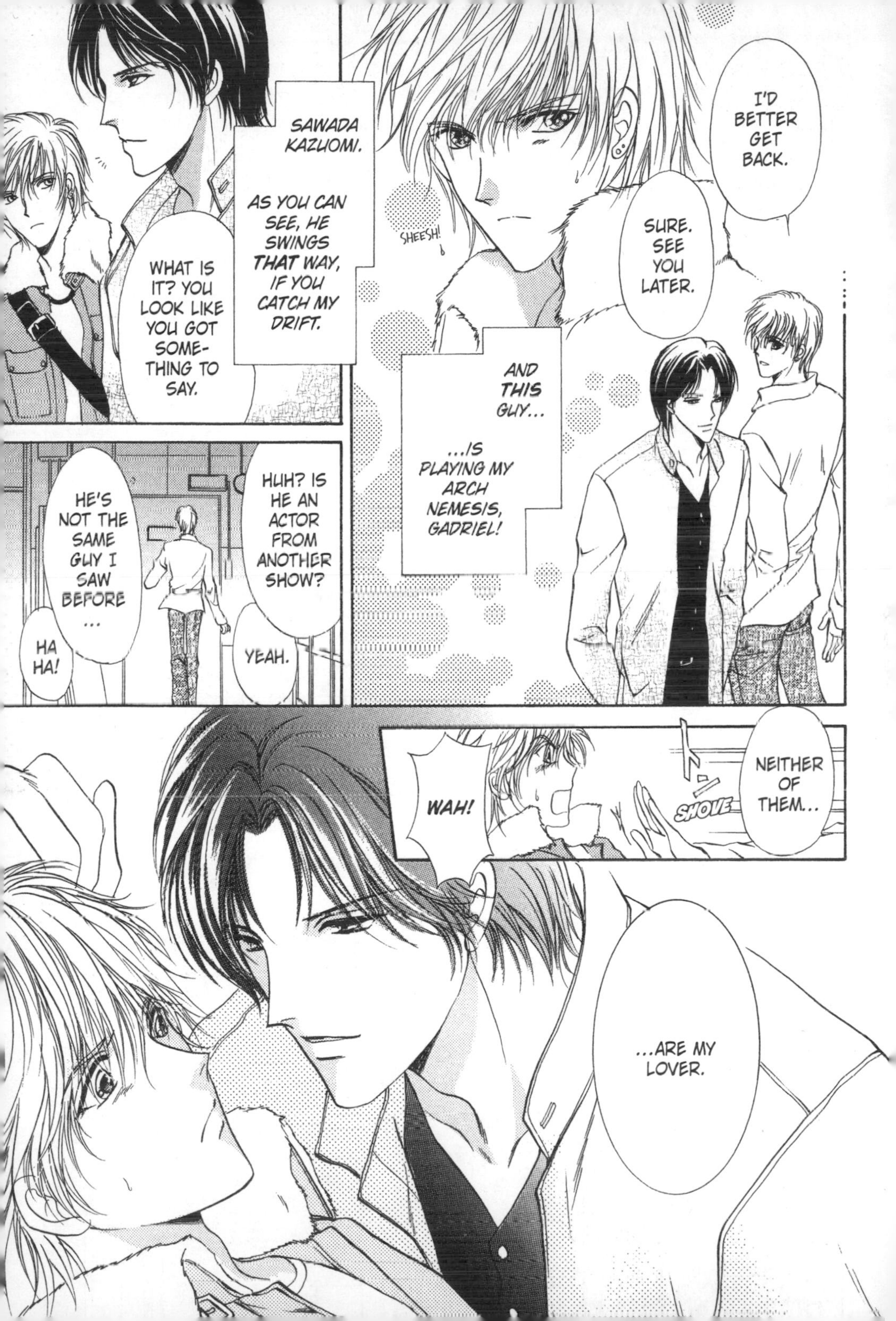
I'D BETTER GET BACK.
SURE. SEE YOU LATER.
SHEESH!
AND THIS GUY...
...IS PLAYING MY ARCH NEMESIS, GADRIEL!
SAWADA KAZUOMI.
AS YOU CAN SEE, HE SWINGS THAT WAY, IF YOU CATCH MY DRIFT.
WHAT IS IT? YOU LOOK LIKE YOU GOT SOME-THING TO SAY.
HUH? IS HE AN ACTOR FROM ANOTHER SHOW?
YEAH.
HE'S NOT THE SAME GUY I SAW BEFORE...
HA HA!
NEITHER OF THEM...
SHOVE
WAH!
...ARE MY LOVER.

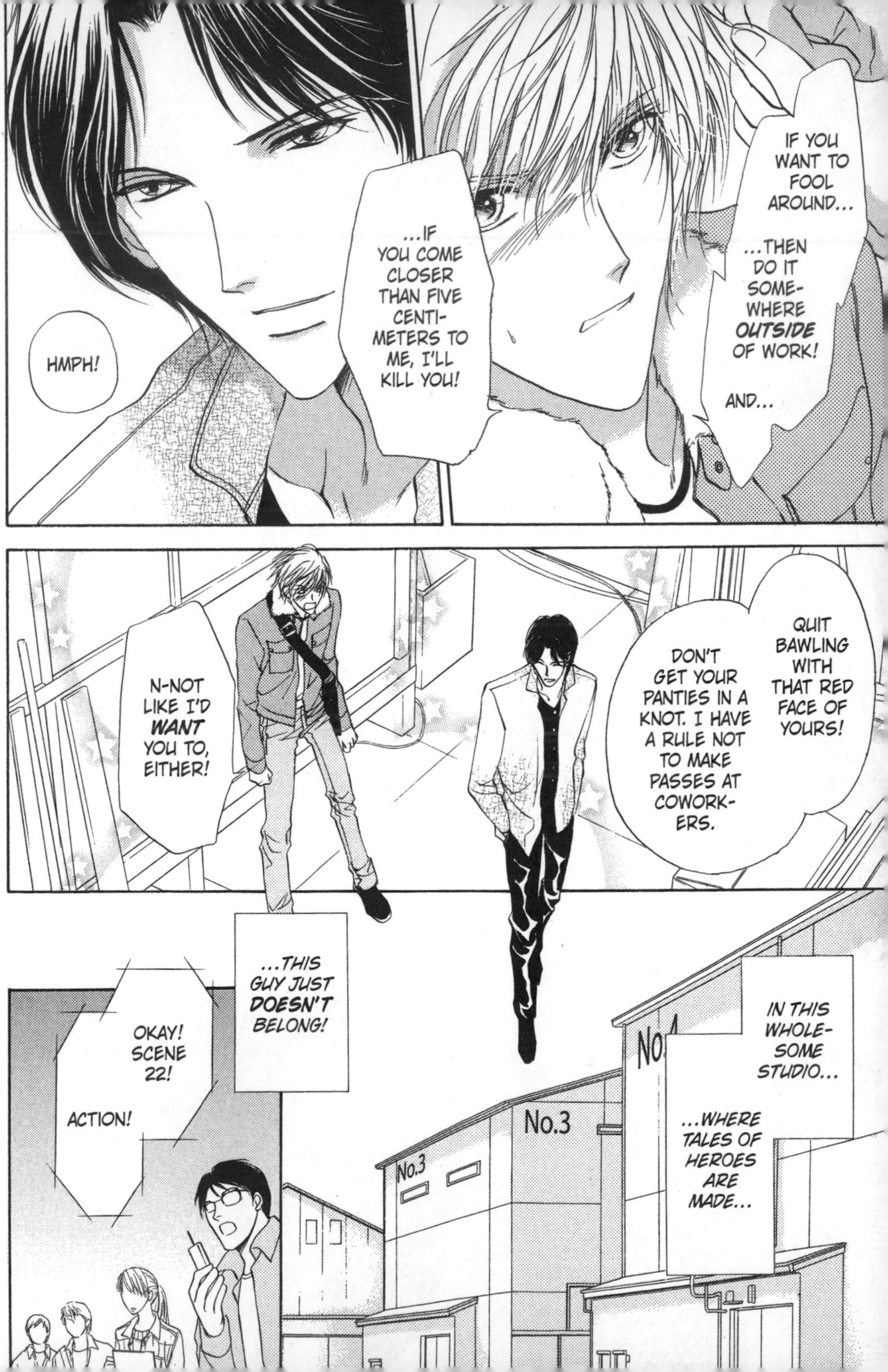
IF YOU WANT TO FOOL AROUND...
...THEN DO IT SOMEWHERE *OUTSIDE* OF WORK!
AND...
...IF YOU COME CLOSER THAN FIVE CENTIMETERS TO ME, I'LL KILL YOU!
HMPH!
QUIT BAWLING WITH THAT RED FACE OF YOURS!
DON'T GET YOUR PANTIES IN A KNOT. I HAVE A RULE NOT TO MAKE PASSES AT COWORKERS.
N-NOT LIKE I'D ***WANT*** YOU TO, EITHER!
IN THIS WHOLESOME STUDIO...
...WHERE TALES OF HEROES ARE MADE...
No.4
No.3
No.3
*...THIS GUY JUST **DOESN'T** BELONG!*
OKAY! SCENE 22!
ACTION!

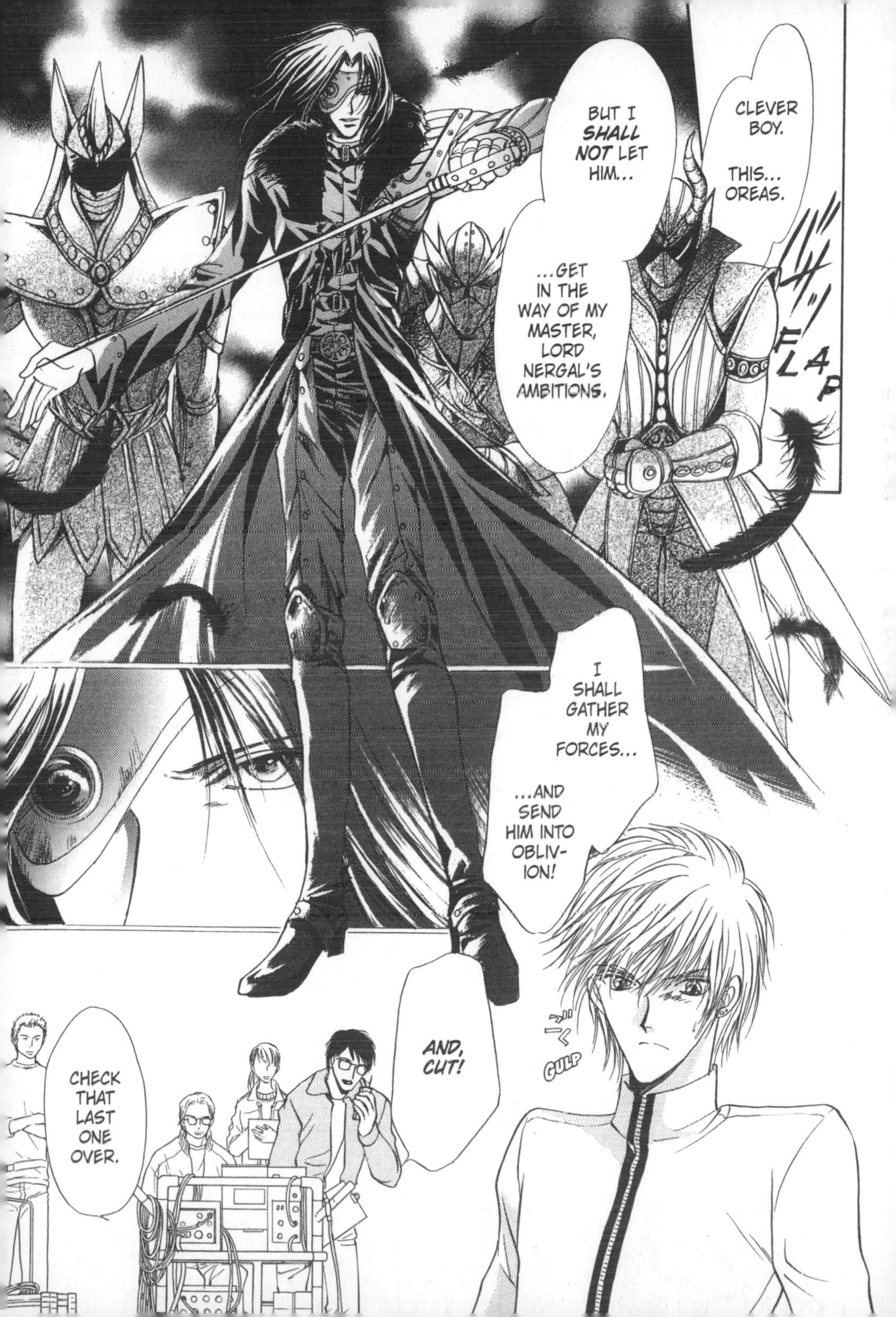
CLEVER BOY.
THIS... OREAS.
FLAP
BUT I SHALL NOT LET HIM...
...GET IN THE WAY OF MY MASTER, LORD NERGAL'S AMBITIONS.
I SHALL GATHER MY FORCES...
...AND SEND HIM INTO OBLIV-ION!
AND, CUT!
GULP
CHECK THAT LAST ONE OVER.

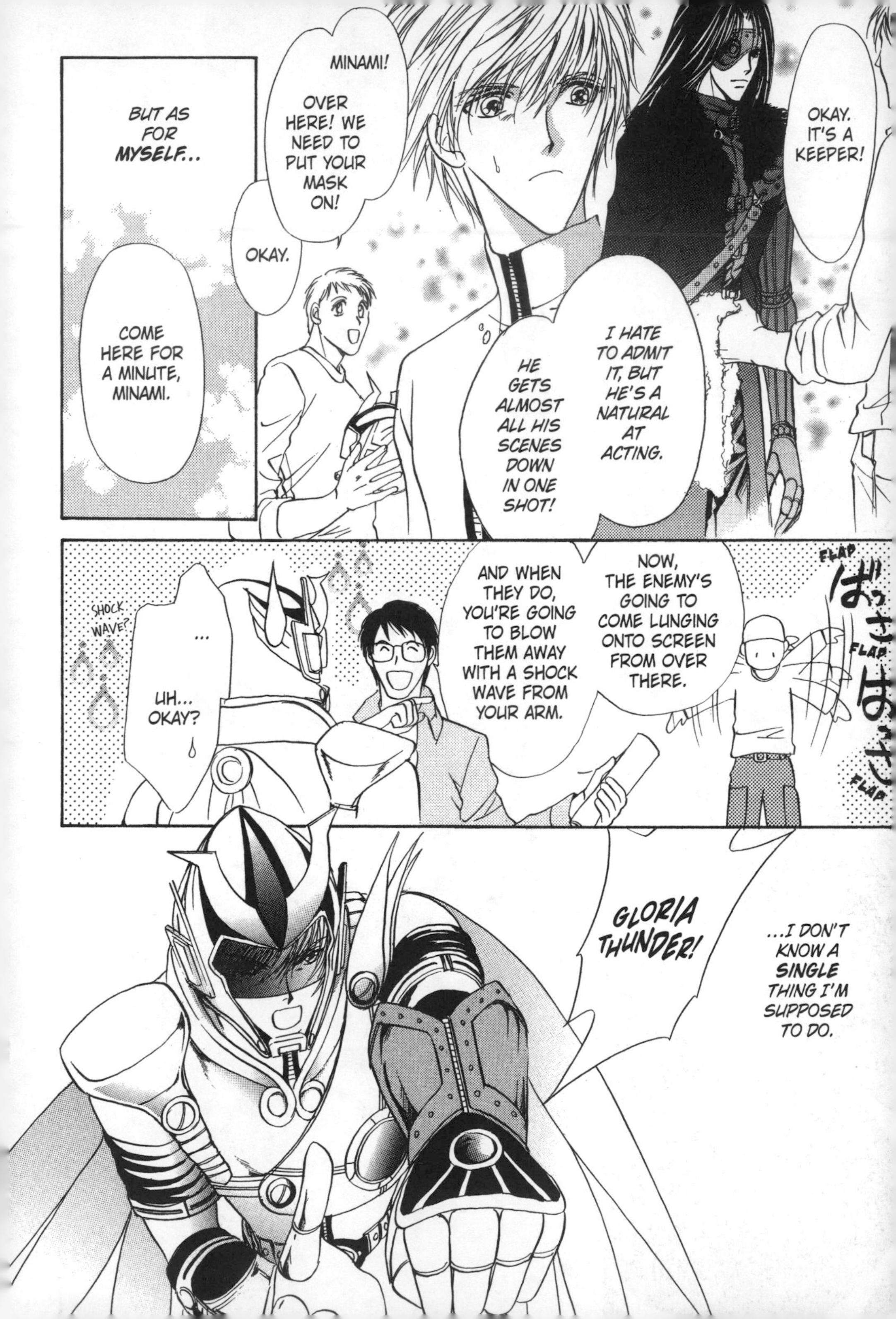
OKAY. IT'S A KEEPER!
MINAMI! OVER HERE! WE NEED TO PUT YOUR MASK ON!
I HATE TO ADMIT IT, BUT HE'S A NATURAL AT ACTING.
HE GETS ALMOST ALL HIS SCENES DOWN IN ONE SHOT!
OKAY.
BUT AS FOR MYSELF...
COME HERE FOR A MINUTE, MINAMI.
FLAP FLAP FLAP
NOW, THE ENEMY'S GOING TO COME LUNGING ONTO SCREEN FROM OVER THERE.
AND WHEN THEY DO, YOU'RE GOING TO BLOW THEM AWAY WITH A SHOCK WAVE FROM YOUR ARM.
...
UH... OKAY?
SHOCK WAVE?
...I DON'T KNOW A SINGLE THING I'M SUPPOSED TO DO.
GLORIA THUNDER!

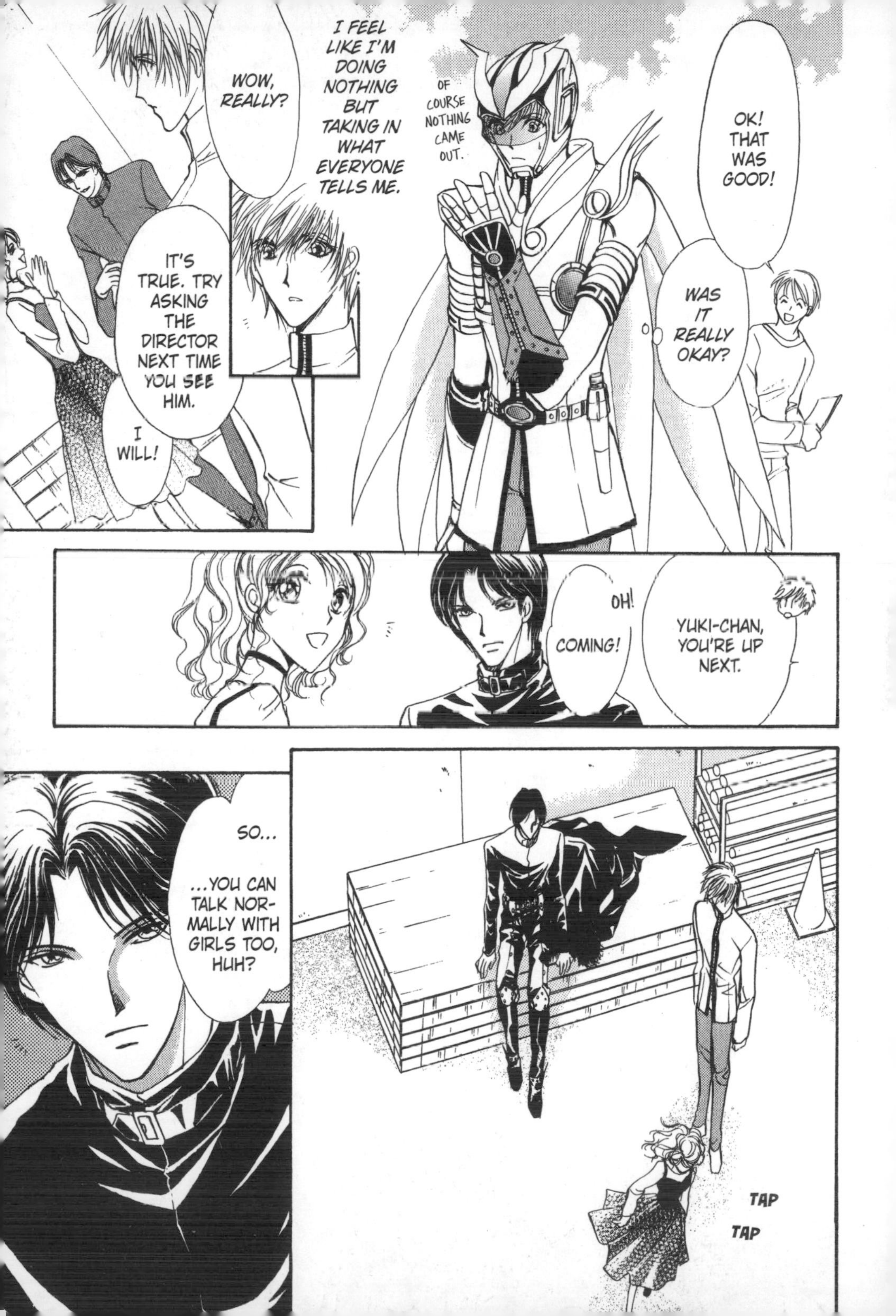
OK! THAT WAS GOOD!
WAS IT REALLY OKAY?
OF COURSE NOTHING CAME OUT.
I FEEL LIKE I'M DOING NOTHING BUT TAKING IN WHAT EVERYONE TELLS ME.
WOW, REALLY?
IT'S TRUE. TRY ASKING THE DIRECTOR NEXT TIME YOU SEE HIM.
I WILL!
YUKI-CHAN, YOU'RE UP NEXT.
OH!
COMING!
TAP
TAP
SO...
...YOU CAN TALK NOR-MALLY WITH GIRLS TOO, HUH?

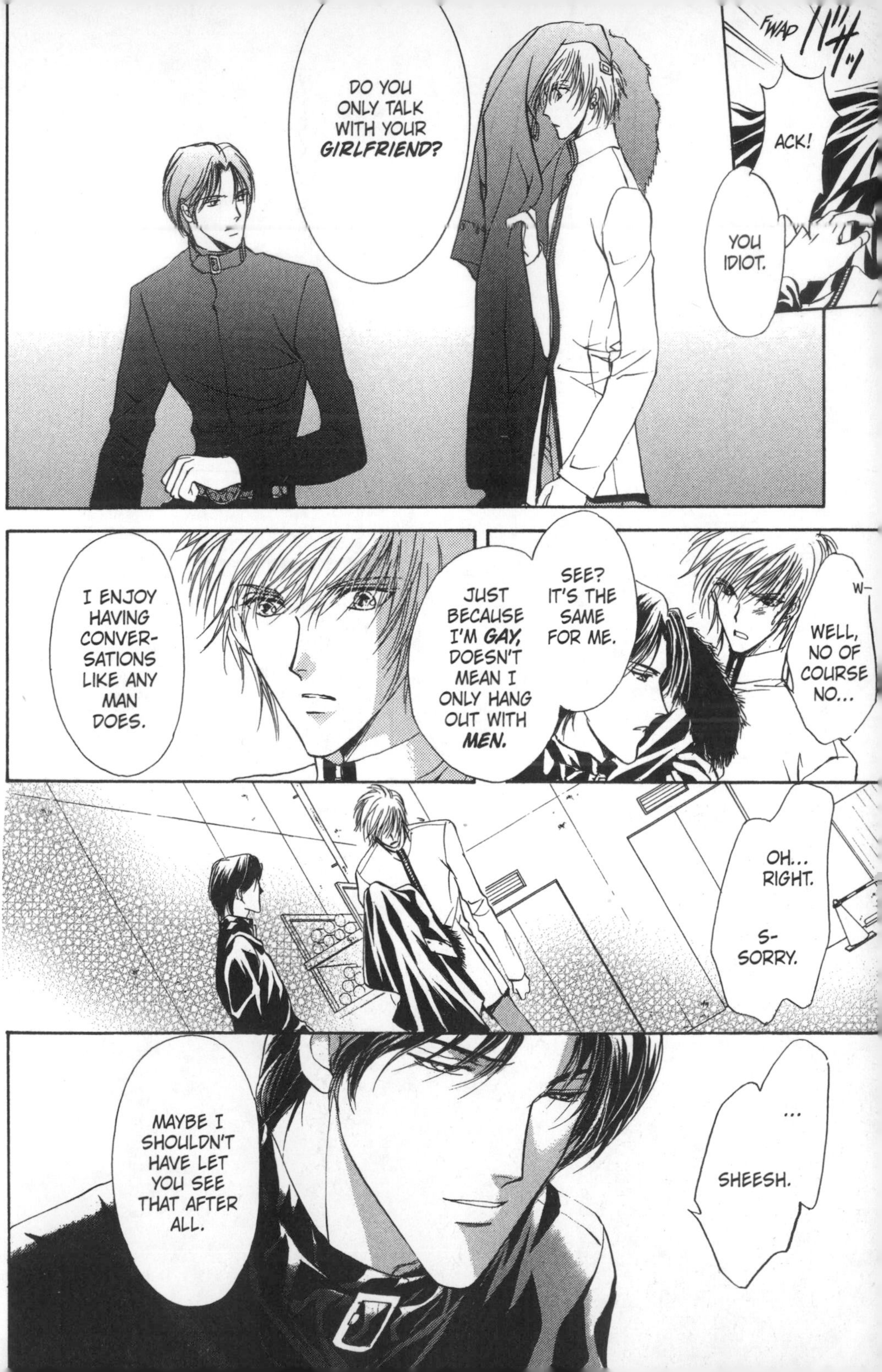
FWAP
ACK!
YOU IDIOT.
DO YOU ONLY TALK WITH YOUR *GIRLFRIEND?*
W-
WELL, NO OF COURSE NO...
SEE? IT'S THE SAME FOR ME.
JUST BECAUSE I'M ***GAY,*** DOESN'T MEAN I ONLY HANG OUT WITH ***MEN.***
I ENJOY HAVING CONVER-SATIONS LIKE ANY MAN DOES.
OH... RIGHT.
S- SORRY.
...
SHEESH.
MAYBE I SHOULDN'T HAVE LET YOU SEE THAT AFTER ALL.

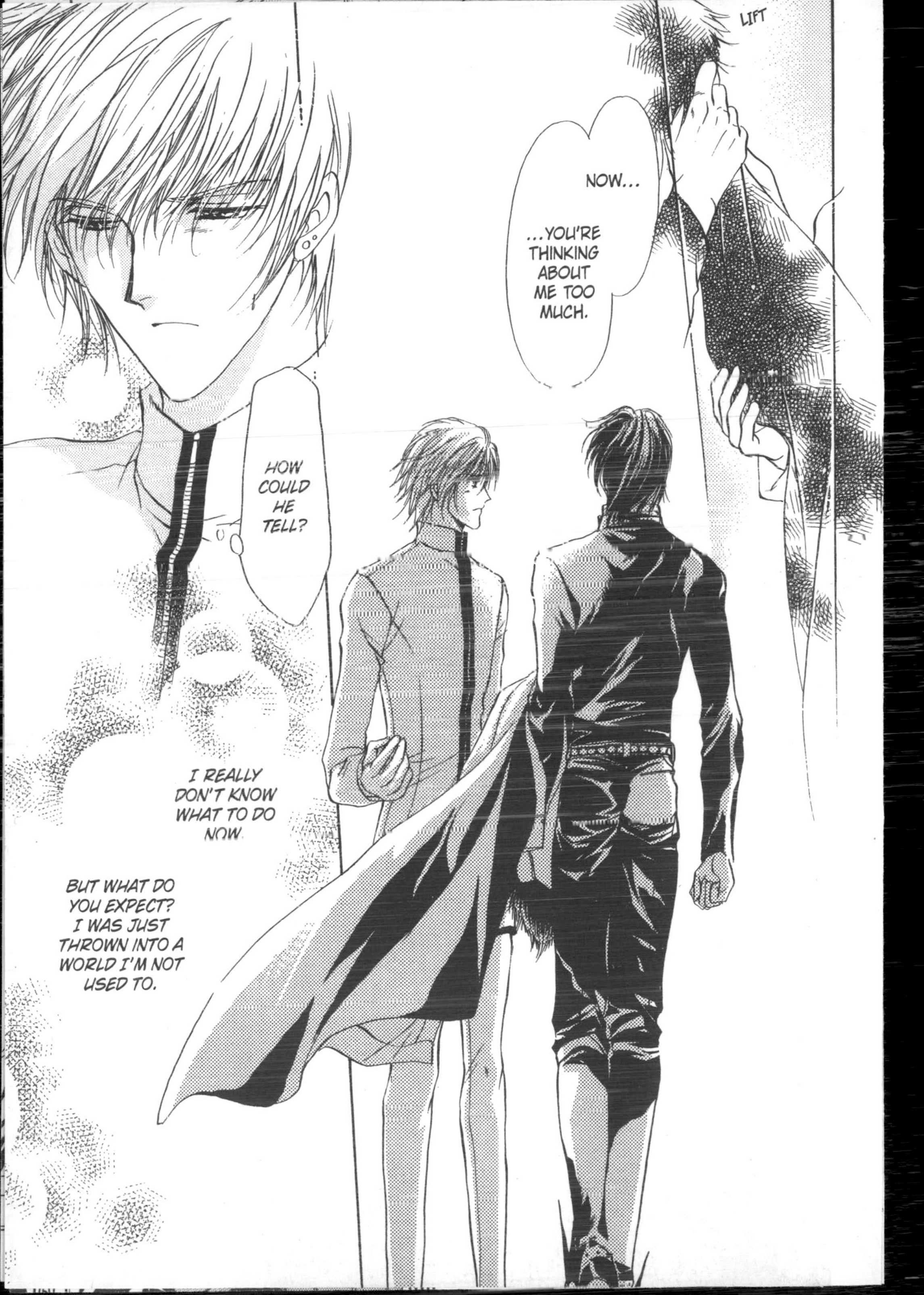
LIFT
NOW...
...YOU'RE THINKING ABOUT ME TOO MUCH.
HOW COULD HE TELL?
I REALLY DON'T KNOW WHAT TO DO NOW.
BUT WHAT DO YOU EXPECT? I WAS JUST THROWN INTO A WORLD I'M NOT USED TO.

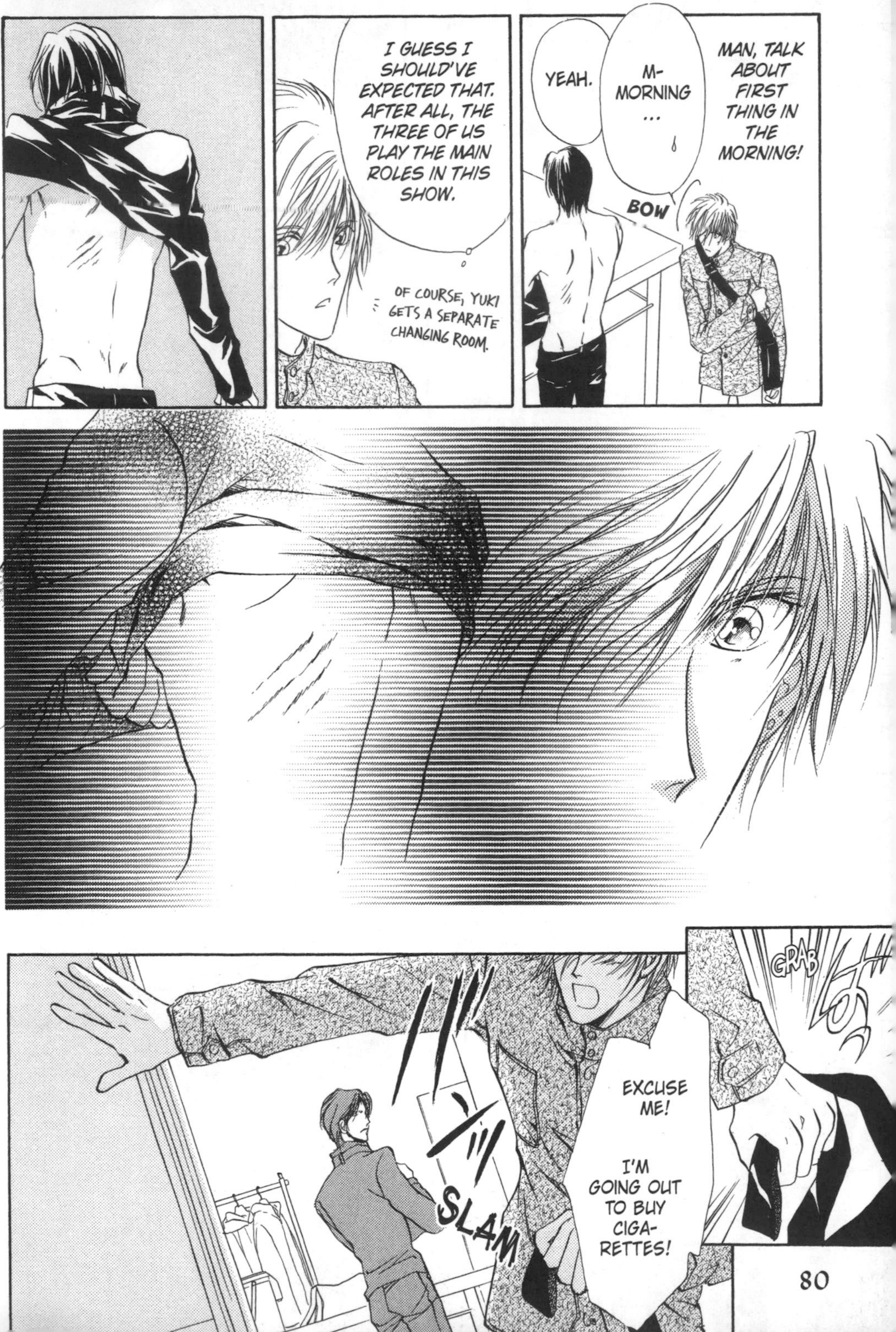
MAN, TALK ABOUT FIRST THING IN THE MORNING!
M-MORNING ...
BOW
YEAH.
I GUESS I SHOULD'VE EXPECTED THAT. AFTER ALL, THE THREE OF US PLAY THE MAIN ROLES IN THIS SHOW.
OF COURSE, YUKI GETS A SEPARATE CHANGING ROOM.
GRAB
EXCUSE ME!
I'M GOING OUT TO BUY CIGA-RETTES!
SLAM

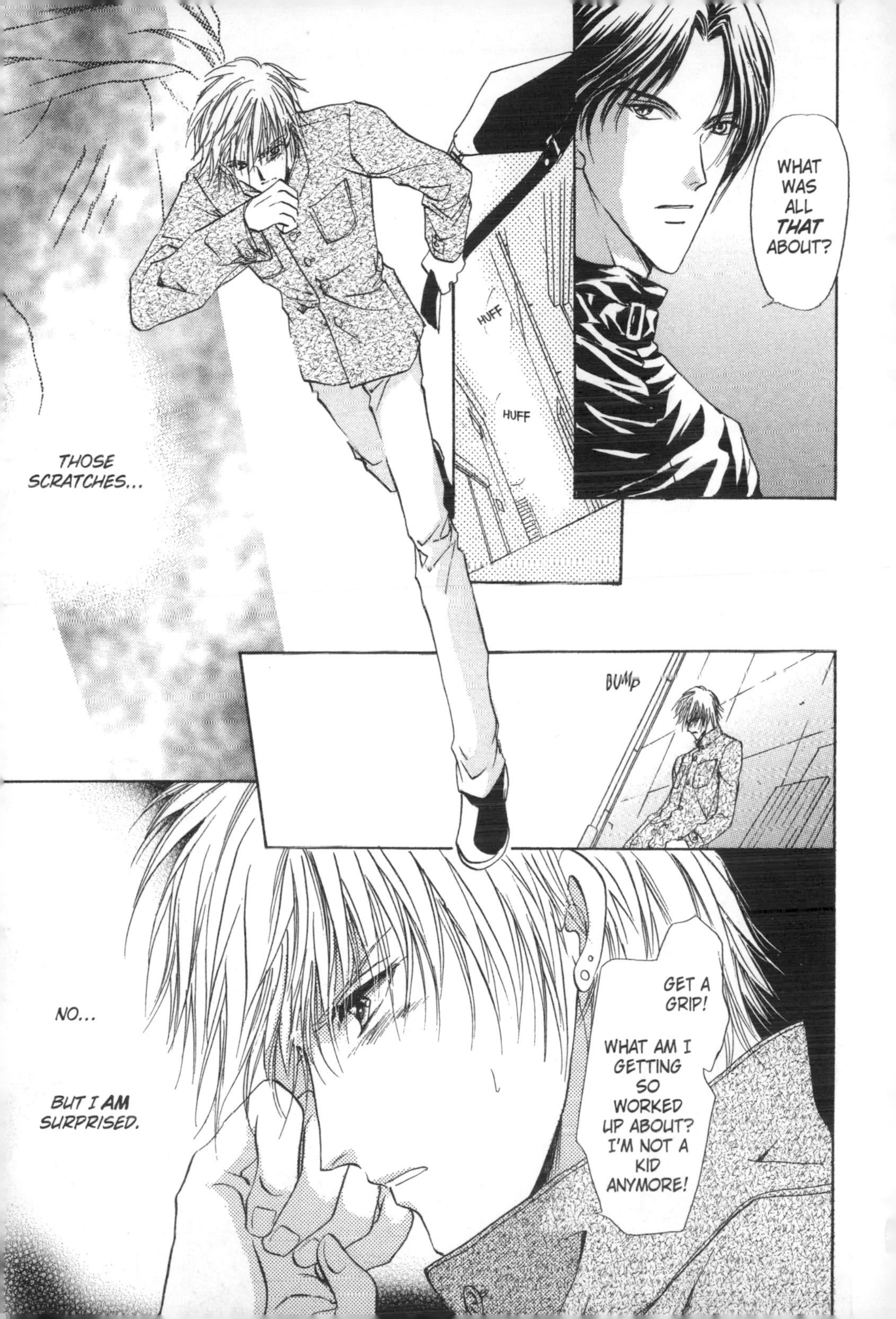
WHAT WAS ALL THAT ABOUT?
HUFF
HUFF
THOSE SCRATCHES...
BUMP
GET A GRIP!
WHAT AM I GETTING SO WORKED UP ABOUT? I'M NOT A KID ANYMORE!
NO...
BUT I AM SURPRISED.

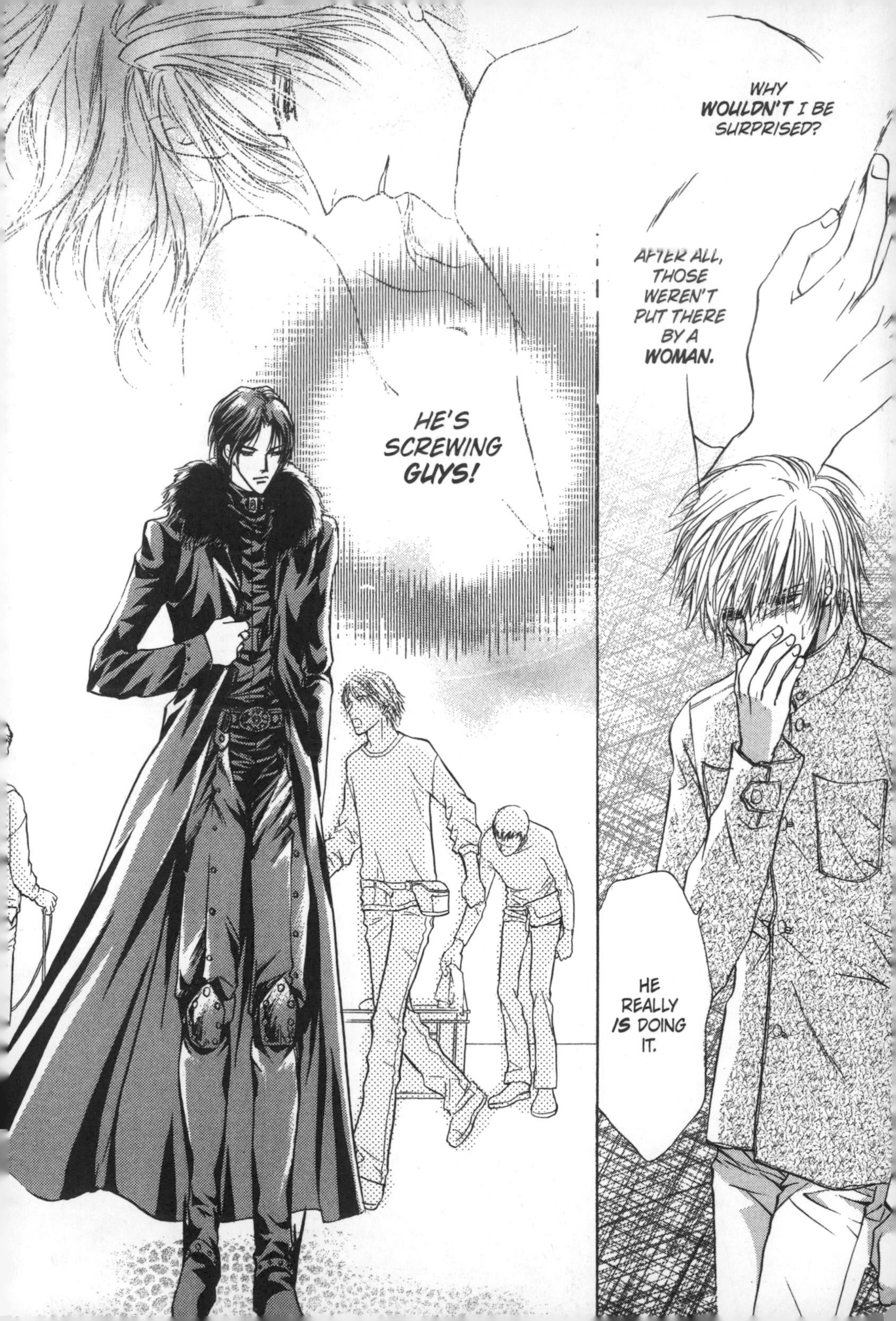
WHY WOULDN'T I BE SURPRISED?
AFTER ALL, THOSE WEREN'T PUT THERE BY A WOMAN.
HE REALLY IS DOING IT.
HE'S SCREWING GUYS!

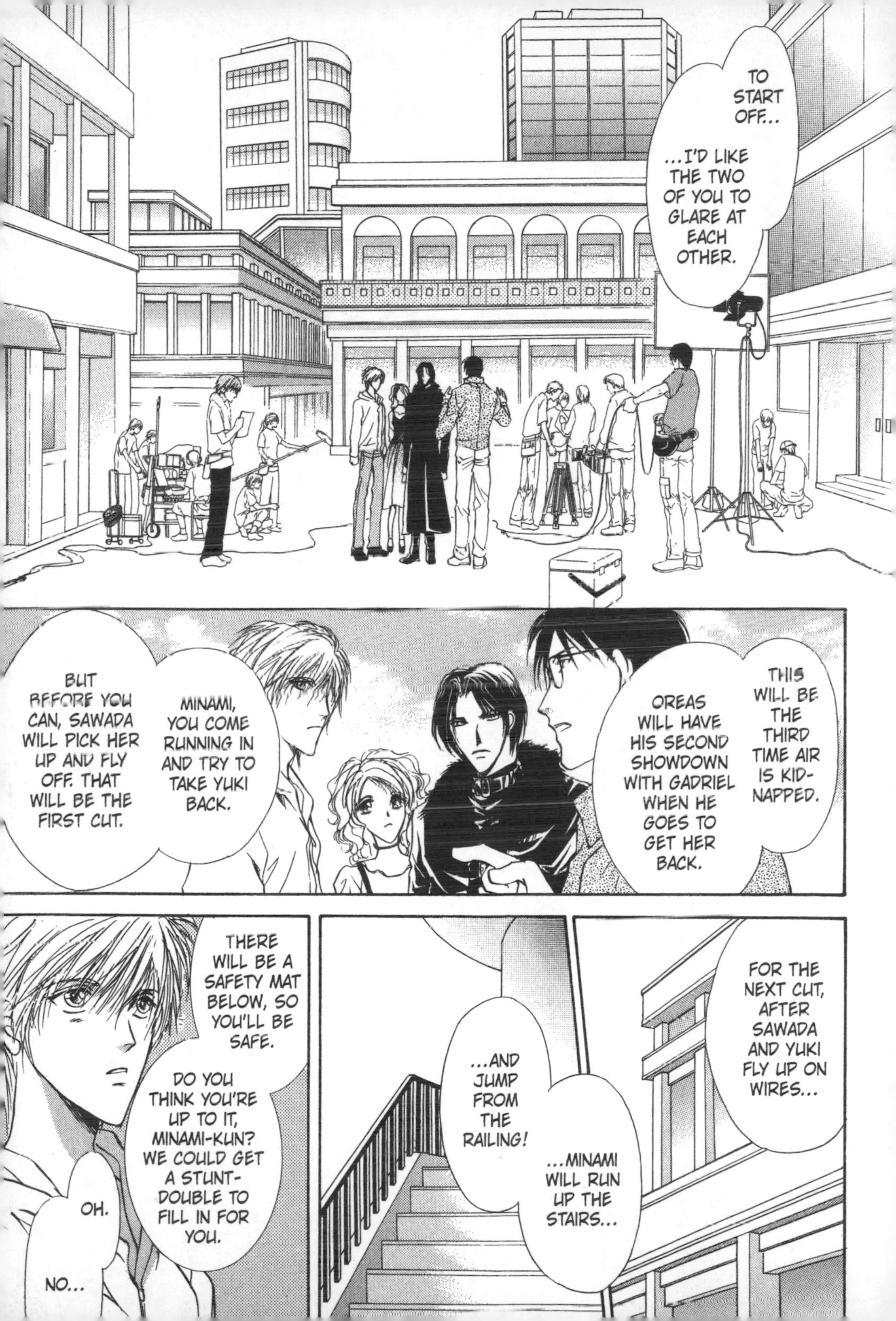
TO START OFF...
...I'D LIKE THE TWO OF YOU TO GLARE AT EACH OTHER.
THIS WILL BE THE THIRD TIME AIR IS KID-NAPPED.
OREAS WILL HAVE HIS SECOND SHOWDOWN WITH GADRIEL WHEN HE GOES TO GET HER BACK.
MINAMI, YOU COME RUNNING IN AND TRY TO TAKE YUKI BACK.
BUT BEFORE YOU CAN, SAWADA WILL PICK HER UP AND FLY OFF. THAT WILL BE THE FIRST CUT.
FOR THE NEXT CUT, AFTER SAWADA AND YUKI FLY UP ON WIRES...
...MINAMI WILL RUN UP THE STAIRS...
...AND JUMP FROM THE RAILING!
THERE WILL BE A SAFETY MAT BELOW, SO YOU'LL BE SAFE.
DO YOU THINK YOU'RE UP TO IT, MINAMI-KUN? WE COULD GET A STUNT-DOUBLE TO FILL IN FOR YOU.
OH.
NO...

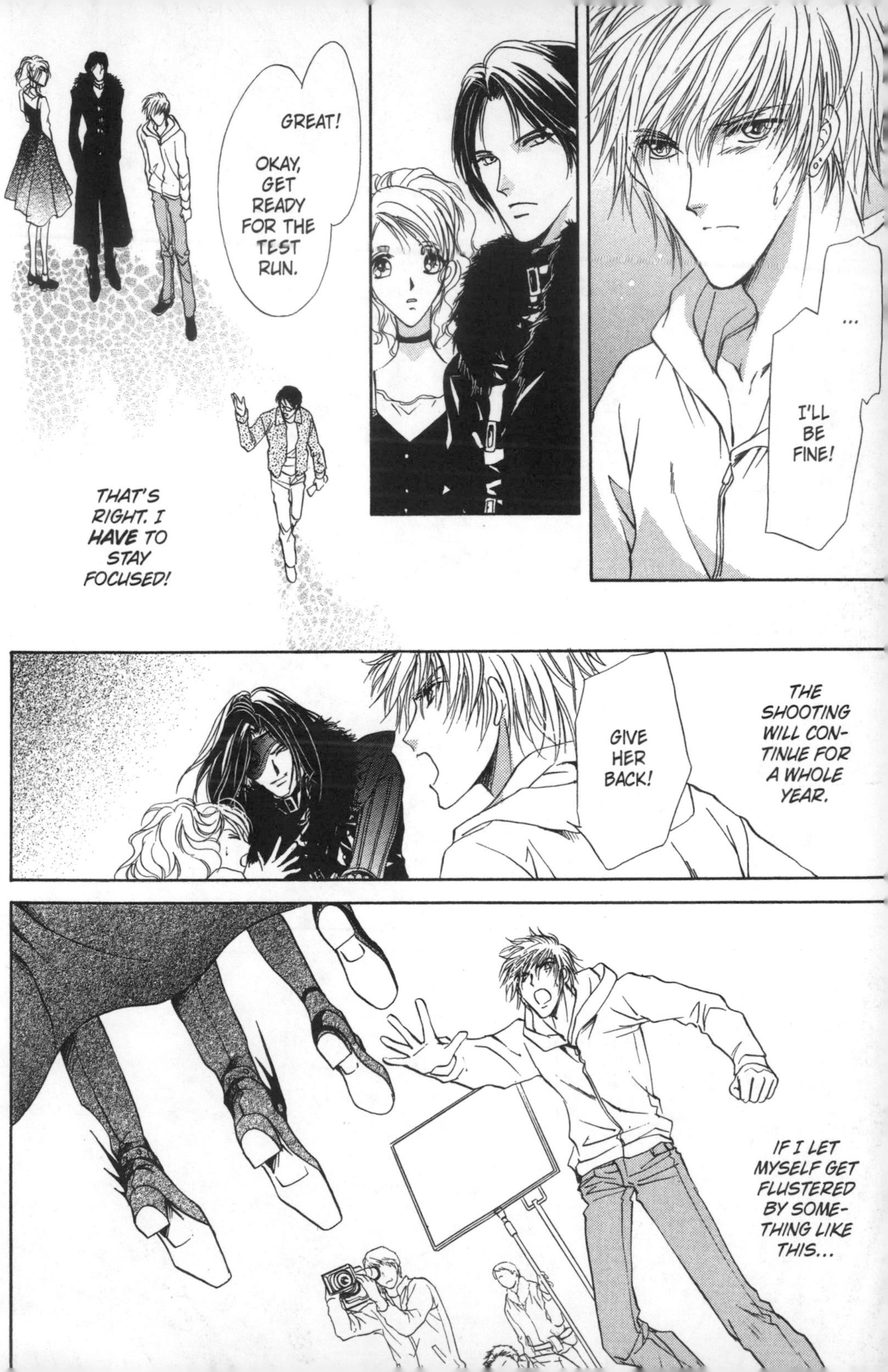
...
I'LL BE FINE!
GREAT!
OKAY, GET READY FOR THE TEST RUN.
THAT'S RIGHT. I **HAVE** TO STAY FOCUSED!
THE SHOOTING WILL CONTINUE FOR A WHOLE YEAR.
GIVE HER BACK!
IF I LET MYSELF GET FLUSTERED BY SOMETHING LIKE THIS...

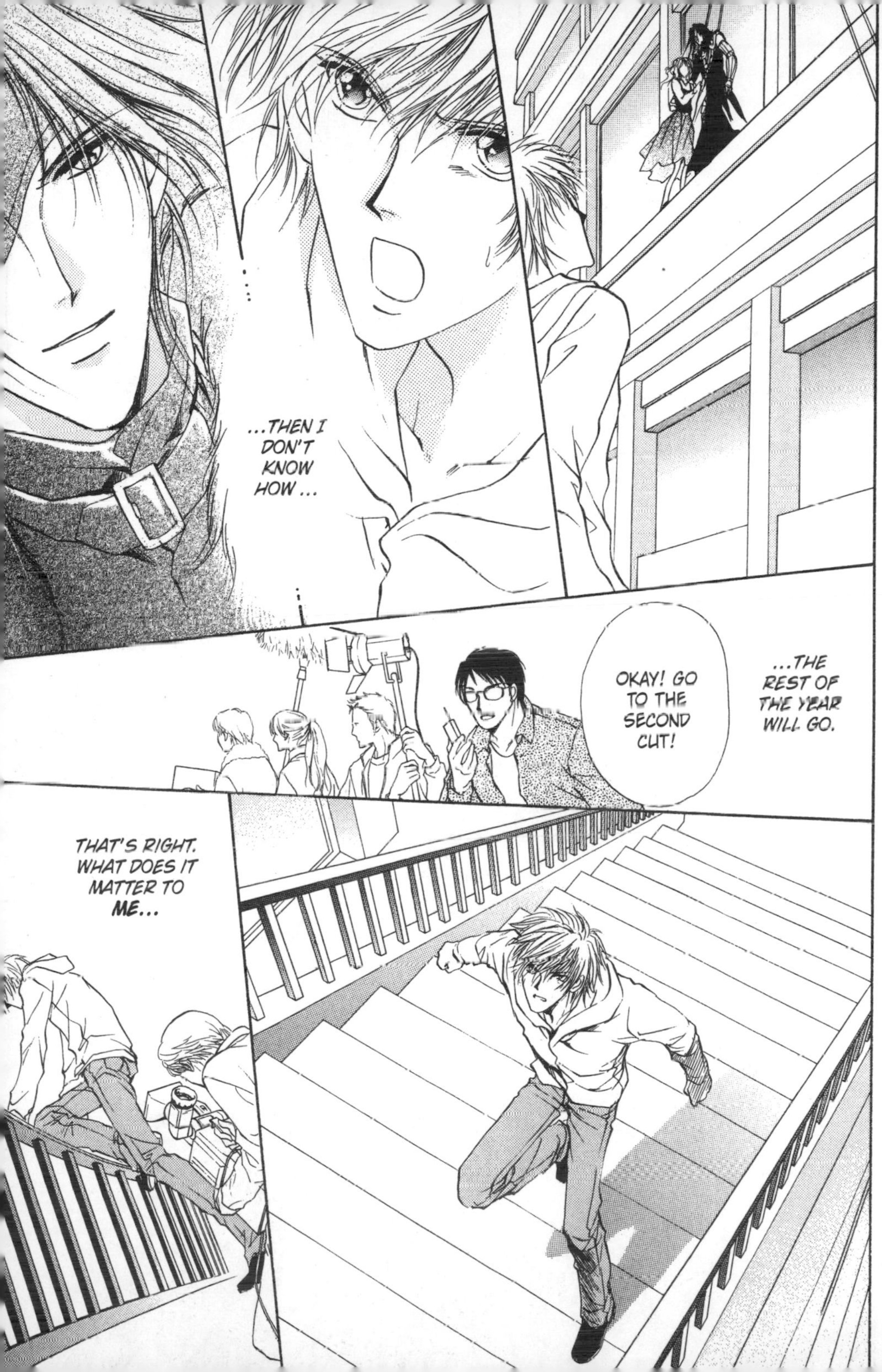
...THEN I DON'T KNOW HOW...
...THE REST OF THE YEAR WILL GO.
OKAY! GO TO THE SECOND CUT!
THAT'S RIGHT. WHAT DOES IT MATTER TO ME...

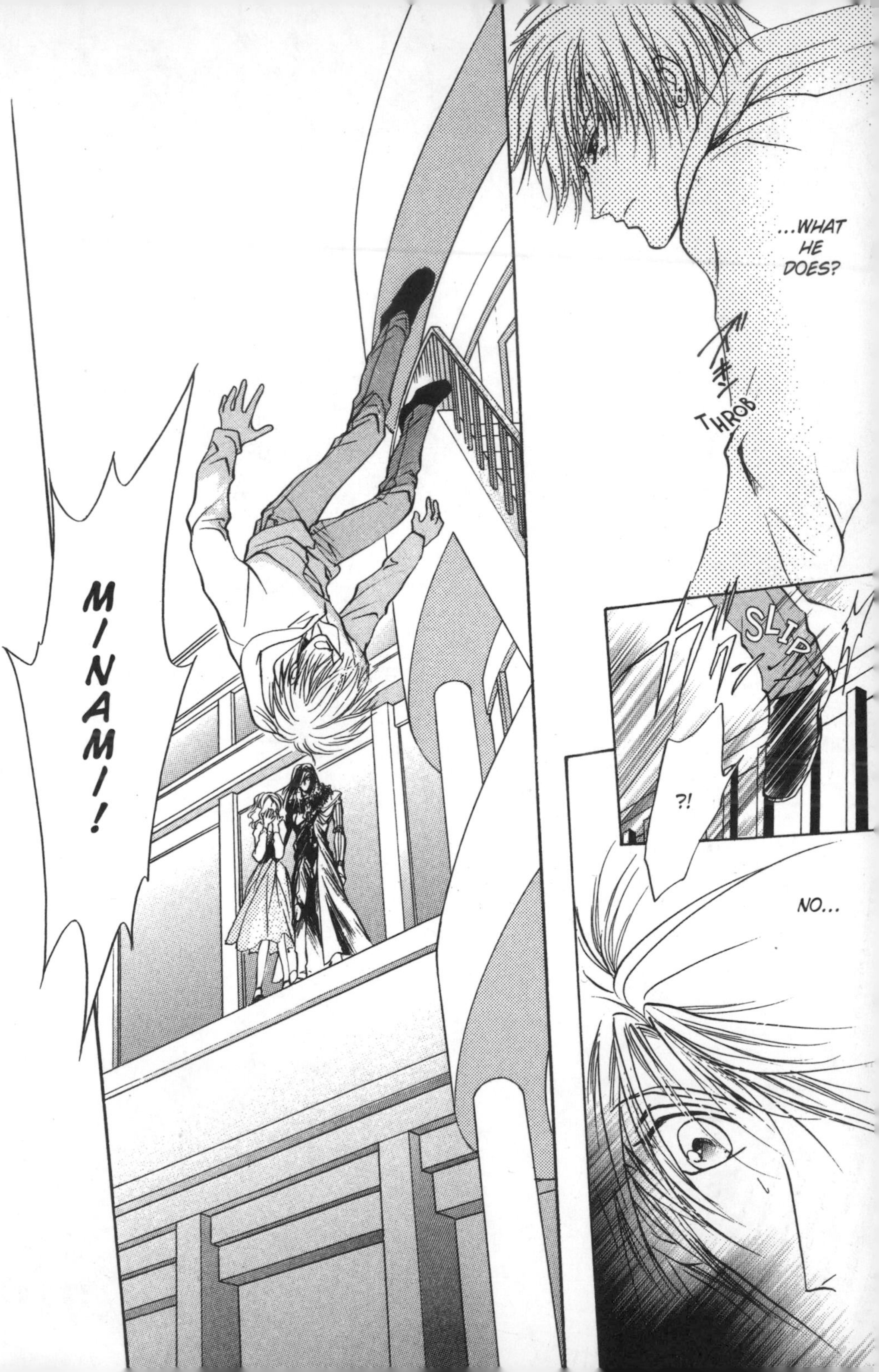
...WHAT HE DOES?
THROB
SLIP
?!
NO...
MINAMI!!

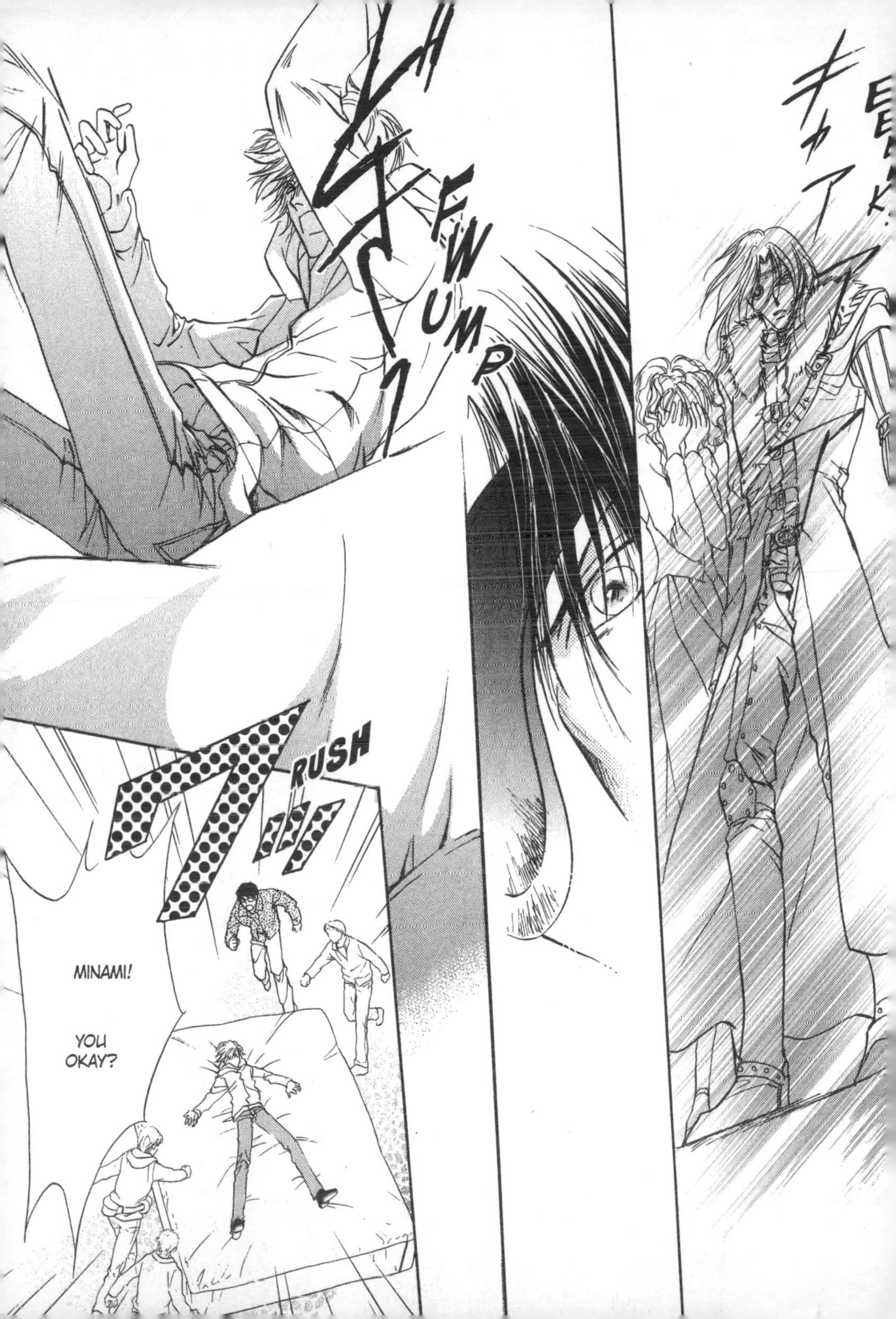
EEEK!
FWUMP
RUSH
MINAMI!
YOU OKAY?

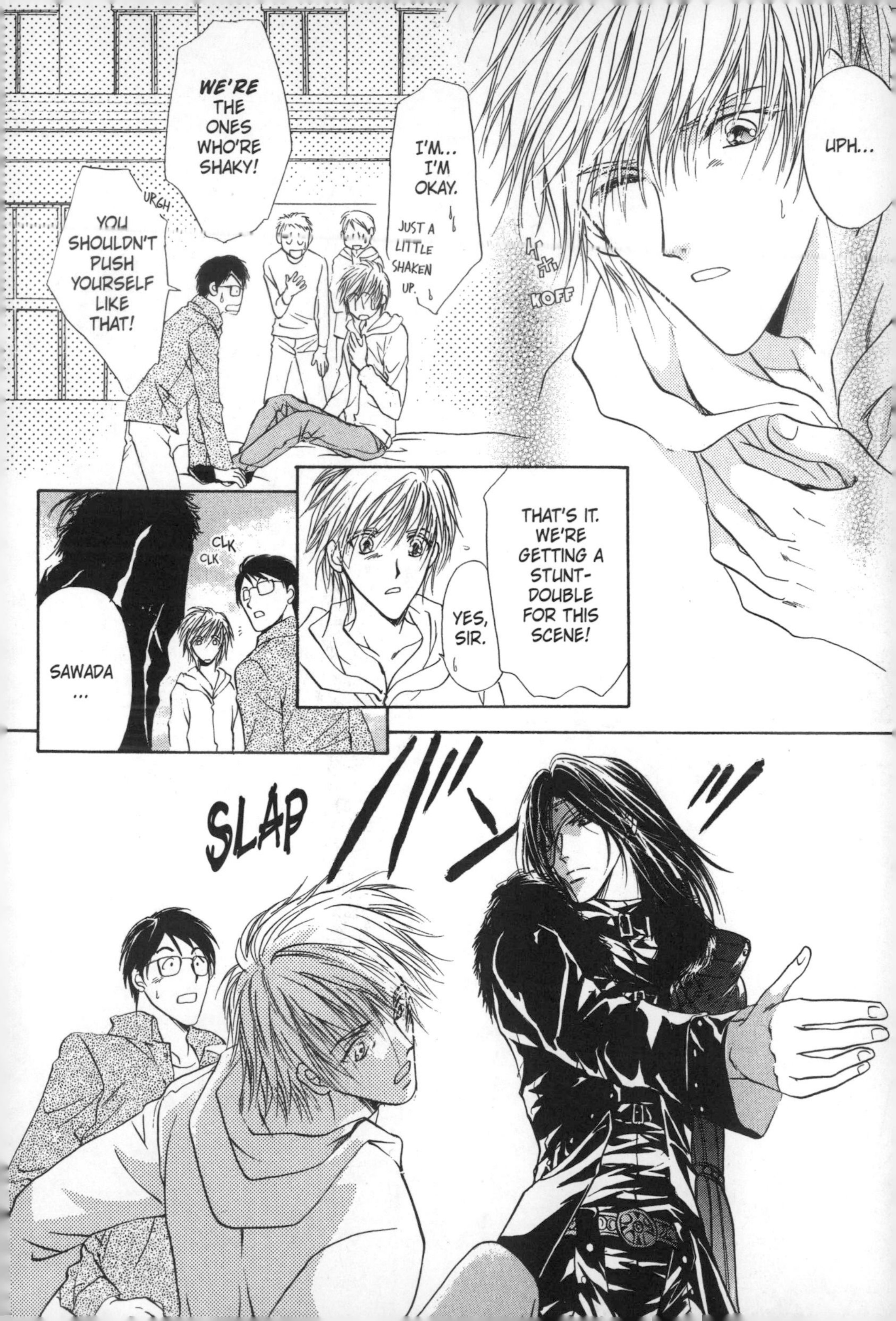
UPH...
KOFF
I'M... I'M OKAY.
JUST A LITTLE SHAKEN UP.
WE'RE THE ONES WHO'RE SHAKY!
URGH
YOU SHOULDN'T PUSH YOURSELF LIKE THAT!
THAT'S IT. WE'RE GETTING A STUNT-DOUBLE FOR THIS SCENE!
YES, SIR.
CLK
CLK
SAWADA ...
SLAP

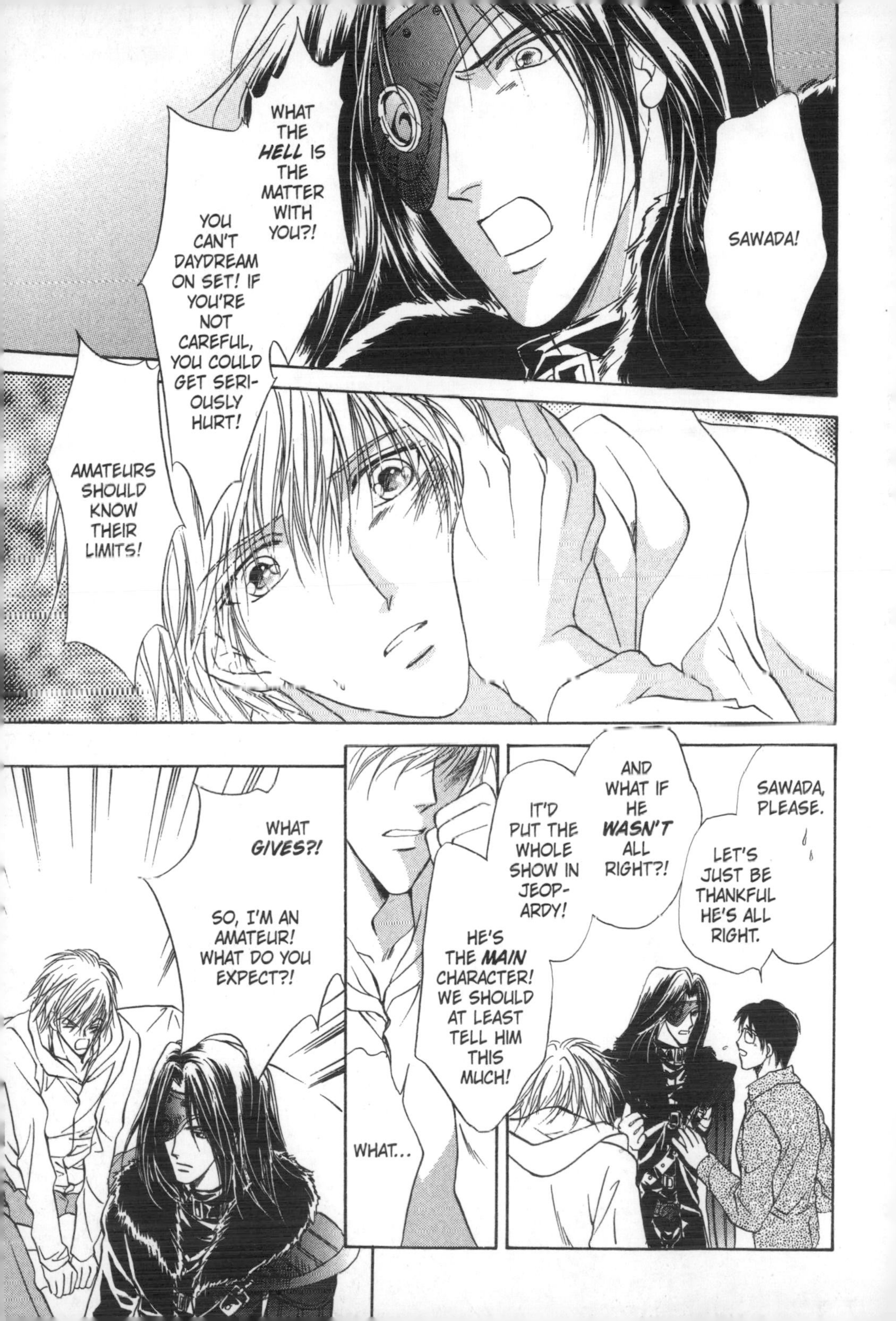
SAWADA!
WHAT THE HELL IS THE MATTER WITH YOU?!
YOU CAN'T DAYDREAM ON SET! IF YOU'RE NOT CAREFUL, YOU COULD GET SERIOUSLY HURT!
AMATEURS SHOULD KNOW THEIR LIMITS!
SAWADA, PLEASE.
LET'S JUST BE THANKFUL HE'S ALL RIGHT.
AND WHAT IF HE WASN'T ALL RIGHT?!
IT'D PUT THE WHOLE SHOW IN JEOPARDY!
HE'S THE MAIN CHARACTER! WE SHOULD AT LEAST TELL HIM THIS MUCH!
WHAT...
WHAT GIVES?!
SO, I'M AN AMATEUR! WHAT DO YOU EXPECT?!

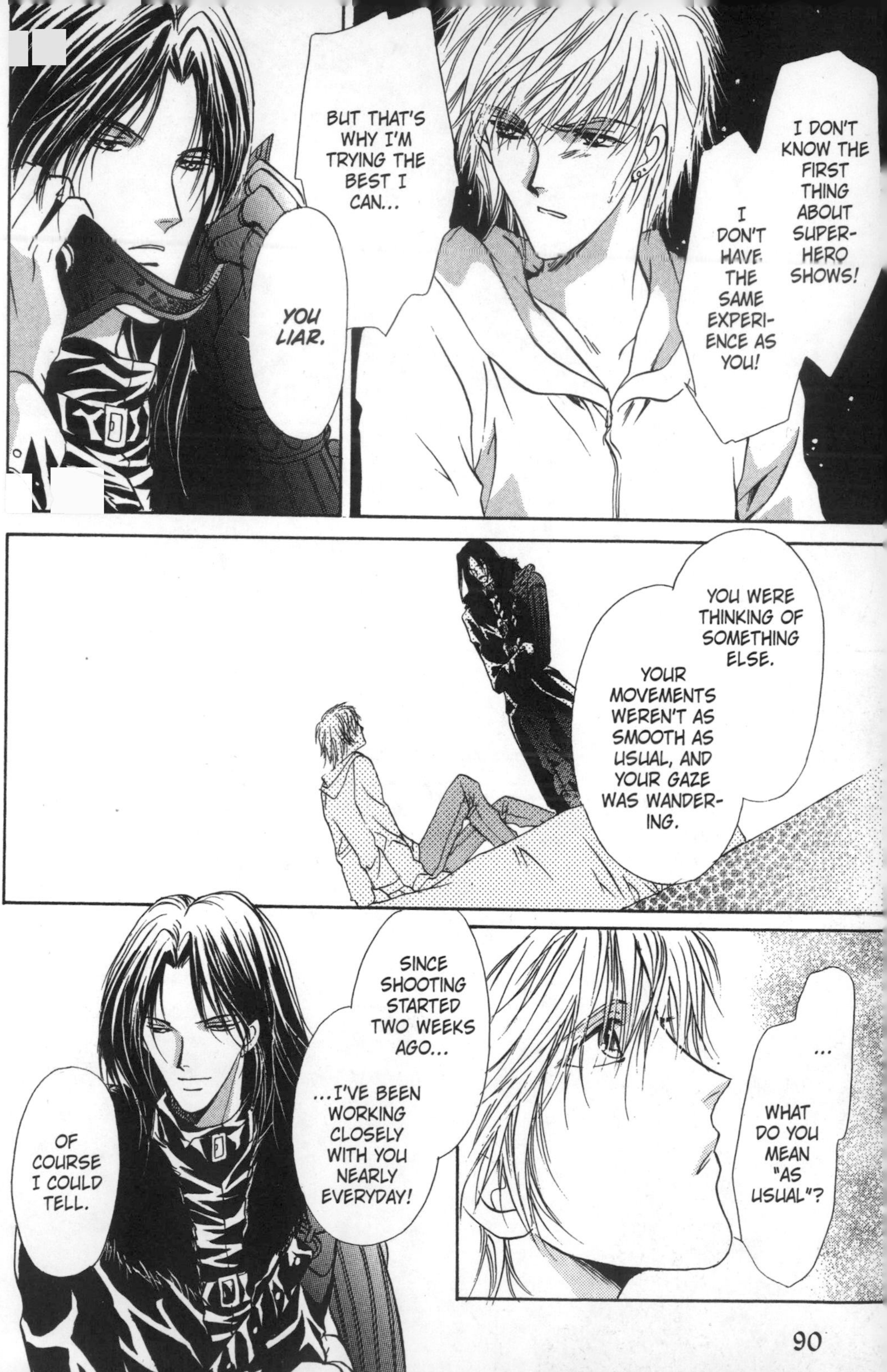
I DON'T KNOW THE FIRST THING ABOUT SUPER-HERO SHOWS!
I DON'T HAVE THE SAME EXPERIENCE AS YOU!
BUT THAT'S WHY I'M TRYING THE BEST I CAN...
YOU LIAR.
YOU WERE THINKING OF SOMETHING ELSE.
YOUR MOVEMENTS WEREN'T AS SMOOTH AS USUAL, AND YOUR GAZE WAS WANDER-ING.
... WHAT DO YOU MEAN "AS USUAL"?
SINCE SHOOTING STARTED TWO WEEKS AGO...
...I'VE BEEN WORKING CLOSELY WITH YOU NEARLY EVERYDAY!
OF COURSE I COULD TELL.

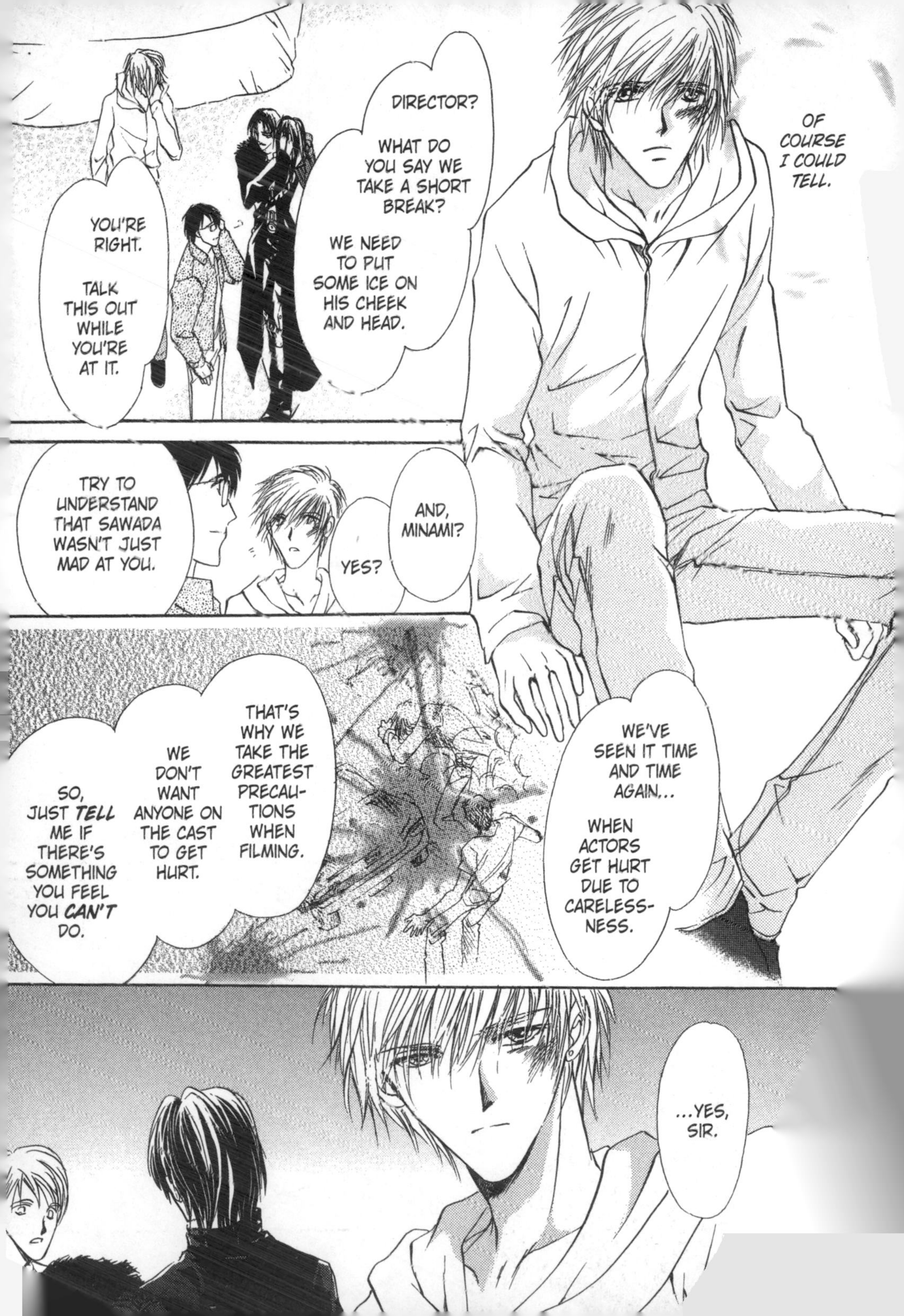
OF COURSE I COULD TELL.
WE'VE SEEN IT TIME AND TIME AGAIN... WHEN ACTORS GET HURT DUE TO CARELESS-NESS.
DIRECTOR? WHAT DO YOU SAY WE TAKE A SHORT BREAK? WE NEED TO PUT SOME ICE ON HIS CHEEK AND HEAD.
YOU'RE RIGHT. TALK THIS OUT WHILE YOU'RE AT IT.
AND, MINAMI?
YES?
TRY TO UNDERSTAND THAT SAWADA WASN'T JUST MAD AT YOU.
THAT'S WHY WE TAKE THE GREATEST PRECAU-TIONS WHEN FILMING.
WE DON'T WANT ANYONE ON THE CAST TO GET HURT.
SO, JUST TELL ME IF THERE'S SOMETHING YOU FEEL YOU CAN'T DO.
...YES, SIR.

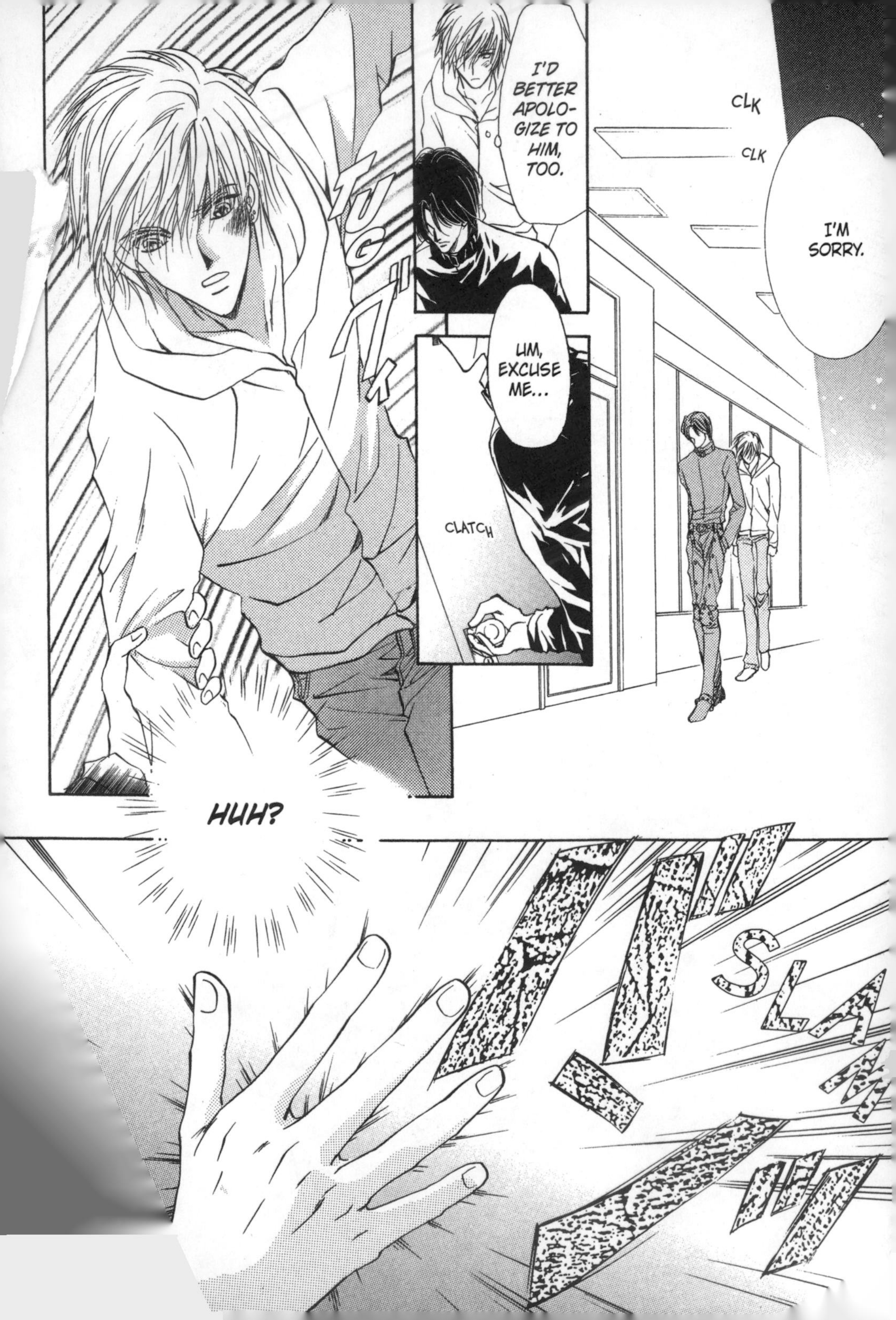
CLK
CLK
I'M SORRY.
I'D BETTER APOLO-GIZE TO HIM, TOO.
UM, EXCUSE ME...
CLATCH
TUG
HUH?
SLAM

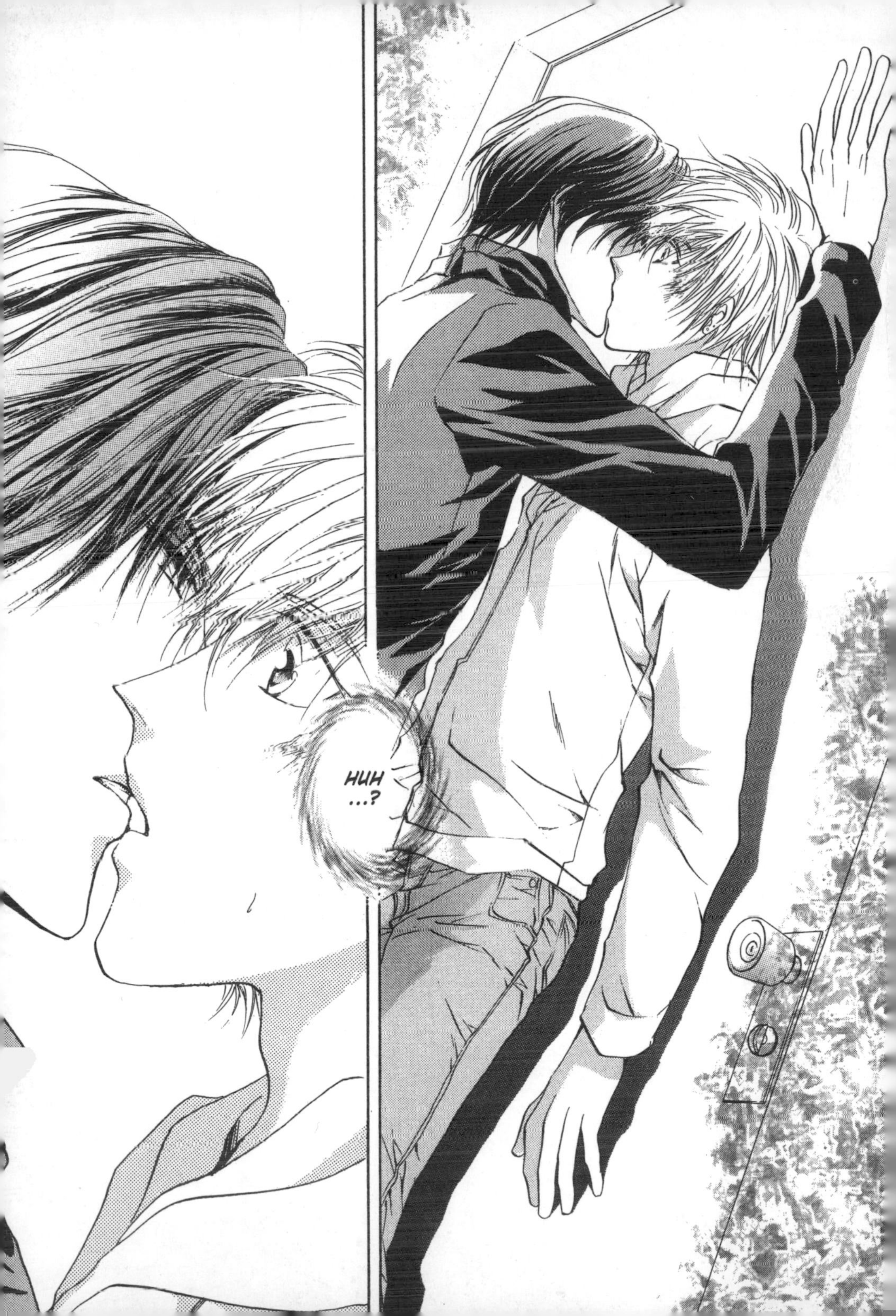
HUH ...?

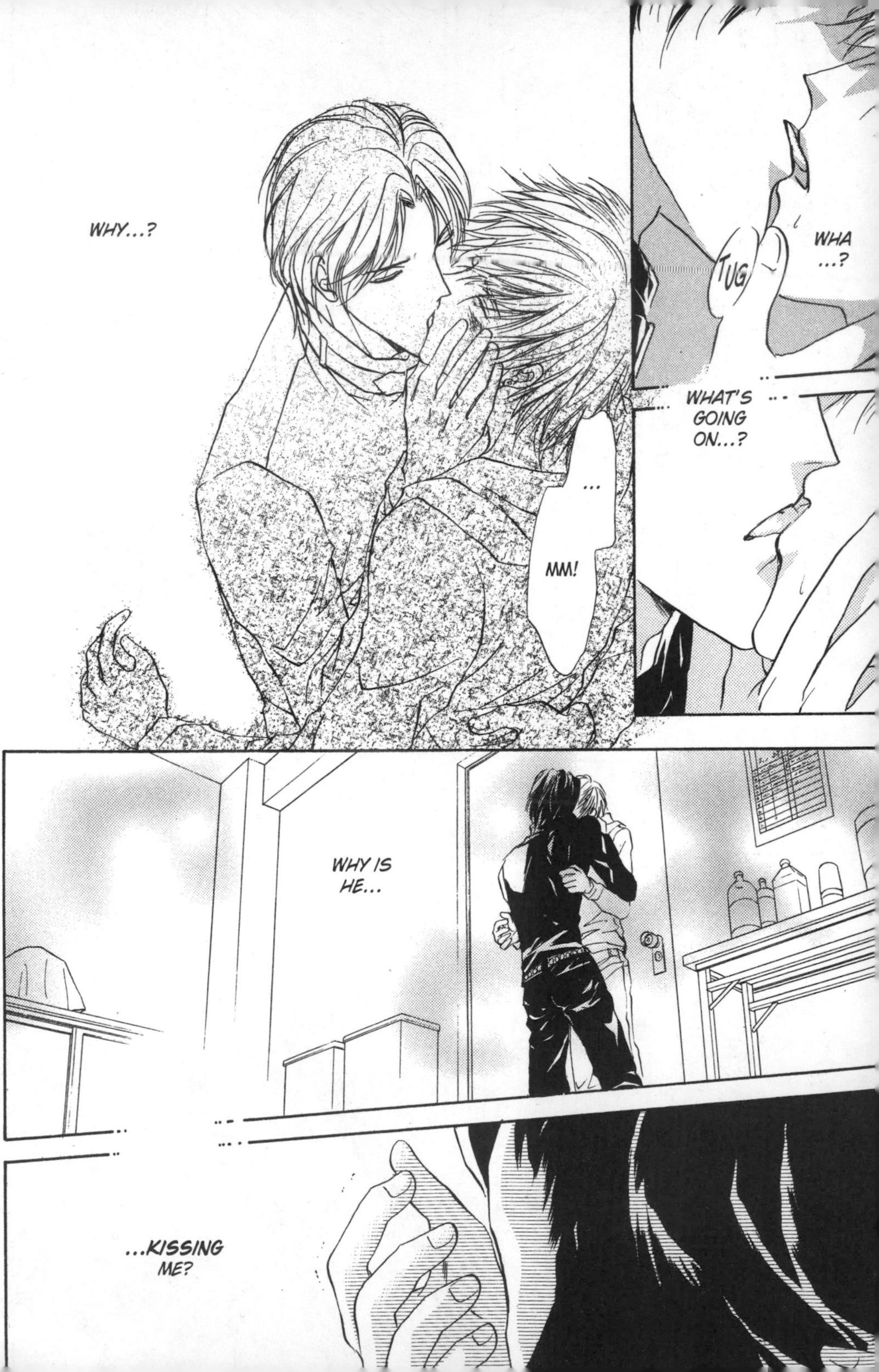
WHA ...?
TUG
WHAT'S GOING ON...?
WHY...?
...
MM!
WHY IS HE...
...KISSING ME?

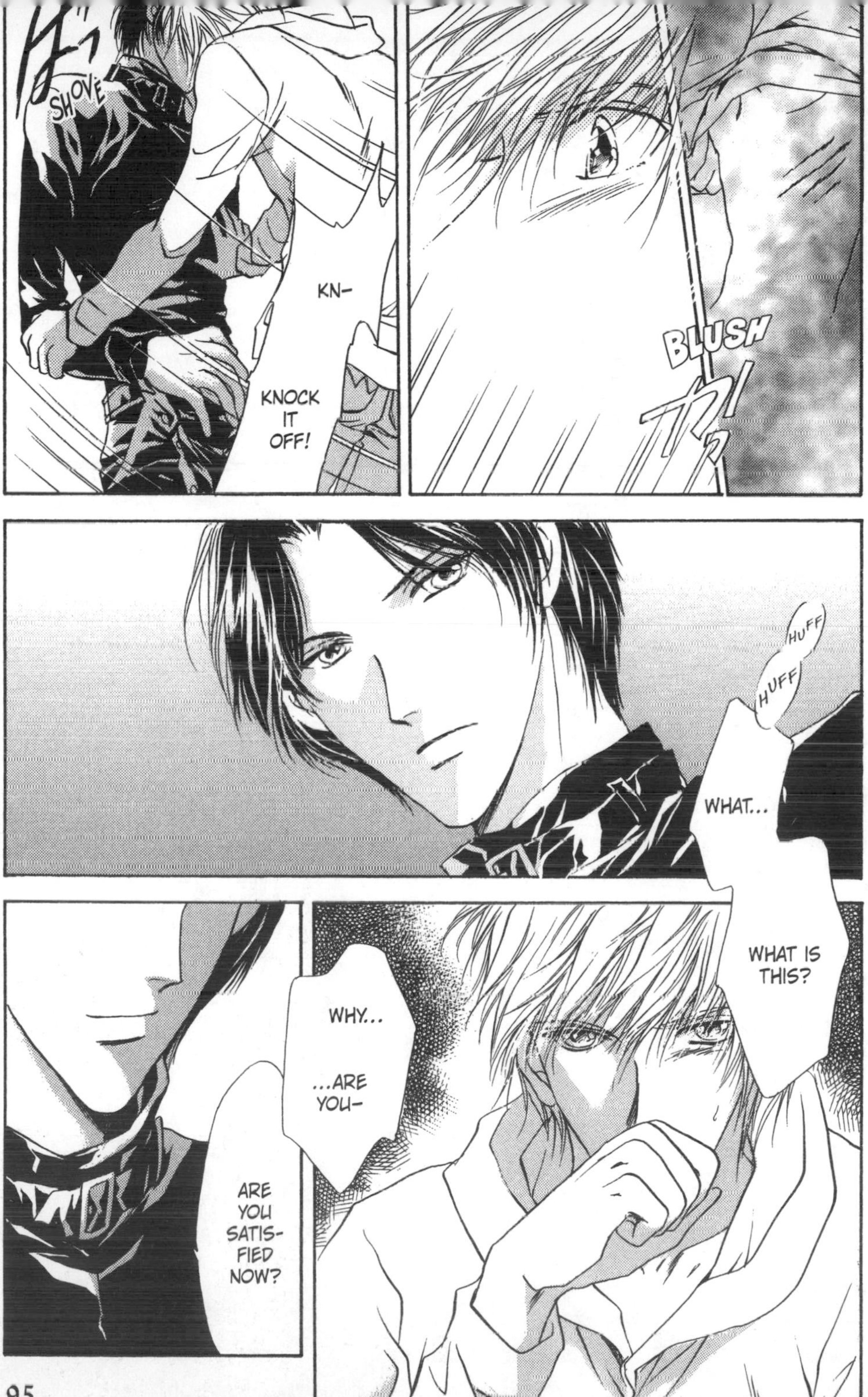
BLUSH
SHOVE
KN-
KNOCK IT OFF!
HUFF HUFF
WHAT...
WHAT IS THIS?
WHY...
...ARE YOU-
ARE YOU SATISFIED NOW?

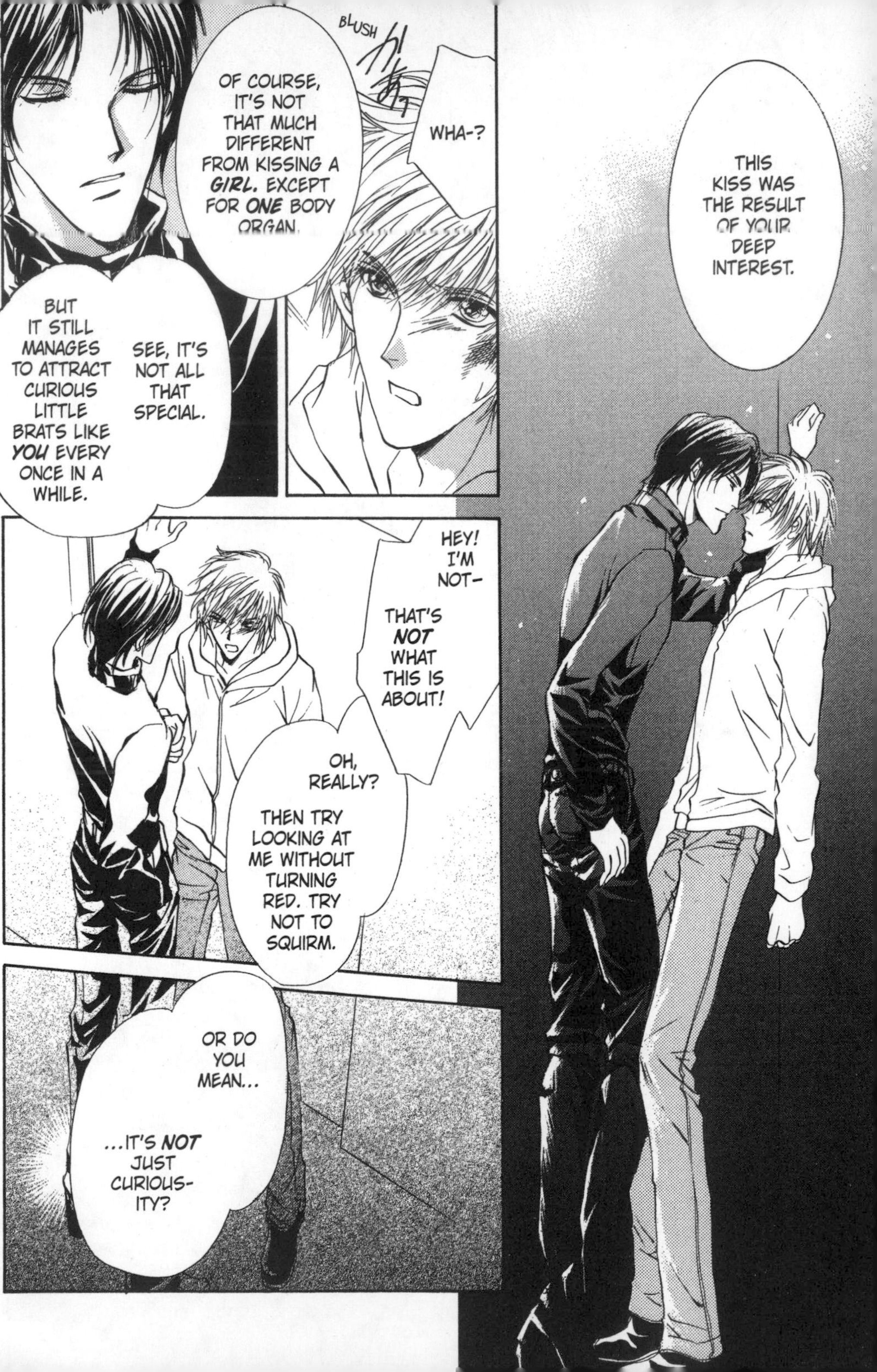
THIS KISS WAS THE RESULT OF YOUR DEEP INTEREST.
BLUSH
WHA-?
OF COURSE, IT'S NOT THAT MUCH DIFFERENT FROM KISSING A GIRL. EXCEPT FOR ONE BODY ORGAN.
SEE, IT'S NOT ALL THAT SPECIAL.
BUT IT STILL MANAGES TO ATTRACT CURIOUS LITTLE BRATS LIKE YOU EVERY ONCE IN A WHILE.
HEY! I'M NOT-
THAT'S NOT WHAT THIS IS ABOUT!
OH, REALLY?
THEN TRY LOOKING AT ME WITHOUT TURNING RED. TRY NOT TO SQUIRM.
OR DO YOU MEAN...
...IT'S NOT JUST CURIOUS-ITY?

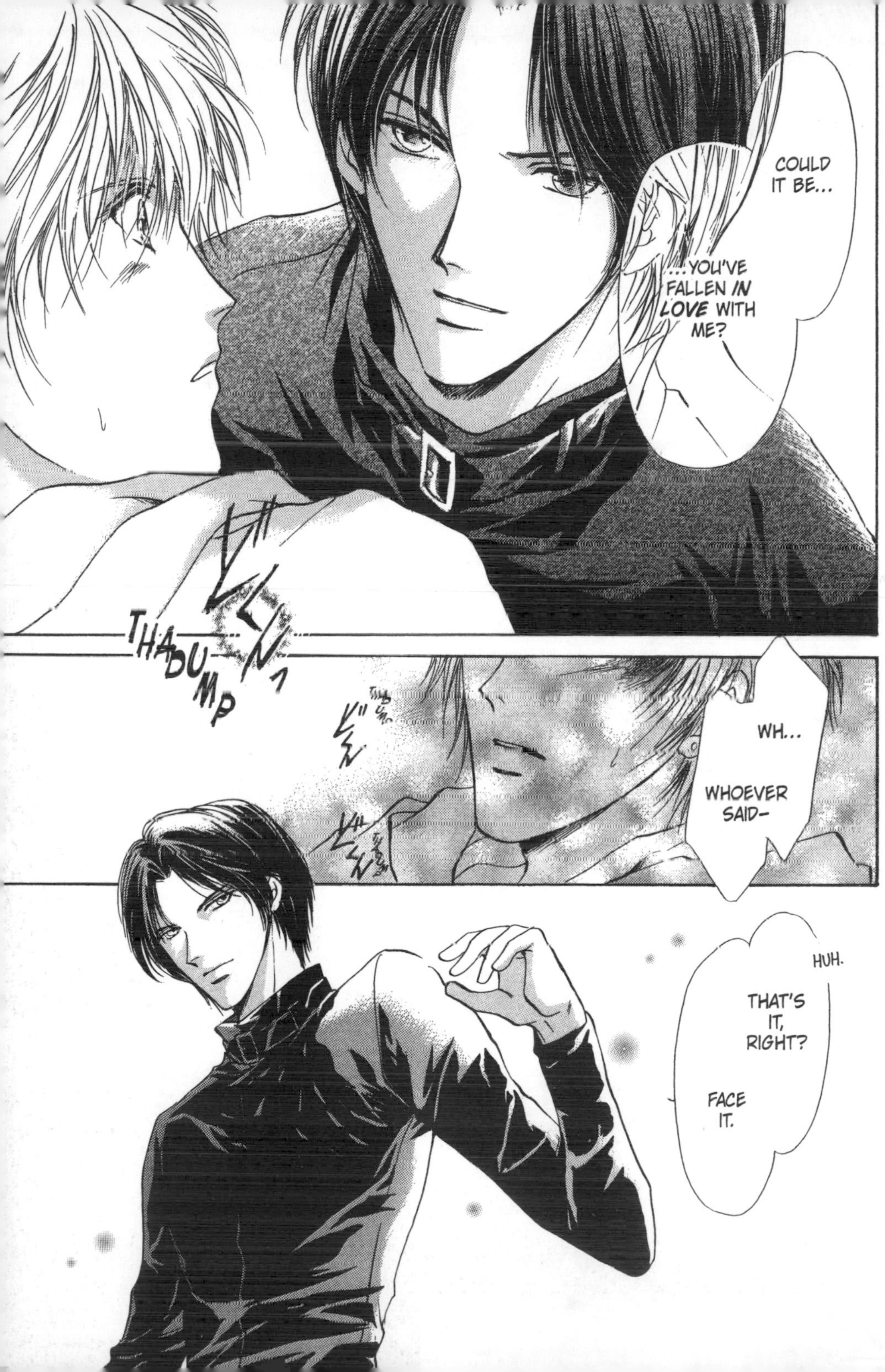
COULD IT BE...
...YOU'VE FALLEN *IN LOVE* WITH ME?
THADUMP
WH...
WHOEVER SAID-
HUH.
THAT'S IT, RIGHT?
FACE IT.

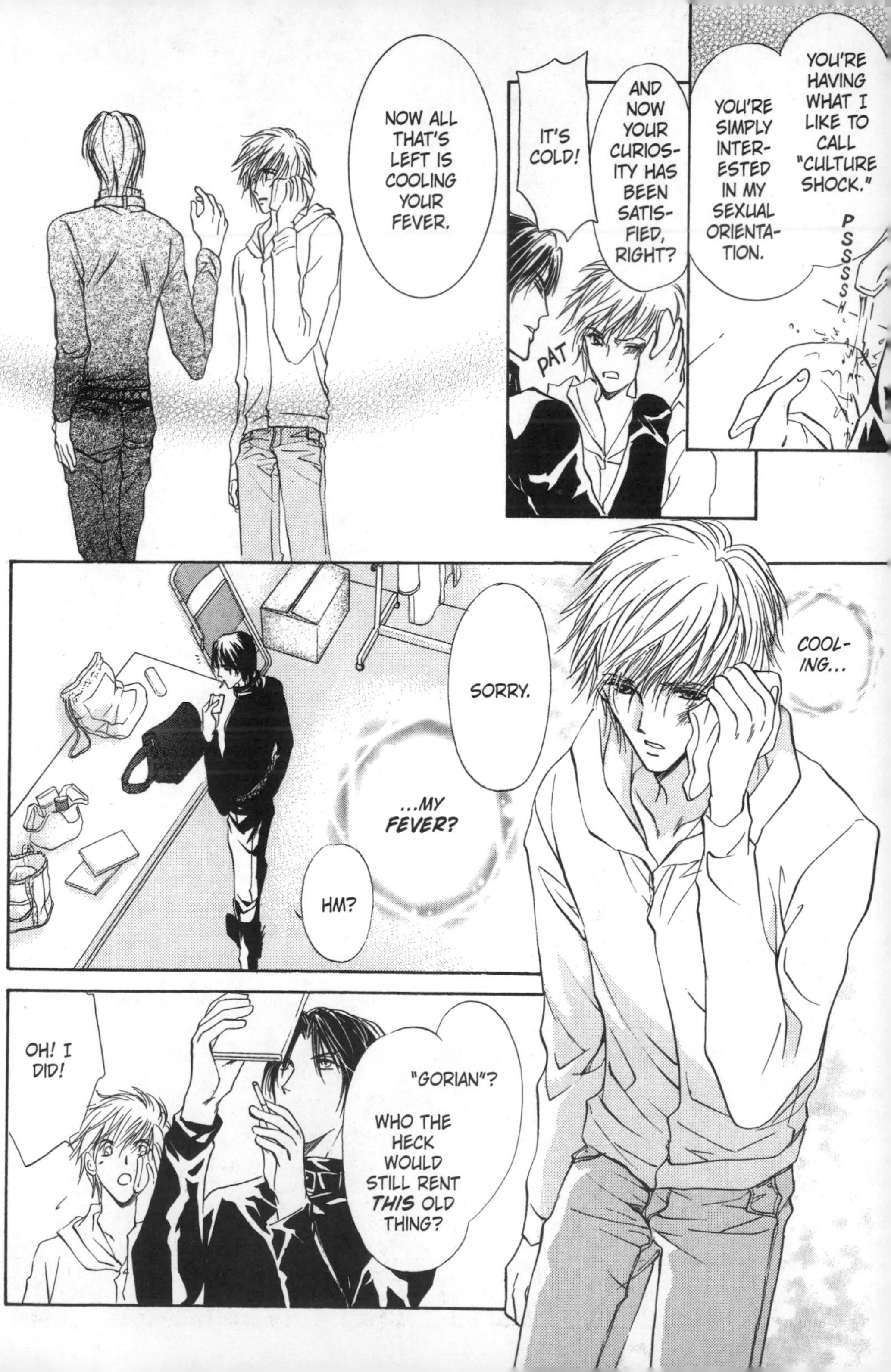
YOU'RE HAVING WHAT I LIKE TO CALL "CULTURE SHOCK."
YOU'RE SIMPLY INTER-ESTED IN MY SEXUAL ORIENTA-TION.
PSSSSH
AND NOW YOUR CURIOS-ITY HAS BEEN SATIS-FIED, RIGHT?
IT'S COLD!
PAT
NOW ALL THAT'S LEFT IS COOLING YOUR FEVER.
COOL-ING...
SORRY.
...MY *FEVER?*
HM?
"GORIAN"?
WHO THE HECK WOULD STILL RENT *THIS* OLD THING?
OH! I DID!

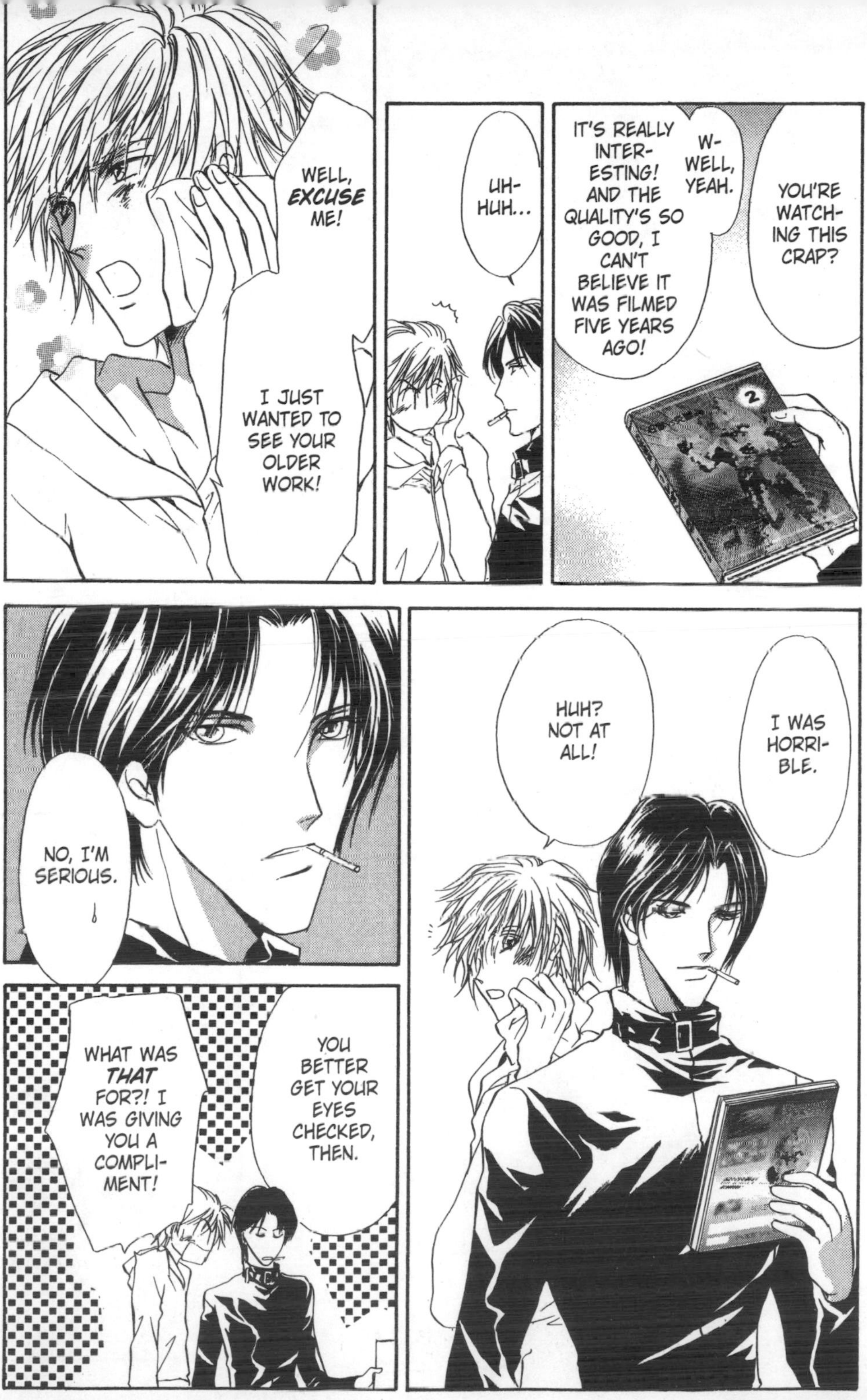
YOU'RE WATCHING THIS CRAP?
W-WELL, YEAH.
IT'S REALLY INTERESTING! AND THE QUALITY'S SO GOOD, I CAN'T BELIEVE IT WAS FILMED FIVE YEARS AGO!
UH-HUH...
WELL, EXCUSE ME!
I JUST WANTED TO SEE YOUR OLDER WORK!
I WAS HORRIBLE.
HUH? NOT AT ALL!
NO, I'M SERIOUS.
YOU BETTER GET YOUR EYES CHECKED, THEN.
WHAT WAS THAT FOR?! I WAS GIVING YOU A COMPLIMENT!

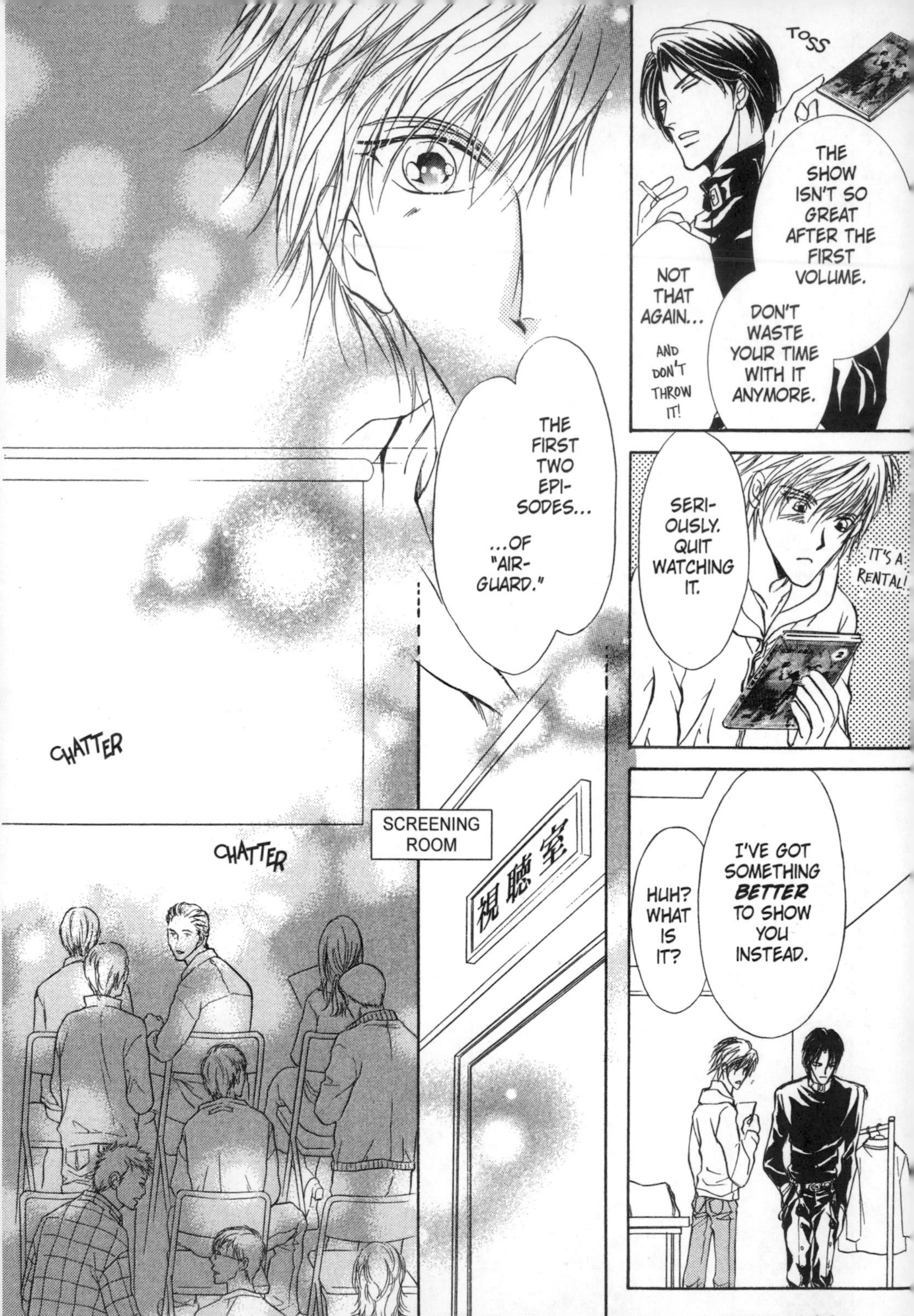
TOSS
THE SHOW ISN'T SO GREAT AFTER THE FIRST VOLUME.
NOT THAT AGAIN...
AND DON'T THROW IT!
DON'T WASTE YOUR TIME WITH IT ANYMORE.
SERIOUSLY. QUIT WATCHING IT.
IT'S A RENTAL!
I'VE GOT SOMETHING **BETTER** TO SHOW YOU INSTEAD.
HUH? WHAT IS IT?
THE FIRST TWO EPISODES...
...OF "AIR-GUARD."
SCREENING ROOM
視聴室
CHATTER
CHATTER

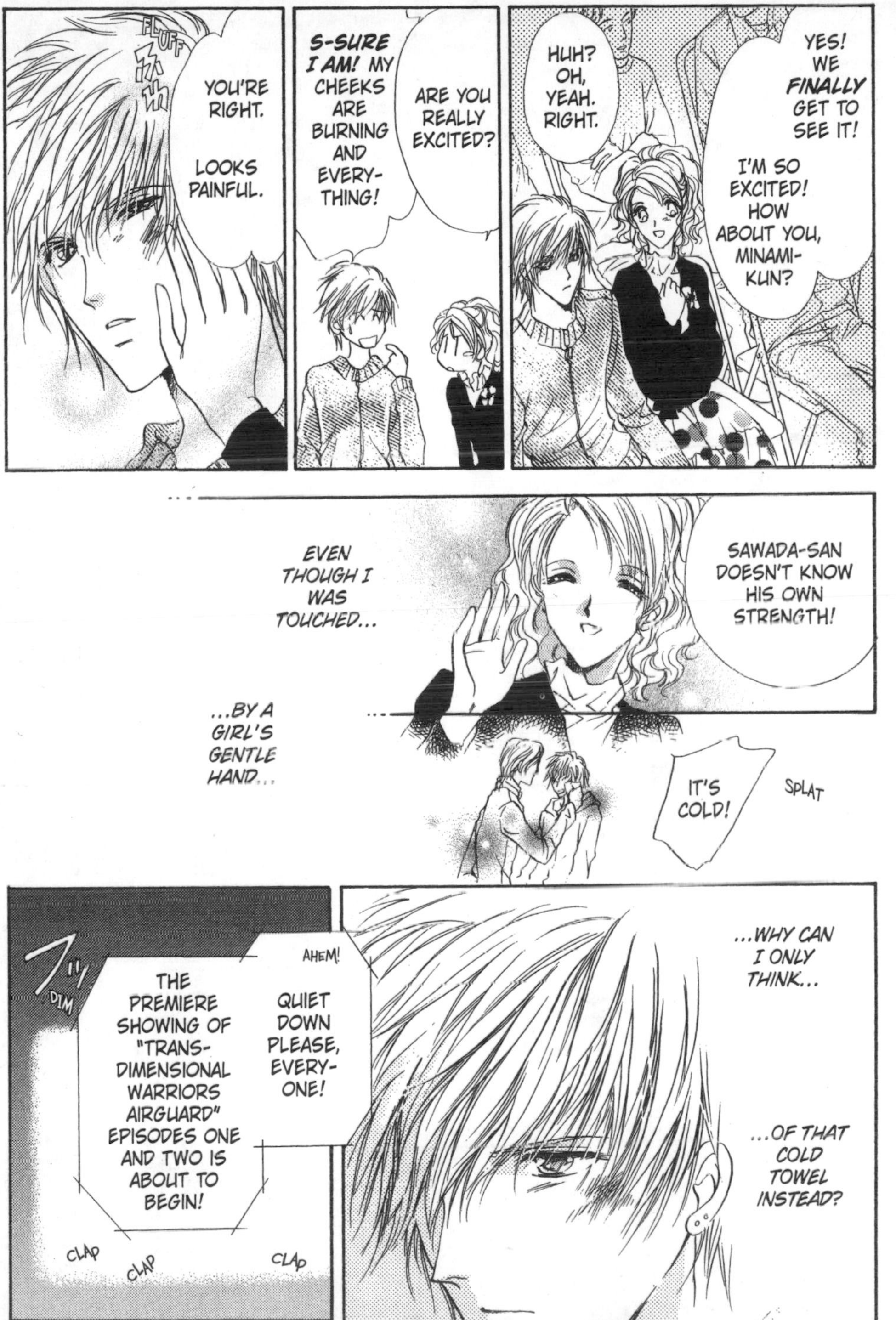
YES! WE FINALLY GET TO SEE IT!
I'M SO EXCITED! HOW ABOUT YOU, MINAMI-KUN?
HUH? OH, YEAH. RIGHT.
ARE YOU REALLY EXCITED?
S-SURE I AM! MY CHEEKS ARE BURNING AND EVERYTHING!
FLUFF
ふわ
YOU'RE RIGHT.
LOOKS PAINFUL.
SAWADA-SAN DOESN'T KNOW HIS OWN STRENGTH!
EVEN THOUGH I WAS TOUCHED...
...BY A GIRL'S GENTLE HAND...
SPLAT
IT'S COLD!
...WHY CAN I ONLY THINK...
...OF THAT COLD TOWEL INSTEAD?
AHEM!
QUIET DOWN PLEASE, EVERYONE!
THE PREMIERE SHOWING OF "TRANS-DIMENSIONAL WARRIORS AIRGUARD" EPISODES ONE AND TWO IS ABOUT TO BEGIN!
DIM
CLAP
CLAP
CLAP

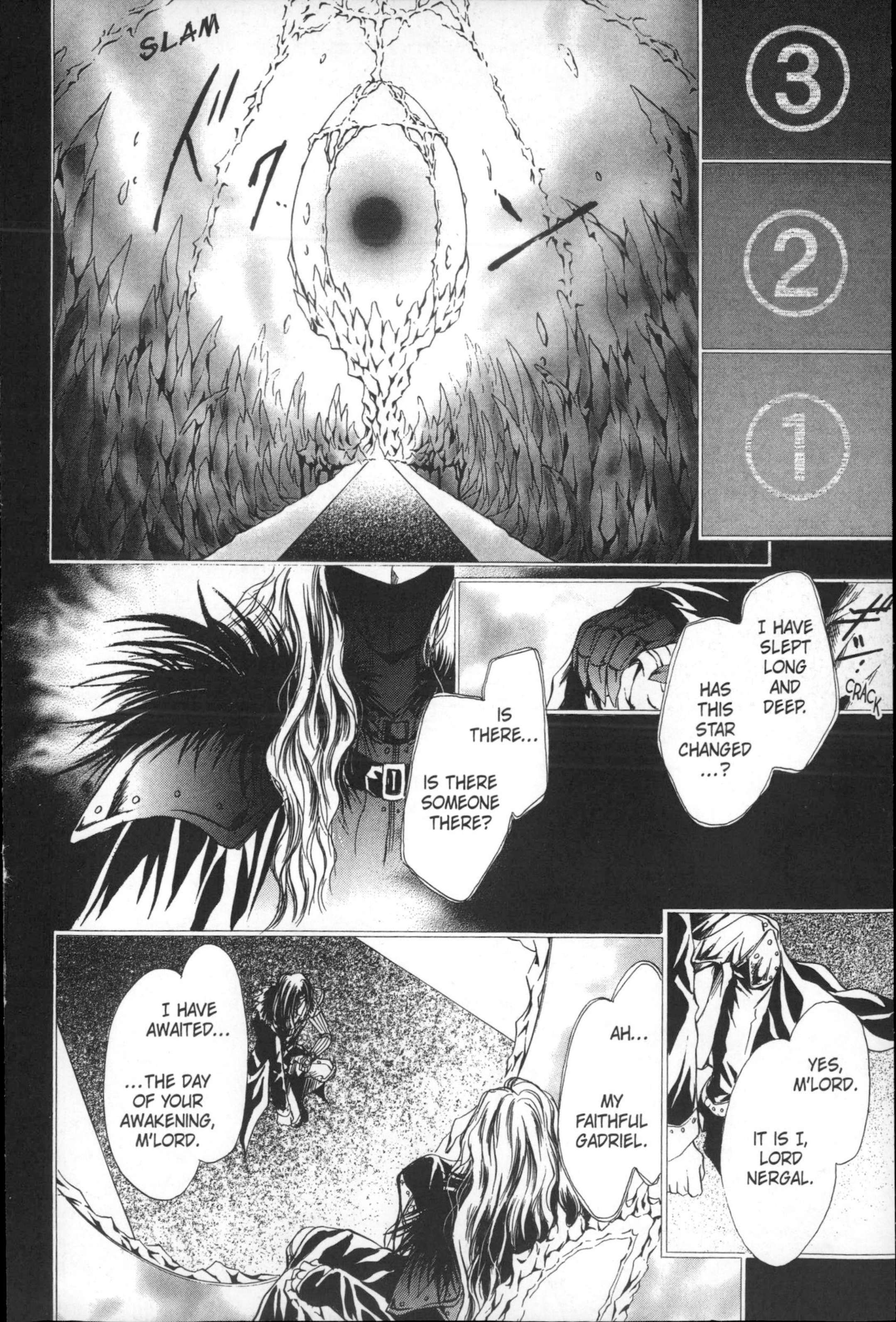
3
2
1
SLAM
CRACK
I HAVE SLEPT LONG AND DEEP.
HAS THIS STAR CHANGED ...?
IS THERE...
IS THERE SOMEONE THERE?
YES, M'LORD.
IT IS I, LORD NERGAL.
AH...
MY FAITHFUL GADRIEL.
I HAVE AWAITED...
...THE DAY OF YOUR AWAKENING, M'LORD.

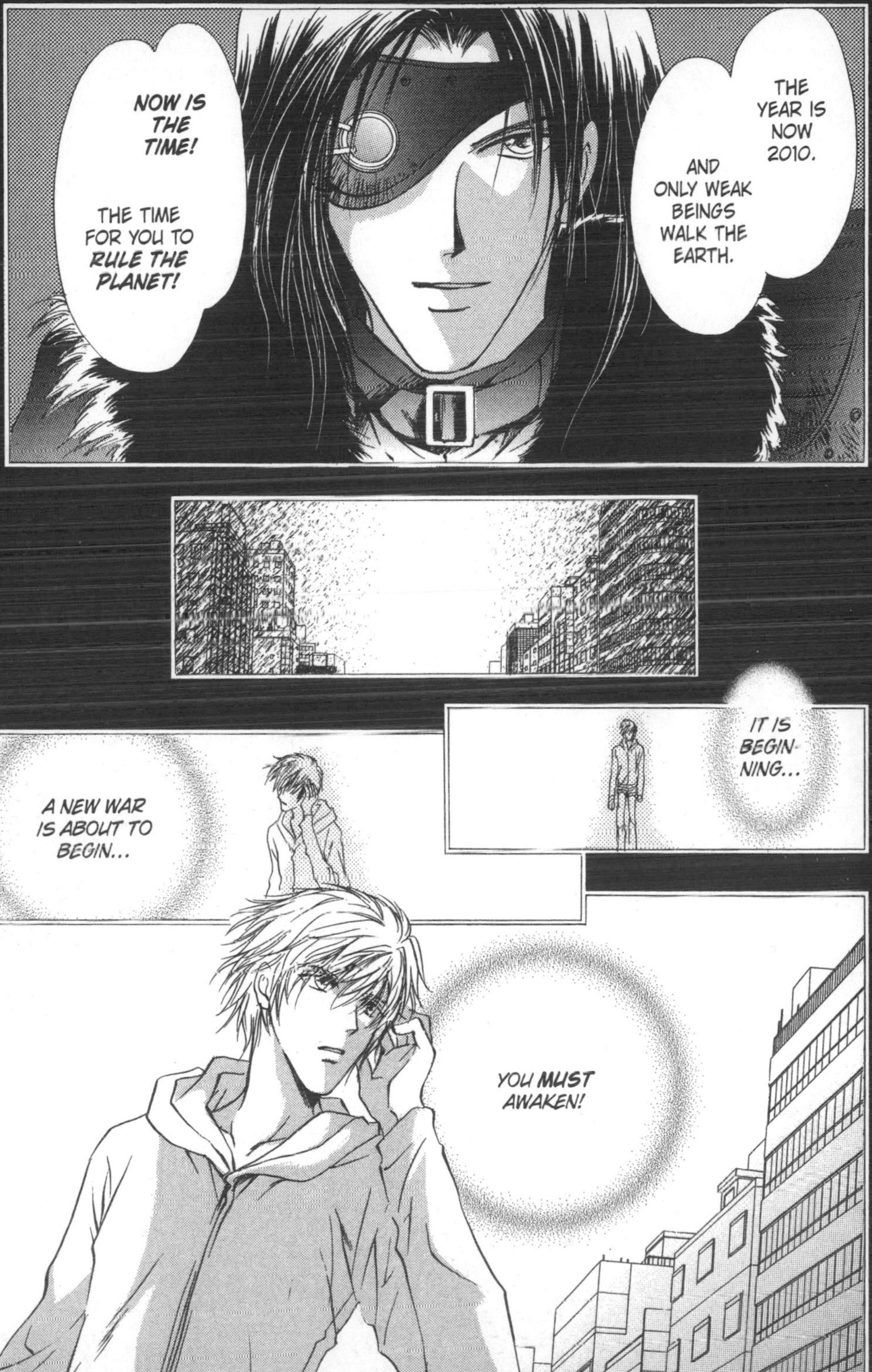
THE YEAR IS NOW 2010.
AND ONLY WEAK BEINGS WALK THE EARTH.
NOW IS THE TIME!
THE TIME FOR YOU TO RULE THE PLANET!
IT IS BEGINNING...
A NEW WAR IS ABOUT TO BEGIN...
YOU MUST AWAKEN!

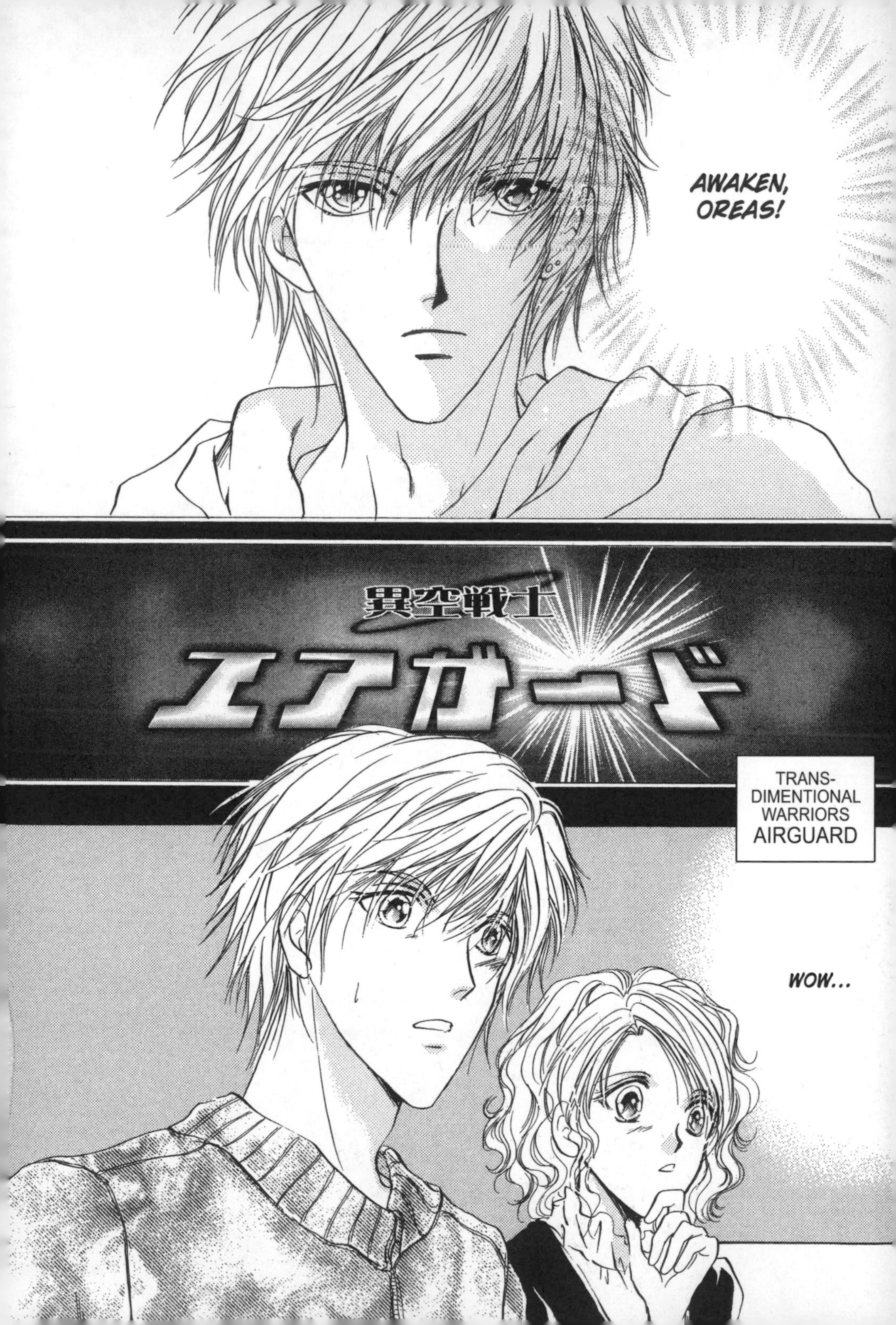
AWAKEN, OREAS!
異空戦士
エアガード
TRANS-DIMENTIONAL WARRIORS AIRGUARD
WOW...

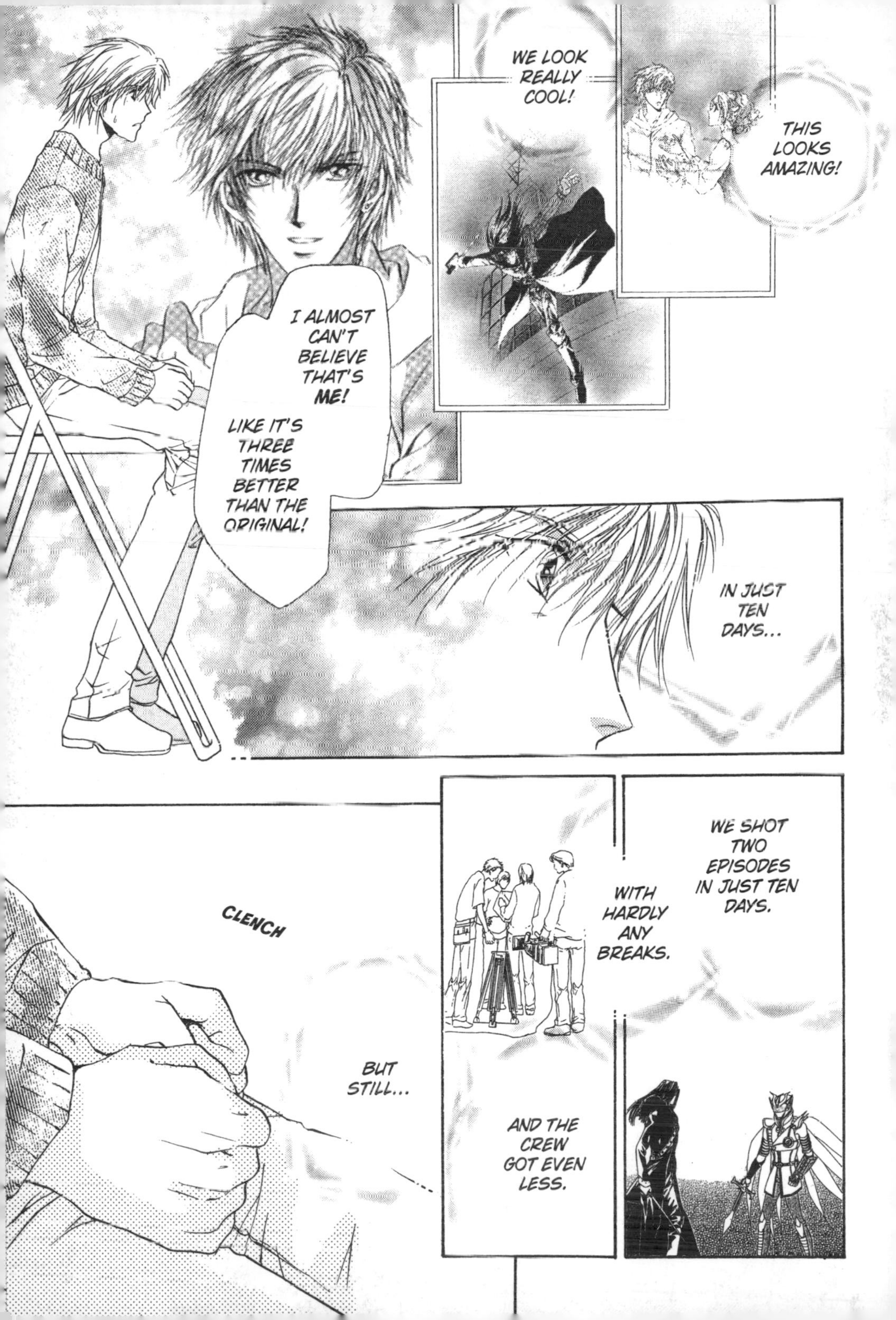
THIS LOOKS AMAZING!
WE LOOK REALLY COOL!
I ALMOST CAN'T BELIEVE THAT'S ME!
LIKE IT'S THREE TIMES BETTER THAN THE ORIGINAL!
IN JUST TEN DAYS...
WE SHOT TWO EPISODES IN JUST TEN DAYS.
WITH HARDLY ANY BREAKS.
AND THE CREW GOT EVEN LESS.
CLENCH
BUT STILL...

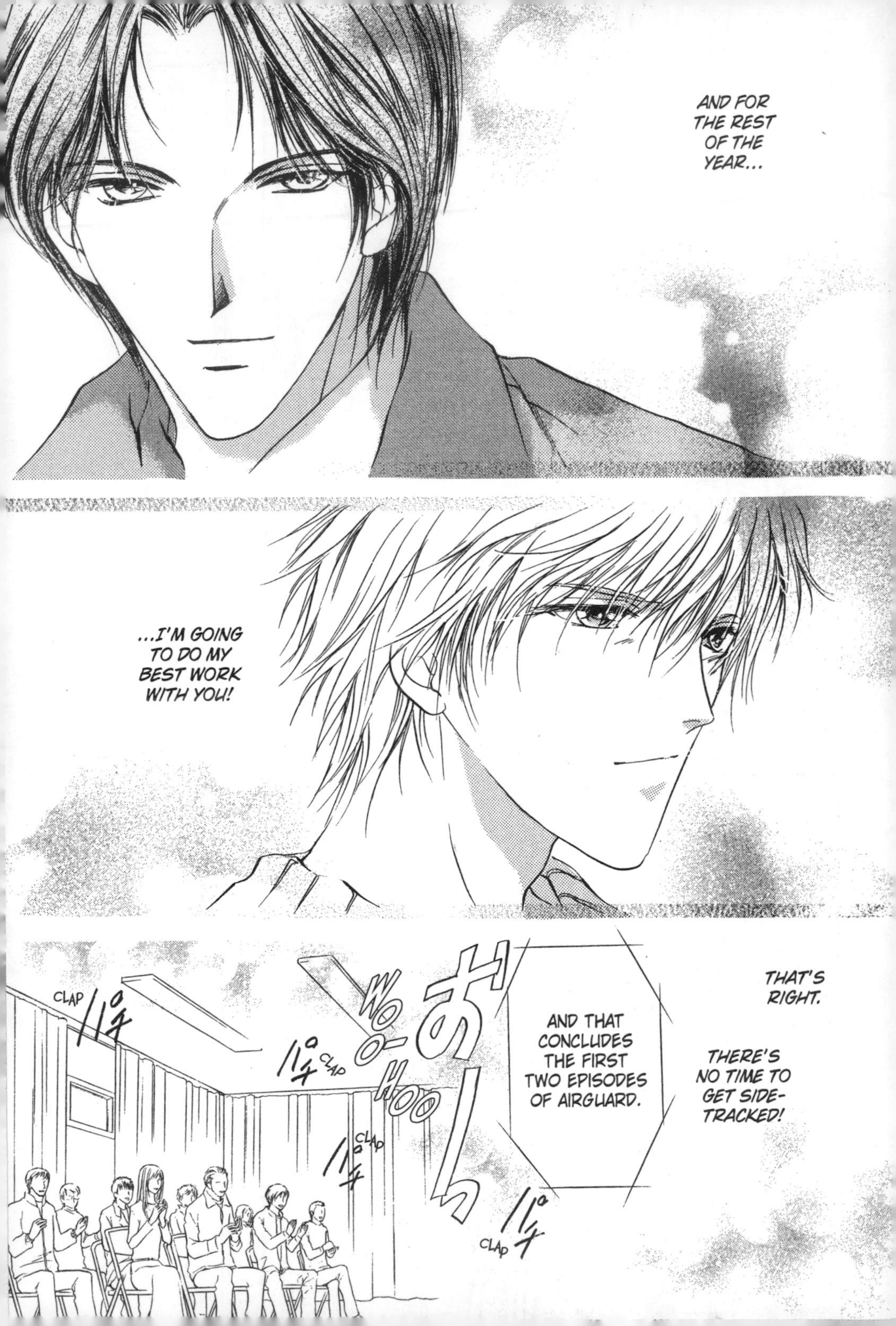
AND FOR THE REST OF THE YEAR...
...I'M GOING TO DO MY BEST WORK WITH YOU!
THAT'S RIGHT.
THERE'S NO TIME TO GET SIDE-TRACKED!
AND THAT CONCLUDES THE FIRST TWO EPISODES OF AIRGUARD.
WOO-HOO
CLAP
CLAP
CLAP
CLAP

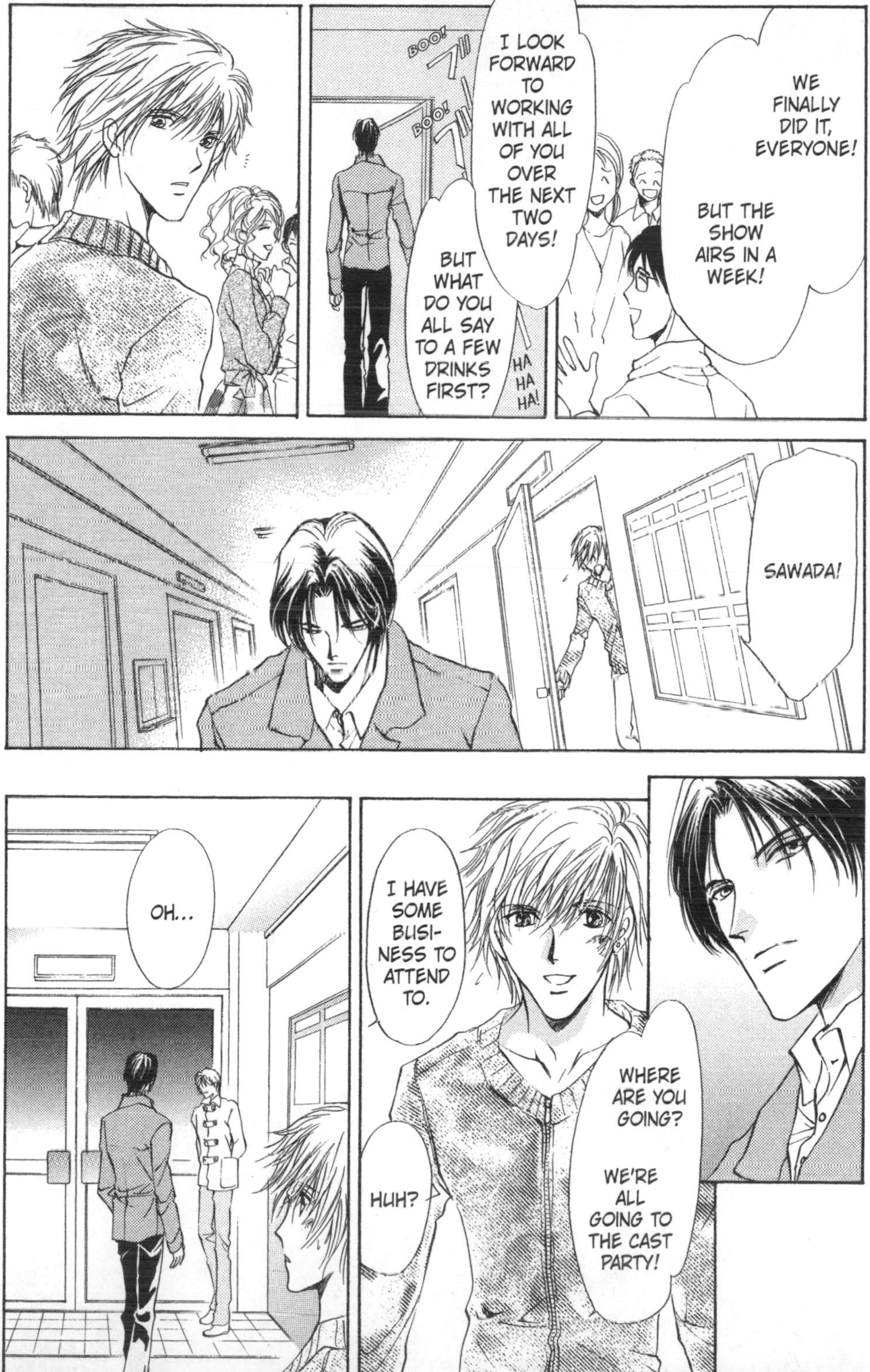
WE FINALLY DID IT, EVERYONE!
BUT THE SHOW AIRS IN A WEEK!
I LOOK FORWARD TO WORKING WITH ALL OF YOU OVER THE NEXT TWO DAYS!
BUT WHAT DO YOU ALL SAY TO A FEW DRINKS FIRST?
HA HA HA!
BOO! BOO!
SAWADA!
WHERE ARE YOU GOING?
WE'RE ALL GOING TO THE CAST PARTY!
I HAVE SOME BUSI-NESS TO ATTEND TO.
HUH?
OH...

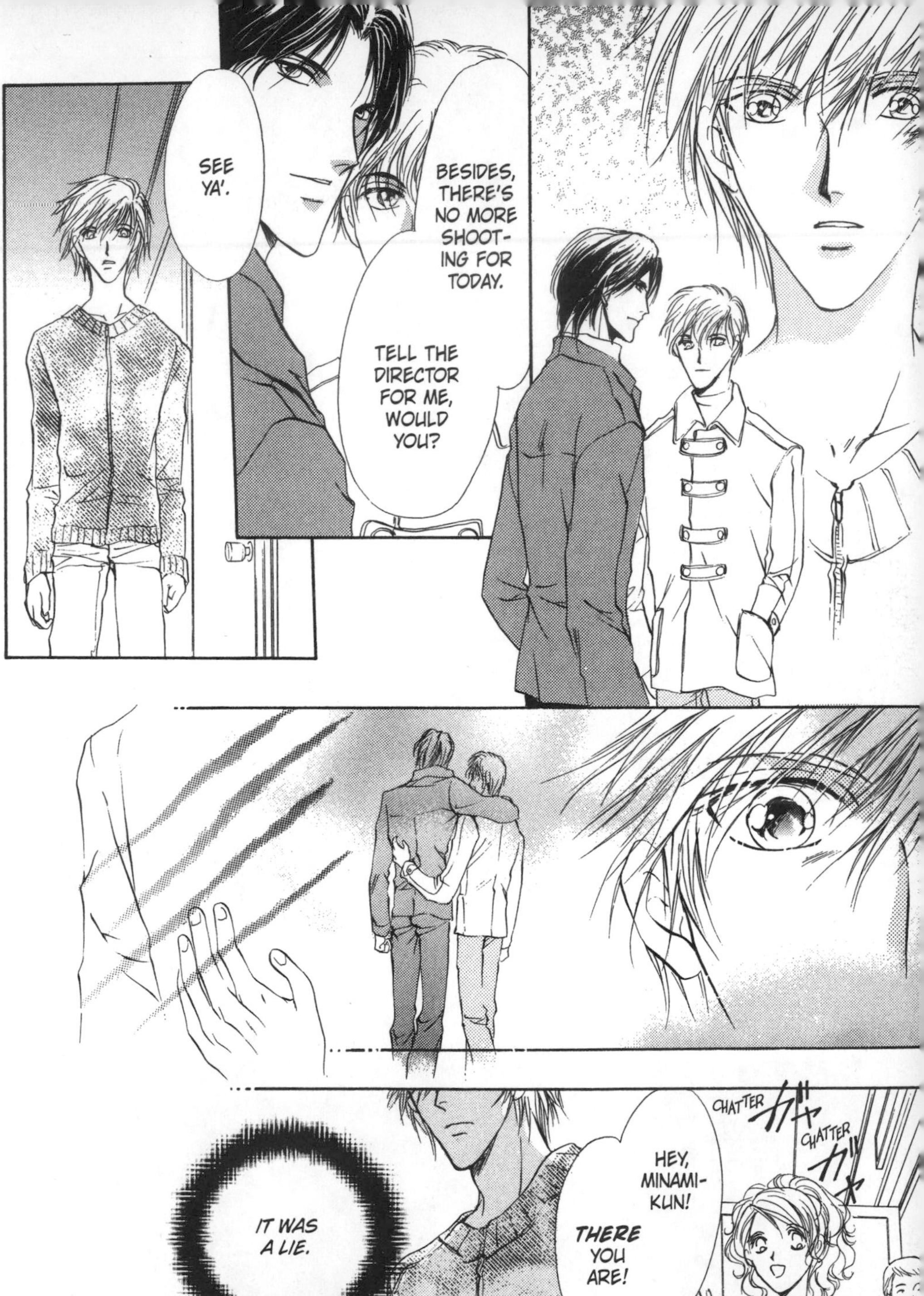
BESIDES, THERE'S NO MORE SHOOT-ING FOR TODAY.
TELL THE DIRECTOR FOR ME, WOULD YOU?
SEE YA'.
CHATTER
CHATTER
HEY, MINAMI-KUN!
THERE YOU ARE!
IT WAS A LIE.

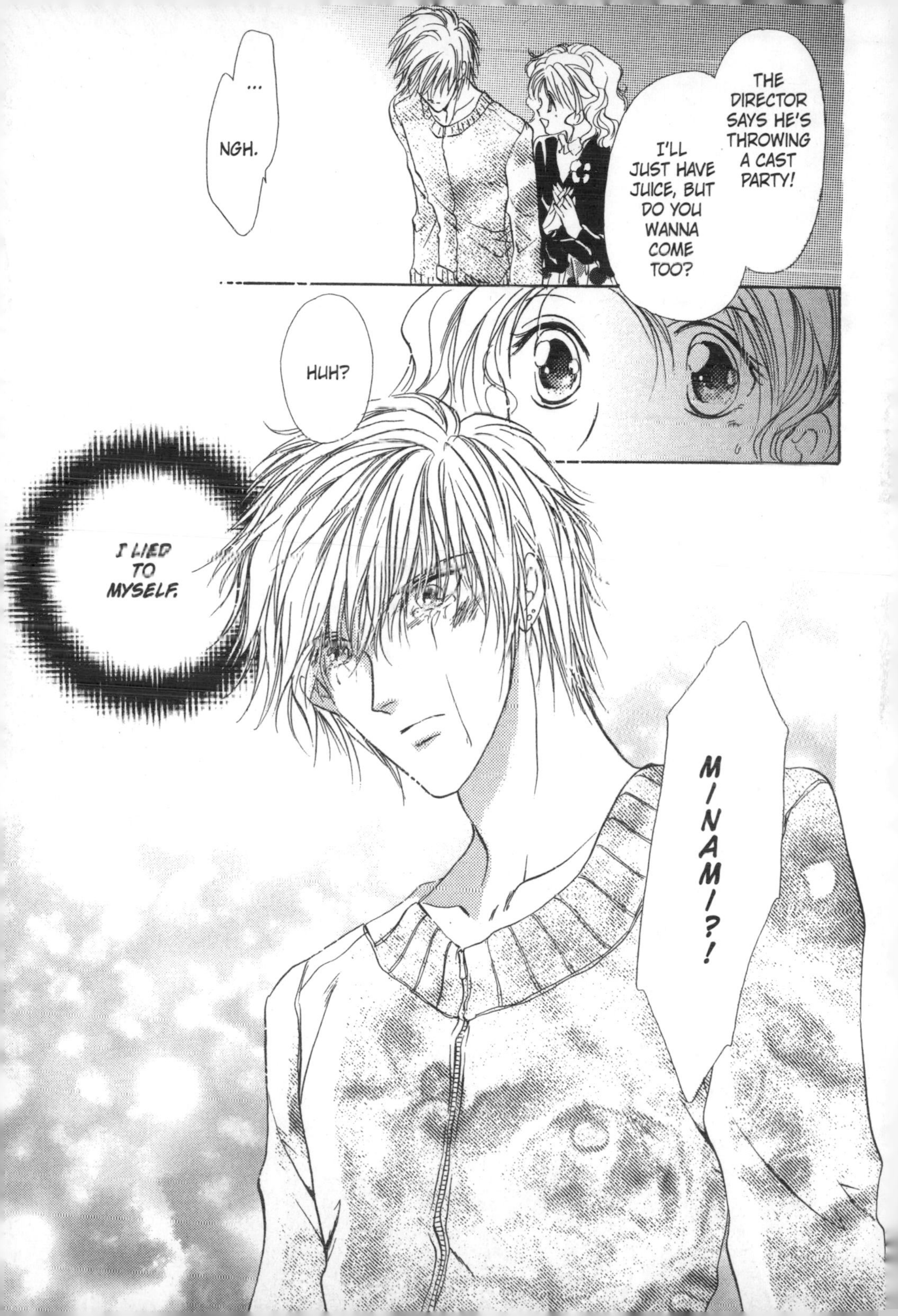
THE DIRECTOR SAYS HE'S THROWING A CAST PARTY!
I'LL JUST HAVE JUICE, BUT DO YOU WANNA COME TOO?
... NGH.
HUH?
MINAMI?!
I LIED TO MYSELF.

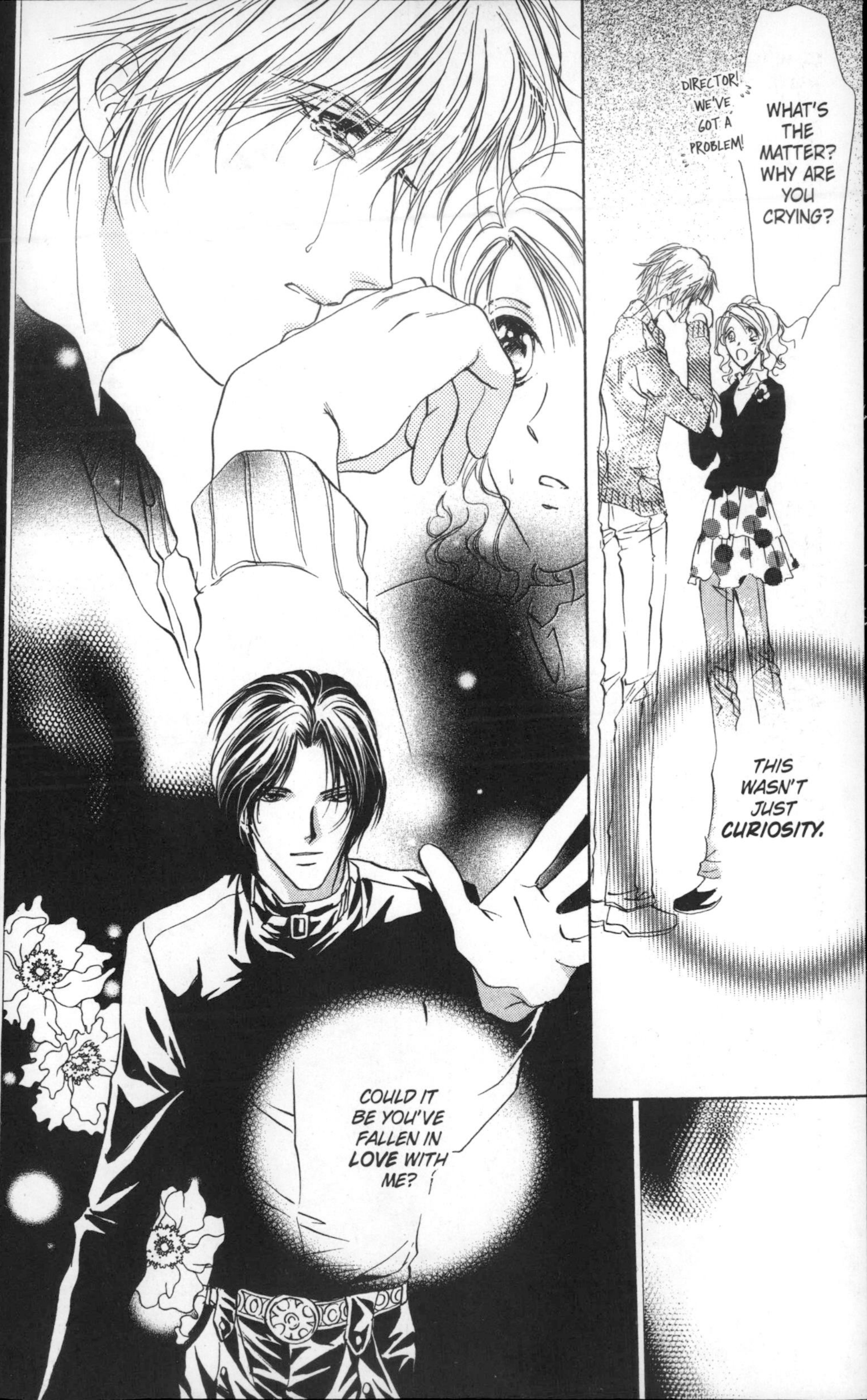
WHAT'S THE MATTER? WHY ARE YOU CRYING?
DIRECTOR! WE'VE GOT A PROBLEM!
THIS WASN'T JUST CURIOSITY.
COULD IT BE YOU'VE FALLEN IN LOVE WITH ME?

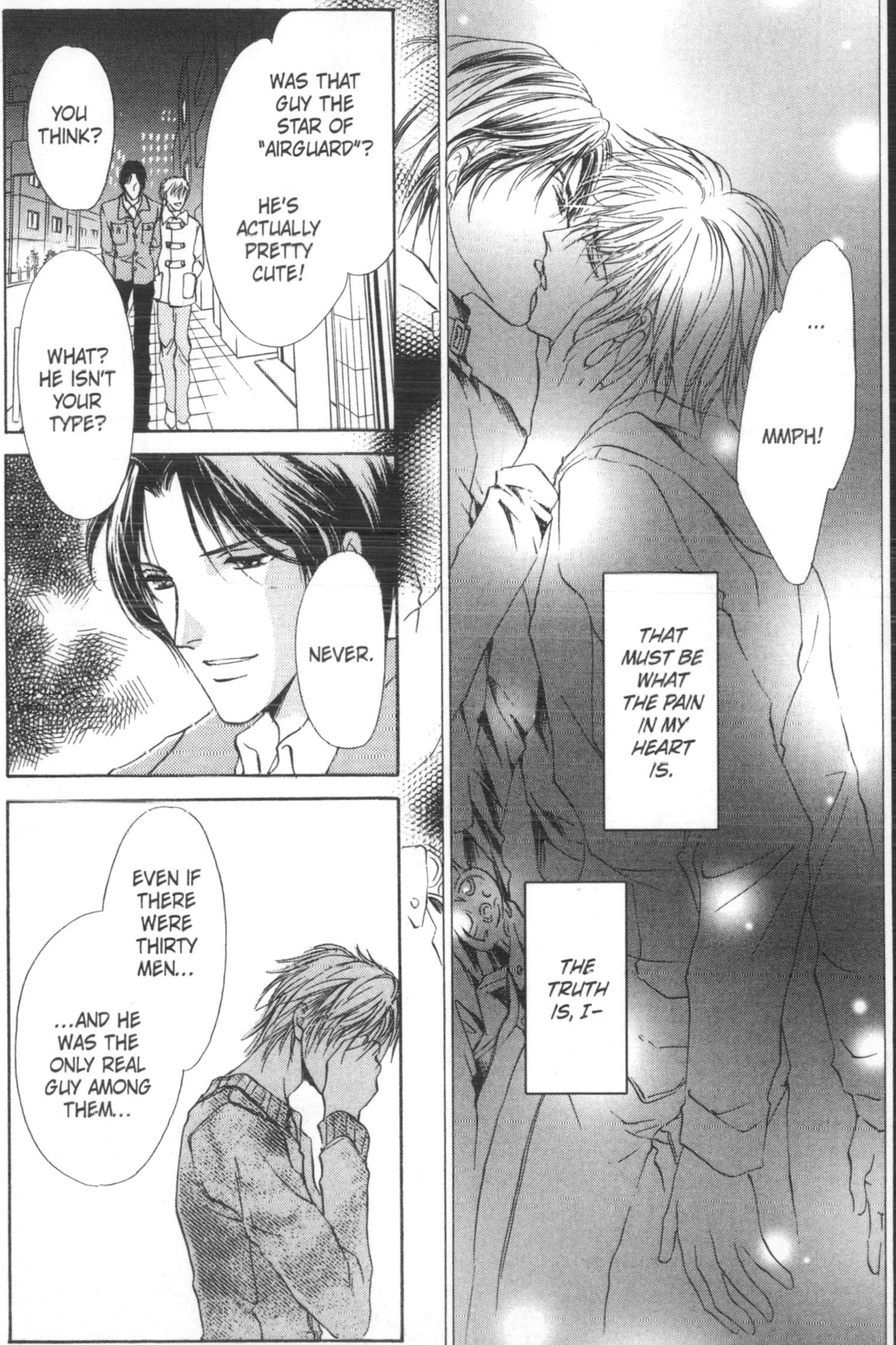
...
MMPH!
THAT MUST BE WHAT THE PAIN IN MY HEART IS.
THE TRUTH IS, I-
WAS THAT GUY THE STAR OF "AIRGUARD"?
HE'S ACTUALLY PRETTY CUTE!
YOU THINK?
WHAT? HE ISN'T YOUR TYPE?
NEVER.
EVEN IF THERE WERE THIRTY MEN...
...AND HE WAS THE ONLY REAL GUY AMONG THEM...

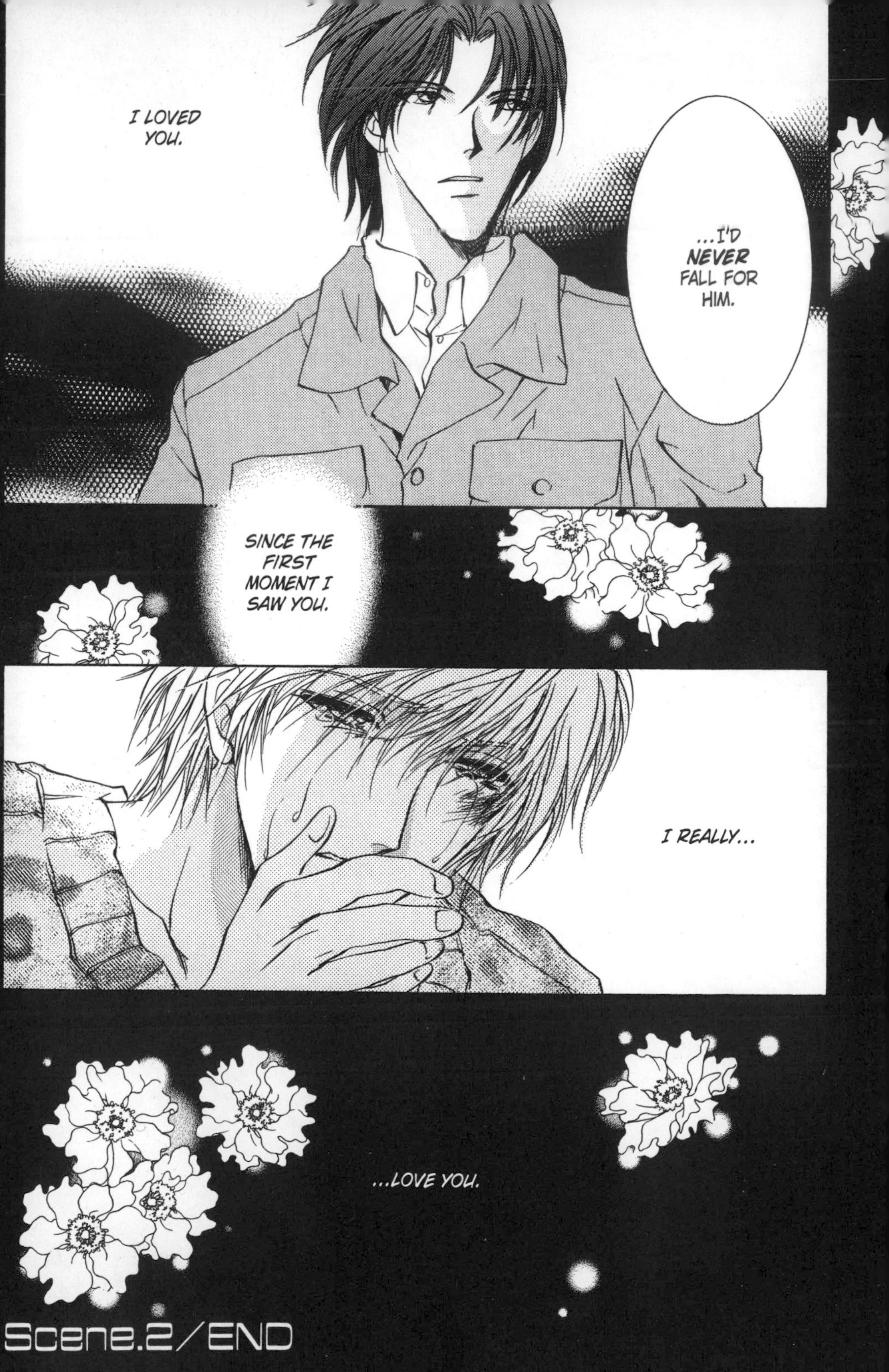
...I'D NEVER FALL FOR HIM.
I LOVED YOU.
SINCE THE FIRST MOMENT I SAW YOU.
I REALLY...
...LOVE YOU.
Scene.2/END

MASAKI MINAMI

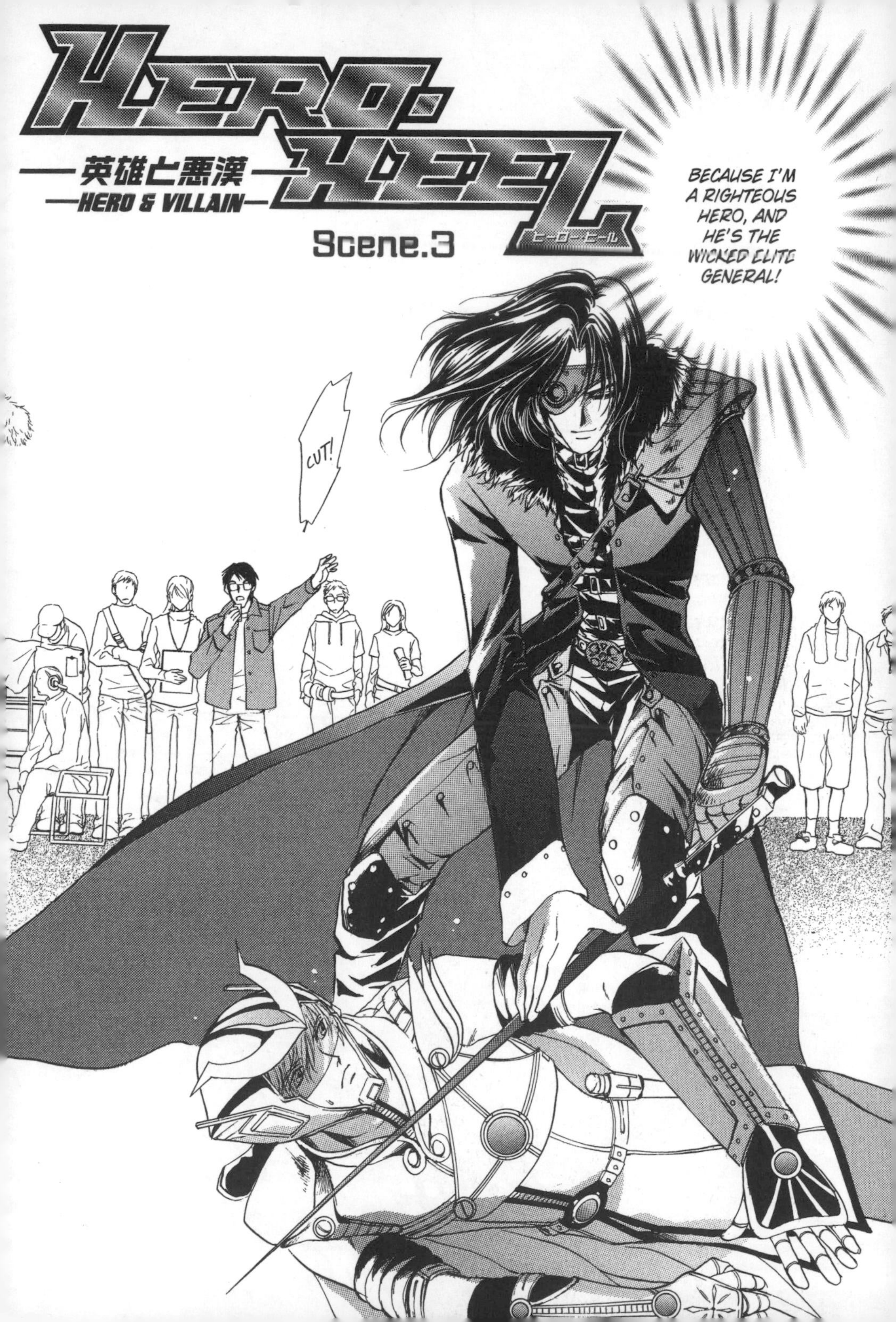
HERO HEEL
—英雄と悪漢—
—HERO & VILLAIN—
ヒーローヒール
Scene.3
BECAUSE I'M A RIGHTEOUS HERO, AND HE'S THE WICKED ELITE GENERAL!
CUT!

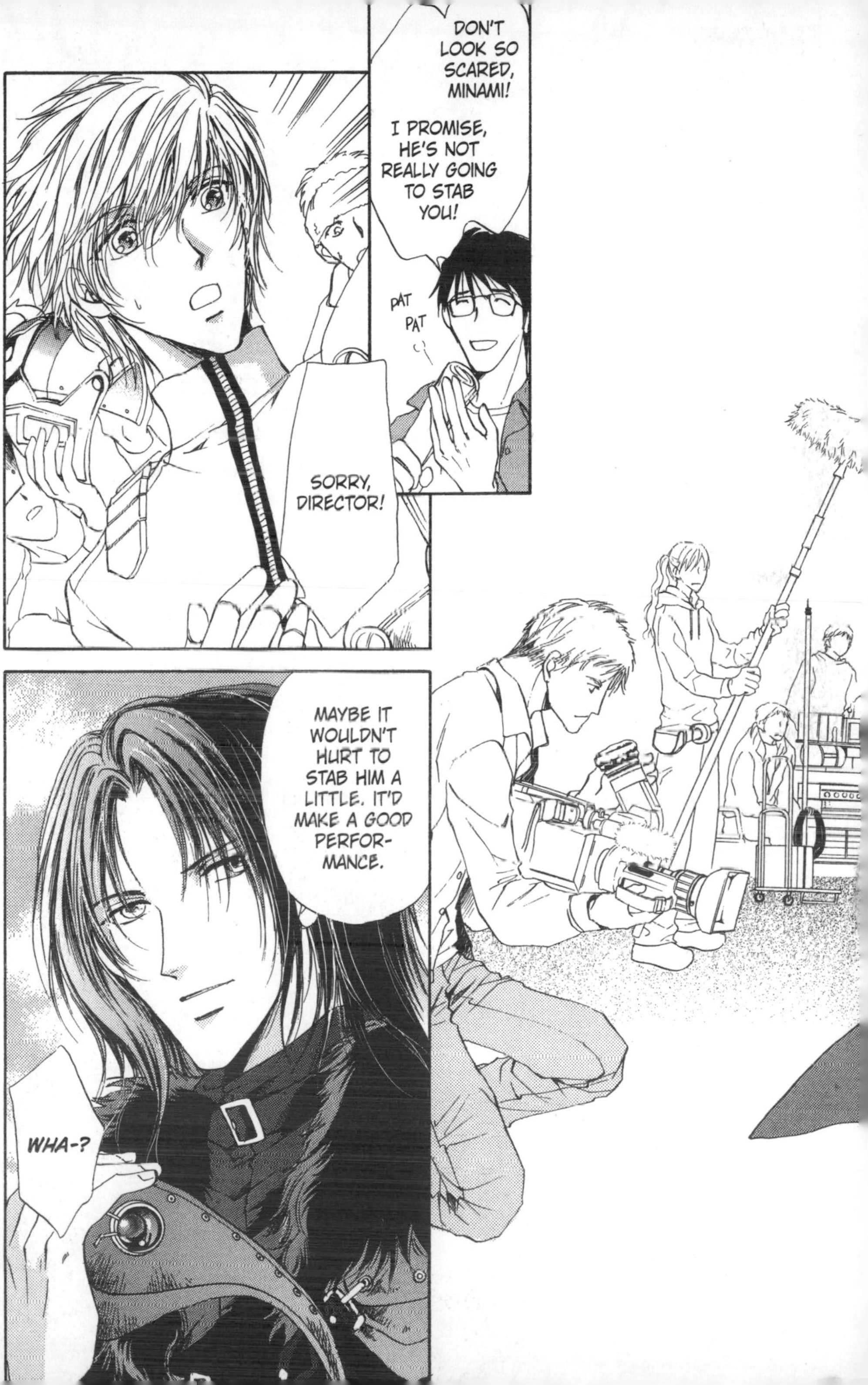
DON'T LOOK SO SCARED, MINAMI!
I PROMISE, HE'S NOT REALLY GOING TO STAB YOU!
PAT PAT
SORRY, DIRECTOR!
MAYBE IT WOULDN'T HURT TO STAB HIM A LITTLE. IT'D MAKE A GOOD PERFORMANCE.
WHA-?

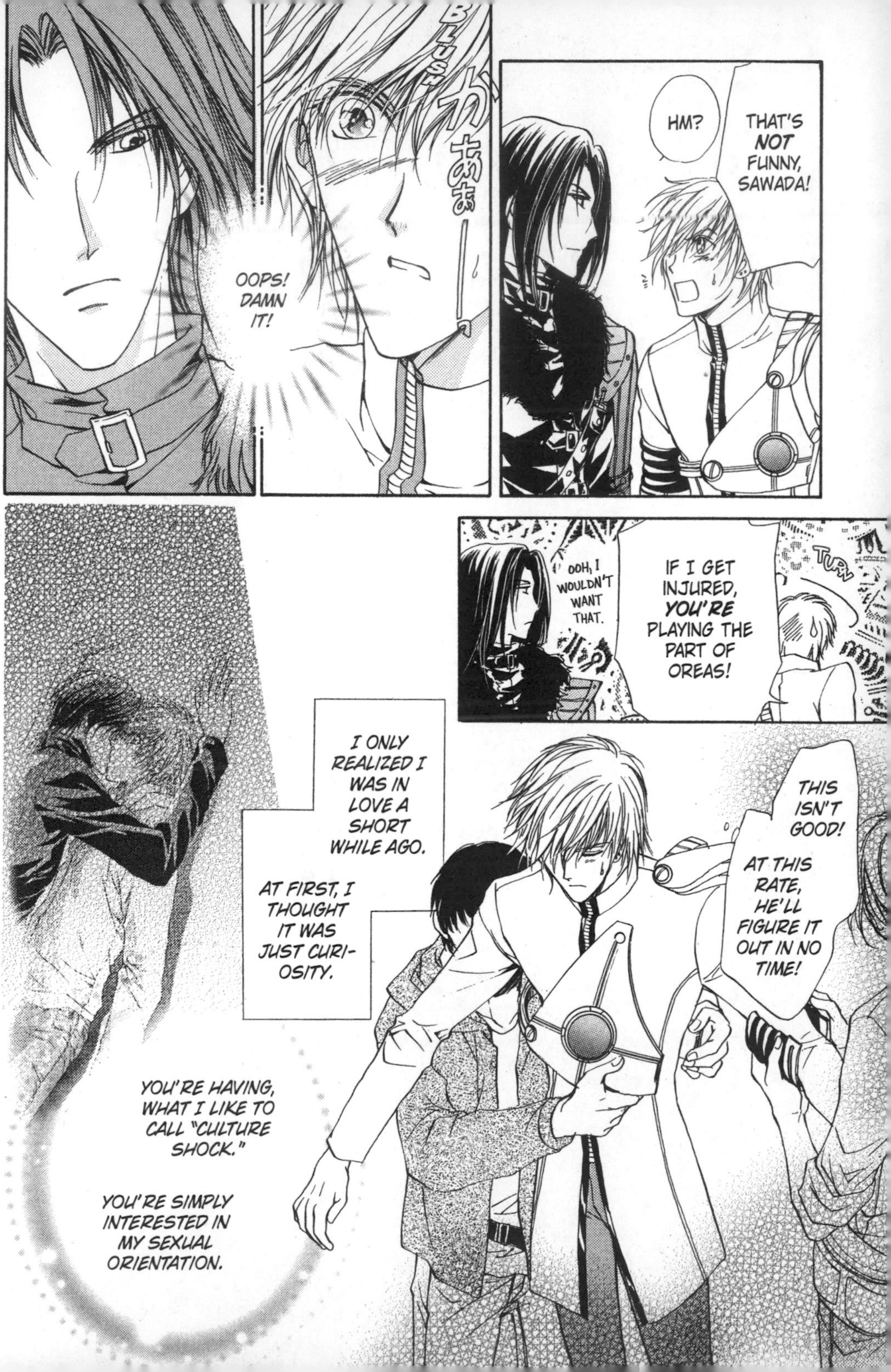
THAT'S **NOT** FUNNY, SAWADA!
HM?
BLUSH
OOPS! DAMN IT!
TURN
IF I GET INJURED, ***YOU'RE*** PLAYING THE PART OF OREAS!
OOH, I WOULDN'T WANT THAT.
THIS ISN'T GOOD!
AT THIS RATE, HE'LL FIGURE IT OUT IN NO TIME!
I ONLY REALIZED I WAS IN LOVE A SHORT WHILE AGO.
AT FIRST, I THOUGHT IT WAS JUST CURI-OSITY.
YOU'RE HAVING, WHAT I LIKE TO CALL "CULTURE SHOCK."
YOU'RE SIMPLY INTERESTED IN MY SEXUAL ORIENTATION.

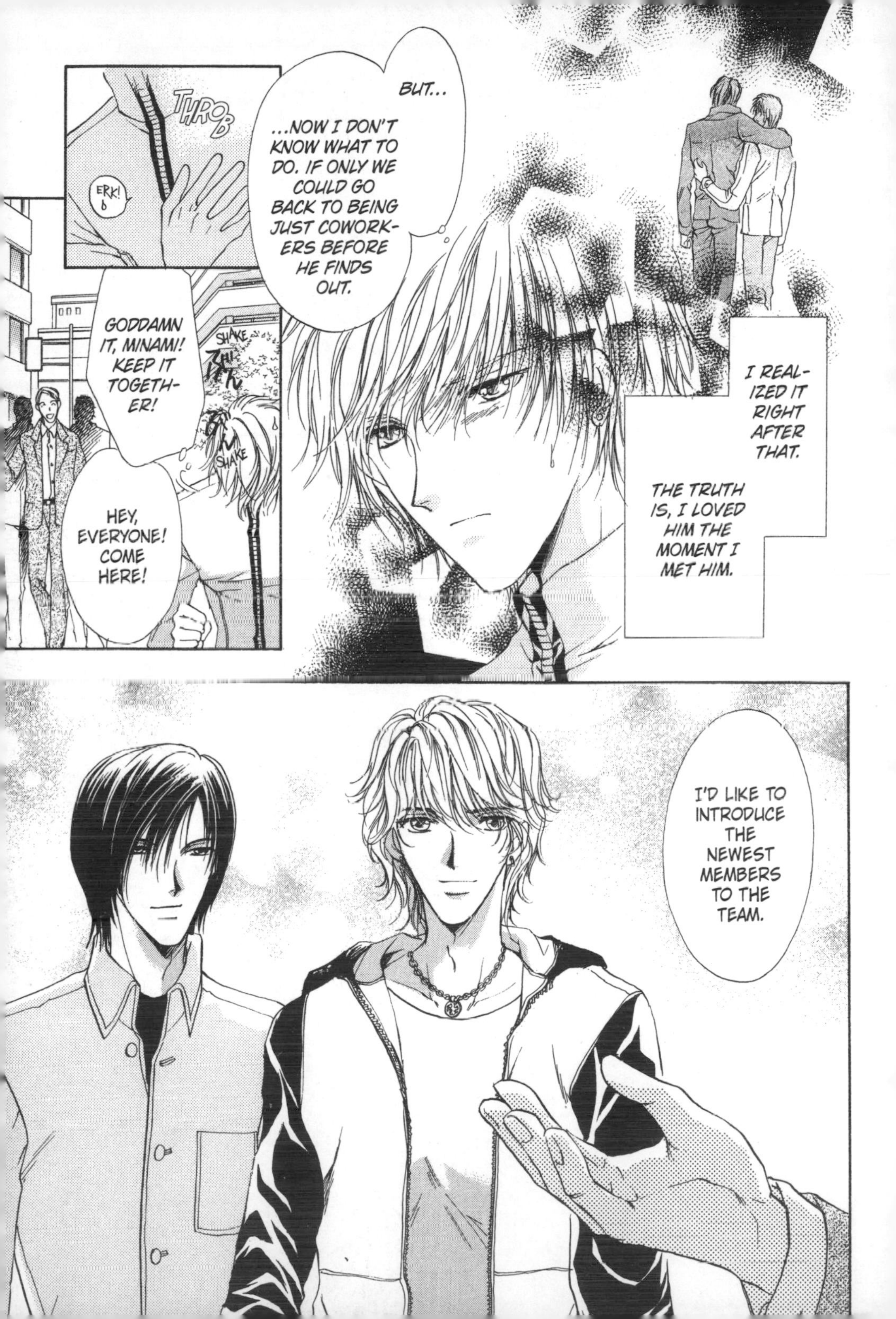
BUT...
...NOW I DON'T KNOW WHAT TO DO. IF ONLY WE COULD GO BACK TO BEING JUST COWORKERS BEFORE HE FINDS OUT.
I REALIZED IT RIGHT AFTER THAT.
THE TRUTH IS, I LOVED HIM THE MOMENT I MET HIM.
THROB
ERK!
GODDAMN IT, MINAMI! KEEP IT TOGETHER!
SHAKE
SHAKE
HEY, EVERYONE! COME HERE!
I'D LIKE TO INTRODUCE THE NEWEST MEMBERS TO THE TEAM.

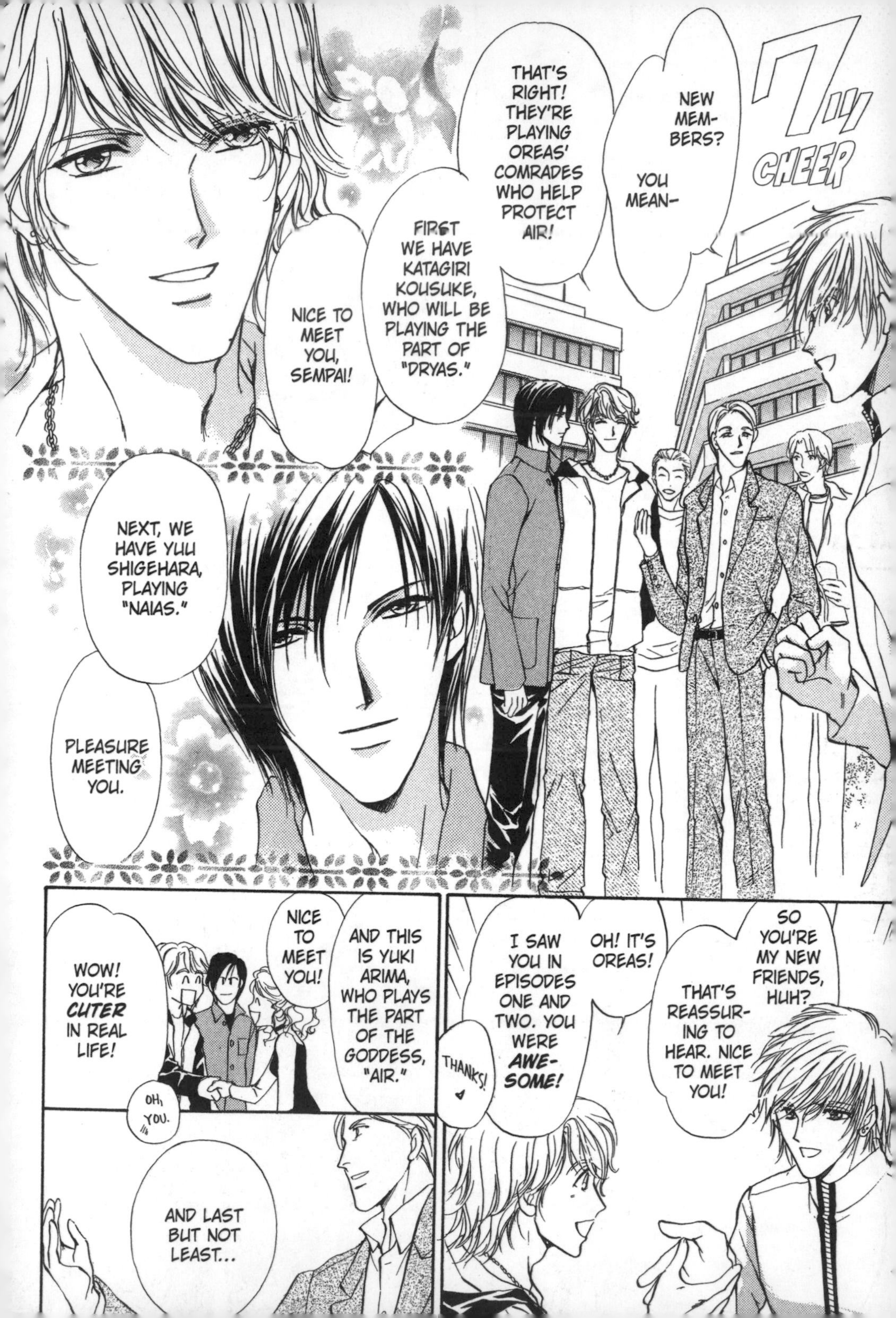
CHEER
NEW MEMBERS?
YOU MEAN-
THAT'S RIGHT! THEY'RE PLAYING OREAS' COMRADES WHO HELP PROTECT AIR!
FIRST WE HAVE KATAGIRI KOUSUKE, WHO WILL BE PLAYING THE PART OF "DRYAS."
NICE TO MEET YOU, SEMPAI!
NEXT, WE HAVE YUU SHIGEHARA, PLAYING "NAIAS."
PLEASURE MEETING YOU.
SO YOU'RE MY NEW FRIENDS, HUH?
THAT'S REASSURING TO HEAR. NICE TO MEET YOU!
OH! IT'S OREAS!
I SAW YOU IN EPISODES ONE AND TWO. YOU WERE **AWESOME!**
THANKS!
AND THIS IS YUKI ARIMA, WHO PLAYS THE PART OF THE GODDESS, "AIR."
NICE TO MEET YOU!
WOW! YOU'RE **CUTER** IN REAL LIFE!
OH, YOU.
AND LAST BUT NOT LEAST...

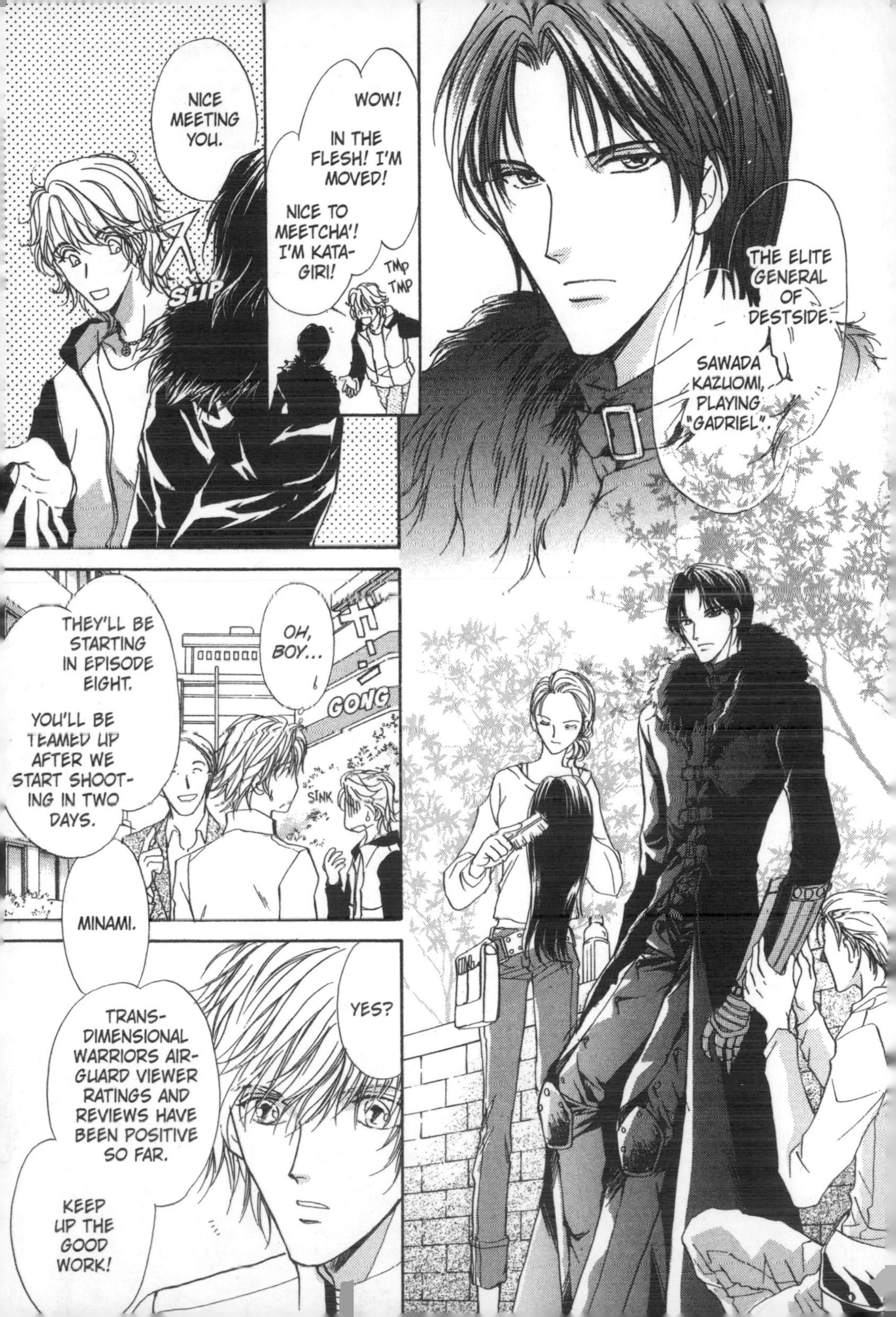
THE ELITE GENERAL OF DESTSIDE.
SAWADA KAZUOMI, PLAYING "GADRIEL".
WOW!
IN THE FLESH! I'M MOVED!
NICE TO MEETCHA'! I'M KATA-GIRI!
TMP TMP
NICE MEETING YOU.
SLIP
OH, BOY...
GONG
THEY'LL BE STARTING IN EPISODE EIGHT.
YOU'LL BE TEAMED UP AFTER WE START SHOOTING IN TWO DAYS.
SINK
MINAMI.
YES?
TRANS-DIMENSIONAL WARRIORS AIR-GUARD VIEWER RATINGS AND REVIEWS HAVE BEEN POSITIVE SO FAR.
KEEP UP THE GOOD WORK!

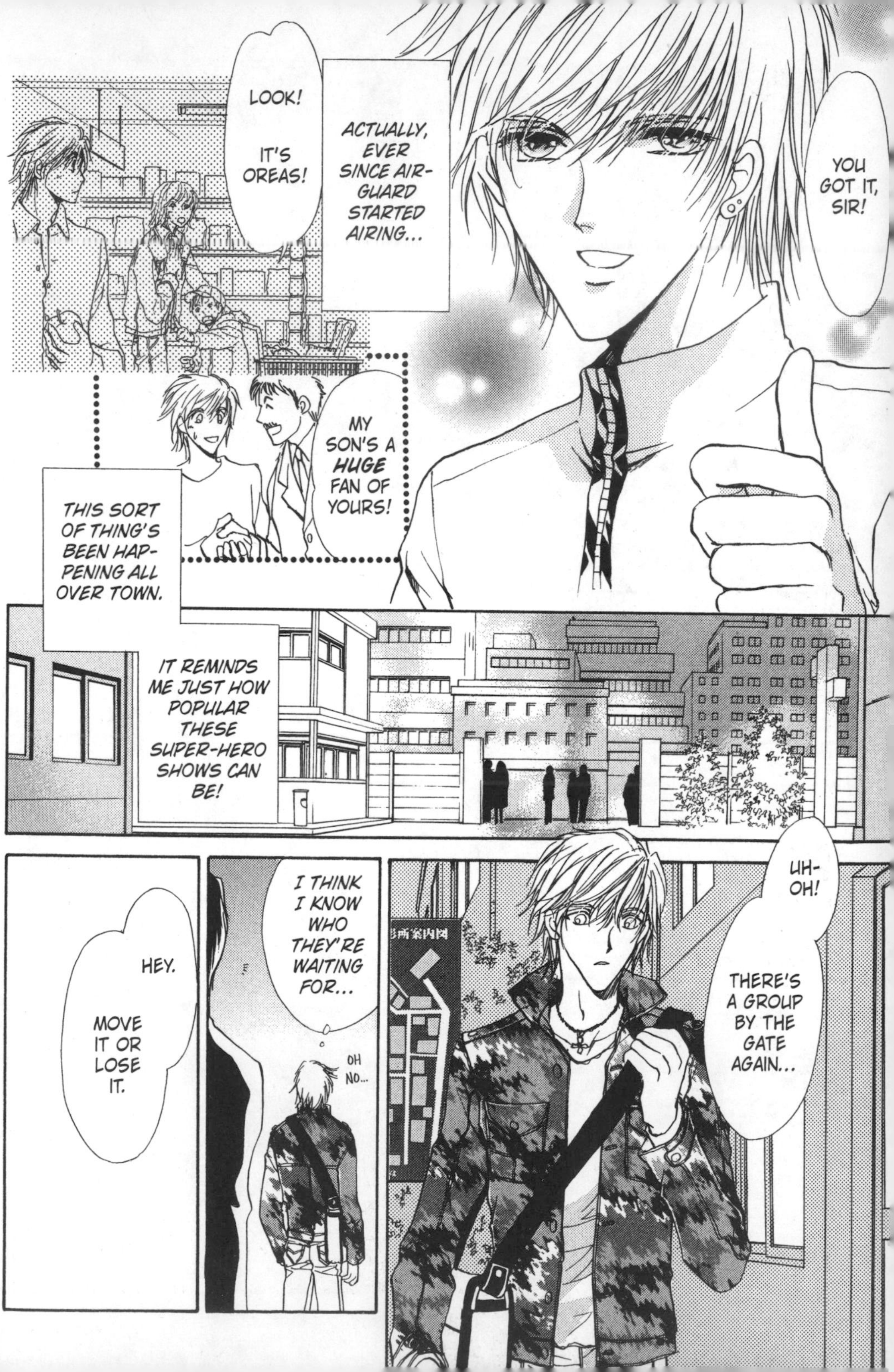
YOU GOT IT, SIR!
ACTUALLY, EVER SINCE AIR-GUARD STARTED AIRING...
LOOK!
IT'S OREAS!
MY SON'S A HUGE FAN OF YOURS!
THIS SORT OF THING'S BEEN HAPPENING ALL OVER TOWN.
IT REMINDS ME JUST HOW POPULAR THESE SUPER-HERO SHOWS CAN BE!
UH-OH!
THERE'S A GROUP BY THE GATE AGAIN...
I THINK I KNOW WHO THEY'RE WAITING FOR...
OH NO...
HEY.
MOVE IT OR LOSE IT.

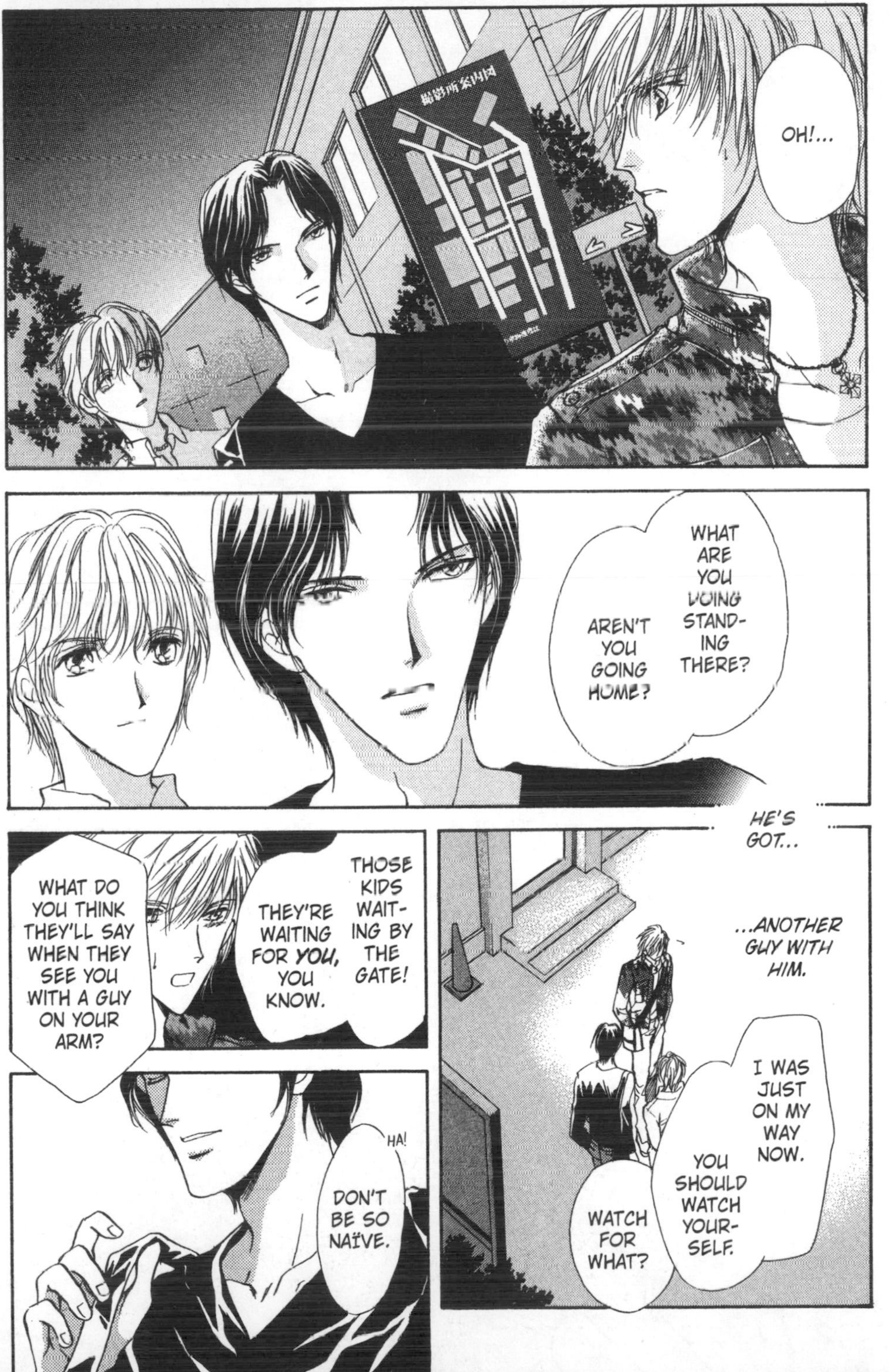
OH!...
WHAT ARE YOU DOING STANDING-ING THERE?
AREN'T YOU GOING HOME?
HE'S GOT...
...ANOTHER GUY WITH HIM.
I WAS JUST ON MY WAY NOW.
YOU SHOULD WATCH YOUR-SELF.
WATCH FOR WHAT?
THOSE KIDS WAIT-ING BY THE GATE!
THEY'RE WAITING FOR YOU, YOU KNOW.
WHAT DO YOU THINK THEY'LL SAY WHEN THEY SEE YOU WITH A GUY ON YOUR ARM?
HA!
DON'T BE SO NAÏVE.

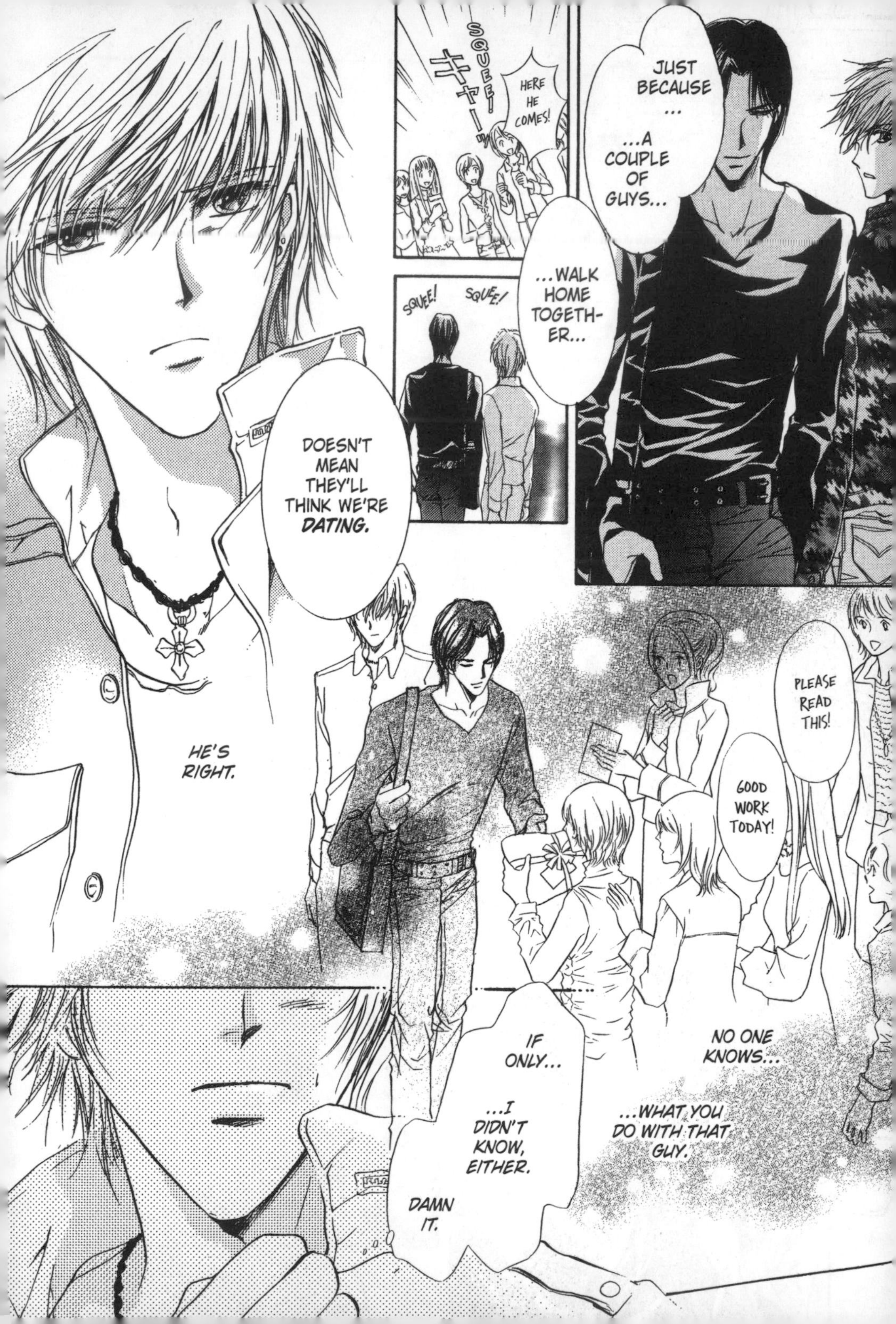
JUST BECAUSE...
...A COUPLE OF GUYS...
...WALK HOME TOGETH-ER...
SQUEE!
キャーッ
HERE HE COMES!
SQUEE!
SQUEE!
DOESN'T MEAN THEY'LL THINK WE'RE *DATING.*
HE'S RIGHT.
PLEASE READ THIS!
GOOD WORK TODAY!
NO ONE KNOWS...
...WHAT YOU DO WITH THAT GUY.
IF ONLY...
...I DIDN'T KNOW, EITHER.
DAMN IT.

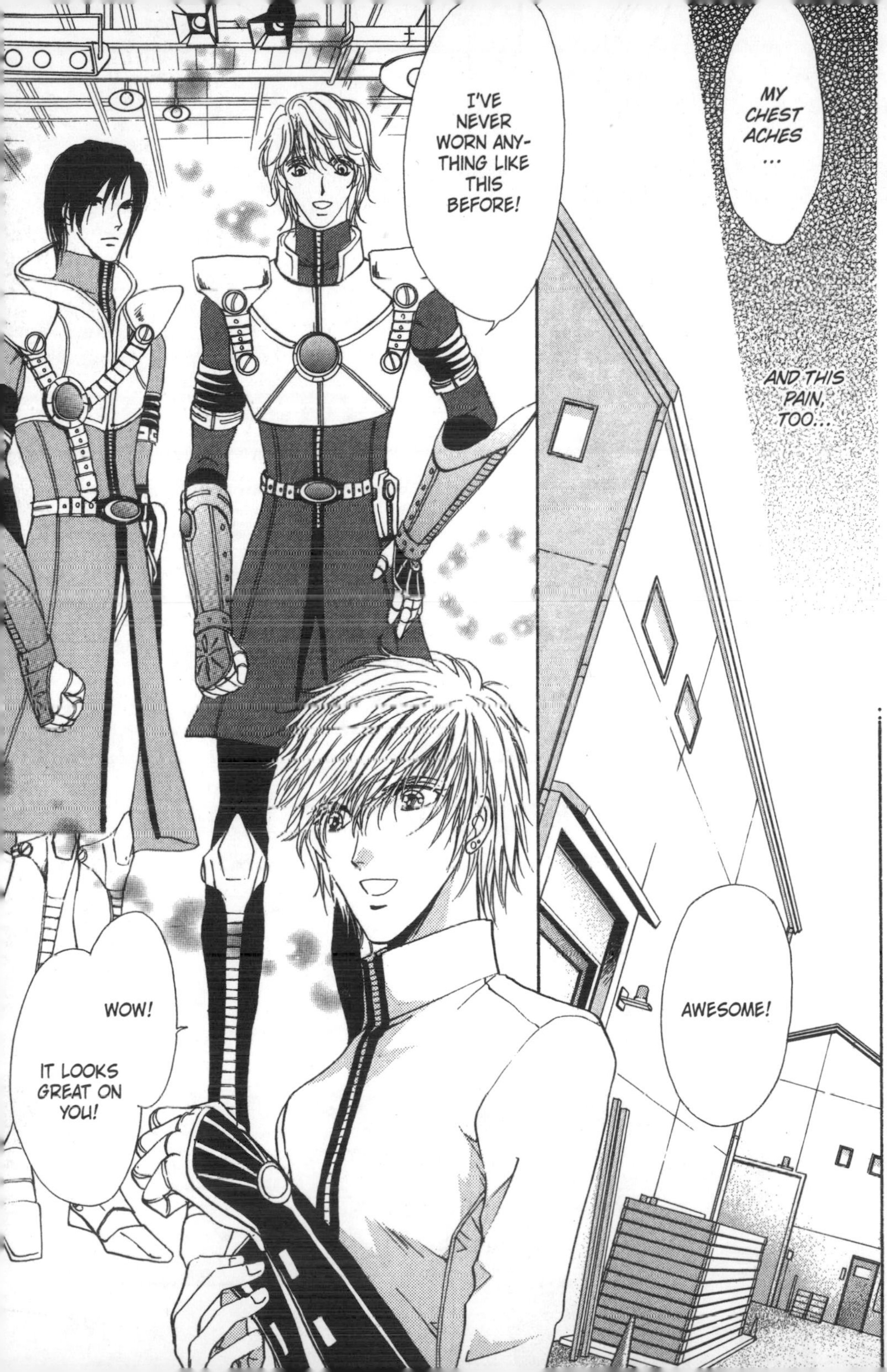
MY CHEST ACHES ...
AND THIS PAIN, TOO...
I'VE NEVER WORN ANY-THING LIKE THIS BEFORE!
AWESOME!
WOW!
IT LOOKS GREAT ON YOU!

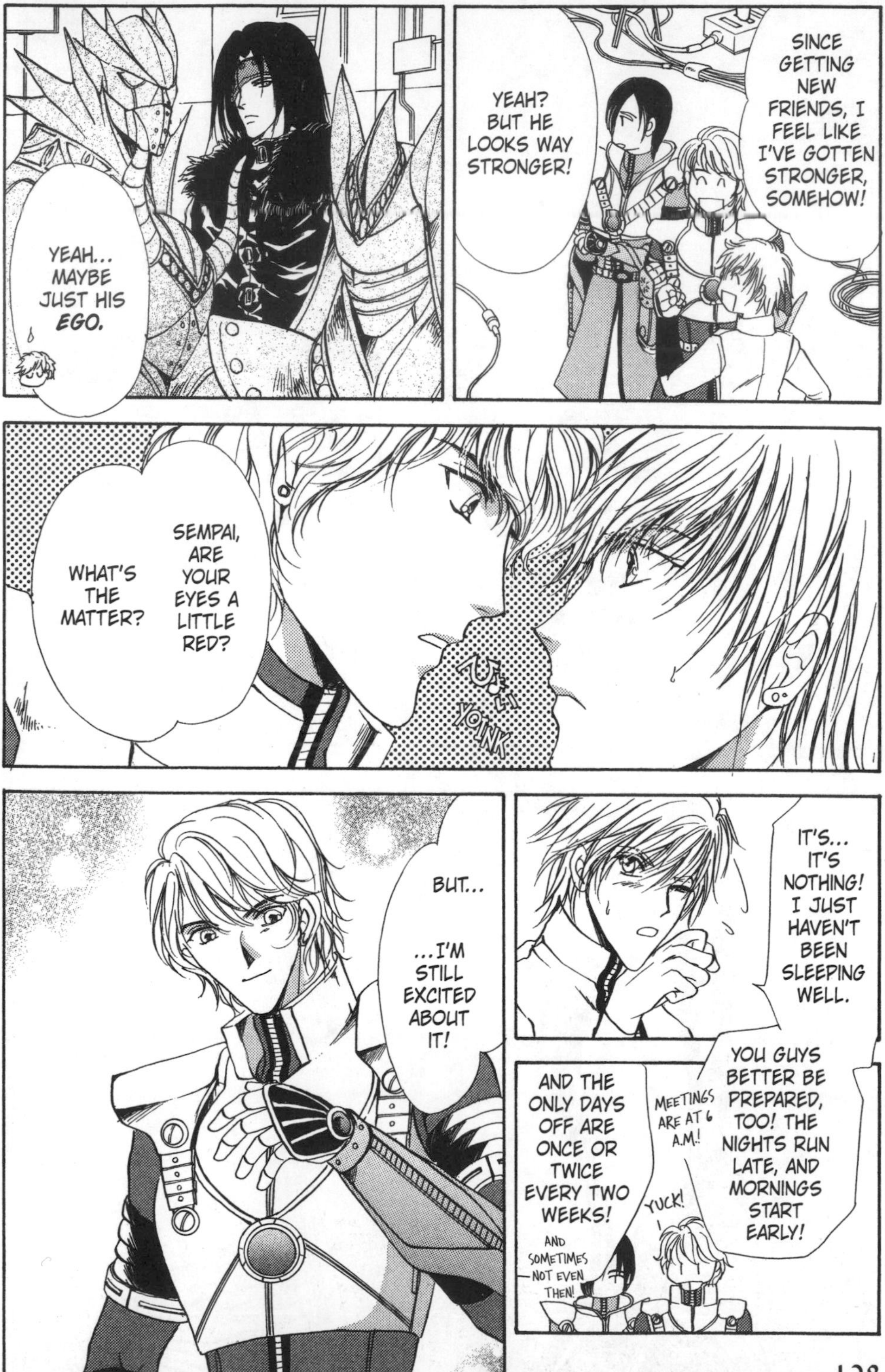
SINCE GETTING NEW FRIENDS, I FEEL LIKE I'VE GOTTEN STRONGER, SOMEHOW!
YEAH? BUT HE LOOKS WAY STRONGER!
YEAH... MAYBE JUST HIS **EGO.**
YOINK
SEMPAI, ARE YOUR EYES A LITTLE RED?
WHAT'S THE MATTER?
IT'S... IT'S NOTHING! I JUST HAVEN'T BEEN SLEEPING WELL.
YOU GUYS BETTER BE PREPARED, TOO! THE NIGHTS RUN LATE, AND MORNINGS START EARLY!
MEETINGS ARE AT 6 A.M.!
AND THE ONLY DAYS OFF ARE ONCE OR TWICE EVERY TWO WEEKS!
YUCK!
AND SOMETIMES NOT EVEN THEN!
BUT...
...I'M STILL EXCITED ABOUT IT!

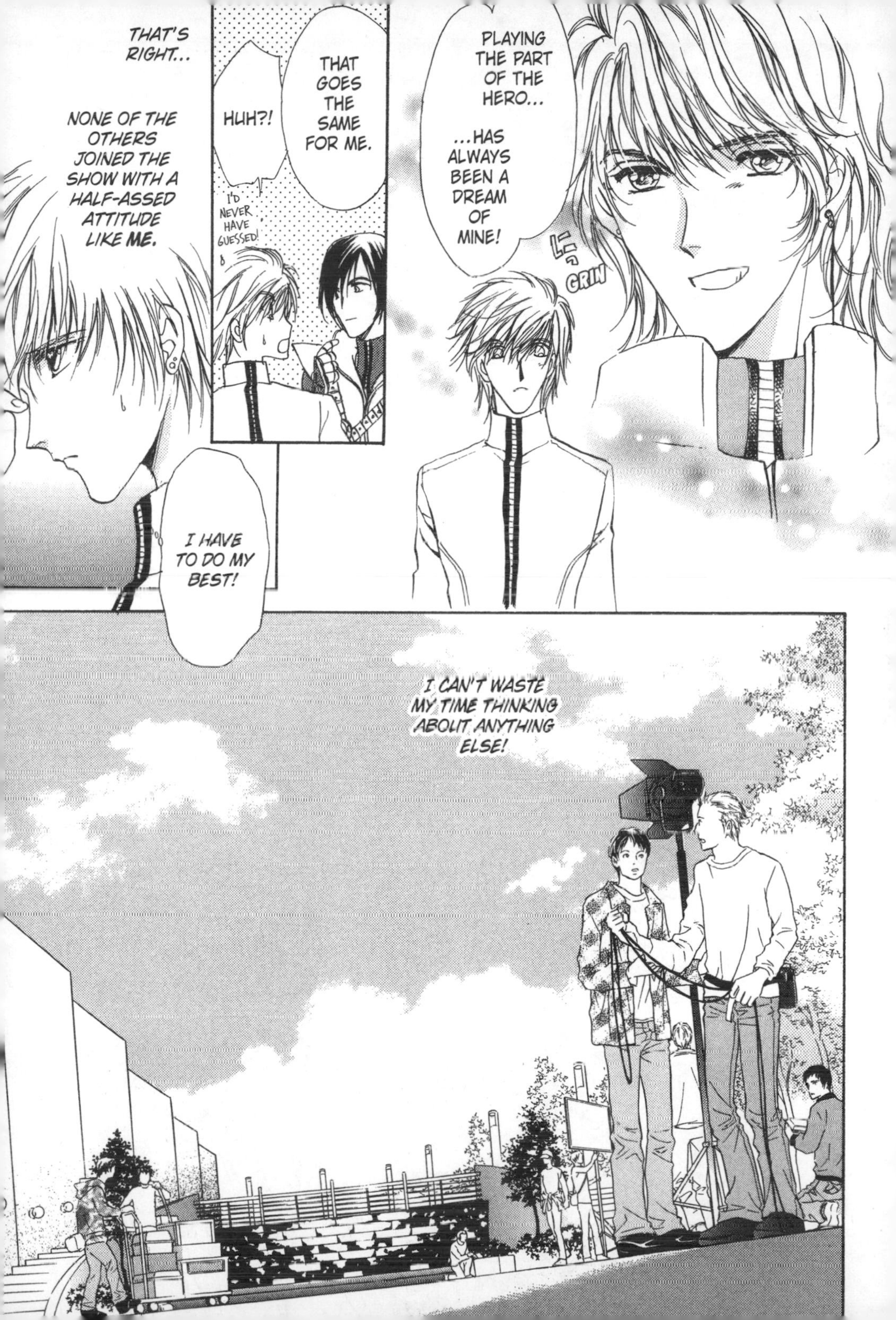
PLAYING THE PART OF THE HERO...
...HAS ALWAYS BEEN A DREAM OF MINE!
GRIN
THAT GOES THE SAME FOR ME.
HUH?!
I'D NEVER HAVE GUESSED!
THAT'S RIGHT...
NONE OF THE OTHERS JOINED THE SHOW WITH A HALF-ASSED ATTITUDE LIKE ME.
I HAVE TO DO MY BEST!
I CAN'T WASTE MY TIME THINKING ABOUT ANYTHING ELSE!

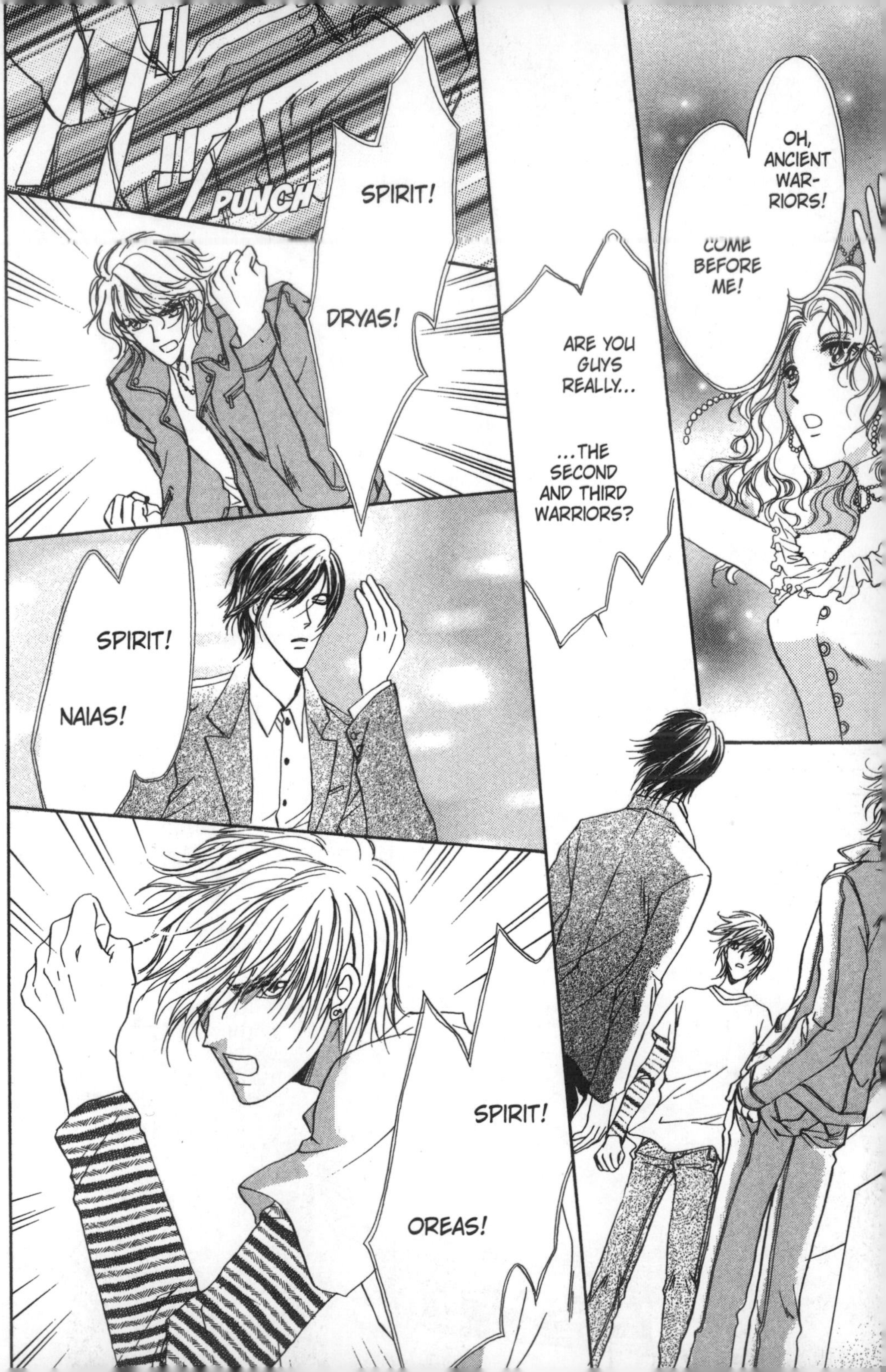
OH, ANCIENT WAR-RIORS!
COME BEFORE ME!
ARE YOU GUYS REALLY...
...THE SECOND AND THIRD WARRIORS?
PUNCH
SPIRIT!
DRYAS!
SPIRIT!
NAIAS!
SPIRIT!
OREAS!

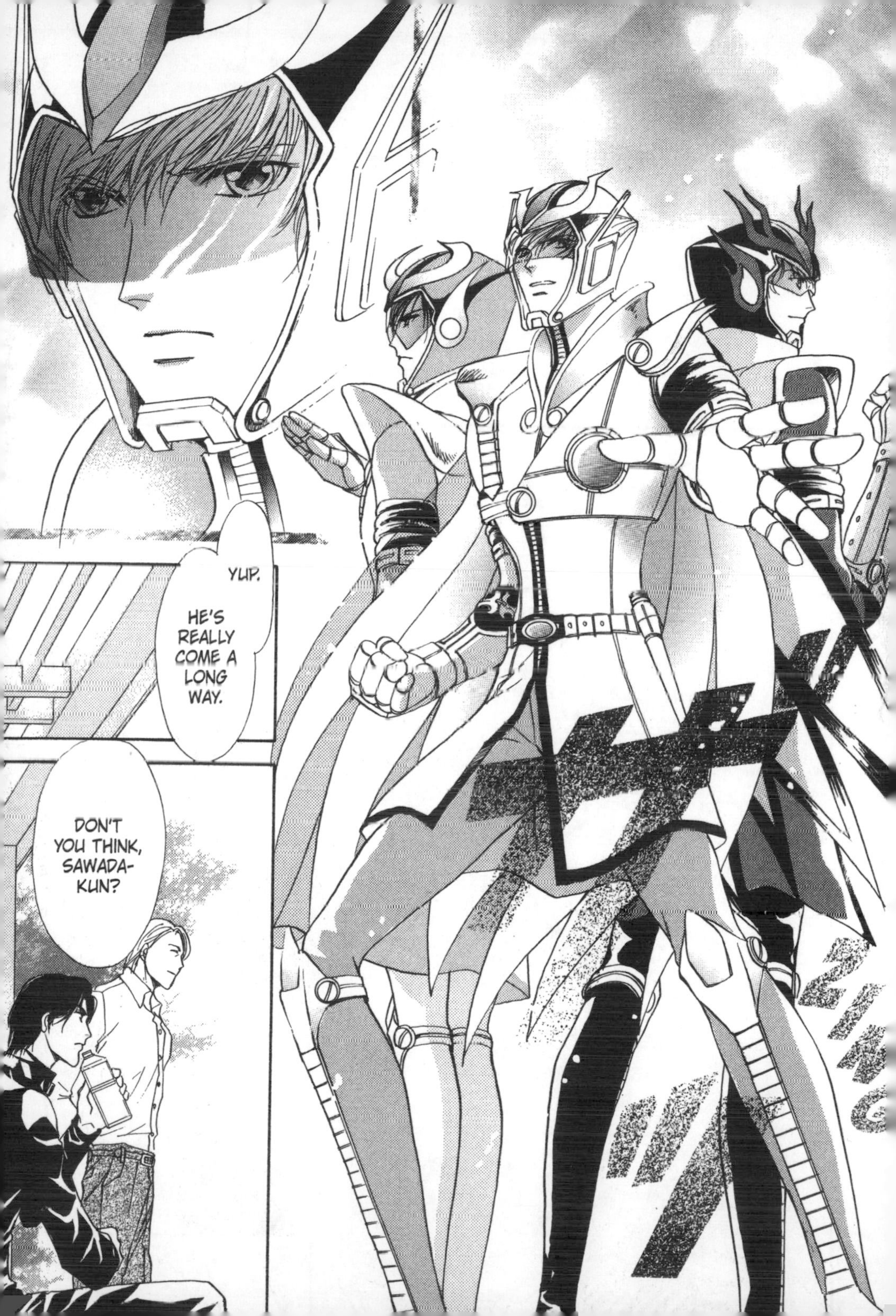
YUP.
HE'S REALLY COME A LONG WAY.
DON'T YOU THINK, SAWADA-KUN?

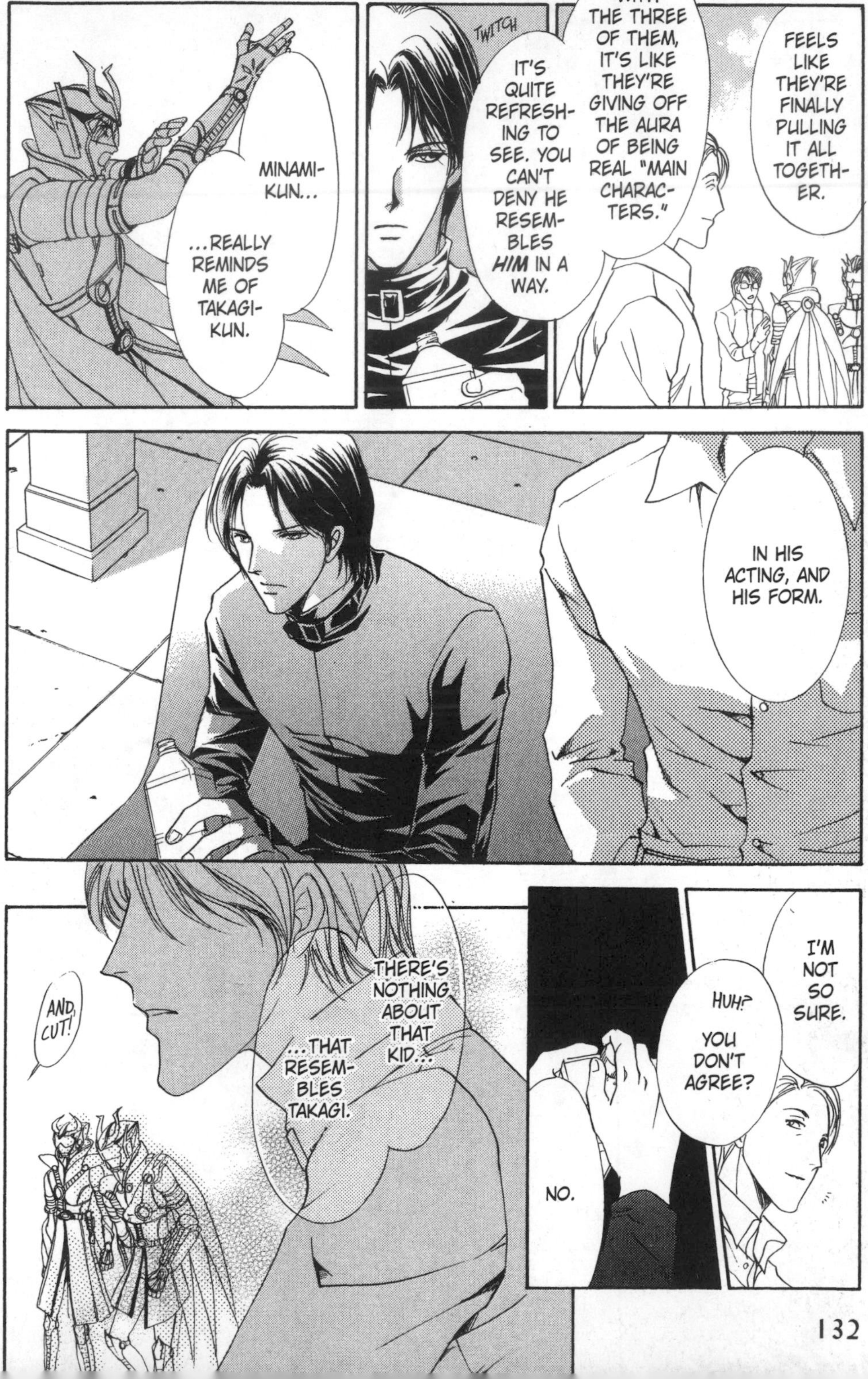
FEELS LIKE THEY'RE FINALLY PULLING IT ALL TOGETH-ER.
WITH THE THREE OF THEM, IT'S LIKE THEY'RE GIVING OFF THE AURA OF BEING REAL "MAIN CHARAC-TERS."
TWITCH
IT'S QUITE REFRESH-ING TO SEE. YOU CAN'T DENY HE RESEM-BLES *HIM* IN A WAY.
MINAMI-KUN...
...REALLY REMINDS ME OF TAKAGI-KUN.
IN HIS ACTING, AND HIS FORM.
I'M NOT SO SURE.
HUH?
YOU DON'T AGREE?
NO.
THERE'S NOTHING ABOUT THAT KID...
...THAT RESEM-BLES TAKAGI.
AND, CUT!

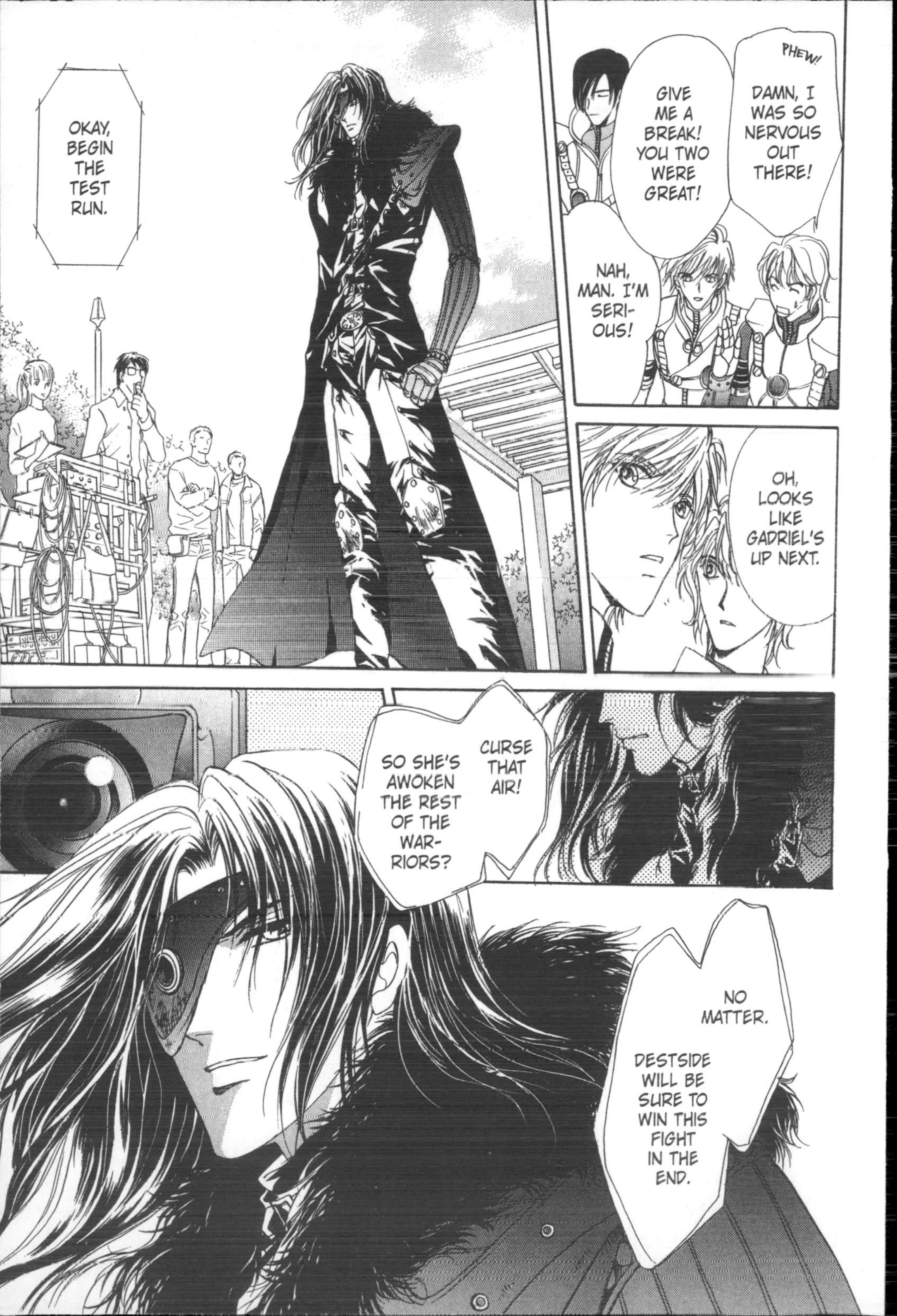
PHEW!
DAMN, I WAS SO NERVOUS OUT THERE!
GIVE ME A BREAK! YOU TWO WERE GREAT!
NAH, MAN. I'M SERI-OUS!
OH, LOOKS LIKE GADRIEL'S UP NEXT.
OKAY, BEGIN THE TEST RUN.
CURSE THAT AIR!
SO SHE'S AWOKEN THE REST OF THE WAR-RIORS?
NO MATTER.
DESTSIDE WILL BE SURE TO WIN THIS FIGHT IN THE END.

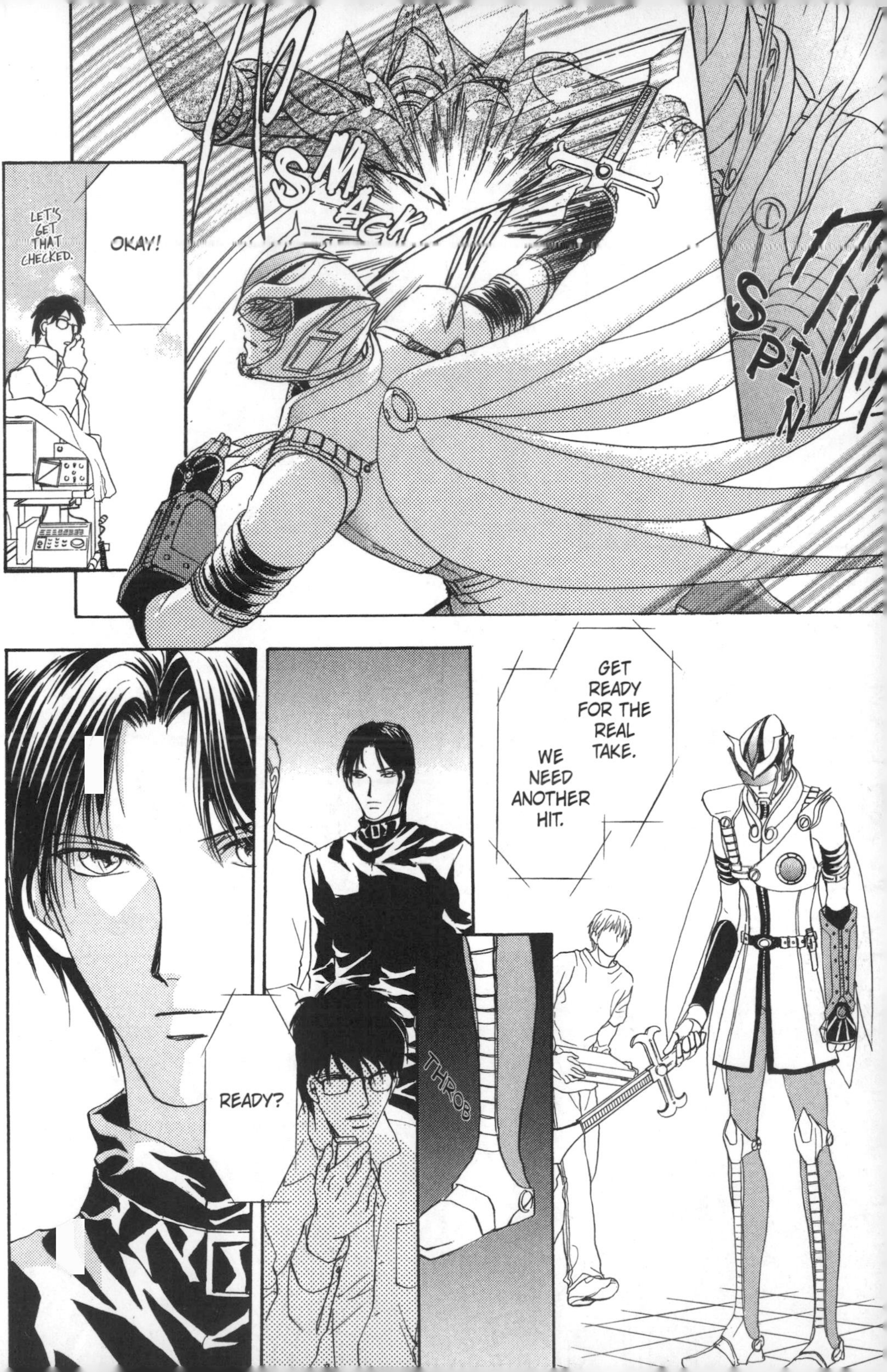
SPIN
SMACK
OKAY!
LET'S GET THAT CHECKED.
GET READY FOR THE REAL TAKE.
WE NEED ANOTHER HIT.
READY?
THROB

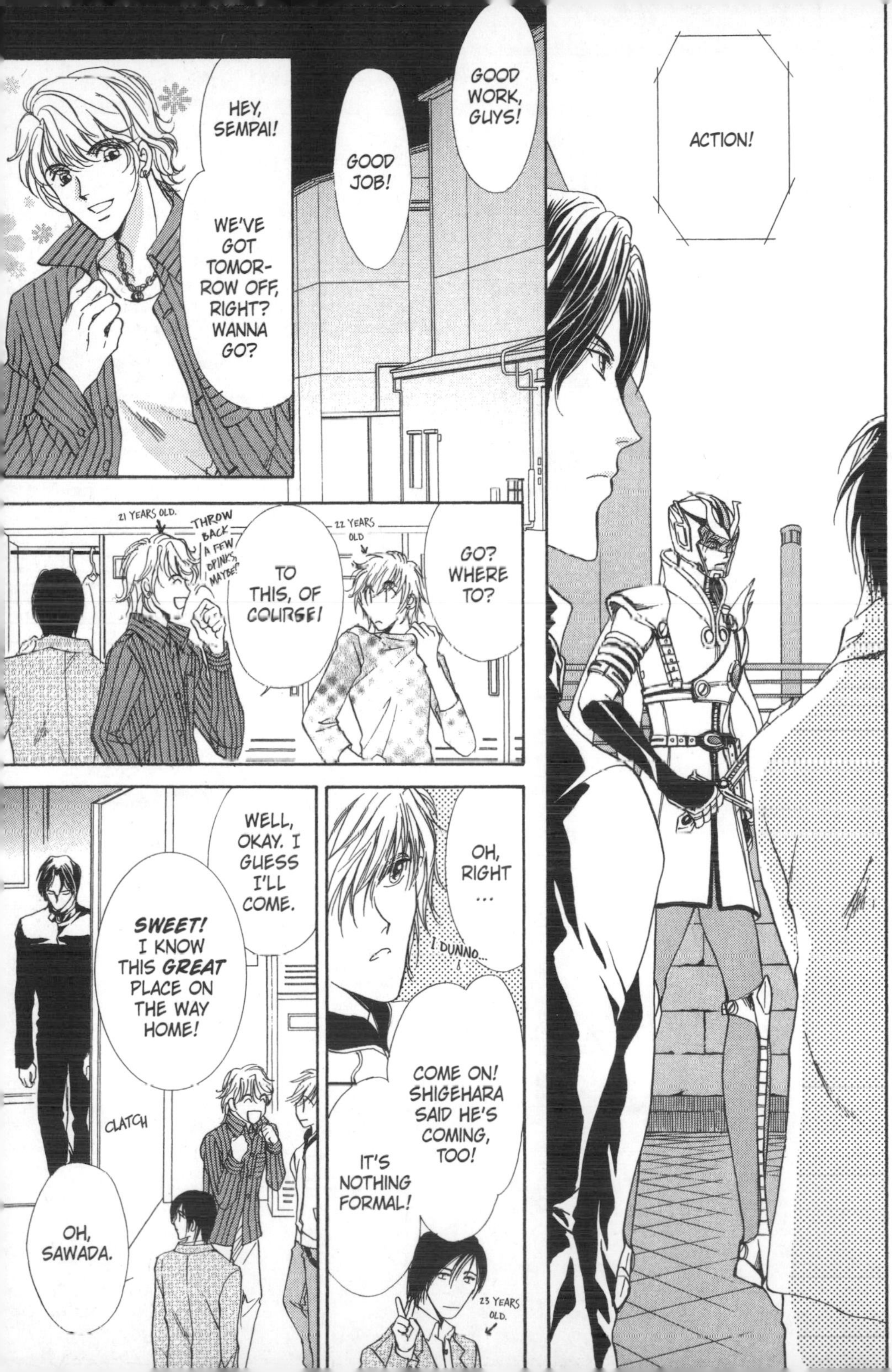
ACTION!
GOOD WORK, GUYS!
GOOD JOB!
HEY, SEMPAI!
WE'VE GOT TOMORROW OFF, RIGHT? WANNA GO?
GO? WHERE TO?
22 YEARS OLD
TO THIS, OF COURSE!
THROW BACK A FEW DRINKS, MAYBE?
21 YEARS OLD.
OH, RIGHT...
I DUNNO...
COME ON! SHIGEHARA SAID HE'S COMING, TOO!
IT'S NOTHING FORMAL!
23 YEARS OLD.
WELL, OKAY. I GUESS I'LL COME.
SWEET! I KNOW THIS GREAT PLACE ON THE WAY HOME!
CLATCH
OH, SAWADA.

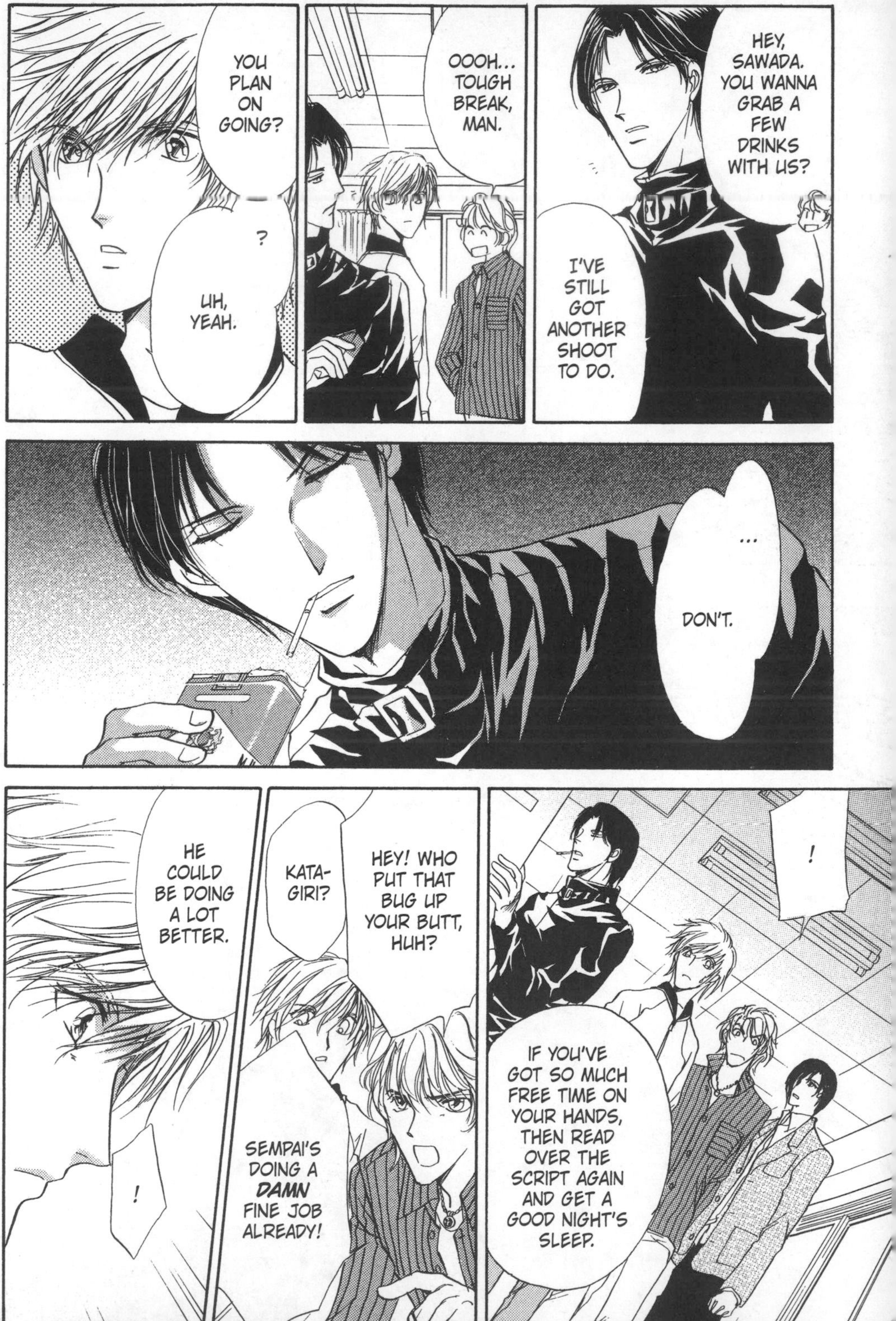
HEY, SAWADA. YOU WANNA GRAB A FEW DRINKS WITH US?
I'VE STILL GOT ANOTHER SHOOT TO DO.
OOOH... TOUGH BREAK, MAN.
YOU PLAN ON GOING?
?
UH, YEAH.
...
DON'T.
!
IF YOU'VE GOT SO MUCH FREE TIME ON YOUR HANDS, THEN READ OVER THE SCRIPT AGAIN AND GET A GOOD NIGHT'S SLEEP.
HEY! WHO PUT THAT BUG UP YOUR BUTT, HUH?
KATA-GIRI?
SEMPAI'S DOING A DAMN FINE JOB ALREADY!
HE COULD BE DOING A LOT BETTER.
!

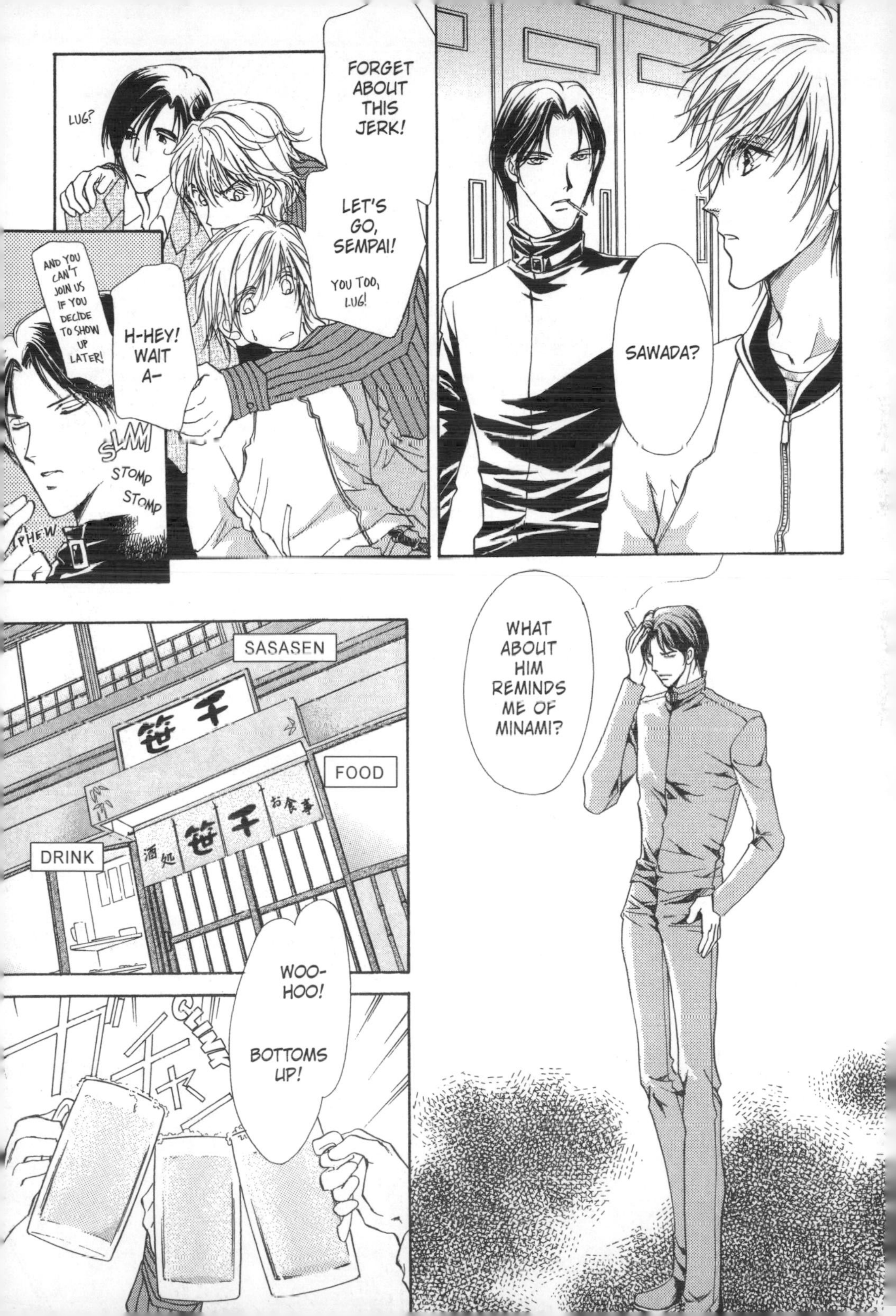
SAWADA?
LUG?
FORGET ABOUT THIS JERK!
LET'S GO, SEMPAI!
YOU TOO, LUG!
H-HEY! WAIT A-
AND YOU CAN'T JOIN US IF YOU DECIDE TO SHOW UP LATER!
SLMM
STOMP
STOMP
PHEW
WHAT ABOUT HIM REMINDS ME OF MINAMI?
SASASEN
笹千
FOOD
お食事
笹千
酒処
DRINK
WOO-HOO!
BOTTOMS UP!
CLINK

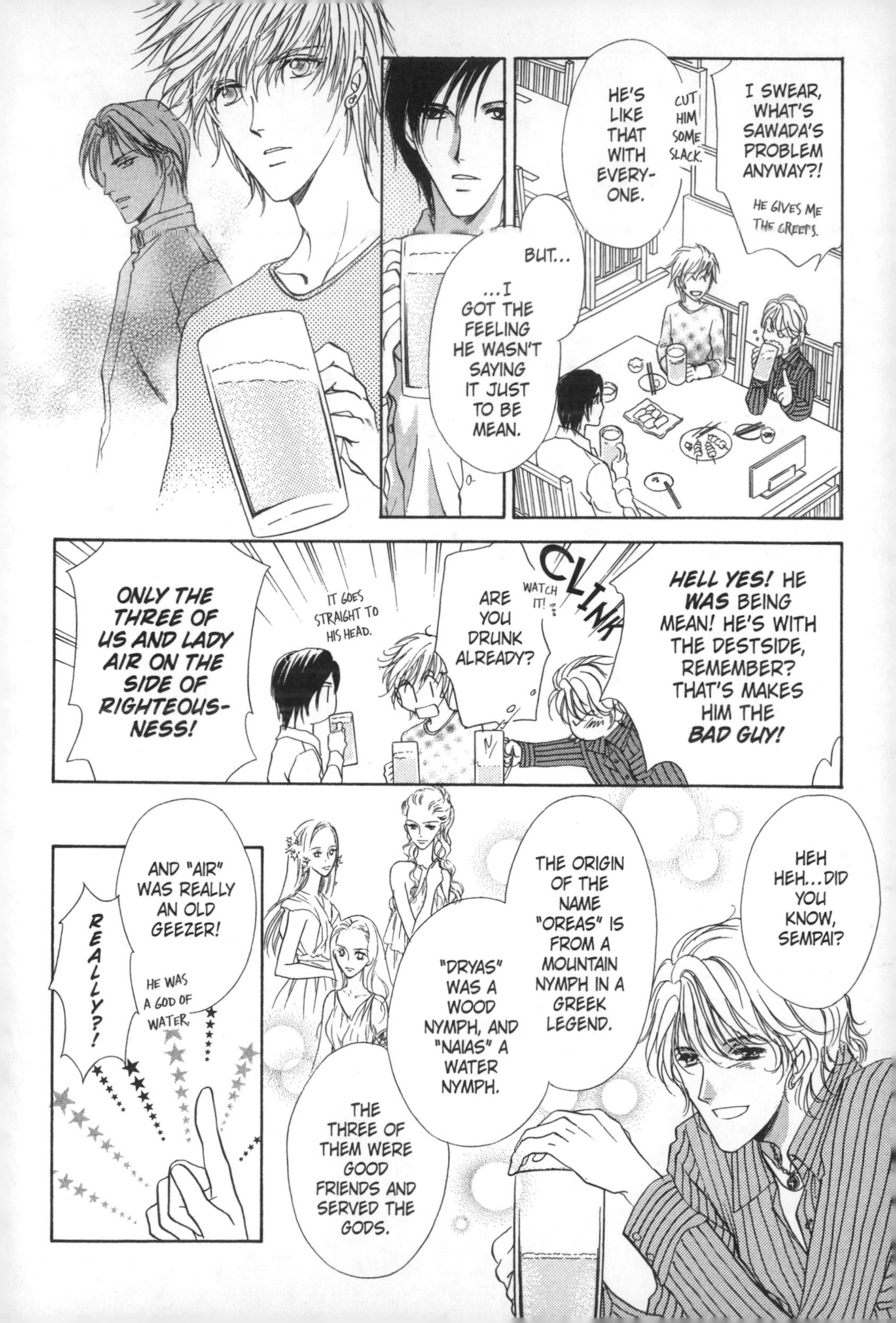
I SWEAR, WHAT'S SAWADA'S PROBLEM ANYWAY?!
HE GIVES ME THE CREEPS.
HE'S LIKE THAT WITH EVERY-ONE.
CUT HIM SOME SLACK.
BUT...
...I GOT THE FEELING HE WASN'T SAYING IT JUST TO BE MEAN.
HELL YES! HE WAS BEING MEAN! HE'S WITH THE DESTSIDE, REMEMBER? THAT'S MAKES HIM THE BAD GUY!
CLINK
WATCH IT!
ARE YOU DRUNK ALREADY?
IT GOES STRAIGHT TO HIS HEAD.
ONLY THE THREE OF US AND LADY AIR ON THE SIDE OF RIGHTEOUS-NESS!
HEH HEH...DID YOU KNOW, SEMPAI?
THE ORIGIN OF THE NAME "OREAS" IS FROM A MOUNTAIN NYMPH IN A GREEK LEGEND.
"DRYAS" WAS A WOOD NYMPH, AND "NAIAS" A WATER NYMPH.
THE THREE OF THEM WERE GOOD FRIENDS AND SERVED THE GODS.
AND "AIR" WAS REALLY AN OLD GEEZER!
HE WAS A GOD OF WATER.
REALLY?!

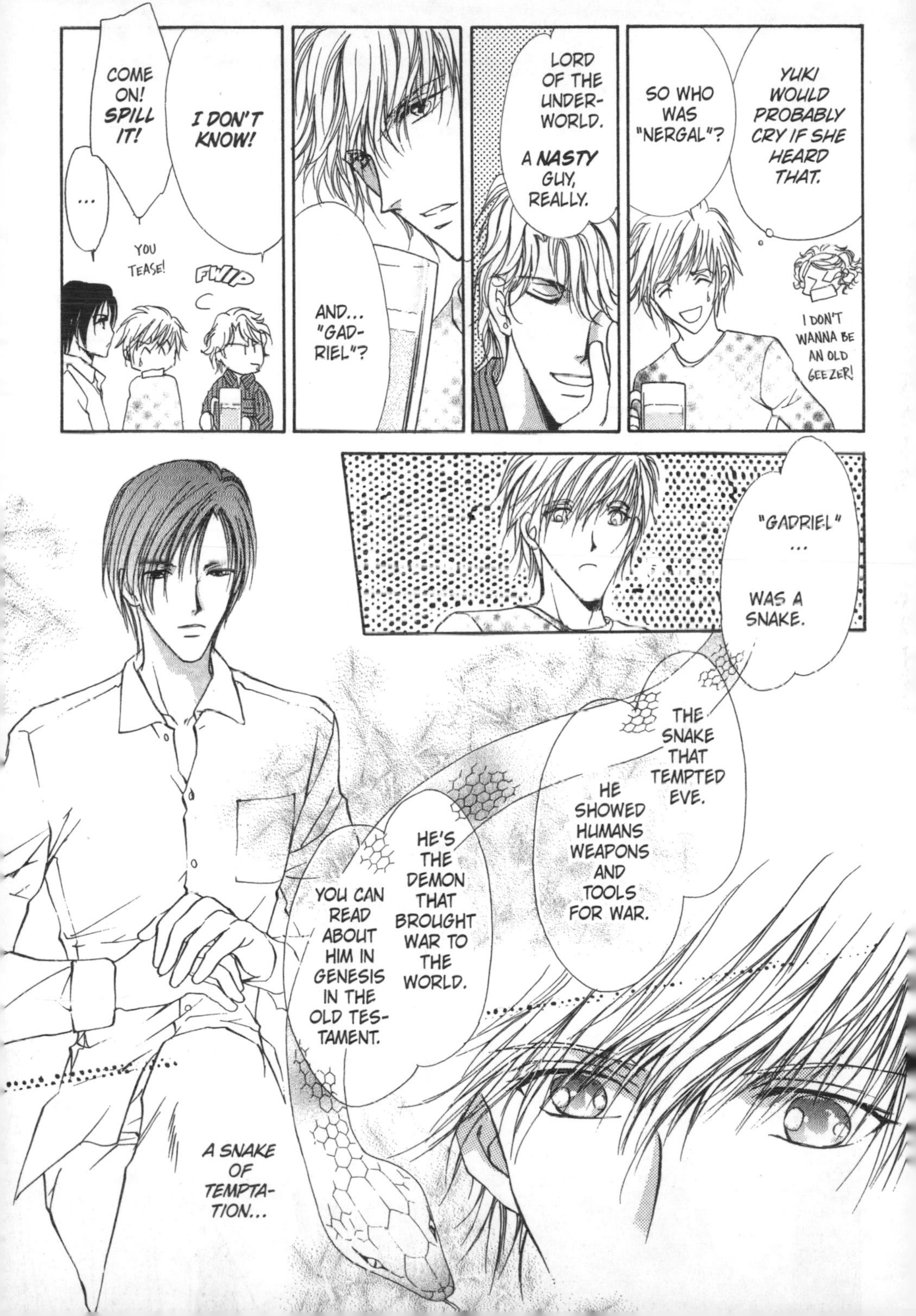
YUKI WOULD PROBABLY CRY IF SHE HEARD THAT.
SO WHO WAS "NERGAL"?
I DON'T WANNA BE AN OLD GEEZER!
LORD OF THE UNDER-WORLD.
A **NASTY** GUY, REALLY.
AND... "GAD-RIEL"?
I DON'T KNOW!
COME ON! **SPILL IT!**
...
FWIP
YOU TEASE!
"GADRIEL"...
WAS A SNAKE.
THE SNAKE THAT TEMPTED EVE.
HE SHOWED HUMANS WEAPONS AND TOOLS FOR WAR.
HE'S THE DEMON THAT BROUGHT WAR TO THE WORLD.
YOU CAN READ ABOUT HIM IN GENESIS IN THE OLD TES-TAMENT.
A SNAKE OF TEMPTA-TION...

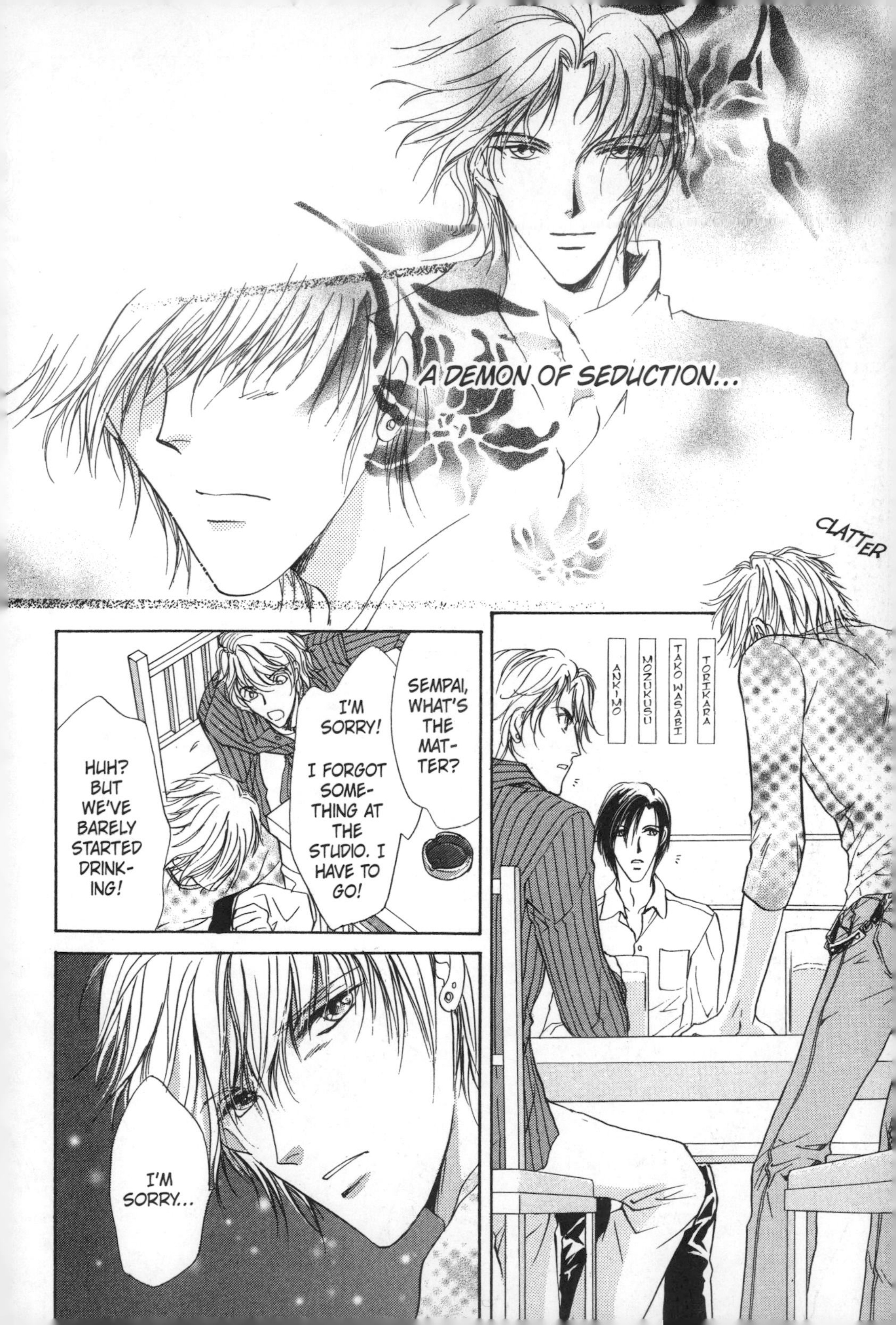

A DEMON OF SEDUCTION...
CLATTER
TORIKARA
TAKO WASABI
MOZUKUSU
ANKIMO
SEMPAI, WHAT'S THE MAT-TER?
I'M SORRY!
I FORGOT SOME-THING AT THE STUDIO. I HAVE TO GO!
HUH? BUT WE'VE BARELY STARTED DRINK-ING!
I'M SORRY...

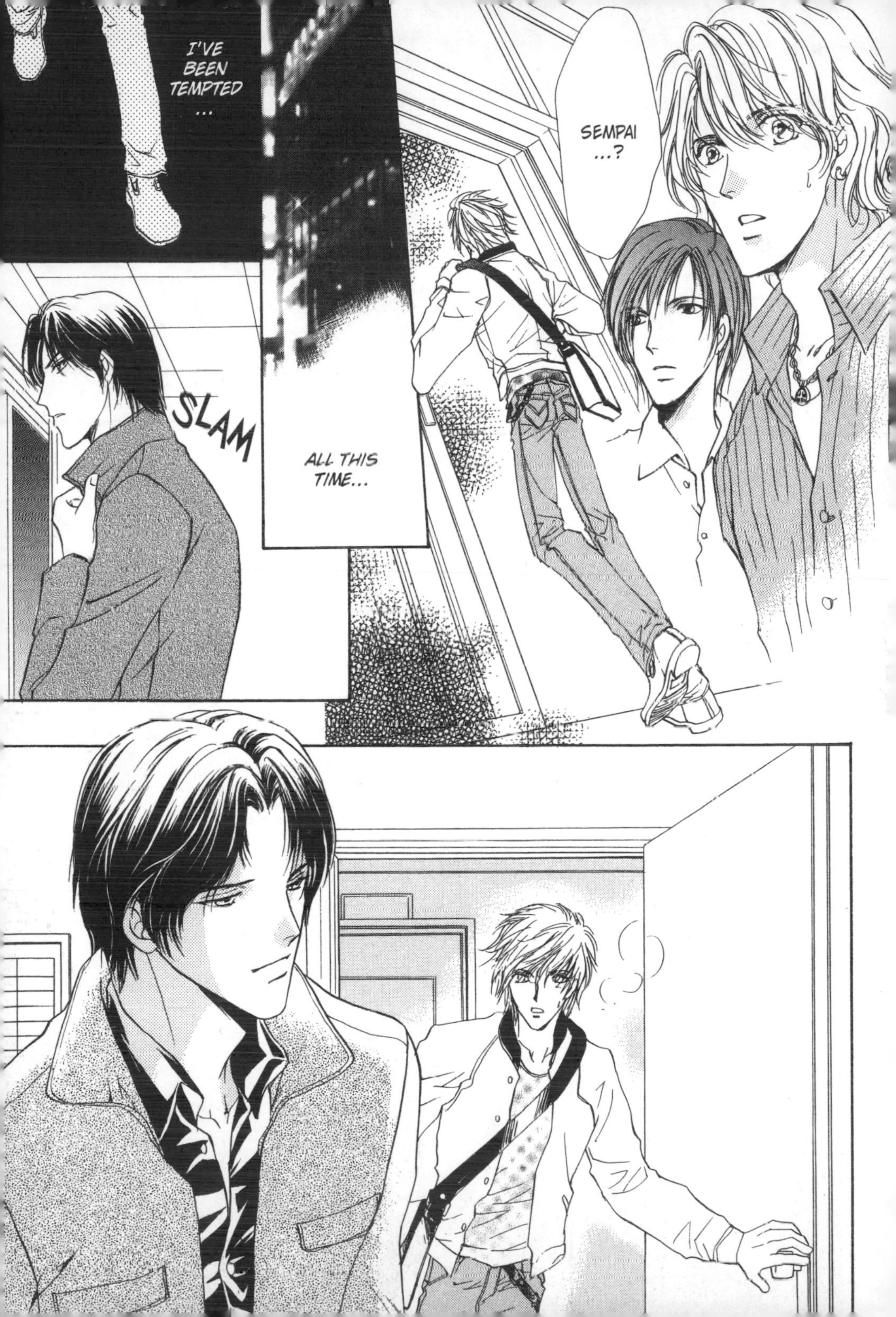
SEMPAI ...?
I'VE BEEN TEMPTED ...
ALL THIS TIME...
SLAM

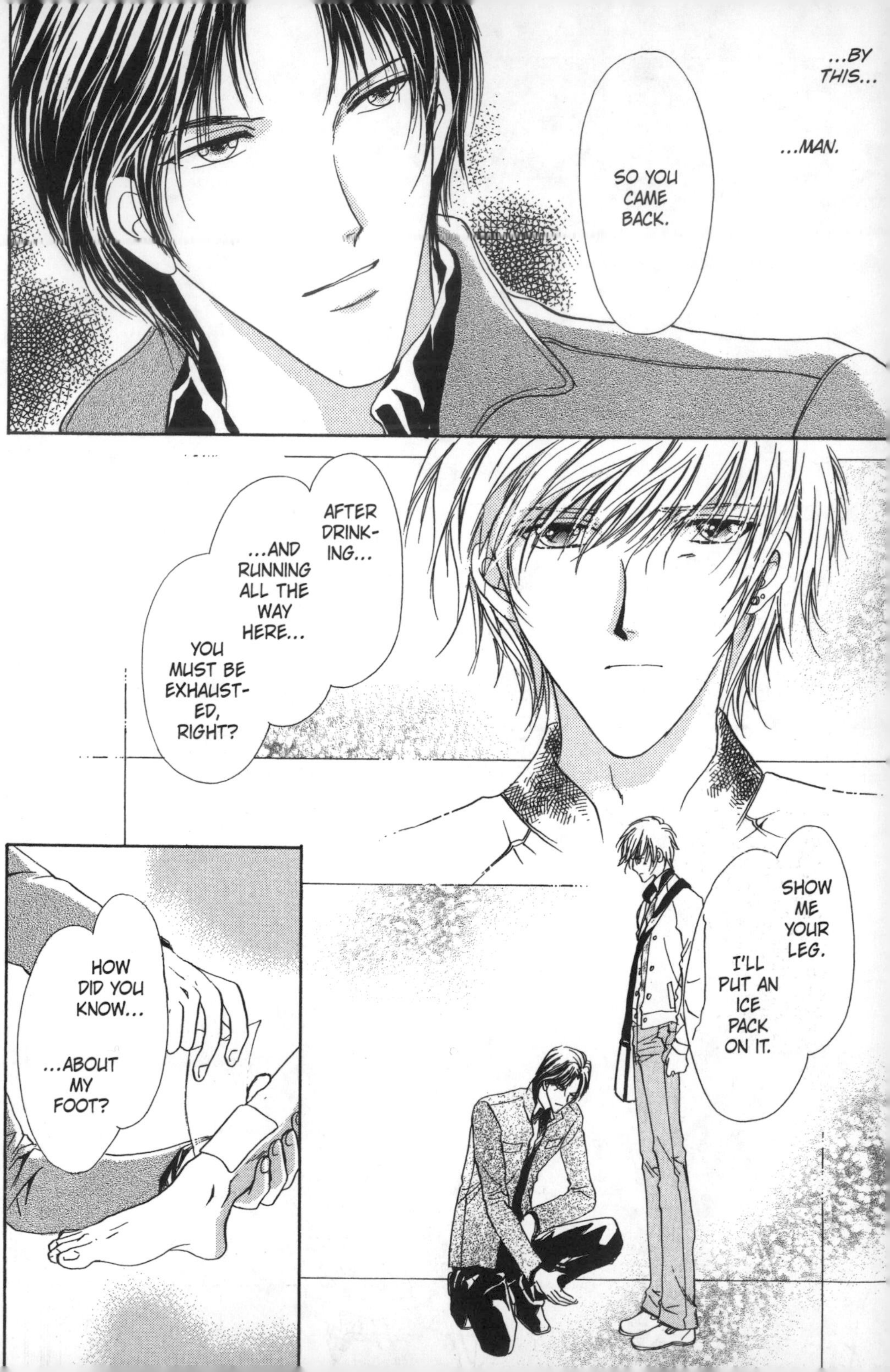
...BY THIS...
...MAN.
SO YOU CAME BACK.
AFTER DRINKING...
...AND RUNNING ALL THE WAY HERE...
YOU MUST BE EXHAUSTED, RIGHT?
SHOW ME YOUR LEG.
I'LL PUT AN ICE PACK ON IT.
HOW DID YOU KNOW...
...ABOUT MY FOOT?

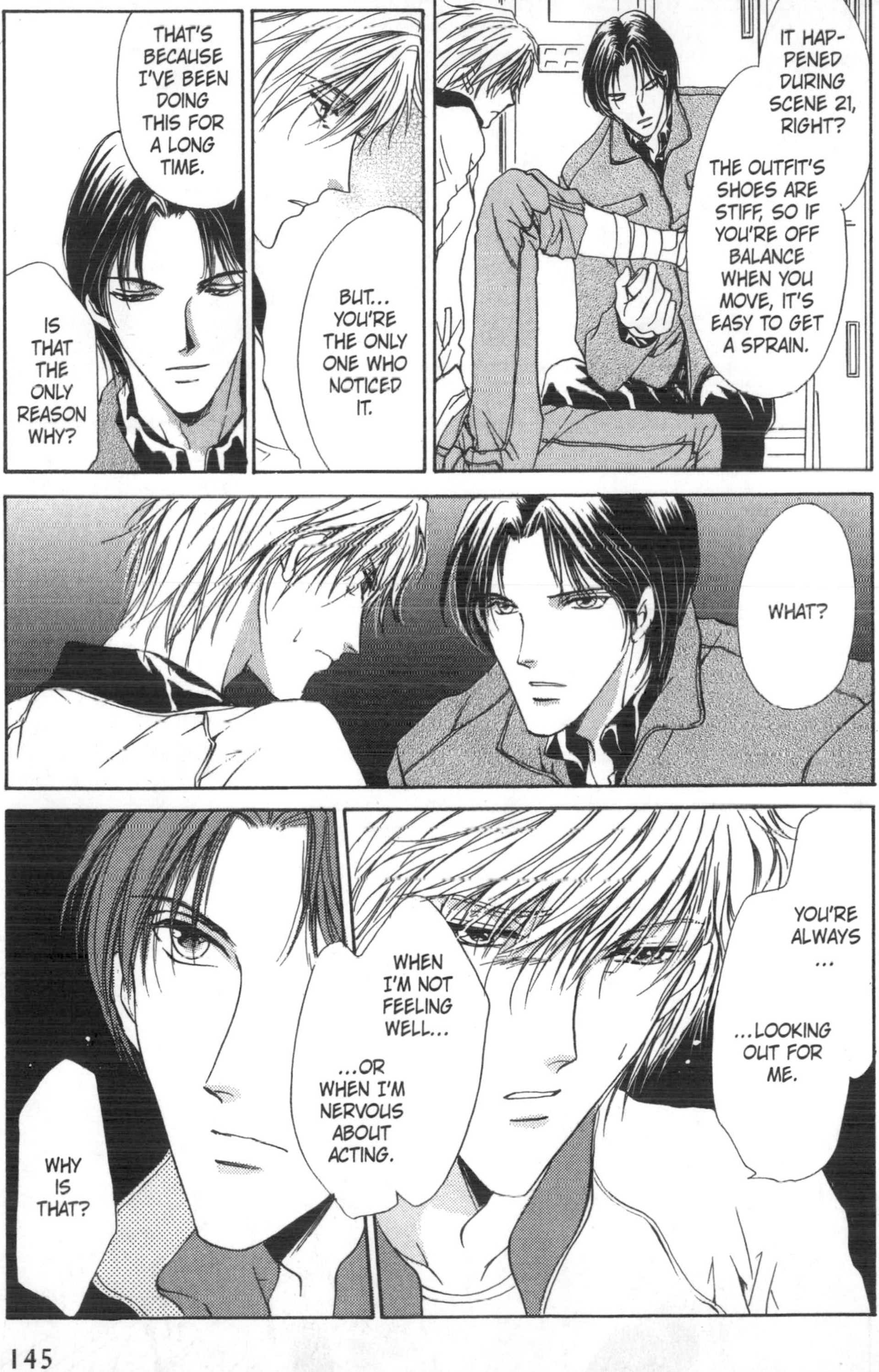
IT HAP-PENED DURING SCENE 21, RIGHT?
THE OUTFIT'S SHOES ARE STIFF, SO IF YOU'RE OFF BALANCE WHEN YOU MOVE, IT'S EASY TO GET A SPRAIN.
BUT... YOU'RE THE ONLY ONE WHO NOTICED IT.
THAT'S BECAUSE I'VE BEEN DOING THIS FOR A LONG TIME.
IS THAT THE ONLY REASON WHY?
WHAT?
YOU'RE ALWAYS ...
...LOOKING OUT FOR ME.
WHEN I'M NOT FEELING WELL...
...OR WHEN I'M NERVOUS ABOUT ACTING.
WHY IS THAT?

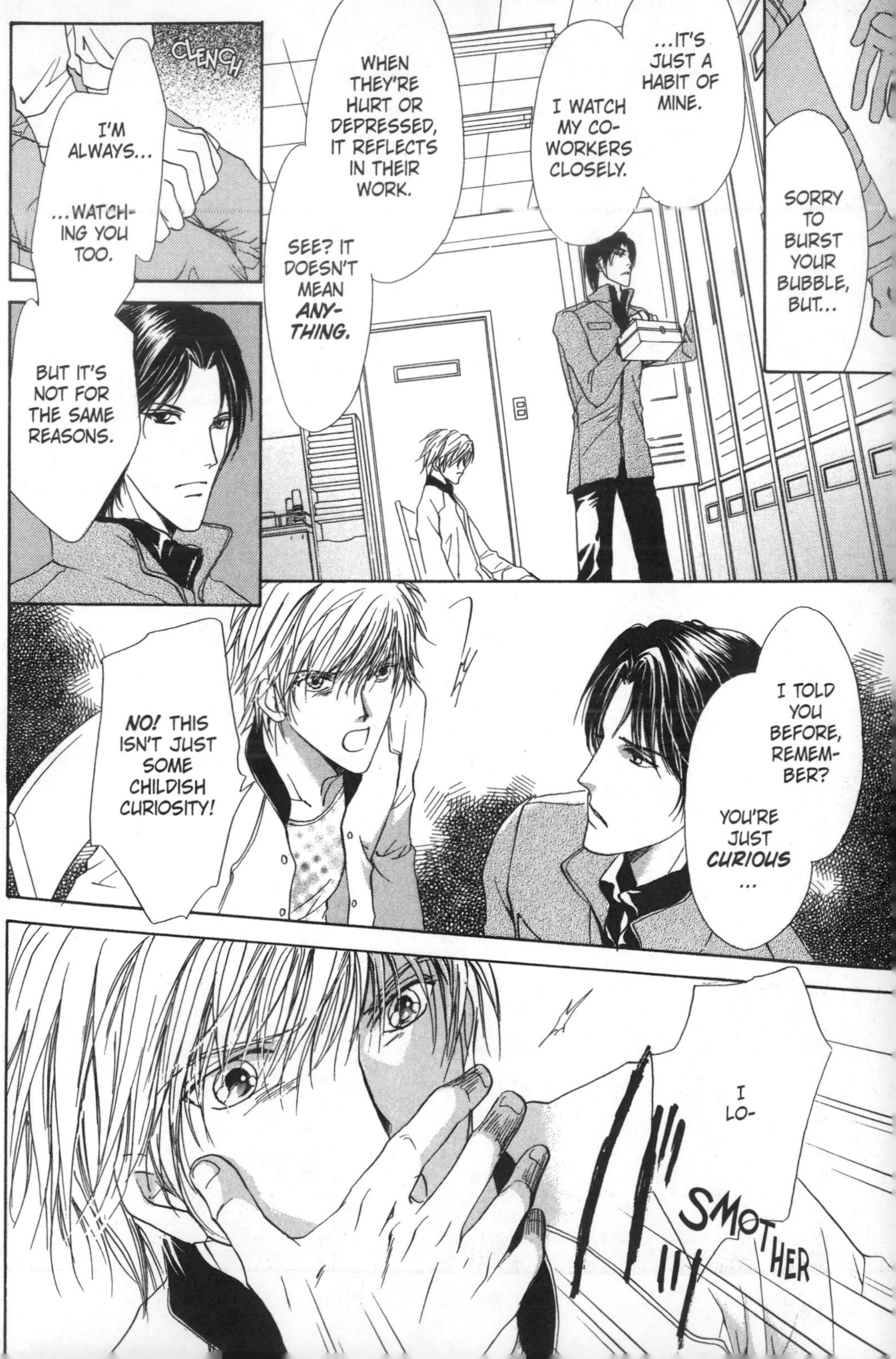
SORRY TO BURST YOUR BUBBLE, BUT...
...IT'S JUST A HABIT OF MINE.
I WATCH MY CO-WORKERS CLOSELY.
WHEN THEY'RE HURT OR DEPRESSED, IT REFLECTS IN THEIR WORK.
SEE? IT DOESN'T MEAN ANYTHING.
CLENCH
I'M ALWAYS...
...WATCHING YOU TOO.
BUT IT'S NOT FOR THE SAME REASONS.
I TOLD YOU BEFORE, REMEMBER?
YOU'RE JUST CURIOUS...
NO! THIS ISN'T JUST SOME CHILDISH CURIOSITY!
I LO-
SMOTHER

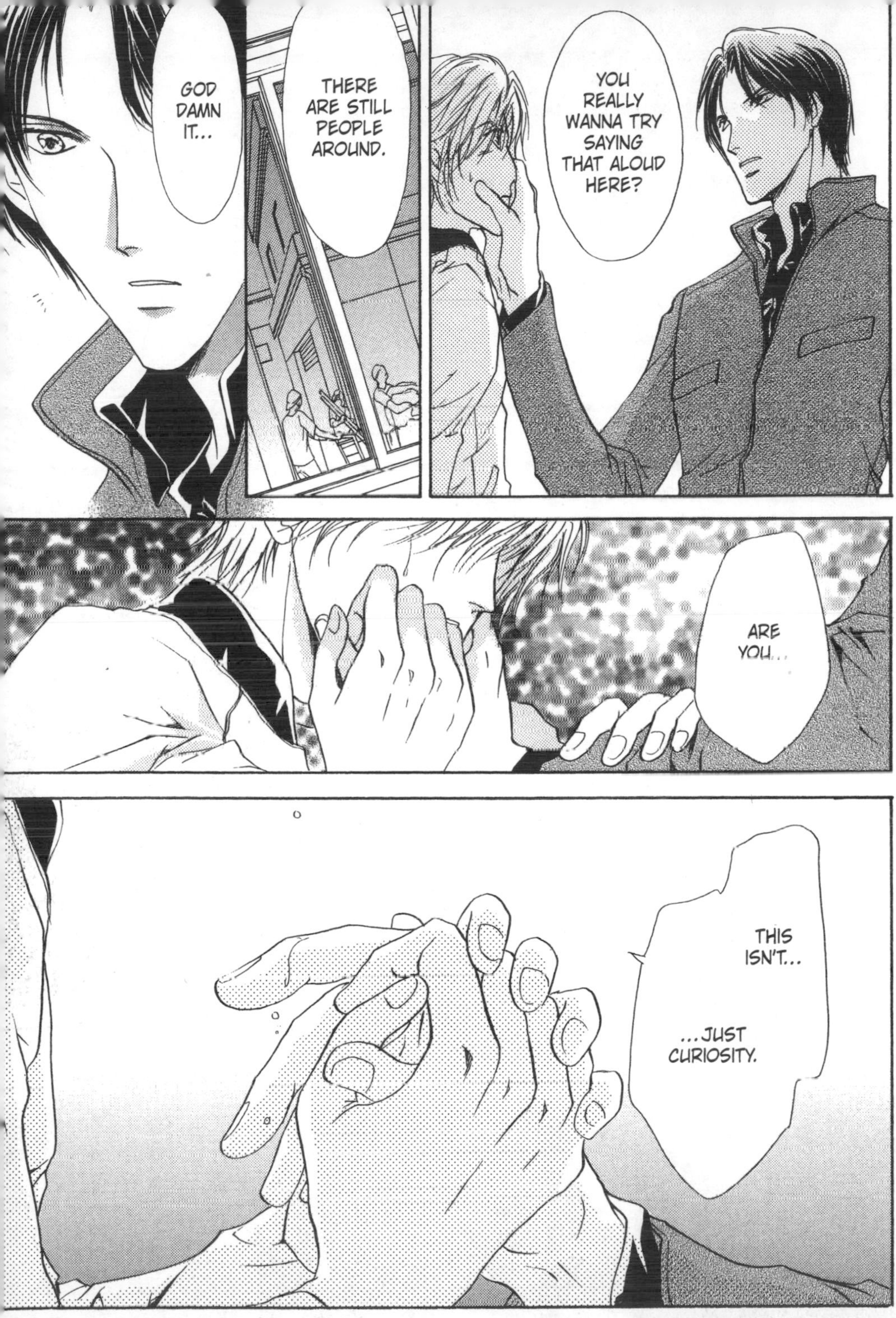
YOU REALLY WANNA TRY SAYING THAT ALOUD HERE?
THERE ARE STILL PEOPLE AROUND.
GOD DAMN IT...
ARE YOU...
THIS ISN'T...
...JUST CURIOSITY.

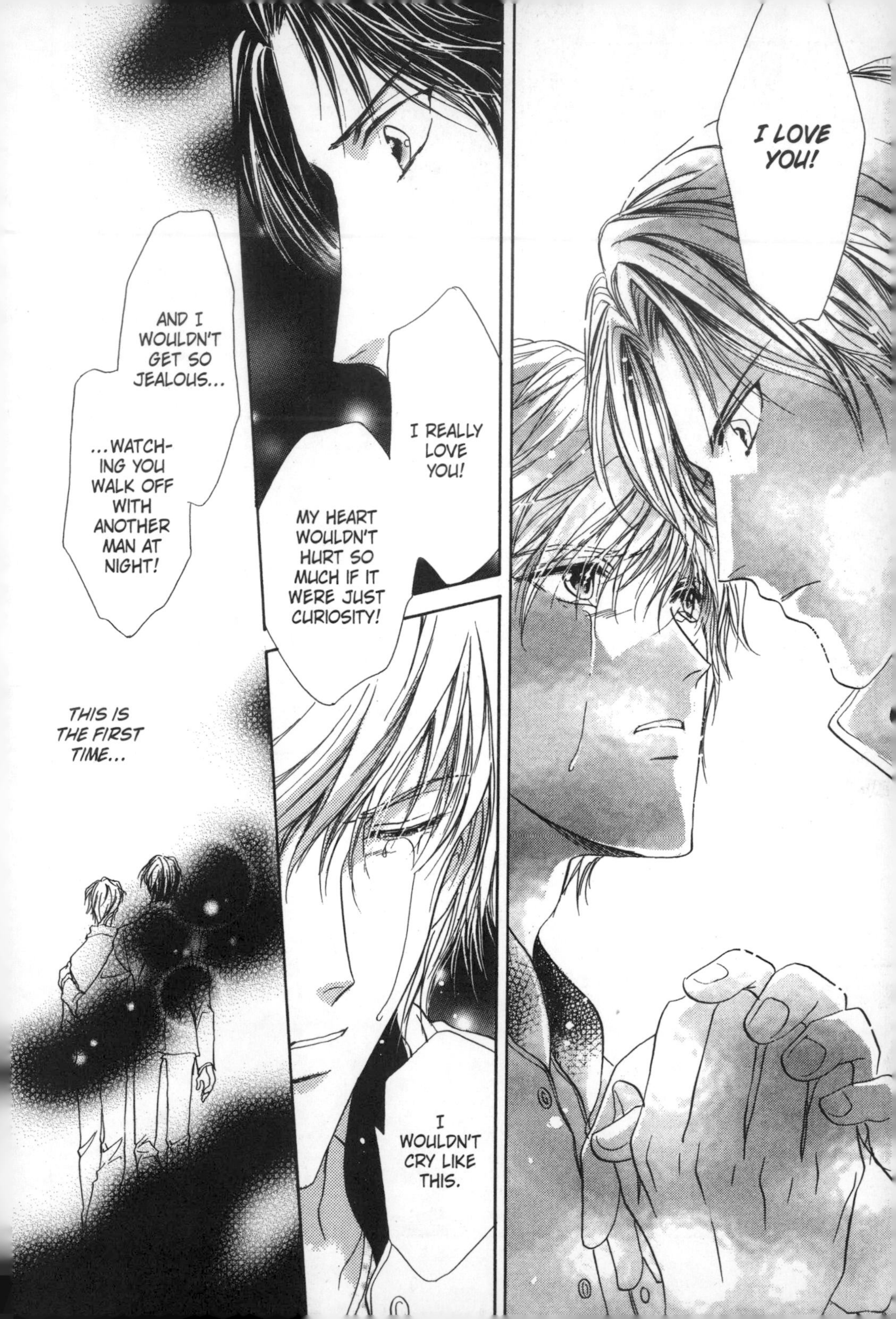
I LOVE YOU!
I REALLY LOVE YOU!
MY HEART WOULDN'T HURT SO MUCH IF IT WERE JUST CURIOSITY!
I WOULDN'T CRY LIKE THIS.
AND I WOULDN'T GET SO JEALOUS...
...WATCHING-ING YOU WALK OFF WITH ANOTHER MAN AT NIGHT!
THIS IS THE FIRST TIME...

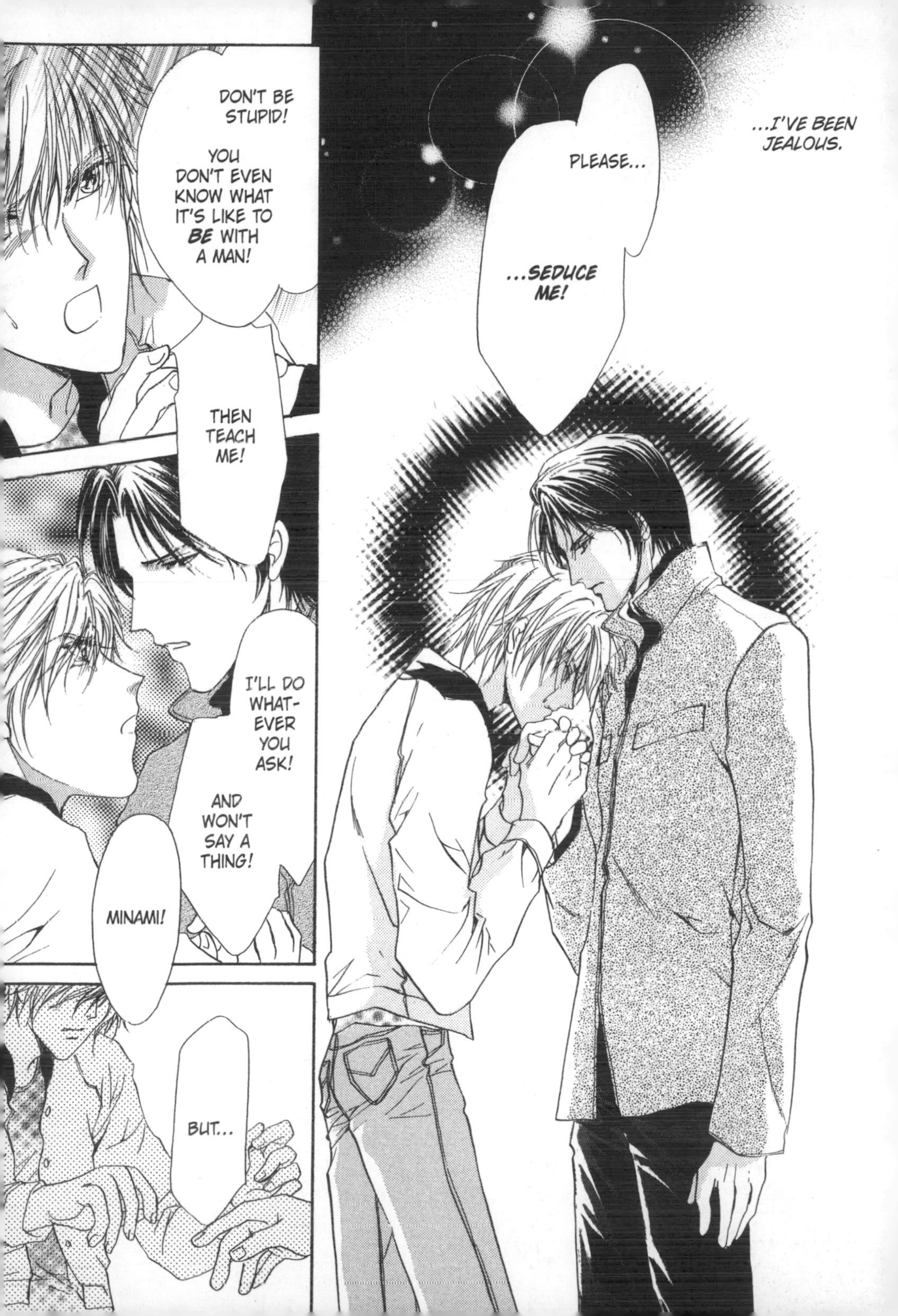
...I'VE BEEN JEALOUS.
PLEASE...
...SEDUCE ME!
DON'T BE STUPID!
YOU DON'T EVEN KNOW WHAT IT'S LIKE TO BE WITH A MAN!
THEN TEACH ME!
I'LL DO WHAT-EVER YOU ASK!
AND WON'T SAY A THING!
MINAMI!
BUT...

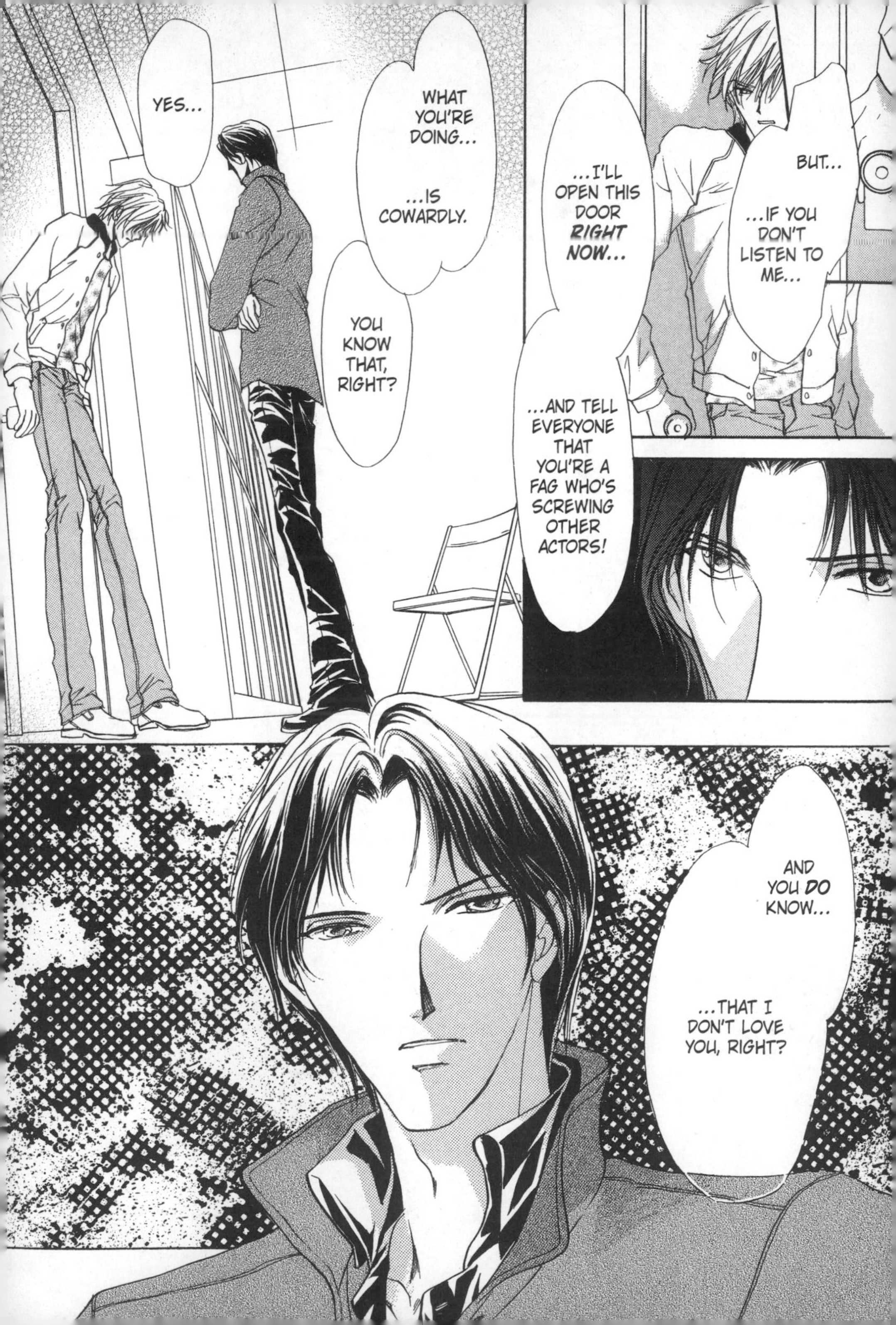
BUT...
...IF YOU DON'T LISTEN TO ME...
...I'LL OPEN THIS DOOR **RIGHT NOW**...
...AND TELL EVERYONE THAT YOU'RE A FAG WHO'S SCREWING OTHER ACTORS!
WHAT YOU'RE DOING...
...IS COWARDLY.
YOU KNOW THAT, RIGHT?
YES...
AND YOU **DO** KNOW...
...THAT I DON'T LOVE YOU, RIGHT?

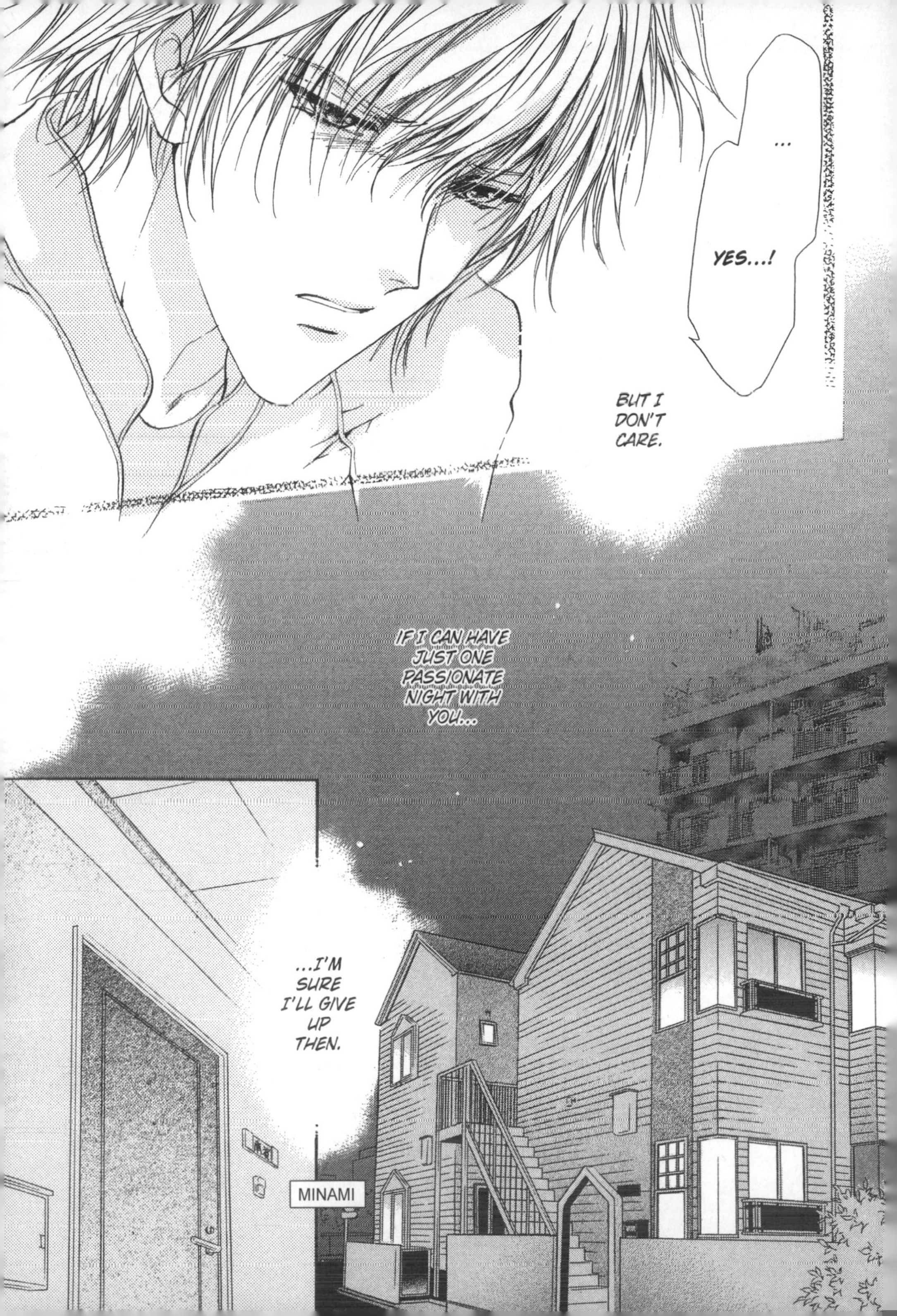
...
YES...!
BUT I DON'T CARE.
IF I CAN HAVE JUST ONE PASSIONATE NIGHT WITH YOU...
...I'M SURE I'LL GIVE UP THEN.
MINAMI

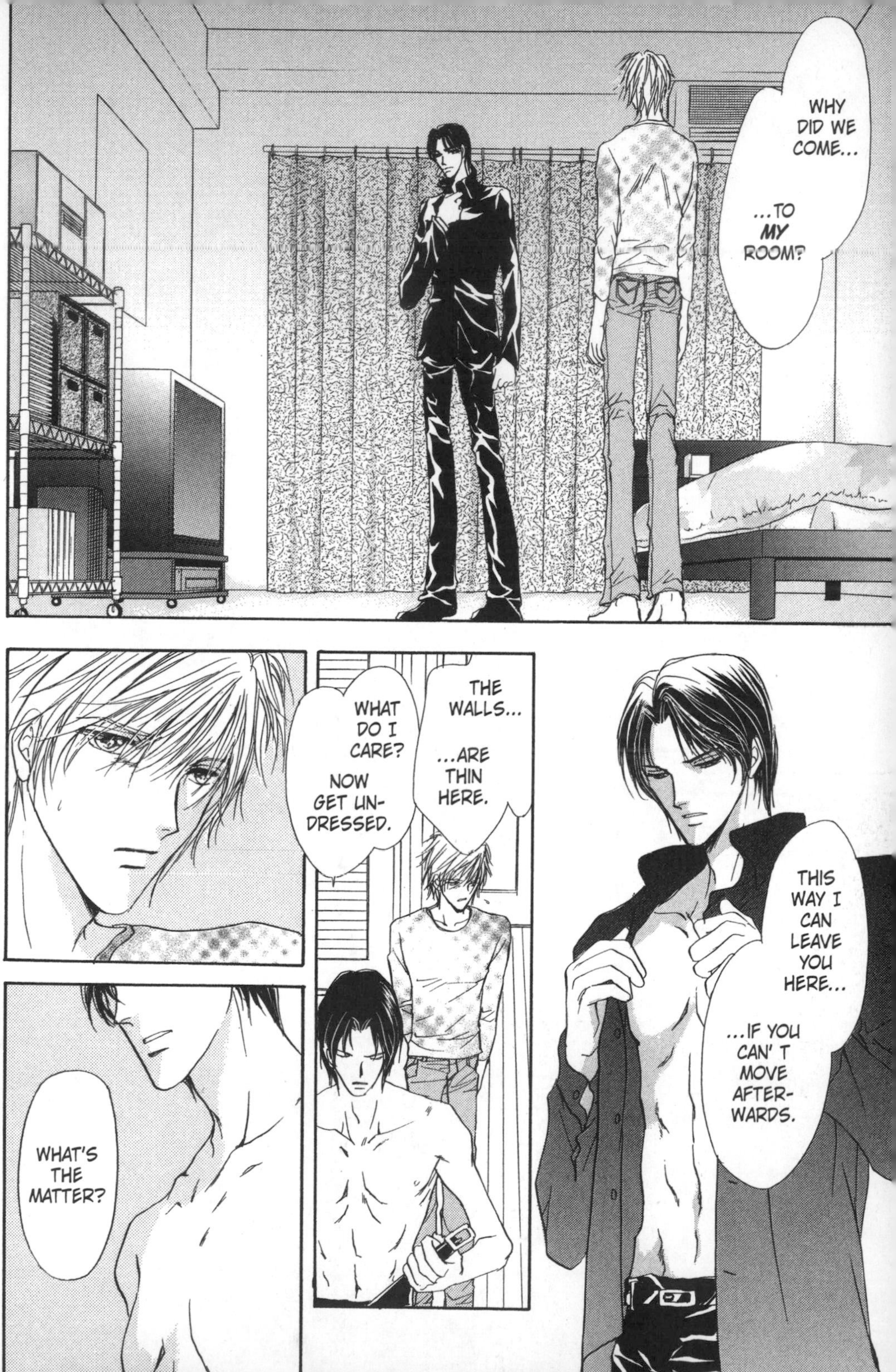
WHY DID WE COME...
...TO MY ROOM?
THIS WAY I CAN LEAVE YOU HERE...
...IF YOU CAN'T MOVE AFTER-WARDS.
THE WALLS...
...ARE THIN HERE.
WHAT DO I CARE?
NOW GET UN-DRESSED.
WHAT'S THE MATTER?

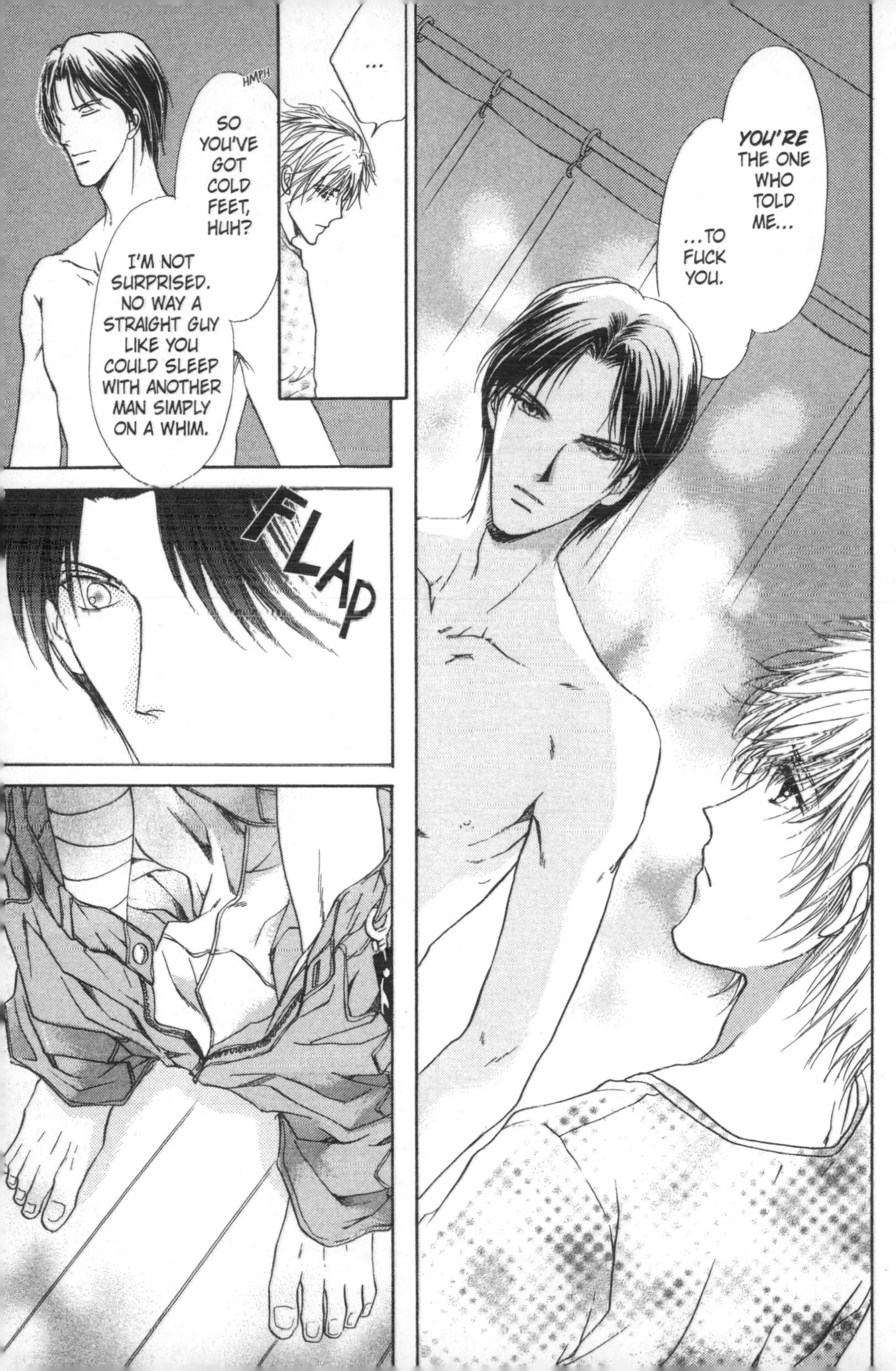
YOU'RE THE ONE WHO TOLD ME...
...TO FUCK YOU.
...
HMPH
SO YOU'VE GOT COLD FEET, HUH?
I'M NOT SURPRISED. NO WAY A STRAIGHT GUY LIKE YOU COULD SLEEP WITH ANOTHER MAN SIMPLY ON A WHIM.
FLAP

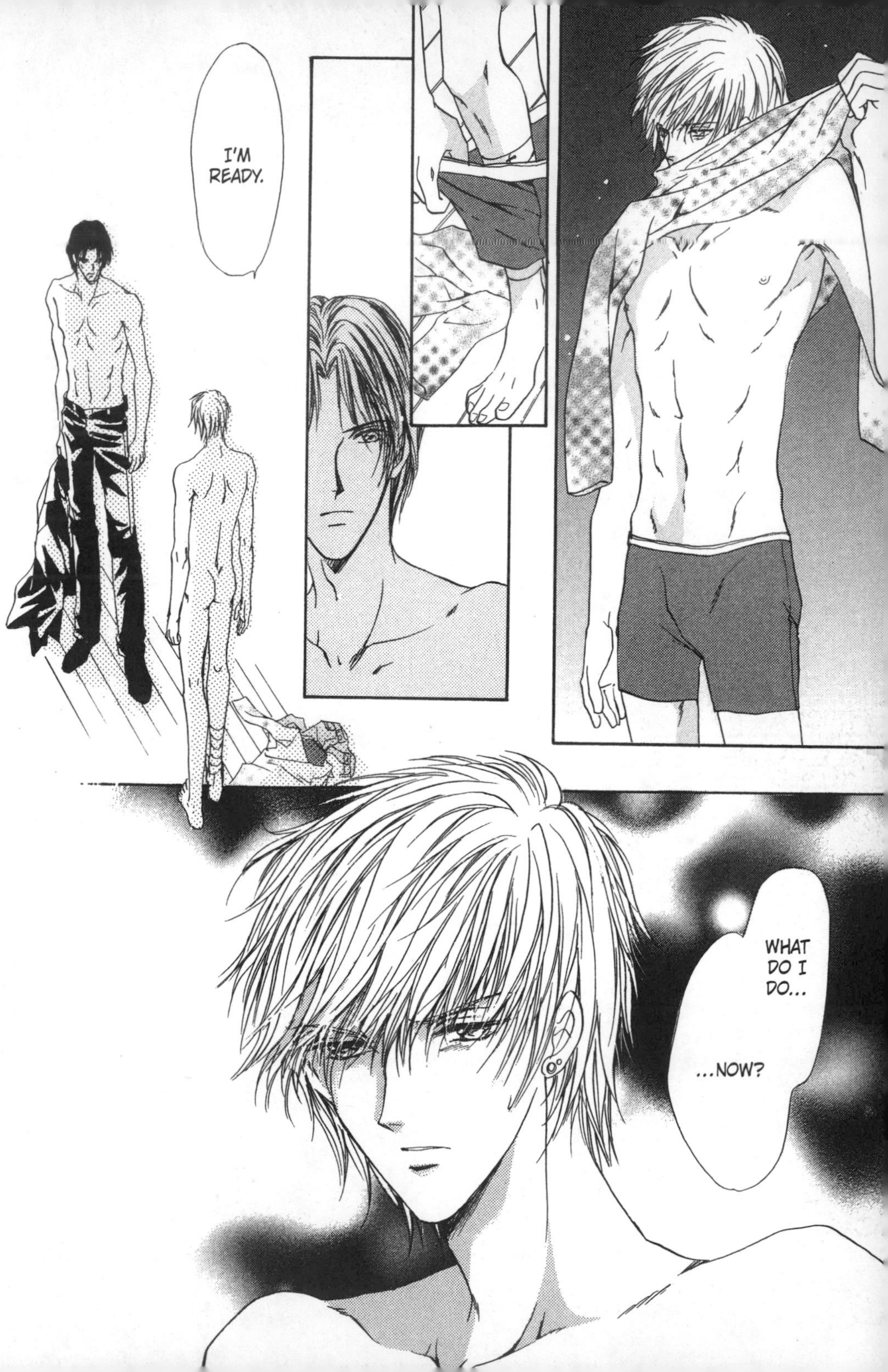
I'M READY.
WHAT DO I DO...
...NOW?

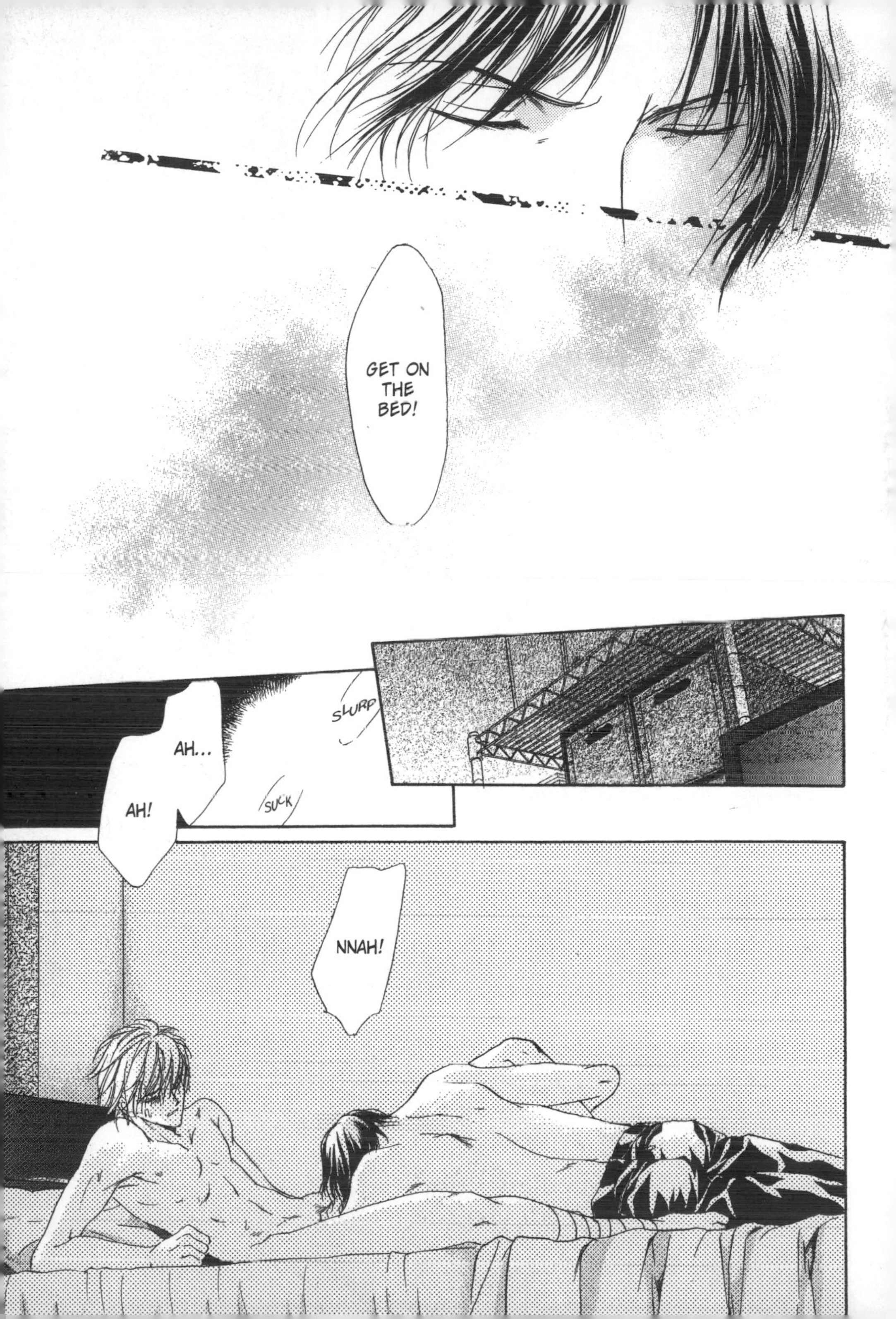
GET ON THE BED!
SLURP
AH... AH!
SUCK
NNAH!

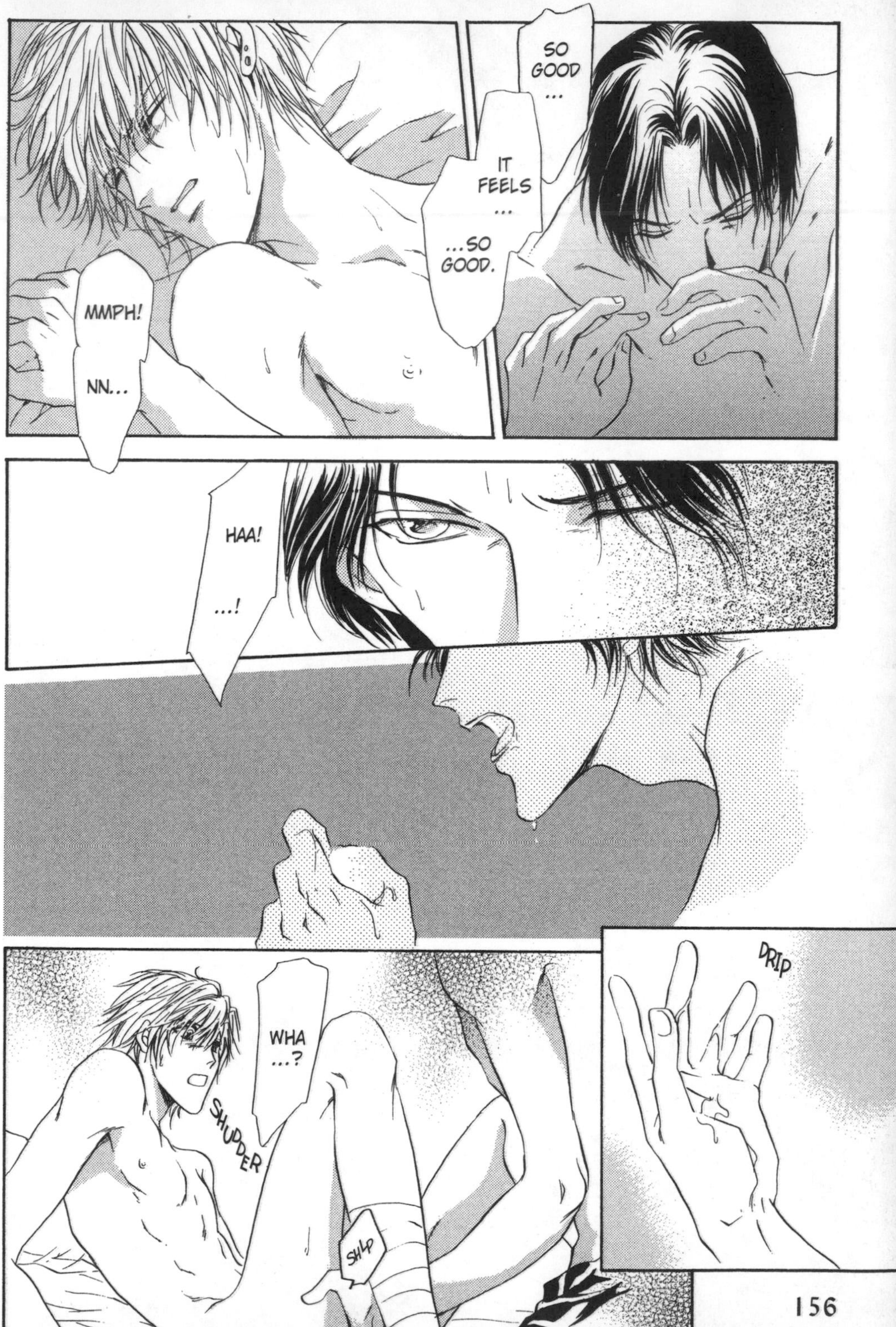
SO GOOD ...
IT FEELS ...
...SO GOOD.
MMPH!
NN...
HAA!
...!
DRIP
WHA ...?
SHUDDER
SHLP

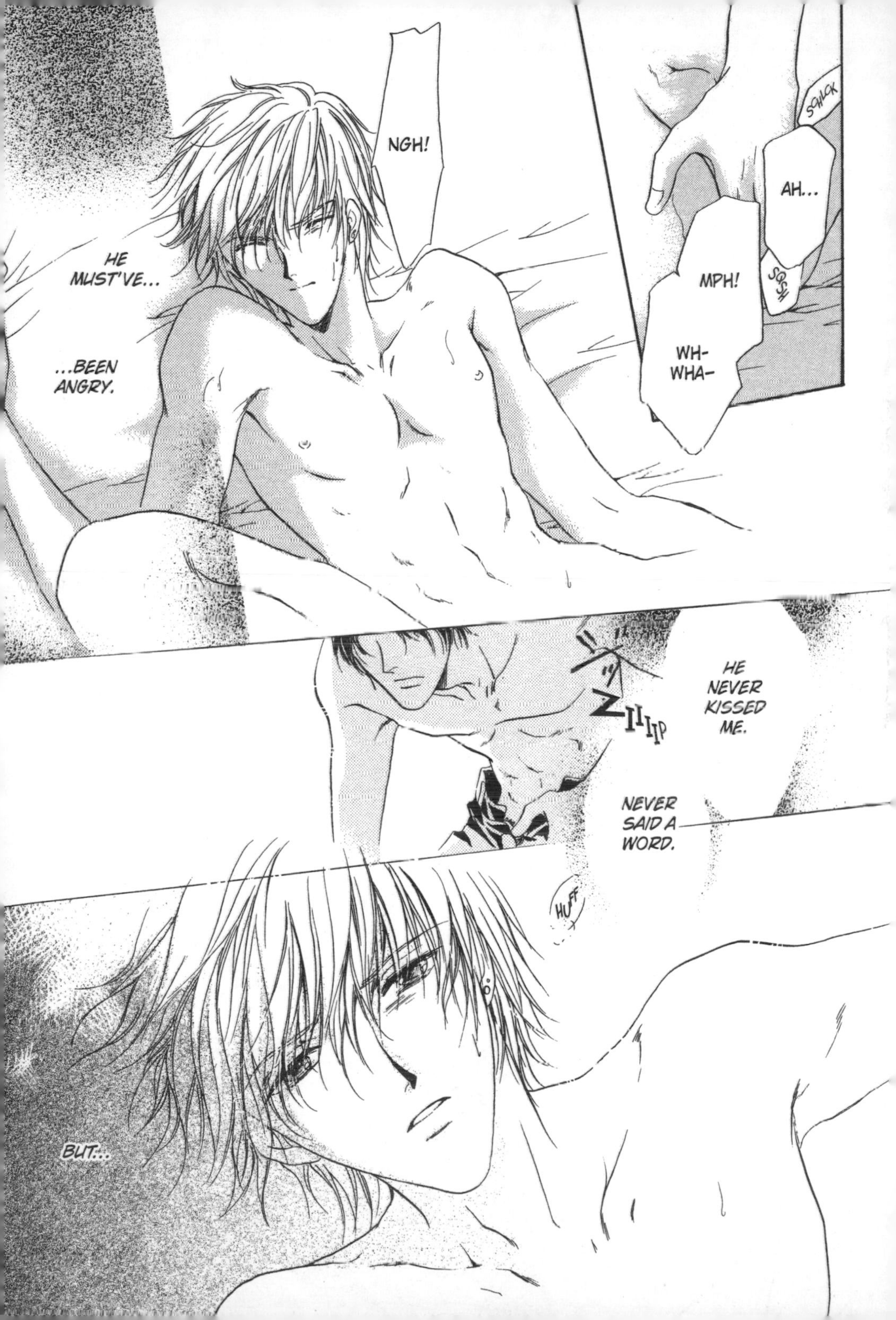
SCHLCK
AH...
MPH!
SQSH
WH-
WHA-
NGH!
HE MUST'VE...
...BEEN ANGRY.
ZIIIP
HE NEVER KISSED ME.
NEVER SAID A WORD.
HUFF
BUT...

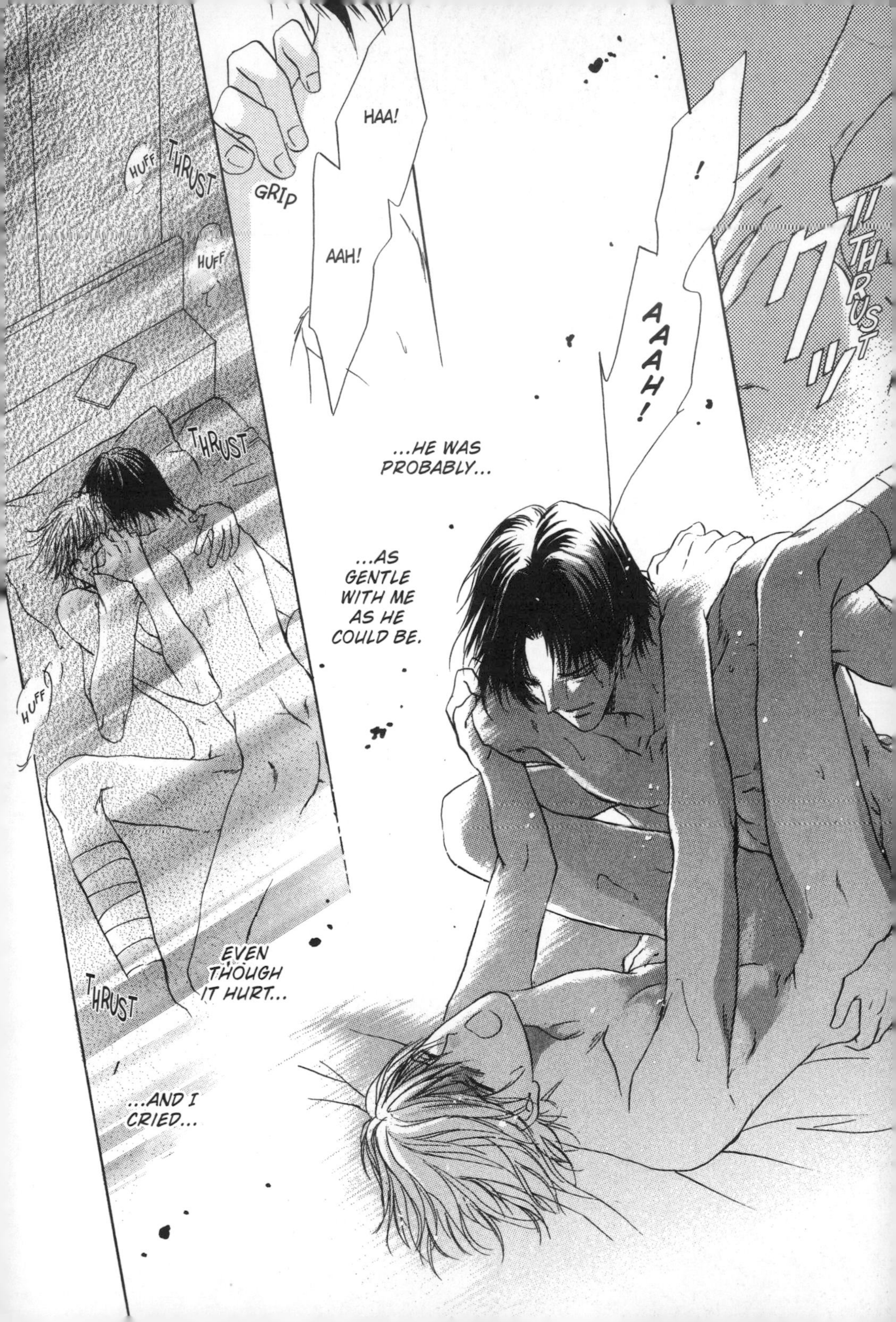
クッ
THRUST
!
AAAH!
HAA!
GRIP
AAH!
...HE WAS PROBABLY...
...AS GENTLE WITH ME AS HE COULD BE.
HUFF
THRUST
HUFF
THRUST
HUFF
THRUST
EVEN THOUGH IT HURT...
...AND I CRIED...

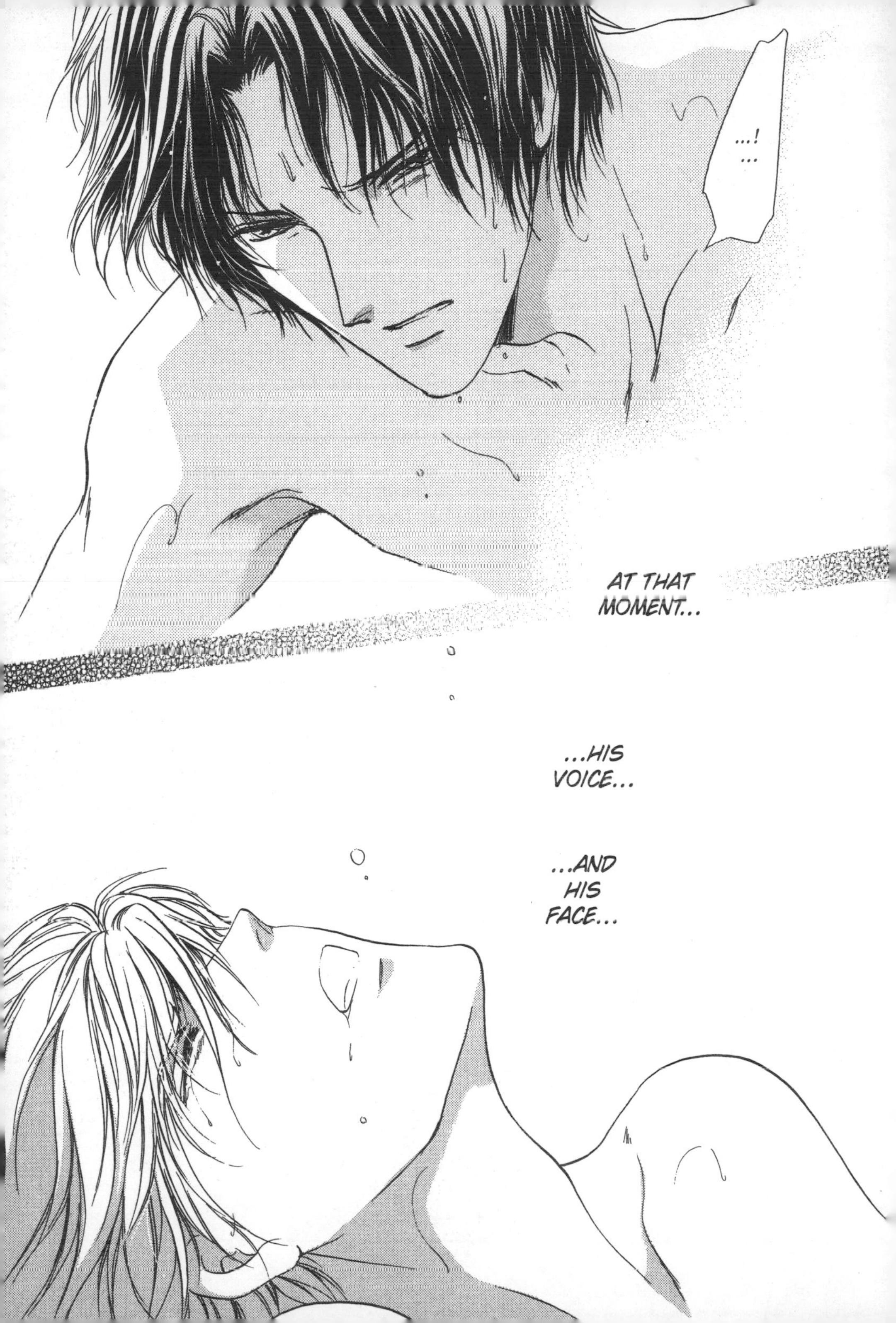
...!
...
AT THAT MOMENT...
...HIS VOICE...
...AND HIS FACE...

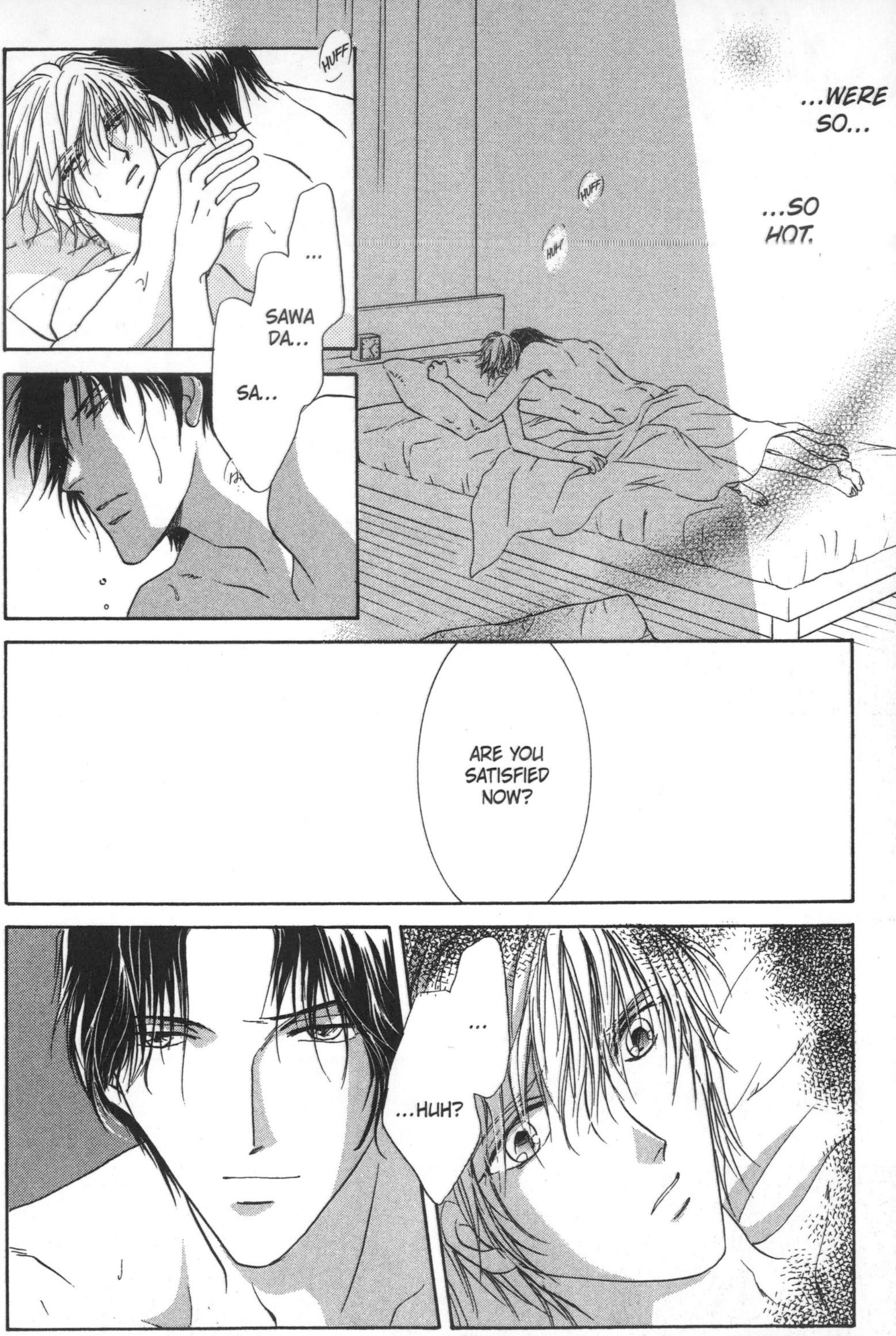
...WERE SO...
...SO HOT.
HUFF
HUH
HUFF
...
SAWA DA...
SA...
ARE YOU SATISFIED NOW?
...
...HUH?

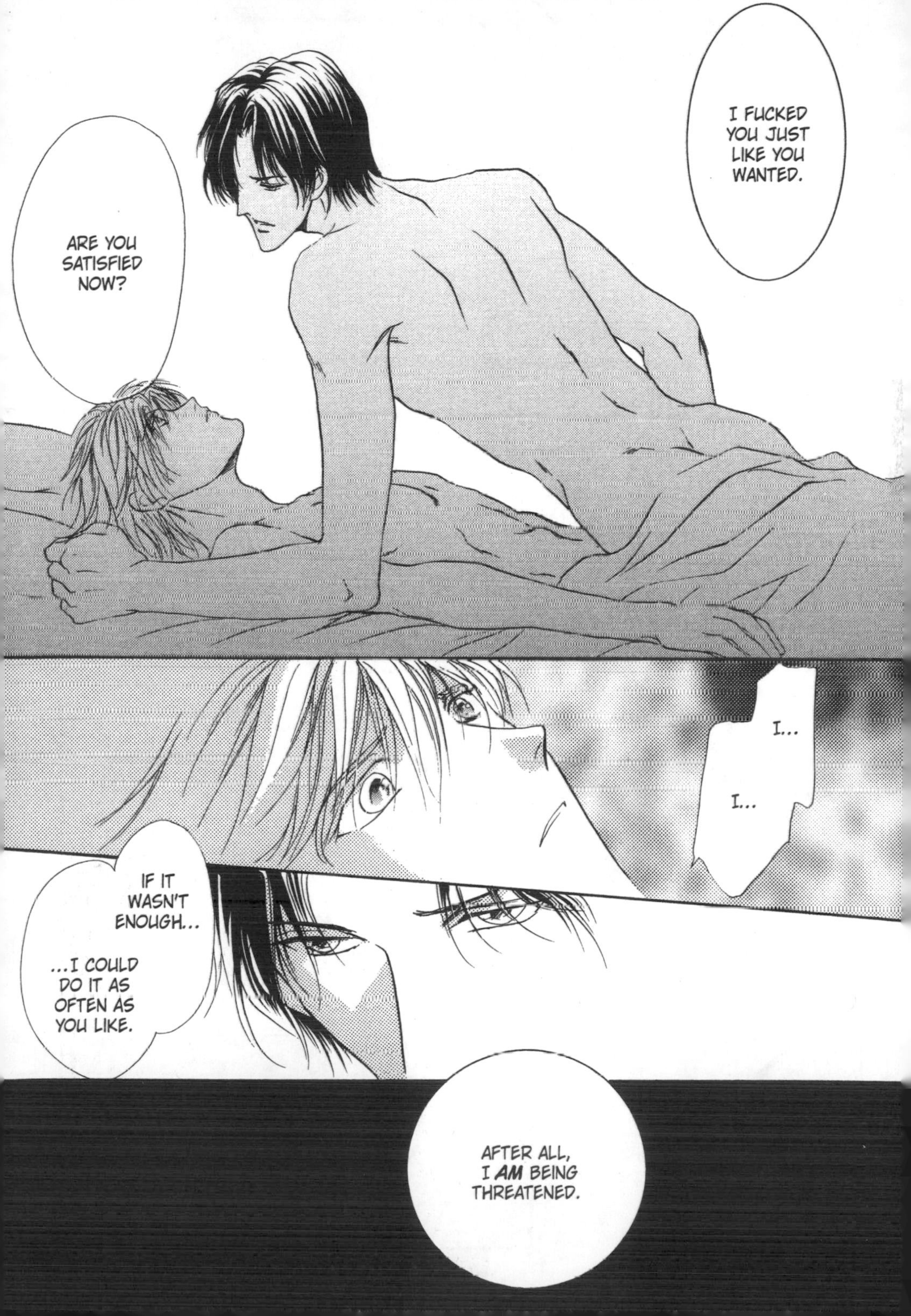
I FUCKED YOU JUST LIKE YOU WANTED.
ARE YOU SATISFIED NOW?
I...
I...
IF IT WASN'T ENOUGH...
...I COULD DO IT AS OFTEN AS YOU LIKE.
AFTER ALL, I *AM* BEING THREATENED.

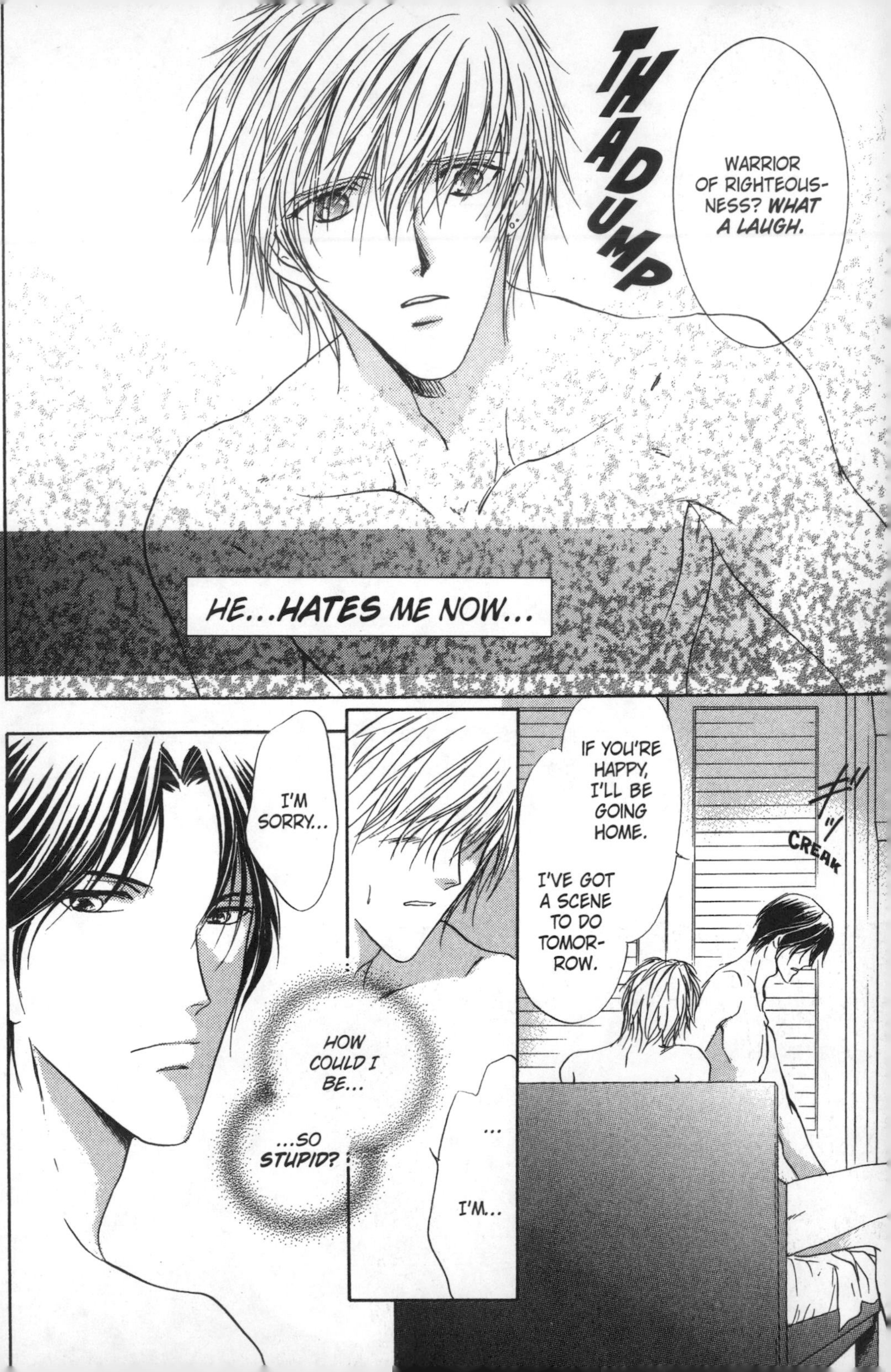
THADUMP
WARRIOR OF RIGHTEOUSNESS? WHAT A LAUGH.
HE...HATES ME NOW...
CREAK
IF YOU'RE HAPPY, I'LL BE GOING HOME.
I'VE GOT A SCENE TO DO TOMORROW.
I'M SORRY...
...
I'M...
HOW COULD I BE...
...SO STUPID?

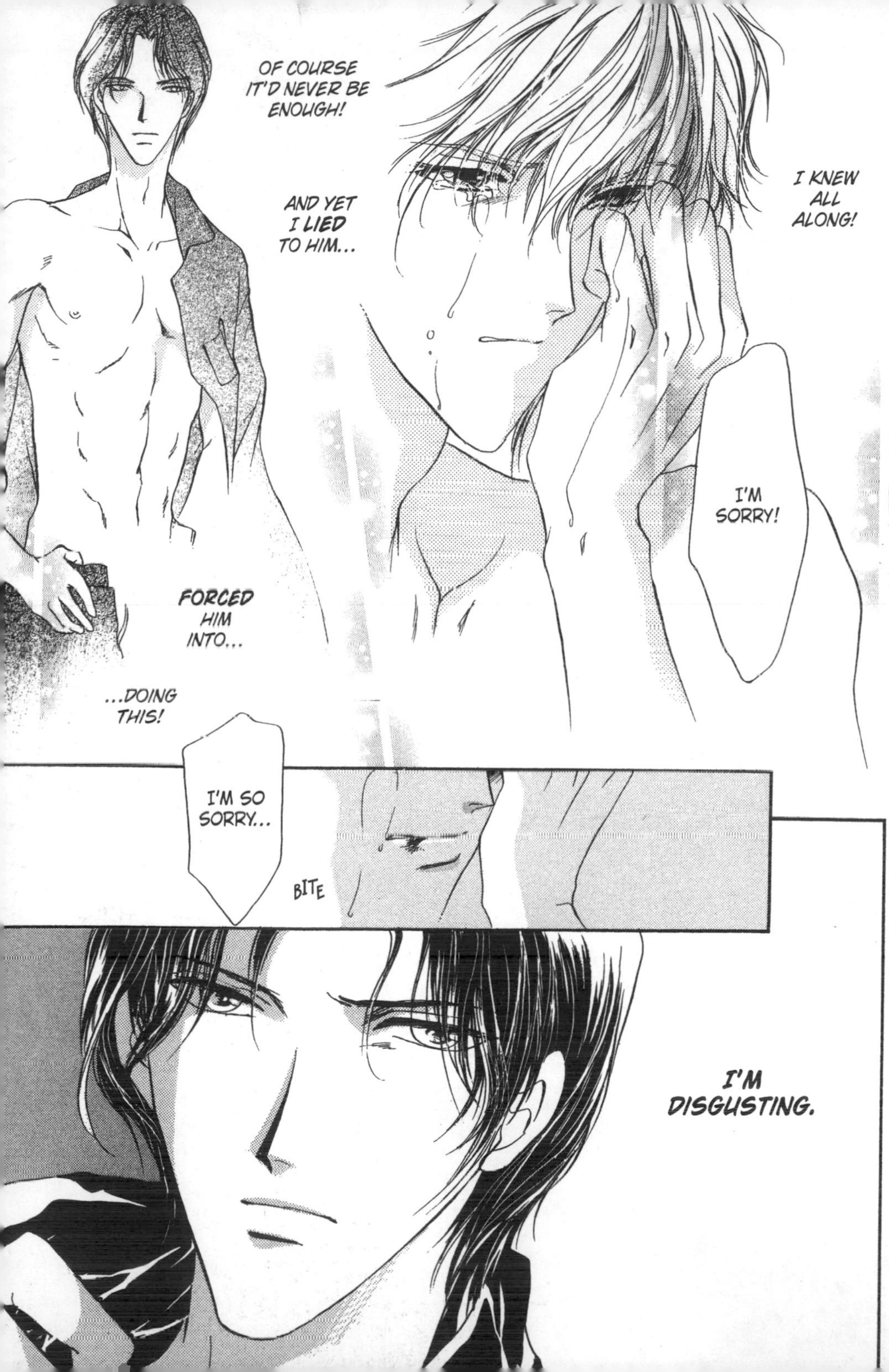
I KNEW ALL ALONG!
OF COURSE IT'D NEVER BE ENOUGH!
AND YET I **LIED** TO HIM...
FORCED HIM INTO...
...DOING THIS!
I'M SORRY!
I'M SO SORRY...
BITE
I'M DISGUSTING.

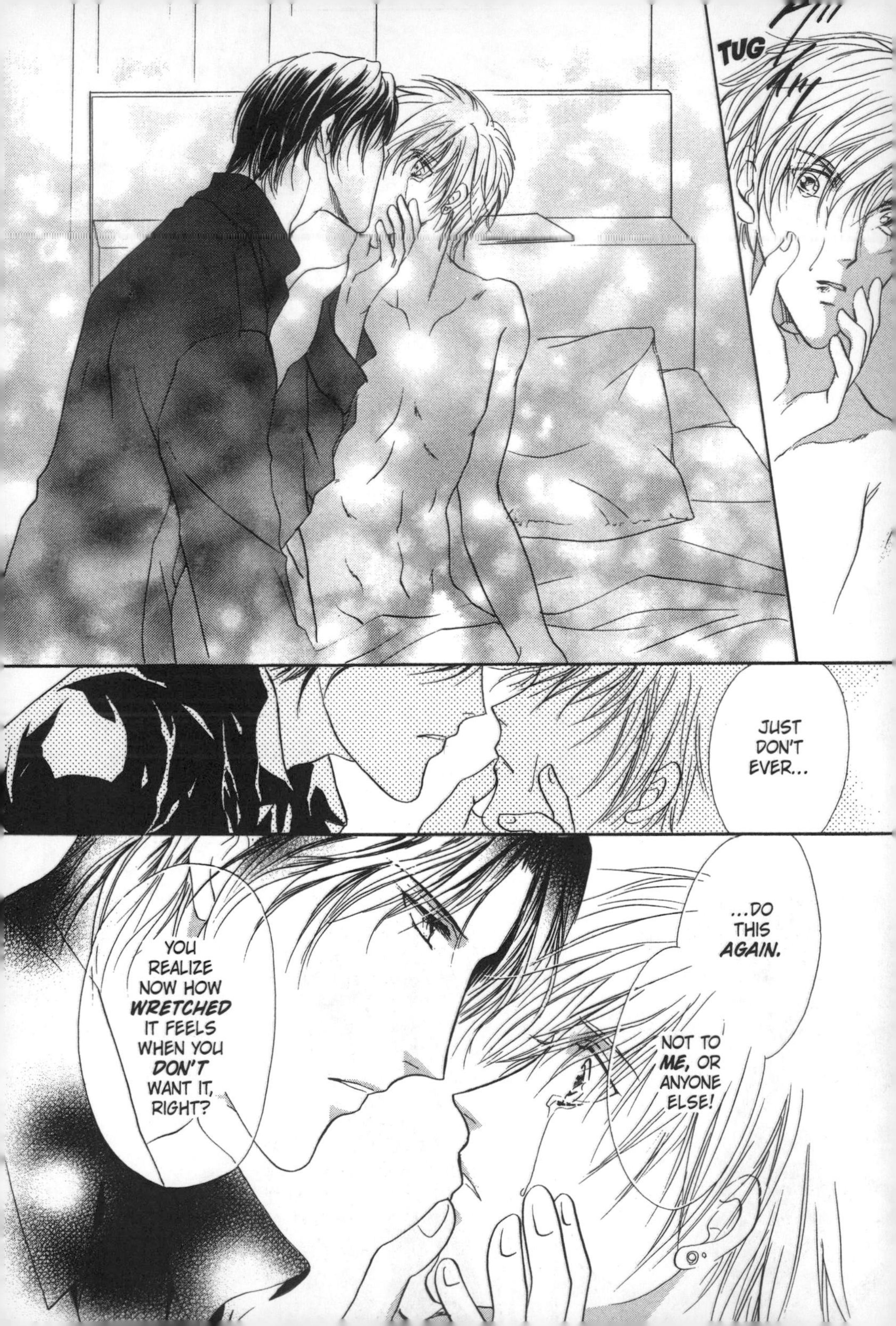
TUG
JUST DON'T EVER...
...DO THIS AGAIN.
NOT TO ME, OR ANYONE ELSE!
YOU REALIZE NOW HOW WRETCHED IT FEELS WHEN YOU DON'T WANT IT, RIGHT?

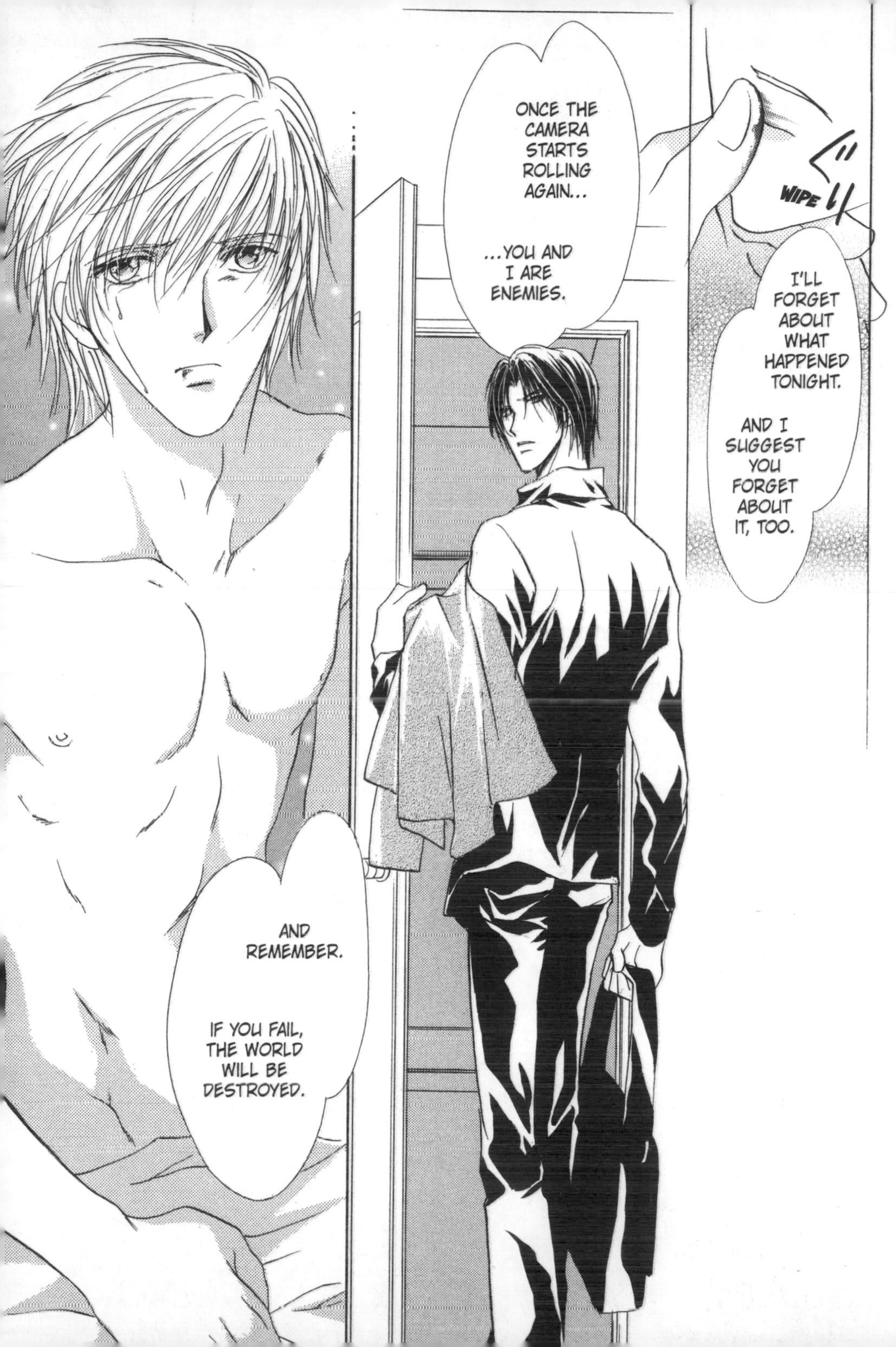
WIPE
I'LL FORGET ABOUT WHAT HAPPENED TONIGHT.
AND I SUGGEST YOU FORGET ABOUT IT, TOO.
ONCE THE CAMERA STARTS ROLLING AGAIN...
...YOU AND I ARE ENEMIES.
AND REMEMBER.
IF YOU FAIL, THE WORLD WILL BE DESTROYED.

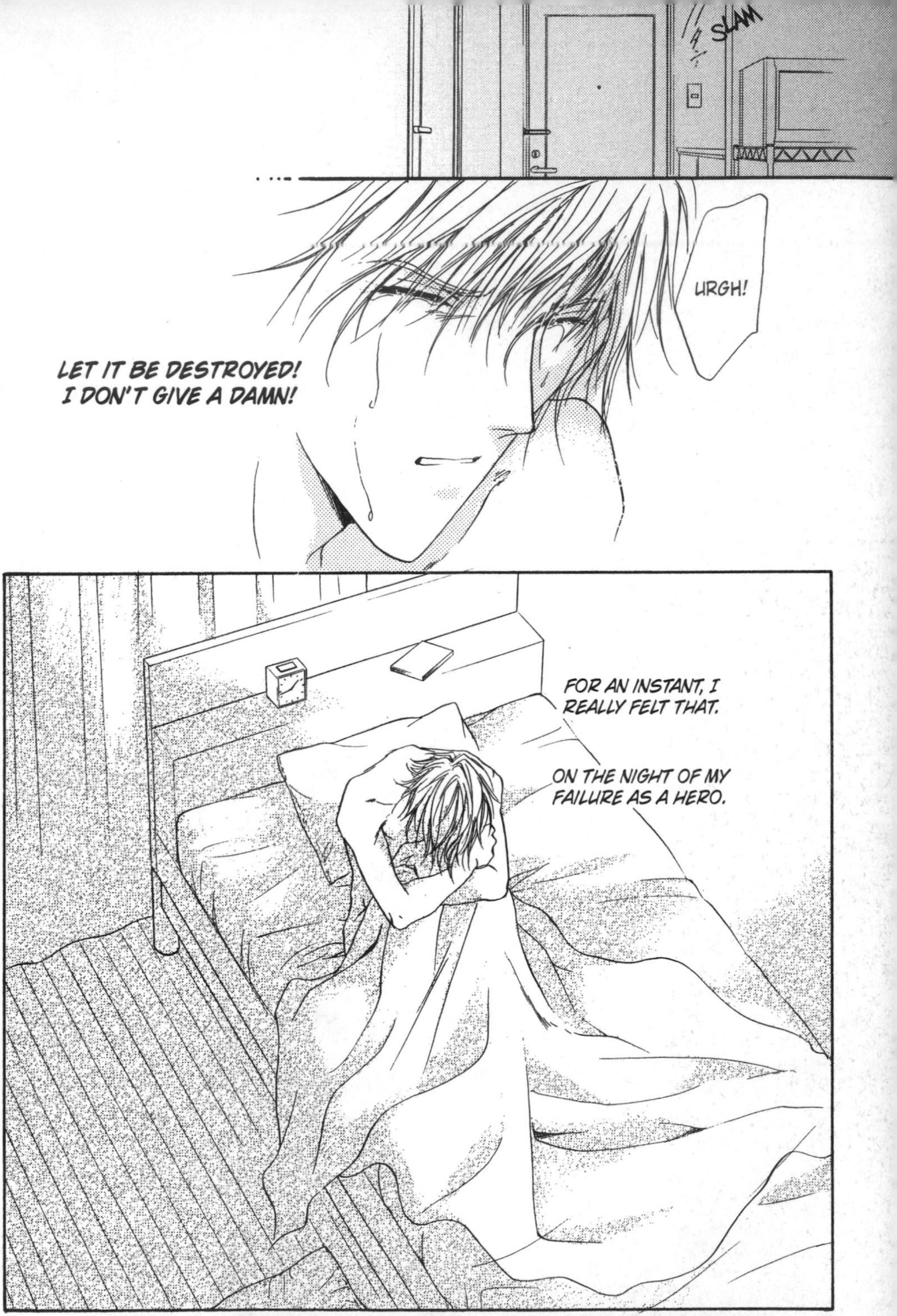
SLAM
URGH!
LET IT BE DESTROYED! I DON'T GIVE A DAMN!
FOR AN INSTANT, I REALLY FELT THAT.
ON THE NIGHT OF MY FAILURE AS A HERO.

HERO · HEEL —英雄と悪漢— HERO & VILLIAN Scene.3/END

KAZUOMI SAWADA

HERO HEEL

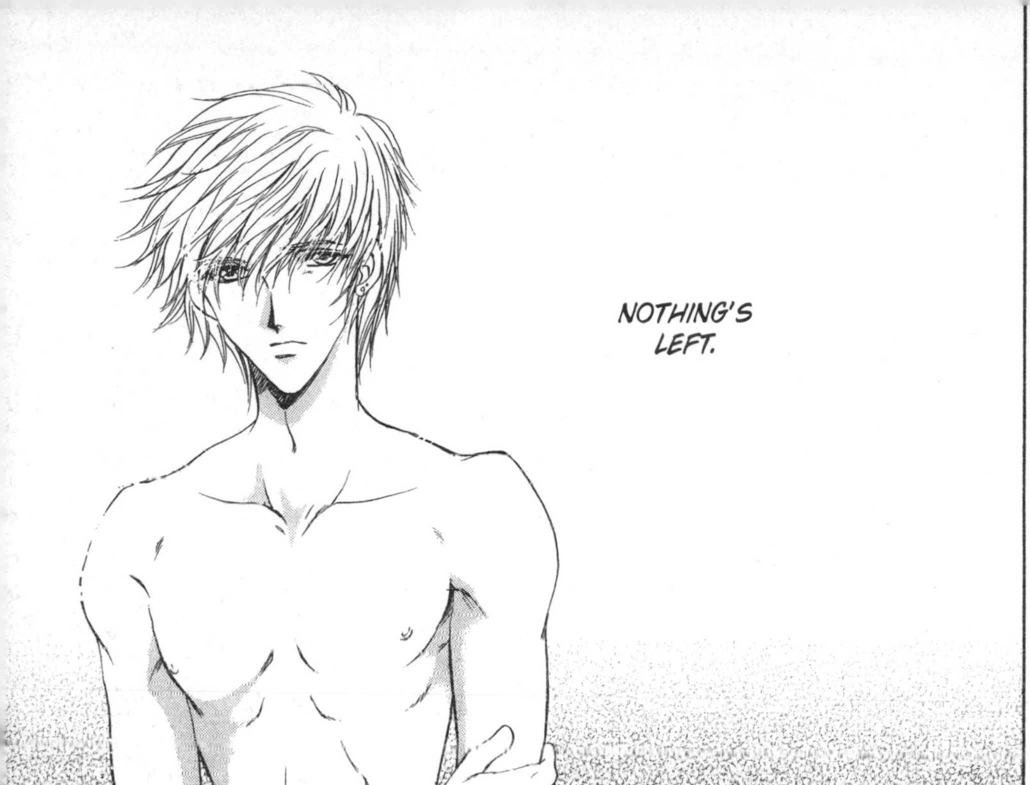
NOTHING'S LEFT.
PAIN

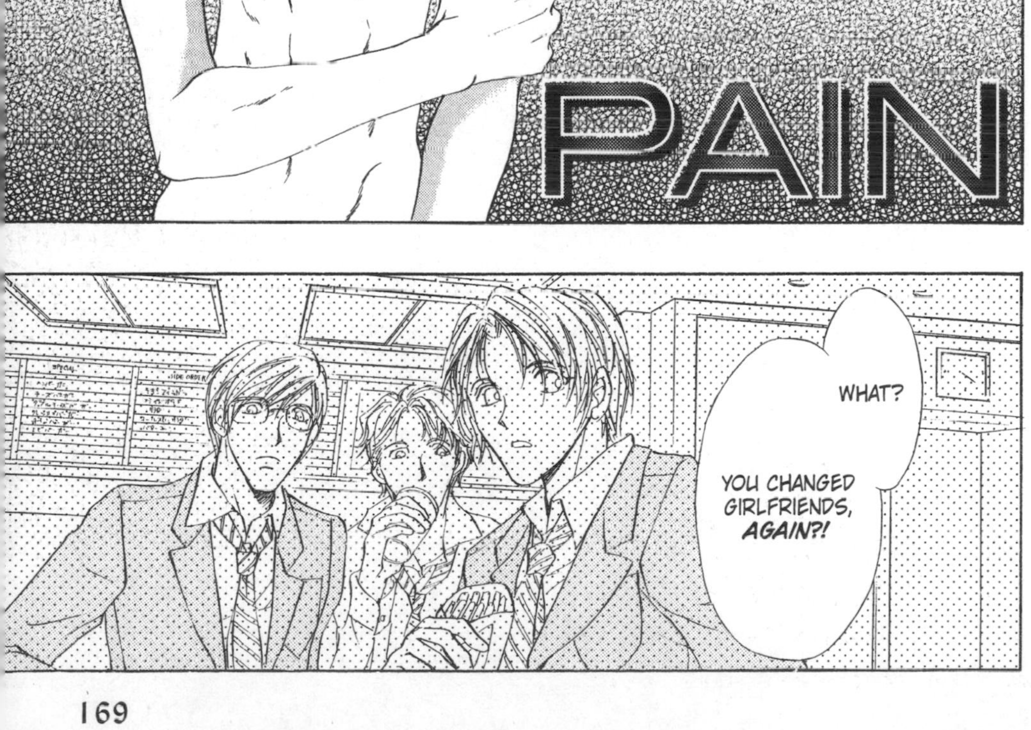
WHAT?
YOU CHANGED GIRLFRIENDS, AGAIN?!

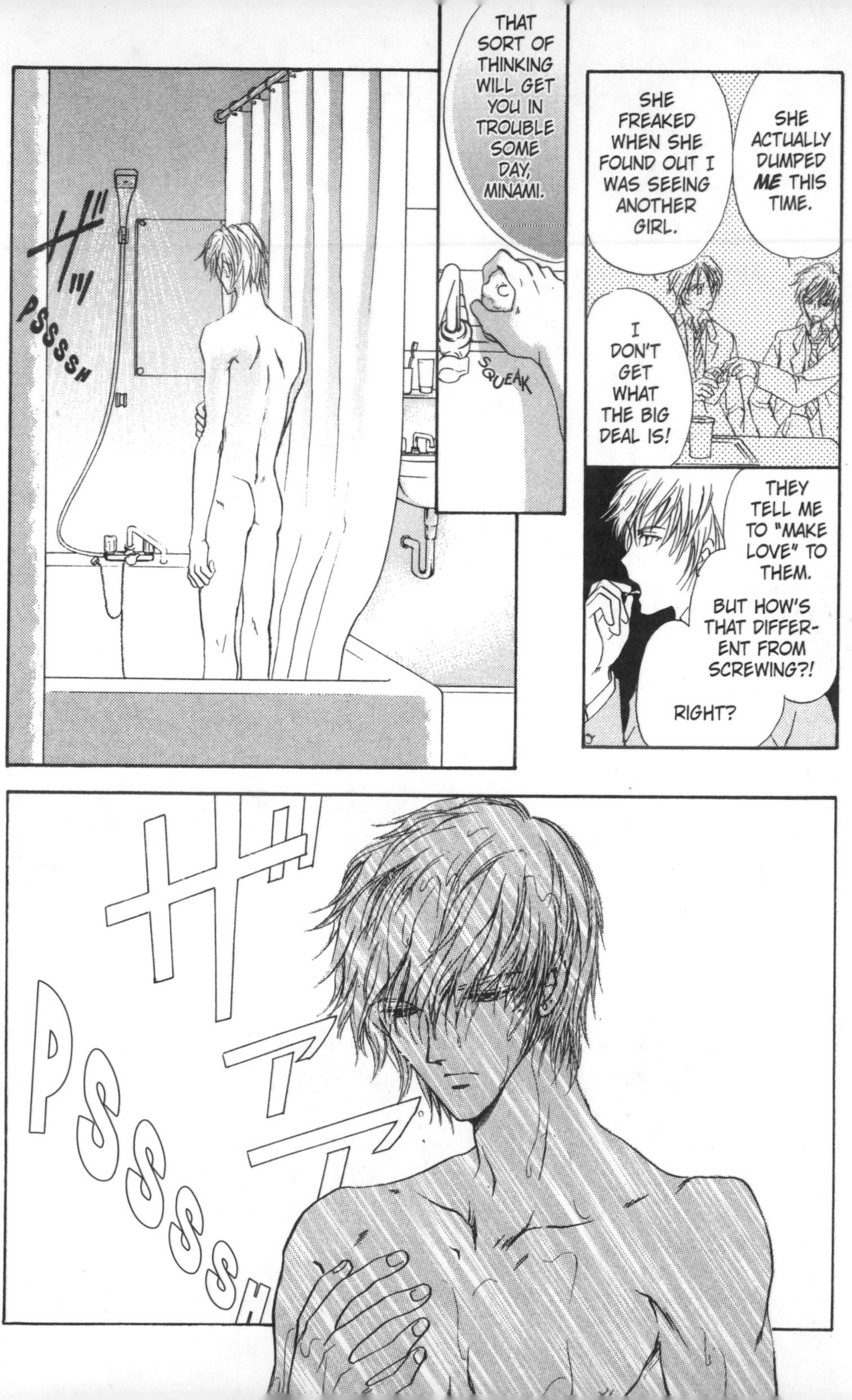
SHE ACTUALLY DUMPED ME THIS TIME.
SHE FREAKED WHEN SHE FOUND OUT I WAS SEEING ANOTHER GIRL.
I DON'T GET WHAT THE BIG DEAL IS!
THEY TELL ME TO "MAKE LOVE" TO THEM.
BUT HOW'S THAT DIFFERENT FROM SCREWING?!
RIGHT?
THAT SORT OF THINKING WILL GET YOU IN TROUBLE SOME DAY, MINAMI.
SQUEAK
PSSSSH
PSSSSSH

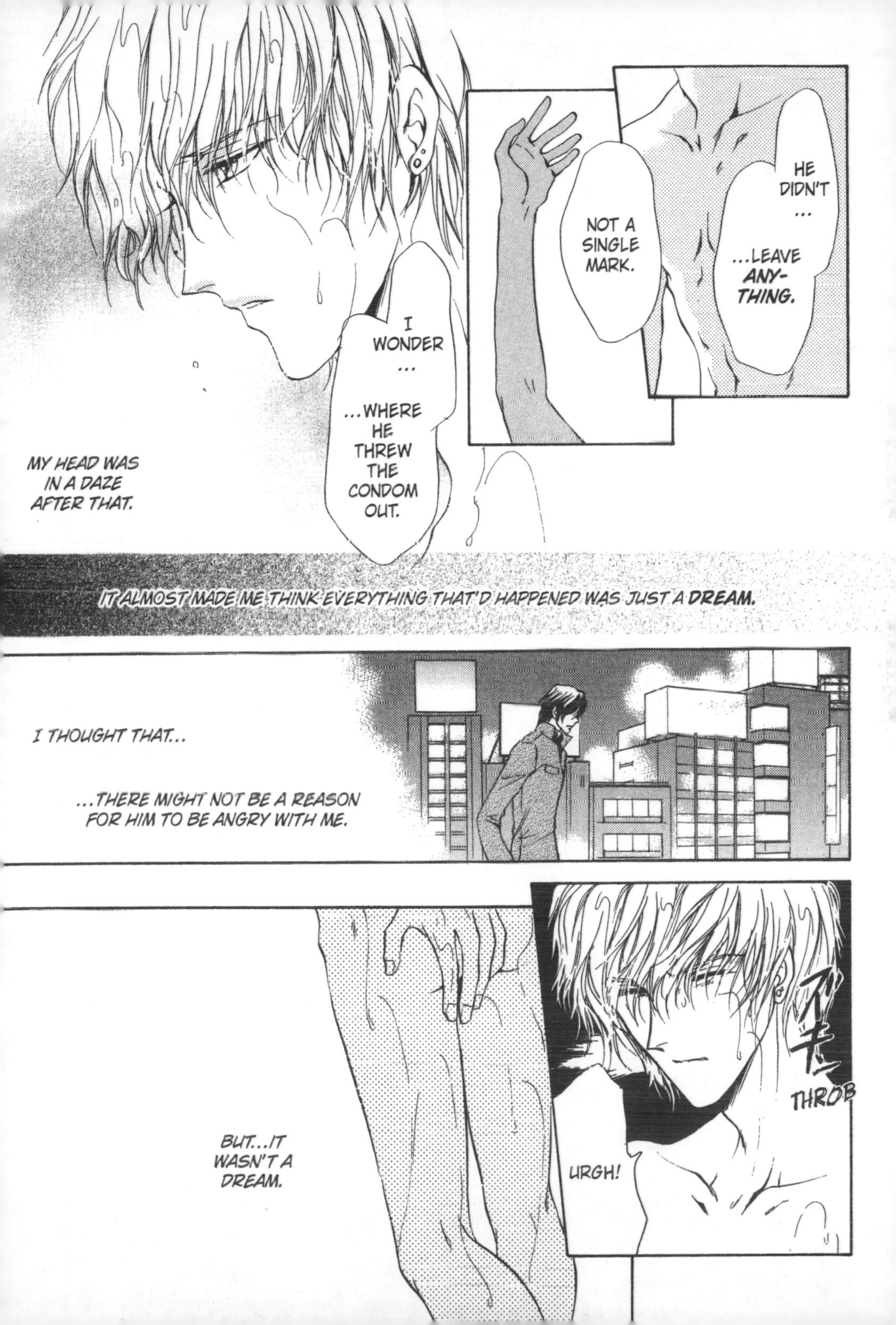
HE DIDN'T ... ...LEAVE ANYTHING.
NOT A SINGLE MARK.
I WONDER ... ...WHERE HE THREW THE CONDOM OUT.
MY HEAD WAS IN A DAZE AFTER THAT.
IT ALMOST MADE ME THINK EVERYTHING THAT'D HAPPENED WAS JUST A DREAM.
I THOUGHT THAT...
...THERE MIGHT NOT BE A REASON FOR HIM TO BE ANGRY WITH ME.
THROB
URGH!
BUT...IT WASN'T A DREAM.

I SEE MYSELF REFLECTED IN THE MIRROR.

...AND I KNOW THAT I'VE DIRTIED MYSELF.

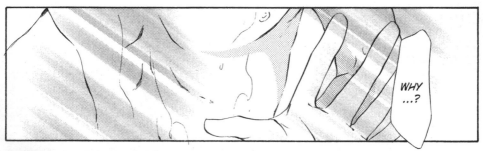

WHY...?

WHY COULDN'T HE AT LEAST LEAVE...

...A HICKEY ON ME?

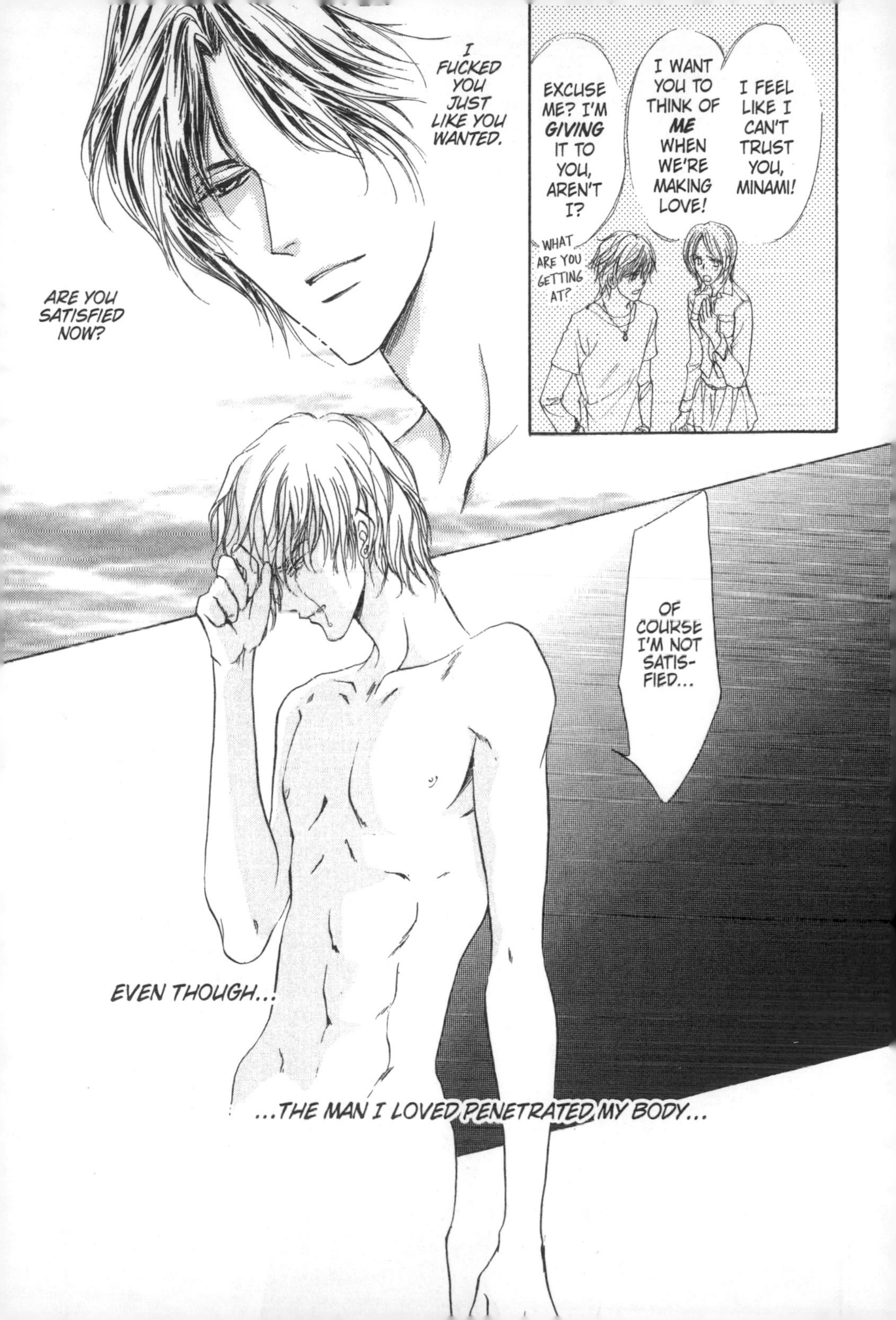
I FEEL LIKE I CAN'T TRUST YOU, MINAMI!
I WANT YOU TO THINK OF ME WHEN WE'RE MAKING LOVE!
EXCUSE ME? I'M GIVING IT TO YOU, AREN'T I?
WHAT ARE YOU GETTING AT?
I FUCKED YOU JUST LIKE YOU WANTED.
ARE YOU SATISFIED NOW?
OF COURSE I'M NOT SATIS-FIED...
EVEN THOUGH...
...THE MAN I LOVED PENETRATED MY BODY...

*...THERE'S NOTHING LEFT.*

OW...

...

NOT A SINGLE TRACE THAT I'D BEEN LOVED.

ALL THAT'S LEFT IS PAIN.

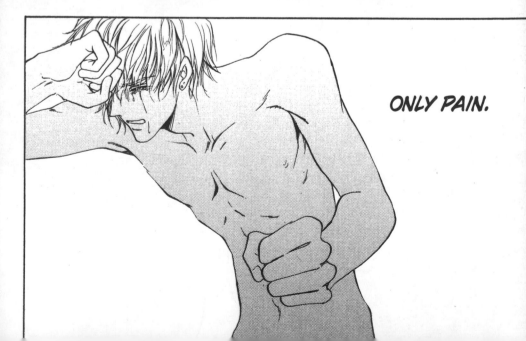

ONLY PAIN.

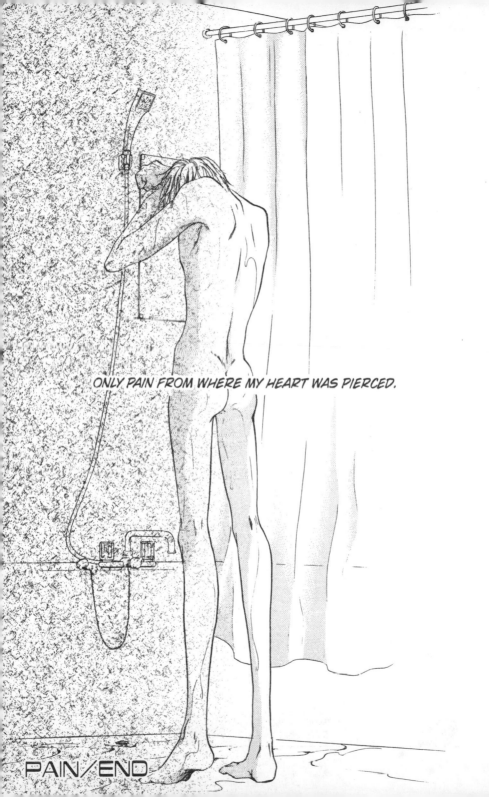

ONLY PAIN FROM WHERE MY HEART WAS PIERCED.

PAIN/END

POSTSCRIPT

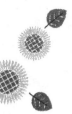

HELLO, EVERYONE! THIS IS TATENO SPEAKING.

I CAN'T THANK YOU ENOUGH FOR PICKING UP THIS FIRST INSTALLMENT OF "HERO HEEL"! ♡

SORRY I HAD TO END THE VOLUME WITH A PICTURE OF OUR MAIN CHARACTER NAKED IN THE SHOWER AND BAWLING HIS EYES OUT.

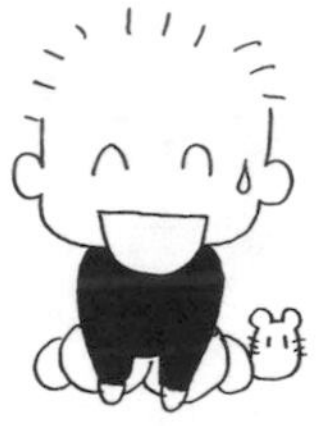

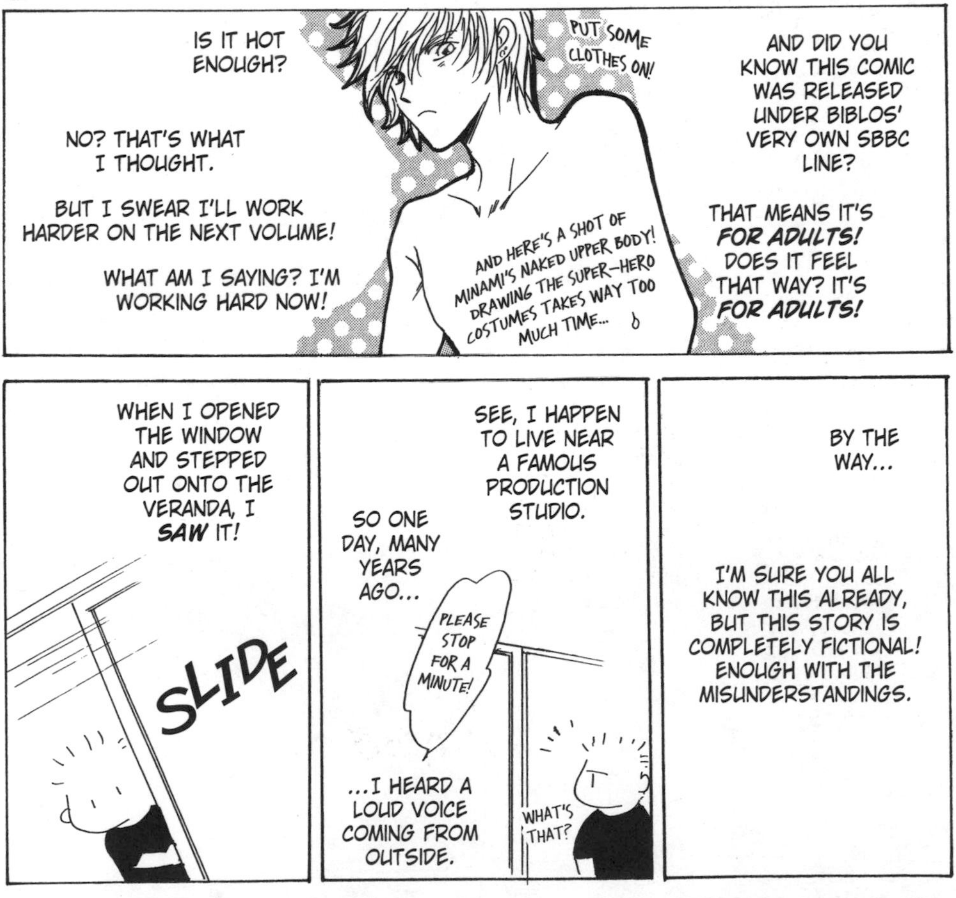
AND DID YOU KNOW THIS COMIC WAS RELEASED UNDER BIBLOS' VERY OWN SBBC LINE?
THAT MEANS IT'S ***FOR ADULTS!*** DOES IT FEEL THAT WAY? IT'S ***FOR ADULTS!***
PUT SOME CLOTHES ON!
AND HERE'S A SHOT OF MINAMI'S NAKED UPPER BODY! DRAWING THE SUPER-HERO COSTUMES TAKES WAY TOO MUCH TIME...
IS IT HOT ENOUGH?
NO? THAT'S WHAT I THOUGHT.
BUT I SWEAR I'LL WORK HARDER ON THE NEXT VOLUME!
WHAT AM I SAYING? I'M WORKING HARD NOW!
BY THE WAY...
I'M SURE YOU ALL KNOW THIS ALREADY, BUT THIS STORY IS COMPLETELY FICTIONAL! ENOUGH WITH THE MISUNDERSTANDINGS.
SEE, I HAPPEN TO LIVE NEAR A FAMOUS PRODUCTION STUDIO.
SO ONE DAY, MANY YEARS AGO...
PLEASE STOP FOR A MINUTE!
...I HEARD A LOUD VOICE COMING FROM OUTSIDE.
WHAT'S THAT?
WHEN I OPENED THE WINDOW AND STEPPED OUT ONTO THE VERANDA, I ***SAW*** IT!
SLIDE

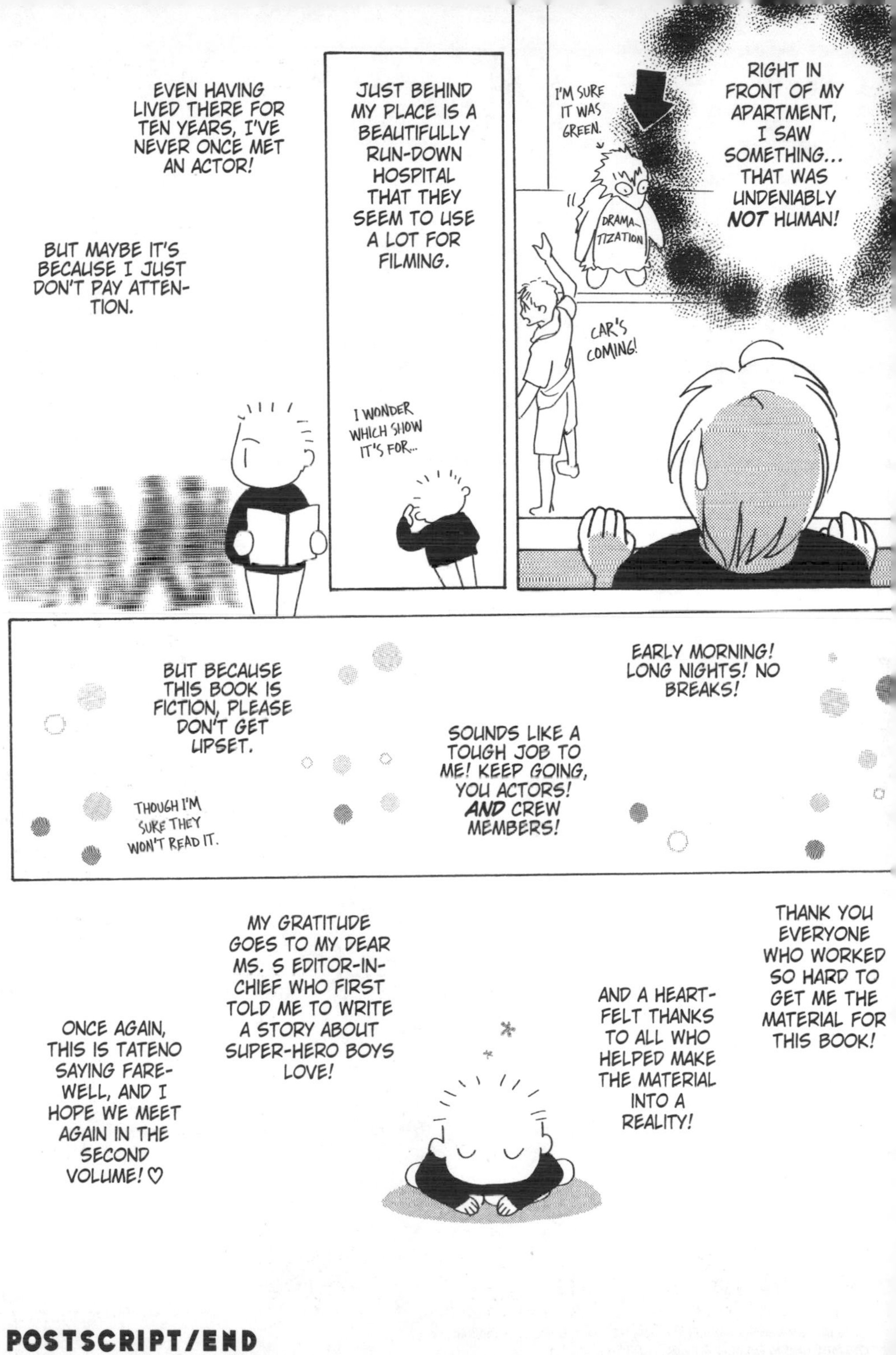
RIGHT IN FRONT OF MY APARTMENT, I SAW SOMETHING... THAT WAS UNDENIABLY **NOT** HUMAN!
I'M SURE IT WAS GREEN.
DRAMATIZATION
CAR'S COMING!
JUST BEHIND MY PLACE IS A BEAUTIFULLY RUN-DOWN HOSPITAL THAT THEY SEEM TO USE A LOT FOR FILMING.
I WONDER WHICH SHOW IT'S FOR...
EVEN HAVING LIVED THERE FOR TEN YEARS, I'VE NEVER ONCE MET AN ACTOR!
BUT MAYBE IT'S BECAUSE I JUST DON'T PAY ATTENTION.
EARLY MORNING! LONG NIGHTS! NO BREAKS!
SOUNDS LIKE A TOUGH JOB TO ME! KEEP GOING, YOU ACTORS! ***AND*** CREW MEMBERS!
BUT BECAUSE THIS BOOK IS FICTION, PLEASE DON'T GET UPSET.
THOUGH I'M SURE THEY WON'T READ IT.
THANK YOU EVERYONE WHO WORKED SO HARD TO GET ME THE MATERIAL FOR THIS BOOK!
AND A HEARTFELT THANKS TO ALL WHO HELPED MAKE THE MATERIAL INTO A REALITY!
MY GRATITUDE GOES TO MY DEAR MS. S EDITOR-IN-CHIEF WHO FIRST TOLD ME TO WRITE A STORY ABOUT SUPER-HERO BOYS LOVE!
ONCE AGAIN, THIS IS TATENO SAYING FAREWELL, AND I HOPE WE MEET AGAIN IN THE SECOND VOLUME! ♡

POSTSCRIPT/END

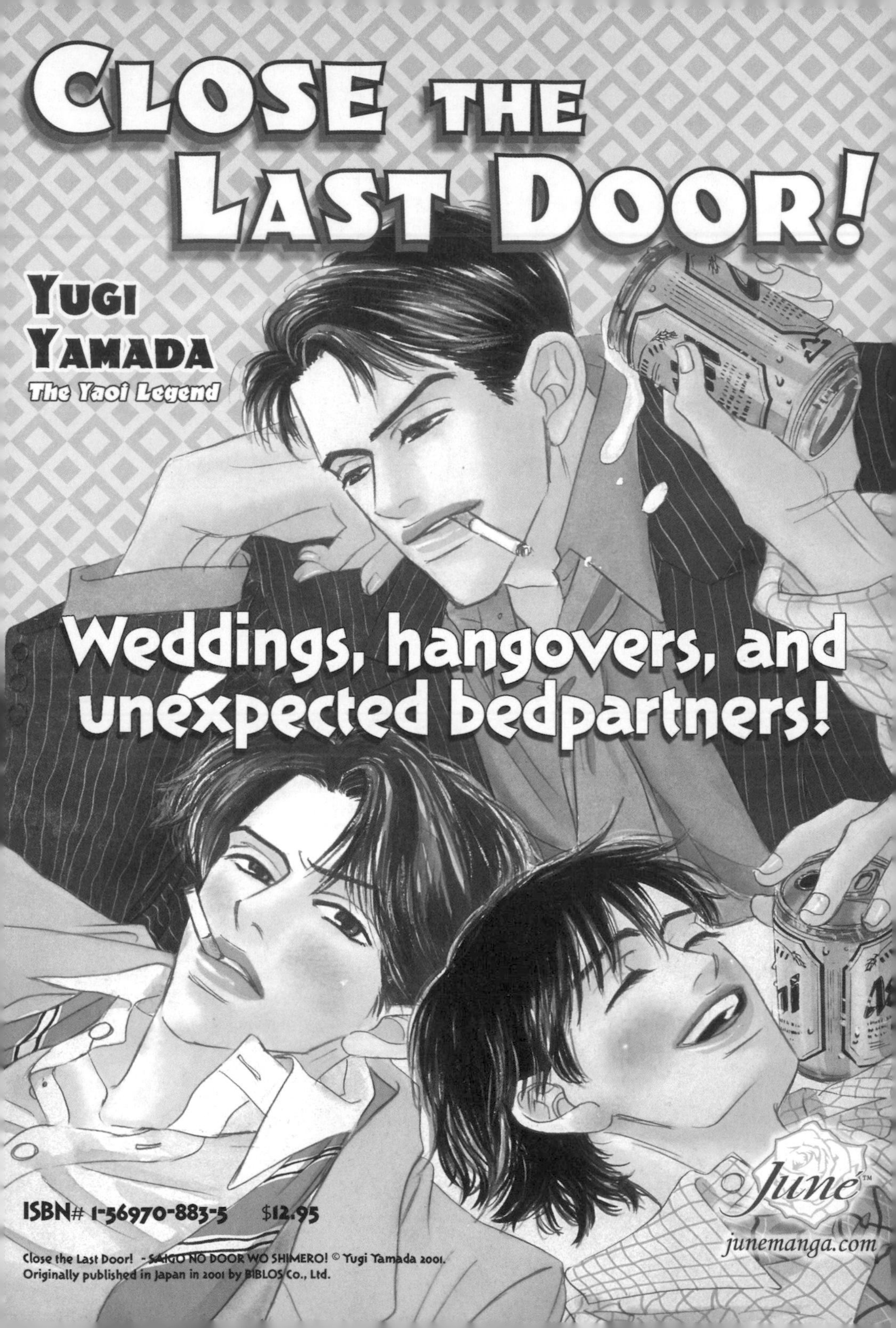
CLOSE THE LAST DOOR!
YUGI YAMADA
The Yaoi Legend
Weddings, hangovers, and unexpected bedpartners!
ISBN# 1-56970-883-5 $12.95
June™
junemanga.com
Close the Last Door! - SAIGO NO DOOR WO SHIMERO! © Yugi Yamada 2001.
Originally published in Japan in 2001 by BIBLOS Co., Ltd.

J-BOY

BY BIBLOS

So much yaoi, all in one place!

Packed full of tantalizing stories by favorite yaoi artists, including Naduki Koujima (*Our Kingdom*), Homerun Ken (*Clan of the Nakagamis*), Natsuho Shino (*Kurashina Sensei's Passion*), and Haruka Minami.

ISBN# 1-56970-875-4 $16.95

june

J-Boy by BIBLOS/Junk! Boy 2004-2005 NATSUYASUMI © BIBLOS 2004-2005.
Originally published in Japan in 2004 2005.

junemanga.com

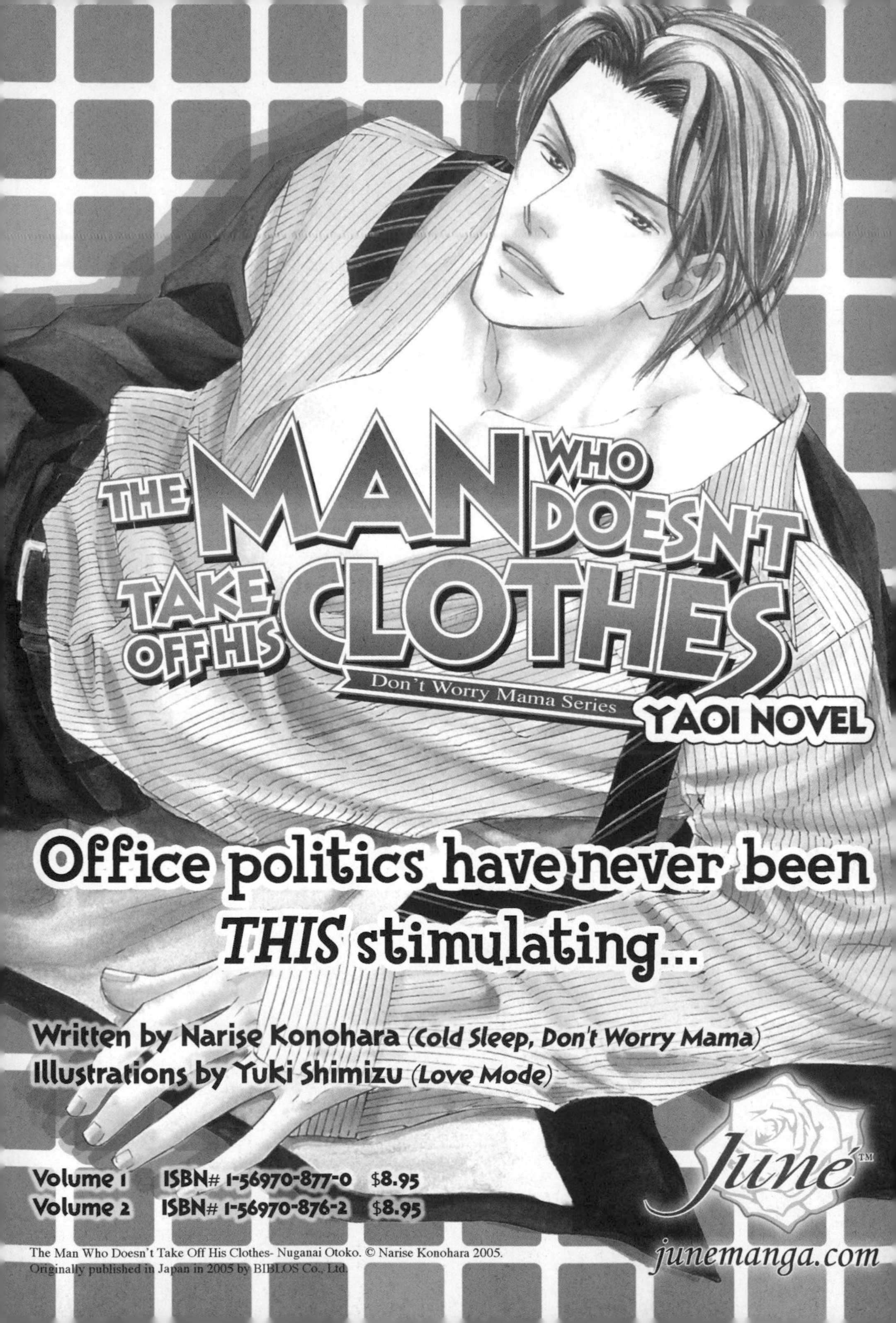
THE MAN WHO DOESN'T TAKE OFF HIS CLOTHES
Don't Worry Mama Series
YAOI NOVEL
Office politics have never been THIS stimulating...
Written by Narise Konohara (Cold Sleep, Don't Worry Mama)
Illustrations by Yuki Shimizu (Love Mode)
Volume 1 ISBN# 1-56970-877-0 $8.95
Volume 2 ISBN# 1-56970-876-2 $8.95
June™
junemanga.com
The Man Who Doesn't Take Off His Clothes- Nuganai Otoko. © Narise Konohara 2005.
Originally published in Japan in 2005 by BIBLOS Co., Ltd.

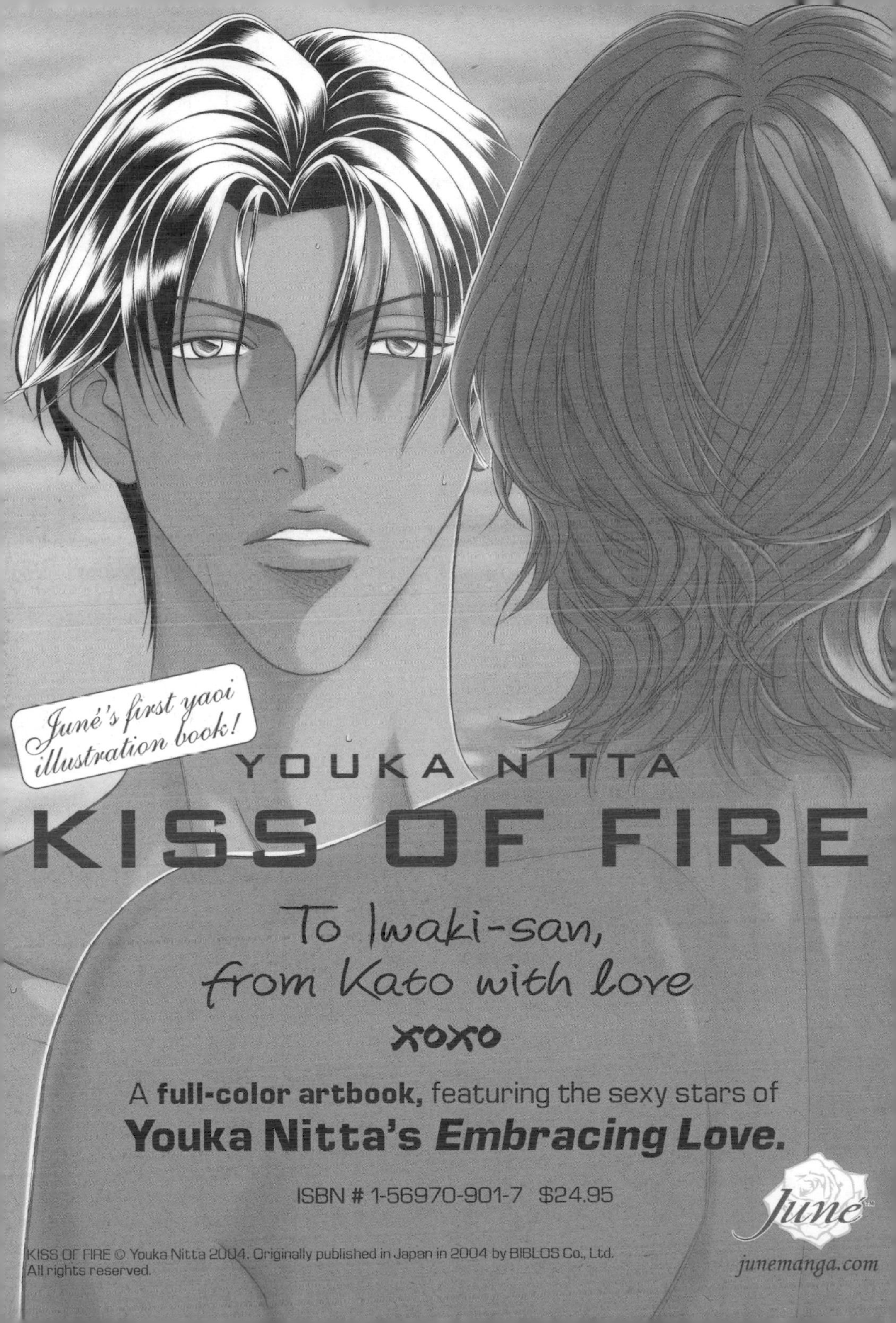
June's first yaoi illustration book!
YOUKA NITTA
KISS OF FIRE
To Iwaki-san, from Kato with love
xoxo
A full-color artbook, featuring the sexy stars of
Youka Nitta's Embracing Love.
ISBN # 1-56970-901-7 $24.95
Juné™
junemanga.com
KISS OF FIRE © Youka Nitta 2004. Originally published in Japan in 2004 by BIBLOS Co., Ltd.
All rights reserved.

STOP

This is the back of the book! Start from the other side.

NATIVE MANGA readers read manga from ***right to left***.

1
2
1
3
2
3
5
4
4
6
5
7
8
6

*If you run into our **Native Manga** logo on any of our books... you'll know that this manga is published in it's true original native Japanese right to left reading format, as it was intended. Turn to the other side of the book and start reading from right to left, top to bottom.*

Follow the diagram to see how its done.
Surf's Up!

NATIVE MANGA
READ RIGHT TO LEFT